DRIVING FORCE

Contents

		Introduction and acknowledgements	6
Chapter	1	Up to 1900	10
Chapter	2	The 1900s: The coming of the multi-cylinder engine	28
Chapter	3	The 1910s: The storm gathers, rages . . . and subsides	44
Chapter	4	The 1920s: Responding to the needs of a mass market	58
Chapter	5	The 1930s: Frying pan to fire – a last flash of glory	76
Chapter	6	The 1940s: The aftermath of the storm – clearing up, sorting out	98
Chapter	7	The 1950s: A farewell to side-valves – and a race for power in the USA	114
Chapter	8	The 1960s: Power and efficiency	136
Chapter	9	The 1970s: Fuel crises, downsizing and uncertainty	158
Chapter	10	The 1980s: Technology takes over	180
Chapter	11	The 1990s: Emissions and efficiency	202
		Index	221

Introduction & Acknowledgements

The idea for this book grew out of a brainstorming session of the best kind, in an English West Country pub. The first notion was to compile a companion volume to Karl Ludvigsen's *Classic Racing Engines*, looking instead at 50 volume-production engines that played a significant role in mass motoring history. That was where the trouble began. Which 50? A handful choose themselves: the Ford Model T, the Austin Seven, the VW Beetle. But which of the multitude of high-quality BMW and Mercedes engines to choose without seeming to denigrate the others? And did General Motors become and remain the world's biggest car builder without making a single classic engine? Of course not, but which are its classics? Have the Japanese engine designers worked diligently since the 1950s without producing a real classic? Again, of course not, but beyond the Honda CVCC and VTEC engines, and maybe the Nissan 240Z unit, would you care to be specific?

Then there is the argument, stronger in the case of volume-production engines than of racers, that immensely valuable lessons were learned from outright disasters like the 'copper-cooled' Chevrolet of the early 1920s. Should such an engine be regarded as a classic – of sorts – because of what was learned from its demise? Hardly – and yet its contribution cannot be denied. So, by degrees the book turned into a history of the passenger car, as distinct from the racing, engine. My Haynes' editors and I were encouraged by the realisation that while many books had been written about racing and individual low-volume, high-performance engines, nobody seemed to have tackled the history of the 'bread and butter' power unit. So I set about writing it.

It has produced some strange perspectives. When I was born, in 1939, only 54 years had elapsed since the first Daimler and Benz engines had sputtered into life. Over half of this history, in fact, has happened in my lifetime and since 1965, when I defected from the aircraft industry, I have been closely associated with it. Yet memory can play tricks and several times, working through my archive and my notes of some 1970s meetings, I was forced to remember not to take it on trust.

The basic structure of the book I determined early on: to devote the first chapter to what happened up to 1900, and then to take the 20th century decade by decade. Within each decade, I began to trace development trends in each of the major car-building countries. Many times I had to remind myself that this was to be a history, not an encyclopedia. What to leave out caused me many more headaches than what to include. All I can offer by way of proof is a pile of reference books which, at one point, I measured at five feet high, and two thick lever-arch files of Internet print-outs, plus the yards of shelf-space of my personal document-archive. If your favourite engine is not mentioned, I apologise – but I also insist it is absent because, in my personal opinion (the buck stops here, and I have no doubt my judgement will be called into question), it did not contribute to the flow of engine design history in any major way, either to the main path or to the many seemingly attractive and logical alternatives which revealed themselves as dead-ends. These include, for example, the generation of huge engines before the First World War, and the straight-8s of the 1920s. Bear in mind, before you condemn, that at the turn of the 19th century, and for at least a decade afterwards, literally hundreds of small companies were working on engines of their own design. I had to go with the ones which survived, prospered and became major forces in our modern world. It didn't happen by accident – or at least, not often.

Nor did I devote any space to engines which were principally built for competition. If it's in Karl Ludvigsen's book, it isn't in this one. So for example, Bugatti and Bentley, who to be sure built wonderful engines, are out, as are Ferrari, Maserati and even Lotus in the post-1945 era. Of course, more specialised books exist which examine such venerated engines in more detail than I had space for, but my argument remains that they contributed little to the thinking of engine designers working on units to be produced cheaply and by the million. Equally, for the most part I have avoided deep discussion of engines which never raced, but were built in penny-packet numbers which hardly justify the word 'production' – except that I was tempted to make an exception for some of the wonderful, if doomed, multi-cylinder engines, the V12s and V16s, of the 1930s.

What remains, in essence, is the way in which passenger car engine designers have always striven for

an ideal. That ideal is to develop an engine which produces satisfactory output for the task in hand, with equally satisfactory economy, durability and 'driveability', for the least weight, bulk and cost (and, since around 1970, with legally limited exhaust emissions). For a racing engine, economy scarcely matters. Satisfactory durability means lasting until the end of the race. Cost is no kind of consideration at all. There are no emission limits. Those are the differences, and together they are the reason why mass-production engines deserve a book of their own.

Within that basic ideal, designers have had to work constantly to exploit the new opportunities which have opened up for them. From the very beginning, there were improved materials and better industrial processes, for example enabling cylinders to be cast in blocks rather than individually. The development of decent gaskets meant that cylinder heads could be made separate. Through the 1920s, the improvement in fuel quality pushed designers towards higher compression ratios and thus, ultimately, to overhead rather than side valves. And so on . . . but that is the point of the book.

Eventually, in telling the story as best I could, I arrived at the end of the 1990s. Naturally, I contemplated writing a final chapter examining the most recent trends and looking as far as possible into the future. The easiest way would have been to edit the Engines' chapter of my 2001 book, *Modern Car Technology*, and throw it in. But that would have been lazy, and in any case, my esteemed editor was already warning me that I was overdrawn on my word allowance. So, if you want to bring the history right up to date and beyond, please look in that book. It is all there – I hope.

Many people helped in the preparation of this book. Not least, there are all the senior engineers in the industry from whom I have learned so much through the last 35 years or so. Those whose advice I cherish most are acknowledged in the foreword to *Modern Car Technology*. Beyond that, above all, I have to thank the Stuttgart-based archive service of DaimlerChrysler, which presented me with a mass of material especially concerning the years up to 1900, even to the extent of providing a CD with sound recordings of the early engines actually running; and apologised that it was the best they could do! Would that some other companies – especially, dare I say, in the USA – took such pride in, and care of their history. So, apart from published books, that was where the Internet came in – and I can only say that there are dozens of sites which are gold-mines of information, and hundreds which yield the odd nugget which is apparently to be found nowhere else. But there are also blanks in the record which indicate that the scope for research has by no means been exhausted.

I suppose all historians experience the sinking feeling which comes when two (or more) apparently impeccable sources contradict each other. It certainly happened to me. Whenever it did, I worked on the basis first, of deciding which source was likely to be the more authoritative, and second, of going for whichever explanation or number seemed the more likely and made the more sense. Even the conversion of American (and early British) inch-measurements into metric equivalents can be a minefield. I have no doubt that buried in this text there will be mistakes. If you find one, please accept my apologies – and please, via my publishers, let me know!

Jeff Daniels
London SW20
July 2002

Opposite: Starting points – the Daimler workshop (above) in Cannstatt, with engine installed in 'the world's first motorcycle' (there was too little power for a car); Benz's original engine (below) with its characteristic bolted-on cylinder head, mechanically operated valves and horizontal flywheel, ready for installation in its designer's lightweight tricycle. (Ludvigsen Library)

1 Up to 1900

During the 1880s, the hopeful inventor of a 'horseless carriage' could have started, more or less literally, with a light carriage minus the shafts and the horse, to which he would add some form of internal combustion engine, plus the means of transmitting its output to one pair of wheels. He might alternatively start with the engine, so to speak, and devise some kind of framework to carry it, topped by a platform with a seat or two. In either case, since no suitable engine existed, the inventor needed either to design and make it himself, or find a kindred spirit to do it for him. Only a little later, during the late 1890s, a number of companies would be formed specifically to make engines for sale to vehicle manufacturers, but in the 1880s the inventor was on his own.

So how would he have started? Almost certainly, he would not have thought beyond a single cylinder. Worries about mechanical imbalance, overcome through the use of multiple cylinders (preferably, at least four) would come later. With a single cylinder, only primary 'up and down' balance can be addressed, through the use of counterweights moving in the opposite direction to the piston. The inventor did not have to worry about the design details of the 'bottom end' of the engine – the crankshaft and the connecting rod – because to a large extent, these could be carried across from the already familiar steam engine. The knowledge needed for making these parts strong enough, and for manufacturing them to high standards of accuracy (if not always of what we would now regard as first-class materials) already existed. One thing which the new engines would quickly need – and which they soon gained – was better lubrication. Steam engines, whether in ships or locomotives, ran slowly and were overseen by skilled operators who could tweak the oil supply as necessary. When a car engine was hidden (as most of the early ones were) beneath the seats, lubrication really needed to be automatic, although there are plenty of veteran cars which provide the driver with a series of drip-feed oil reservoirs whose plungers have to be pressed at regular intervals.

Mostly, however, the early designer's problems would have been concerned almost entirely with the top end of the engine – in preparing the air/fuel mixture, getting it into the combustion chamber, making it burn there and expelling the burned gas afterwards. This called for some kind of valve mechanism. The majority of steam engines, although there are always exceptions, used slide valves which opened and closed ports to admit high-pressure steam from the boiler to the cylinder and to allow it to escape at lower pressure once it had done its work, but the earliest internal combustion inventors chose a more direct approach. Early in the 20th century the slide-valve concept was taken up by some engineers, in the form of the sleeve valve, but its cost and complication, and doubts about its durability (lubrication was always a problem at car-engine operating speeds) meant that it never became widely accepted, even if some determined teams made it work extremely well.

Very early in the life of the internal combustion engine, two alternative approaches emerged: the 4-stroke cycle, in which there were four separate phases of induction, compression, combustion and exhaust, and the 2-stroke cycle in which, by a combination of internal gas flow and carefully positioned porting, covered and uncovered by movement of the piston, plus the use of the crankcase as a 'staging post' for the mixture, the phases were in effect overlapped. The 4-stroke, which eventually became predominant, was invented – or at least, first legally defined – in 1876 by Nicolaus August Otto (1832–1891). Otto, who exhibited a gas-fuelled stationary engine in the Paris Exhibition of 1867, winning a gold medal, was shrewd enough to patent the 4-stroke principle, shutting off that approach to anyone who was unwilling to pay him a licence fee for the best part of a decade, until 1886 when his patent was annulled.

There was another drawback to the early internal combustion engine which affected Otto as much as anyone else. The real key to making an engine suitable for vehicle propulsion is to make it light enough – more accurately, to achieve a sufficiently high power-to-weight ratio. To do this, the engine needs to be run relatively fast. This was simply not possible with the early stationary gas engines, because no reliable high-speed ignition system had been devised. In the mid-19th century, the standard ignition system consisted of keeping a

Opposite: Even by 1890, Daimler had moved on from the single-cylinder 'grandfather clock' engine to this vee-twin variation on the theme. The two pistons rose and fell together rather than alternately, so mechanical balance remained poor, but the arrangement provided more piston area and more output without greatly adding to the engine's weight, much of which was accounted for (as in all early engines) by the heavy flywheel needed to achieve anything like steady running at very low speeds. (Herridge & Sons Collection)

small flame constantly burning in a chamber adjacent to the main combustion chamber, and opening a shutter at a suitable moment to allow the flame to ignite the main charge. For various reasons, this system could not be made to work at more than around 180rpm – fine for a big, heavy, stationary engine powering a factory or pumping out a mine, but a fatal flaw where any vehicle engine was concerned. Electrical spark ignition was an alternative for such engines – Lenoir offered the first practical sparking plug surprisingly early, in 1860 – and initially depended on the make-and-break principle seen in a simple electric buzzer. This weak spark was sufficient to ignite a slow-running gas engine, but the whole system needed drastic improvement before it would work reliably in a fast-running petrol engine. Thus, apart from overturning the Otto patent, one of the key technical challenges which had to be overcome was to devise an ignition system which would allow the engine to operate at much higher speed.

Ignition apart, if petrol rather than gas was to be the fuel, there had to be some means of vaporising the petrol and mixing it with air to form a combustible 'charge'. In other words, apart from a better ignition system, any petrol engine intended for use in a vehicle needed something which we would now call (with a backwards glance to the early 1990s, when it all but died a death) a carburettor.

We are used to the basic – the very basic – idea of a carburettor as an instrument with a narrow throat, dropping the pressure of the air passing through it so as to suck fuel out of one or more jets. The greater, and therefore faster, the airflow, the more fuel is added to the mixture, maintaining something like the correct air-to-fuel ratio for good, reliable combustion. It seems obvious to us now, but it was not so in the 1880s. True, in 1887 an Englishman, Edward Butler, built a one-off tricycle with a single-cylinder engine whose mixture was supplied by a remarkable side-draught carburettor, complete with a float chamber and a venturi suction throat; but either his invention was not widely reported at the time, or its significance was not appreciated. Most of the early engine designers depended either on dipping a wick

In the mid-1880s the English inventor Edward Butler built this single-seat motor tricycle, whose engine included a carburettor with both a float-chamber and a venturi in the air inlet passage to lower the pressure and suck petrol into the airstream. The single-cylinder engine was mounted lengthwise beneath the seat, driving the single back wheel, with the driver sitting between the two front wheels facing the control levers. Like some of his contemporaries, Butler was vigorously discouraged in his activities by the British authorities of the time. (Ludvigsen Library)

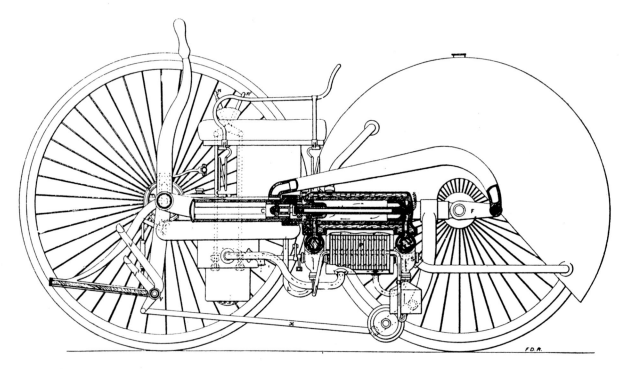

into a reservoir of petrol and drawing air across the wick to form the mixture, or they forced air to bubble through a bath of petrol during the induction stroke. Control of mixture strength was extremely hit-or-miss; most mixtures were probably on the rich side, helping the engine to run cooler. There was always some provision for manual 'tweaking' of mixture strength, before setting out or on the move. Even today, most light aircraft piston engines have manual mixture strength adjustment, allowing the mixture to be leaned-off during the cruise.

Three Germans were among the first to rise to the challenge of finding and combining solutions to these several problems. Two of them became world famous: Karl Benz (1844–1929) and Gottleib Daimler (1834–1900). The third, August Maybach (1846–1929), is revered among engineers as an equally great contributor to the development of the earliest engines, but never became a household name, mainly because he worked most of the time in Daimler's shadow. Astonishing as it now seems, Daimler and Benz, who jointly gave their names to one of the world's most famous car manufacturers, rarely if ever met, and for much of their working lives were competitors following independent paths of development. The Daimler-Benz company was only formed by merger of their original concerns, in 1929 – the year in which Benz died, Daimler having preceded him at the turn of the century. The official history shows that Daimler was the first to demonstrate a vehicle powered by an internal combustion engine of his own devising, but was only a few months ahead of Benz. Purists may argue that the Daimler prototype was literally a horseless carriage – the records show that he ordered such a carriage and installed his engine in it – while Benz developed a complete vehicle; but the Benz was a three-wheeler and in some eyes, perhaps, not a 'proper' car. From the point of view of engine design, however, the interesting thing is that their two designs differed quite markedly, even if they were brought to fruition more or less at the same time.

The histories which led the two men to this point were also markedly different.

Karl Benz had begun his work on engine development by concentrating on the 2-stroke cycle, running his first engine in 1879. By 1883, after a period in which his business interests went through some difficult times, Benz was making 2-stroke stationary gas engines in commercial numbers and had the time and resources to think seriously about

fitting a specially developed small engine to a road vehicle. Through 1885, it being clear that the days of the Otto patent were numbered, Benz developed his first high-speed single-cylinder 4-stroke engine, with trembler-excited electric ignition, and fitted it to his light three-wheeled car. Benz was granted a patent for this vehicle at the end of January 1886, more or less coincidentally with the expiry of the Otto patent. Significantly, despite his knowledge of the 2-stroke engine, Benz had clearly decided that the 4-stroke was the better option for a vehicle power unit.

To begin with, Gottleib Daimler did not face the problem of the Otto 4-stroke patent stranglehold, in that by 1872 he had become technical manager of the Deutz Gas Engine Factory, of which Otto himself was co-founder and owner. By that time, Daimler had already established a close working partnership with August Maybach whom he had 'discovered' in the drawing office of the Reutlingen Bruderhaus – a charitable organisation which partly self-funded itself through commercial activities – when he was that organisation's technical manager. From then on, until Daimler's death, the two effectively worked as a team, with Daimler proposing the broad concepts and Maybach turning them into working machinery.

In 1882, Daimler left the Deutz concern and set up what amounted to a technical development workshop in Cannstatt, where – evidently aware that the Otto patent was under seige and would soon be overturned – he too set about applying the 4-stroke principle to an engine which would be sufficiently light, compact and efficient to power a road vehicle. Maybach soon joined him. Among the practical developments attributed to Maybach and applied to the first Daimler engine – which powered a crude four-wheeled car on a trial run from Cannstatt to Unterturkheim (today home of one of the largest DaimlerChrysler factories) in November 1885 – was a hot-tube ignition system and a float-chamber carburettor.

Daimler's first experimental engine ran in 1883, and its design was based on the inventor's patent No. 28022. It was a horizontal single-cylinder device with a bore of 42mm and stroke of 72mm, thus a swept volume of almost exactly 100cc. For ignition, Daimler ignored electrical spark systems and turned instead to a simple but reliable hot-tube ignition system, in which an external flame kept a platinum tube at constant red heat. This allowed the first Daimler engine to run at 600rpm. However, even when running at this high speed – by the standards of the day – the Daimler engine produced just 0.25hp, in no

Daimler's first running four-stroke petrol engine was built in 1883. Details visible here include the gasketed joint part-way up the cylinder (as distinct from a detachable head), the massive flywheel, the cam operating the exhaust valve, the much more lightly sprung atmospheric inlet valve and, at lower left, the hot-tube ignition system which needed to be lit and warmed through before the engine itself could be started. At the far side is the combined fuel tank and surface-vaporising carburettor. (Ludvigsen Library)

way sufficient to propel any full-sized horseless carriage; but it was a start.

Daimler's design approach, as seen in the original 1883 engine, was to be reflected in many pre-1900 engines. By modern standards there were four especially 'antique' features, three of which became widespread. The first was that his engine had no separate cylinder head as we would understand it, although the cylinder was jointed about halfway up from the crankcase to the top of the combustion chamber. The second was that the mixture was prepared and ignited in a 'prechamber' remote from the main combustion chamber above the piston – a feature in some ways resembling the layout much later adopted for the indirect-injection diesel engine. Once ignited, the burning mixture passed along a passage and into the main chamber. The third antique feature was the use of an 'atmospheric' (or 'automatic') inlet valve. The fourth feature, and the one most quickly abandoned, was the hot-tube ignition system itself. The constant heating of the platinum tube – an expensive item – added to the overall fuel consumption. In addition, the feed tank had to be replenished and the heaters – working on the principle of Bunsen burners – had to be lit and the tubes brought to working temperature before setting out. Simple and reliable it might have been, but from the point of view of convenience hot-tube ignition was a disaster. Its most fundamental drawback, however, was that it was not compatible with really high-speed operation, or with the control of ignition timing – something which many engineers soon realised was crucial. Remarkably, Daimler felt the need to protect the hot-tube system by patent – and for that reason, arguably, remained faithful to it beyond the point at which a change to electric ignition would have been beneficial. It should be added, however, that in the days before anyone thought of equipping a car with an electrical generator, the power for a trembler-coil system had to be drawn from a battery which needed recharging or replacing at intervals, although by 1897 even that objection had been overcome with the invention of the first magneto.

Daimler's complex upper cylinder casting – the cylinder itself plus the curved passage leading from the 'mixture preparation and firing' chamber – was famously supplied by the local bell foundry, accustomed to working to a high standard of accuracy and to achieving sound metal quality. The side chamber contained the two poppet valves, opposite each other, plus the business end of the permanently hot ignition tube. Assembly involved forming the exhaust valve seat, inserting the valve, and then clamping the inlet valve housing into place opposite. Had the engine been vertical rather than horizontal, the inlet valve would have been on top and the exhaust valve underneath; the inlet valve was 'atmospheric', opening against a light spring when downward movement of the piston reduced the pressure in the cylinder, while the inlet valve was operated by a pushrod whose other end ran around an eccentric – a cam – on the flywheel hub. To modern eyes the arrangement looks horribly inefficient, with the curved passage leading from the 'valve chamber' to the main combustion space in the cylinder certain to cause pumping losses to sap still further the engine's minute power output. Remember, though, that this was a team starting from scratch, and undoubtedly attracted by the idea of initially feeding the mixture into a relatively compact space close to the ignition tube.

The combustible mixture was prepared in a surface-evaporation carburettor of Maybach's design, in which a 'bubbling' arrangement was carried in a float to prevent flooding. In effect the carburettor floated on the surface of the fuel in the vertical cylindrical fuel tank, creating the impression that the carburettor was larger than the actual cylinder. Basic mixture strength was determined by the design of the carburettor with precise 'trimming' control a matter of manual adjustment. As already observed, the normal operating mixture strength was well on the rich side, doing nothing for hydrocarbon emissions (but emission controls were almost a hundred years in the future), but bringing the benefit of lower combustion temperatures through the cooling effect of evaporation of the unburned fuel.

As previously explained, the Daimler hot-tube ignition system consisted very simply of a platinum tube maintained at red heat by an external flame. Thus there was no question of timing the ignition: in effect this took place when a combination of compression and the presence of the 'hot spot' created the right conditions for combustion. In any modern sense it was an extremely hit-or-miss approach and recordings of the engine running suggest it misfired about 10 per cent of the time, but at least it enabled the important higher running speed to be achieved. Eventually, it was shown that the hot-tube system itself would not work beyond around 900rpm, but by that time electric spark systems had proved themselves both superior and reliable.

Daimler was so anxious about thermal losses in this first engine that, rather than cooling the cylinder head, he insulated it. This was a miscalculation, as the unit quickly overheated when run, but this was very much a bench engine, an initial demonstrator to prove the principle and to show that high running speeds could be achieved, and that it did.

As for the atmospheric inlet valve, it may seem almost grotesque in the 21st century but it actually worked quite well in the 19th and for some years into the 20th century (apart from car engines, many early aero engines were so equipped). In principle, the valve was sucked open during the induction stroke as soon as the pressure within the cylinder had fallen sufficiently to overcome the loading of the relatively weak spring. Consequently, the valve remained open until close to the bottom of the induction stroke (bottom dead centre, BDC) – or quite possibly, beyond BDC depending on the speed of the engine, the inertia of the valve and the strength of the spring. During the compression, power and exhaust strokes, naturally, internal cylinder pressure held the inlet valve firmly closed. The whole arrangement had the virtue of simplicity, and simplicity usually means lightness and reliability. The only design variables were the valve spring rate (the softer the spring, the longer the valve would remain open) and the weight of the valve (the lighter the better, since high valve inertia means later opening and closing). The drawbacks of the atmospheric inlet valve only became apparent when engineers began to run their power units at higher speeds – above 1,000rpm or so – when the inertia of the valve needed to be checked by a stronger spring, which in turn led to later valve opening; and also when it became clear that positive control of inlet valve timing brought many other benefits in terms of efficient filling of the cylinder with mixture (and eventually, of controlling exhaust emissions).

Daimler's first
vehicle engine

Two years later, in 1885, Daimler and Maybach had prepared a second, much larger engine, still single-cylinder but now vertical rather than horizontal. The cylinder dimensions were 70mm bore by 122mm stroke, for a capacity of 462cc, and while the basic layout remained more or less the same as before, the atmospheric inlet valve was replaced by one operated,

like the exhaust valve, by a pushrod driven by a cam attached directly to the flywheel. The Mercedes-Benz archive records that Maybach had needed to conduct some intensive research into suitable materials for valve springs; maybe he felt it was not worth the effort, because for subsequent engines during the 1890s, he turned again to the atmospheric inlet valve. It was only with the arrival of the first

Benz installed his first road-going engine in this extremely light tricycle. The engine was mounted horizontally, Benz fearing that the gyroscopic effect of the huge flywheel would otherwise affect the vehicle's behaviour. The chain drive to the rear axle is among the features clearly visible. Less obvious is the ingenuity which Benz applied to the cooling system and the exhaust. There is a battery case beneath the seat on the right, since unlike Daimler, Benz used electric ignition from the outset. (Herridge & Sons Collection)

Mercedes at the beginning of the 1900s that he reintroduced mechanical inlet valve operation, and then in a very different form. Another feature of this first vehicle engine was that it precompressed its incoming air charge within the closed crankcase, beneath the descending piston, presumably in the hope of improving airflow into the combustion chamber. This was another idea which was not pursued.

This vertical engine, with its tall, slender single cylinder sitting above a massive lower housing for the crankpin and heavy flywheel, soon gained the name Standuhr (grandfather clock) by virtue of its appearance. Now lacking any insulation, but simply air-cooled and with a compression ratio of 2.6:1, it delivered 1hp at 600rpm, hardly sufficient for any kind of four-wheeled carriage – so Daimler had it installed in what amounted to the world's first motorcycle, a wooden-framed (and, of course, tyreless) device with outrigger wheels. In the following year, 1886, the 'grandfather clock' – uprated to 1.5hp with a year's development, including the addition of water cooling with a jacket around the cylinder – was finally installed in Daimler's specially ordered 4-wheeled carriage, behind and beneath the two seats.

Benz, meanwhile, had developed his own single-cylinder petrol engine, with several features which make it seem more advanced to modern eyes. For example, it had a detachable cylinder head and electric ignition by trembler coil and spark plug, and it was water-cooled using a thermo-siphon system. In addition, the inlet valve was operated mechanically. It was, however, not a poppet valve but an odd sliding shutter device which needed careful lubrication; in subsequent engines, Benz abandoned it in favour of the atmospheric type. Benz's engine had a bore of 90mm and a stroke of 150mm, giving it a capacity of 954cc. With a compression ratio of 2.7:1 it produced 0.75hp at 400rpm, just sufficient to propel its inventor's ultra-light three-wheeled carriage, in which it was installed horizontally, partly because Benz feared the gyroscopic effect of the huge flywheel – which doubled as the handgrip for starting the engine – would affect the handling, a fear which proved groundless.

Nonetheless, it is worth noting that these pioneer engines needed large and heavy flywheels, despite the desperate need to save weight, if they were to run at all. The inertia of the flywheel not only smoothed the shock of each power stroke, but also compensated for the fact that primitive mixture preparation and crude

ignition meant that no two successive power strokes were the same, unless by accident. As already noted, the Daimler engine certainly suffered from frequent misfiring even when it was running 'well'. Equally, they allowed the engines to run at speeds well below the normal idling speed of a modern engine, and thus within their mechanical limits.

Development **begins**

Thus by 1886, both Daimler and Benz had run their first primitive 'horseless carriages' – very different in appearance, and just as different in terms of the details of engine design. The next task was to make the engines more powerful, not only in overall output but also in power-to-weight ratio.

Benz's approach was straightforward. While steadily refining mechanical details (the original slide inlet valve had given way to an atmospheric poppet valve by 1888), he sought greater output simply by making his single-cylinder engine bigger. Intriguingly, he seems to have been torn between relatively narrow-bore, long-stroke engines like his first prototype, and 'square' units with equal bore and stroke. Even in 1886, he had demonstrated an engine with 115mm bore and 160mm stroke, for a capacity of 1,662cc and an output of 2.5hp at 500rpm, but also a 110mm 'square' engine (capacity thus 1,045cc) producing 1.5hp. Very soon he had enlarged this latter unit to 130mm 'square' (1,726cc) and 3hp, still at 500rpm. This 3hp engine was used in the earliest Benz cars produced for sale, but incremental development continued, with further enlargement and a steady increase in running speeds as materials improved and confidence was gained in the mechanical design. A further improvement came in 1894 with Benz's development of a float-type carburettor. By 1898, the cylinder had a bore of 150mm and a stroke of 165mm – huge by modern standards – for a capacity of 2,916cc and an output of 6hp at 700rpm.

Thus after several years of development, the Benz single-cylinder engine was still producing barely 2hp/litre, and the size and inertia of its components (in particular, the weight of its piston) were creating a real challenge. Even by 1898, some customers were asking for a more satisfactory solution – and Benz soon gave it to them.

Meanwhile, Daimler – or more strictly, Maybach – had taken a different approach. He took the original 'grandfather clock' engine and simply added a second

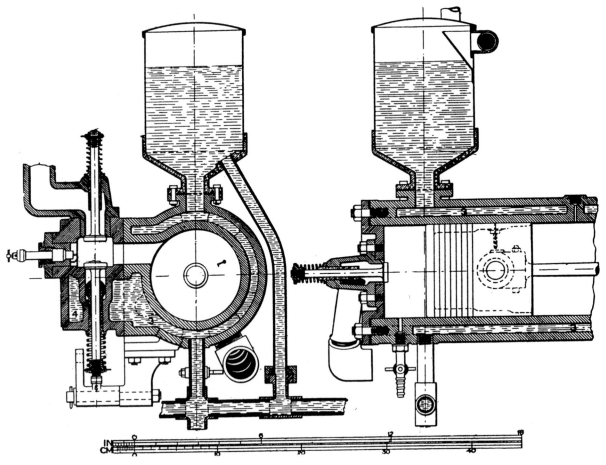

Details, in transverse and lengthwise section view, of a Benz horizontal single-cylinder engine of the early 1890s. Among the noteworthy details are the remarkable two-part construction of the 'detachable head' housing the decompressor to aid starting, the external initial-combustion chamber with atmospheric inlet and mechanical exhaust valve plus sparking plug (and swirl-inducing offset passage into the main chamber), and the cooling system with its header tank and connections to the remote and unseen radiator. (Ludvigsen Library)

cylinder, so that the two formed a 17° vee above the same huge, cylindrical crankcase. This was a neat move, because for the same cylinder dimensions, going from one cylinder to two doubles both the piston area and the piston weight. If on the other hand you keep to a single cylinder and double the piston area, the piston weight (and the mechanical load on the bottom end of the engine) is substantially more than doubled because while the area increases as the square of the cylinder bore dimension, the piston weight increases as its cube. Maybach did not address the complications of firing the two cylinders alternately, which would have led to smoother operation but would also have complicated the design of the engine's top end. The two connecting rods shared a single crankshaft journal and the cylinders fired as one – but the result was still significantly better than an engine with a single large cylinder.

In fact, the cylinders of the Daimler-Maybach vee-twin engine, which appeared in 1889, had a bore of 60mm and a stroke of 100mm, for a capacity of 565cc. It was thus considerably more compact than its single-cylinder predecessor, and with a compression ratio of 2.5:1 it produced 1.5hp (and before long, 2hp) running at 700rpm. Its higher specific output and smaller size meant it weighed only 36kg/hp, compared with the 80kg/hp of the original Standuhr unit. It was sufficiently impressive that Daimler began to sell licences for its construction, notably in France where engines of essentially similar design powered the first-ever Peugeot car in 1890, and the first Panhard et Levassor in 1891. Mercedes proudly notes that in the 1894

Paris–Rouen road race, the first four cars to finish, though bearing French names, were powered by engines using Daimler-licensed technology. Eventually, France would produce original and high-quality engines of its own, but meanwhile Maybach was already working on better concepts.

As early as 1890 Maybach had shown an in-line 4-cylinder engine (with paired cylinders), producing 5hp at 620rpm, weighing a reported 153kg (337lb), and intended for boats rather than cars. Alongside this engine, he was studying the idea of a proper in-line 2-cylinder unit with alternate firing and double-throw crankshaft for car use. As it happened, there was a hiccup in the Daimler fortunes at this point, as both he and Daimler fell out with the partners with whom they had formed Daimler-Motor Gesellschaft (DMG). From 1892 to 1895 Daimler and Maybach took themselves off and worked independently, while DMG struggled to produce a worthwhile product without them. It was however during this period that DMG produced a handful of cars with the new Maybach 2-cylinder engine, initially with a bore and stroke of 67 x 108mm for a capacity of 760cc, producing 1.8hp at 750rpm, and later with a larger unit of 75 x 120mm (1,060cc) with 2.1hp at 720rpm.

Daimler was later invited back by the crestfallen directors of DMG. He and Maybach then continued to develop the 2-cylinder engine, notably improving its efficiency with the aid of a spray-nozzle carburettor (in 1895) and finally abandoning Daimler's beloved hot-tube ignition in 1898, in favour of low-tension magneto sparking which had been invented by Bosch the previous year. The magneto had the advantage of not being dependent on an external electrical power supply. By this time, following the formula first devised in France by Emile Levassor, Daimler switched to a front-engined car, the 'Phoenix', which became the staple product in 1897. The first Phoenix was powered by the 1,060cc 2-cylinder engine, but

the improvements wrought since 1892 meant that it now produced 4hp at 700rpm. Although more powerful and reliable, it still retained many of the characteristics of the 1892 engine including the lack of a separate cylinder head and the use of atmospheric inlet valves. By 1899, Daimler was offering the Phoenix car with an in-line 4-cylinder engine, still archaic in its detail, with bore and stroke of 70 x 120mm, for a capacity of 1,847cc, but with a power output of only 6hp. Better, much better, was to come – but not until the century had turned.

Benz's 2-cylinder Contra engine

As we have seen, Benz persisted with larger and larger single-cylinder engines until by 1898 he was offering a unit of all but 3-litre capacity. That is an awfully large

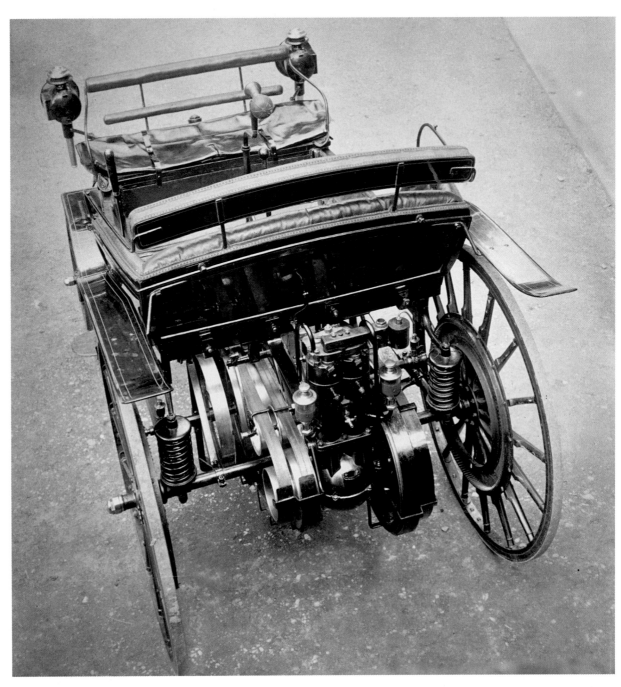

Above: By 1895 Daimler had moved from the narrow vee-twin engine to an in-line twin, seen installed beneath the back seat of this 'face-to-face' four-seater. Despite the mechanically more advanced layout, a massive flywheel is retained.

So too is Daimler's beloved hot-tube ignition system, on which he held the patents. It would not be long before the need for higher engine speeds forced its abandonment, however. (Herridge & Sons Collection)

Opposite: By the late 1890s Benz had evolved his flat-twin engine and was fitting it to Velo cars of the type shown here. Some of the characteristics of earlier Benz engines, including the cylinder head layout and the coolant header-tanks,

can still be seen. The crankshaft is 'open' and is a gear drive to the camshaft beneath, with bell-crank operation of the inlet valves. The exhaust system has been removed for this illustration. (Herridge & Sons Collection)

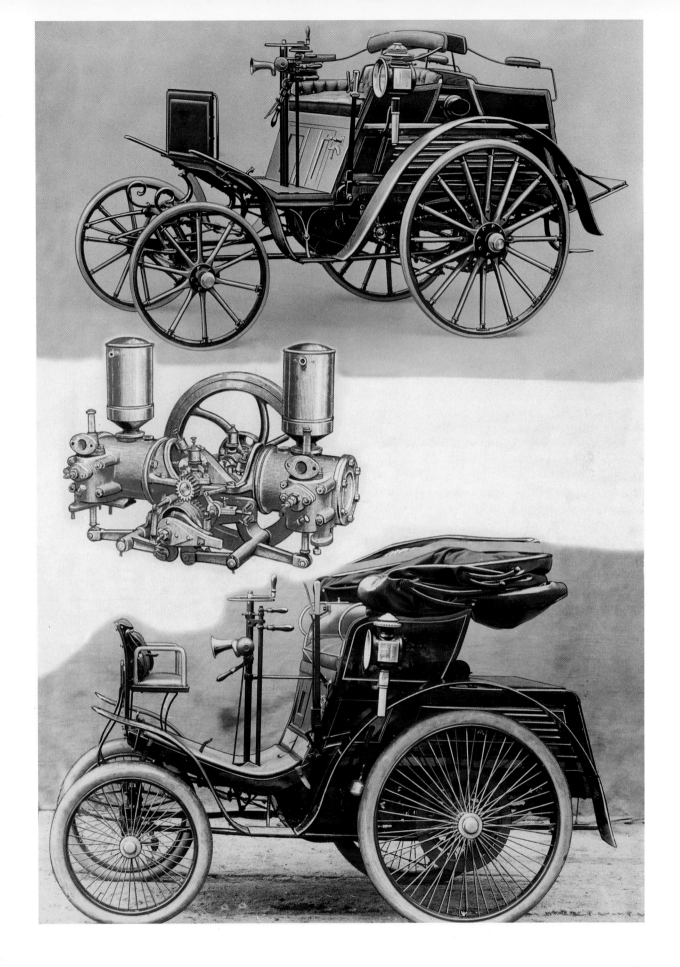

single piston to try to counterbalance, and a hefty bang at the rate of around 12 times a second – a low enough frequency to feel extremely rough. Nor did the engines of those days benefit in any way from vibration-damping mountings. Benz must have known that something better was needed, and he produced it in the form of a mechanically modern flat-twin, with the cylinders offset sufficiently to allow each connecting rod to connect to its own crankshaft throw. Although this Contra engine retained atmospheric inlet valves opposite mechanically operated inlet valves (driven from a gear-driven camshaft beneath the crankcase), and Benz's trembler-type ignition, it also had a number of modern features including a cooling system with a pump, a float-type carburettor and pressure lubrication.

The first Contra engine of 1899 had bore and stroke of 100 x 110mm for a capacity of 1,728cc, and a modest power output of 5hp at 920rpm – still by no means fast, but a lot faster than the single-cylinder. But the formula was sound, and Benz almost immediately enlarged the unit to 120mm 'square', for a capacity of 2,714cc and an output of 8hp. This was an engine which would take Benz into the 20th century – although he retained single-cylinder units, in smaller sizes, for his Velo light cars.

The French challenge

While from 1890, Peugeot and Panhard et Levassor were building cars with licence-built Daimler engines, another French company took a different approach. De Dion-Bouton, jointly administered by the Count de Dion and Georges Bouton, had been building a wide variety of steam-powered vehicles with considerable success. De Dion realised the threat posed to the business by the internal combustion engine, examined a licence-built Daimler vee-twin and decided his company could do better. His key decision was that with suitable ignition, an engine could be

made to run a great deal faster, and therefore with a usefully higher power-to-weight ratio.

De Dion accordingly pressed ahead with the design of a simple, single-cylinder engine whose great virtue was its ignition system, which combined a trembler coil with an ingenious cam-operated contact breaker which made possible much higher operating speeds. On test, the De Dion-Bouton engine would run happily at an unheard-of 3,500rpm, although normally it ran at something less than that, though still a great deal faster than any Daimler (or Benz) engine.

The first De Dion-Bouton engine – at least, the first one to be publicly demonstrated – was small by

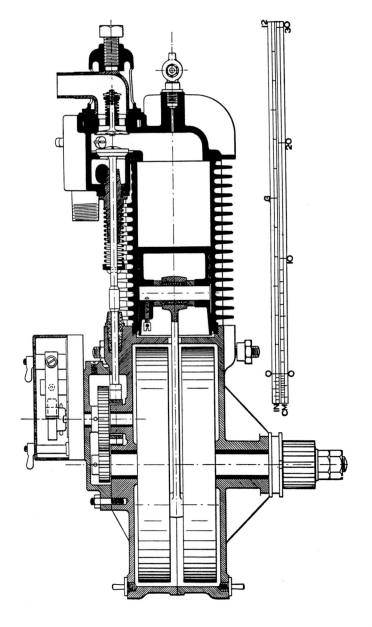

A section through an early De Dion-Bouton single-cylinder engine, showing how the blade-like connecting rod oscillated in the small gap between two large flywheels, whose casing gave the engine its characteristic shape. Note that this engine is air-cooled, with a separately cast, finned cylinder pressed into the crankcase. Note also the geared drive to the cam operating the exhaust valve. These engines were notable for the high speeds they could achieve, giving them an impressive power-to-weight ratio. (Ludvigsen Library)

most standards, with a 50mm bore and a stroke of 70mm, for a capacity of only 137cc. In some ways it remained faithful to the 'Daimler approach' with its surface-evaporation carburettor (floating on top of a 4-litre fuel tank), offset valve-chamber and atmospheric inlet valve opposite a pushrod-operated exhaust valve. But the pushrod itself was operated by a half-speed gear-driven camshaft, and of course there was that ignition system (drawing current from a battery which lasted an average 150 hours, or so it was claimed) which allowed the high operating speed that in turn meant this tiny air-cooled engine produced 0.5hp – a respectable specific output of getting on for 4hp/litre, achieved in an engine notable for being simple, light and extremely compact. Although the De Dion engine bore a certain physical resemblance to the original Daimler 'grandfather clock', the internal arrangement of its bottom end was ingenious, with the webs of the single crankshaft throw enlarged into two massive, symmetrical flywheels which served also as balance weights, leaving only a small separation between them for the blade-like connecting rod.

At this size and output, the De Dion-Bouton engine was not a practical power unit for a full-sized car. Instead, the company began fitting them to powered tricycles. In effect the engine was started first by pedalling the tricycle – with the engine's compression released via a valve provided for the purpose – and then 'bump starting' by closing the compression valve. There was also, naturally, a normal bicycle-type free-wheel. The tricycle rider was provided with three engine controls apart from the decompressor: two of them were connected to the taps in an ingenious arrangement of concentric tubes, one admitting air to the carburettor and the other admitting mixture to the engine itself, thus providing a combined throttle and mixture strength control. There was also a control for varying the ignition timing, a feature made possible by De Dion's cam-operated contact breaker. Although celebrated for its ability to run at high speed, something more moderate was preferable for the sake of refinement and durability, and by 1897 the company had modified the engine's cam profile, enlarged the valves and settled for a maximum speed of 2,000rpm.

De Dion-Bouton proved extremely successful in its engine venture. Not only did its powered tricycles prove popular, but as the company developed slightly larger and more powerful versions of the basic design it

began selling them to other powered-tricycle manufacturers including Clément, Chenard and Peugeot, and to the early inventors of very light cars, the 'voiturettes' beloved of the French at the turn of the century. These included Renault, which used De Dion-Bouton engines until it began making its own in 1902. From the 0.5hp of the original unit in 1895, De Dion-Bouton was able to offer 0.75hp (58 x 70mm, 185cc) in 1896, 1.5hp (62 x 70mm, 211cc) in 1897, and by 1899, the Type A engine of 2.25hp (70 x 70mm,

De Dion-Bouton at first fitted its engines only to light motor-tricycles of the type seen here. The engine could be decompressed until it was needed and then 'bump-started', so long as the vehicle was already in motion (note the visible *bicycle-pedal and chain drive). The box beneath the crossbar is the container housing the battery for De Dion's electric ignition system, and the triangular container is the combined fuel tank and carburettor. (Herridge & Sons Collection)*

269cc). By the turn of the century, the company had delivered 20,000 such engines for its own use and to many other customers. De Dion-Bouton itself stuck to tricycles until in 1899 it showed its first proper car, powered by a further evolution of the single-cylinder design with water cooling – a water jacket was simply welded into place around the cylinder – and with dimensions of 80 x 80mm for a capacity of 402cc and an output of 3.5hp at 1,800prm.

Although most of the early French car manufacturers began life by using either Daimler-licensed or De Dion engines, several of them looked at what was on offer, considered the basic principles and quickly developed their own ideas. Panhard et Levassor, having begun by building Daimler engines, were making 2-cylinder units of their own design by 1895. Peugeot was building its own 2-cylinder engines by 1896, and by 1899 Amédée Bollée had built a remarkably advanced engine with four cylinders cast in a single block, and twin carburettors. Emile Mors was another manufacturer who did well in this decade, building cars with unusual V4 engines – mainly air-cooled, but with water cooling to the cylinder heads – from as early as 1895. Mors's real claim to fame is that in 1899 he seems to have been the first designer to introduce forced-flow lubrication for the crankshaft bearings, paving the way for higher engine speeds and greater loads. Such was the pace of development in this decade, however, that if Mors had not devised the system, somebody else would have done so in short order. Engineering at the turn of the 19th century was like that.

Developments elsewhere

Up to 1900, there is no doubt that technical leadership in the development of internal combustion engines for vehicles resided first in Germany and later to some extent, in France, as we have seen. Engineers in other industrialised countries took a close interest in these developments and conducted experiments of their own, although little came of them on an industrial scale until after the turn of the century.

In Britain, there was no shortage of individuals sufficiently intrigued to overcome all difficulties and build their own self-propelled vehicles. Well, all difficulties except one: whenever they ventured on to the road, they were invariably prosecuted. The attitude of the British establishment to the self-

propelled road vehicle of almost any kind may have been due in part to love of the horse but also, no doubt, to the powerful vested interests of railway shareholders, some of whom must have foreseen the threat which unlimited development of the internal combustion engine would mean. Hence, by the 1890s Britain had its 4mph speed limit and its Red Flag Act, and those who developed one-off road vehicles did so out of simple interest, often combined with the anticipation that the restrictions would soon be overturned, as of course they were, although only to the extent of abandoning the red flag man and raising the limit to 12mph. Even so, the official attitude beyond question set back the nascent British industry by the best part of a decade by comparison with its German and French competitors. Yet the 1890s did throw up one British engineer of real genius, Dr Frederick Lanchester, who analysed the design of the entire car in a more thoughtful and systematic way than anybody before him.

In terms of engine design Lanchester was deeply interested in – one might almost say obsessed by – balance and operating refinement, and his 1896 car ended up with a flat-twin engine, each of whose pistons had two connecting rods driving upper and lower crankshafts rotating in opposite directions, and which were then geared together to produce the output. The twinned connecting rods cancelled out the secondary vibrations to which all other engines were subject, so the Lanchester engine was remarkably smooth in operation – at the expense of considerable added complication, it must be said. Lanchester also decided to use a single poppet valve per cylinder, with a disc-type 'crossover' valve upstream, alternately opening the intake and exhaust passages: not such a good idea, perhaps, when looking back from an age in which valve timing overlap has become an essential tool in any engine developer's workshop. The 'Doctor' also devised his own wick-type carburettor which included an ingenious means of allowing for variations in fuel density – and fuel could be extremely variable in those days.

Meanwhile, an embryo British industry began to arise centred on Coventry, but aside from Lanchester's work there was very little development of significance on the engine side. Indeed, two of the earliest and best-known Coventry-based names, Humber and Riley, both began their car-building existences (having been previously engaged with bicycles and agricultural machinery) buying engines

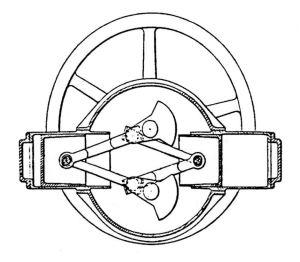

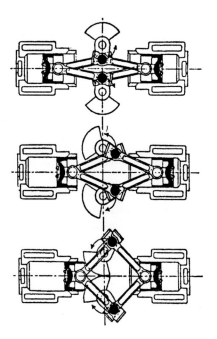

from De Dion-Bouton, while others, such as Allard, licensed that company's technology and built what amounted to adapted near-copies.

In the USA, inevitably, a number of inventors gleaned details of what was happening in Europe and imagined fleets of self-propelled vehicles heading into the wide open spaces. Earliest in the field were the brothers Duryea, who were certainly building cars by the mid-1890s and even set up a British subsidiary in Coventry. In the long term, far more significant contributions came from Henry Ford, who was running prototype single-cylinder engines, and then a 2-cylinder unit, on an improvised test bench in 1893, moving on to demonstrate his original Quadricycle in 1896; and from Ransom S. Olds, who ran his first car in 1898 and whose products were eventually produced by Oldsmobile, the earliest-founded of the five principal product lines (the others being Buick, Cadillac, Chevrolet and Pontiac) which were eventually embraced by General Motors.

The learning curve was steep

In summary, therefore, the final 15 years of the 19th century saw the internal combustion engine evolve, as a power unit for self-propelled vehicles, from the first extremely crude single-cylinder devices, producing

The eminent British pioneer Frederick Lanchester was so obsessed by the notion of perfect mechanical balance that his flat-twin engines had twin counter-rotating crankshafts to which each piston was connected via two rods. The outputs from the two crankshafts were geared together to deliver the final drive. Lanchester's engines did indeed run extremely smoothly and quietly, but the complex layout was difficult and expensive to make, and satisfactory – if not quite as perfect – results were soon achieved by simpler means. (Ludvigsen Library)

extremely small power outputs (especially in relation to the amount of fuel they consumed), into reasonably reliable units with one or two cylinders, producing enough power to propel a light car at up to 50km/h (31mph), sometimes more. All the basic mechanical principles – including some which would not be needed in practice for many years to come – had been determined and set down by Frederick Lanchester and others. Engine designers knew what was needed to provide good, indeed near-perfect balance, even if they often chose on grounds of cost, not to provide it.

Although the majority of engines in production as the 19th century gave way to the 20th had one or two cylinders, it was widely recognised that four cylinders (or even more) were in most respects the obvious way forward. The countervailing factors were cost, complication and sheer engineering ability. Twice as many cylinders meant far more complicated castings, more machining, more components – twice as many valves, pistons, sparking plugs – and thus a great deal more cost for the sake of better operating refinement. It was not an attitude which would persist much longer.

The majority of 1899 engines certainly had their cylinder blocks and heads cast as one; there was scepticism about the reliability of gasket-jointed separate cylinder heads, and as long as the majority of engines used side valves, it was not too much of an issue from the point of view of assembly or of maintenance. The valves could be both on one side of the cylinder (the 'L-head' layout) or inlet on one side and exhaust on the other ('T-head'). The alternative, still, was to have an atmospheric inlet valve sitting opposite, and therefore above the exhaust valve, but the trend was already towards mechanical valve operation. The idea that the side-valve layout could be undesirable because it limited the maximum compression ratio which could be attained, had

Some pioneers clung to the atmospheric inlet valve for a long time, but the advantages of mechanical operation were considerable if the problem of installation could be overcome. The simplest solution in many ways was the 'T-head' side-valve layout seen here, a symmetrical arrangement in which simple gear-driven camshafts operate valves on opposite sides of the head via pushrods. The biggest problem is that the compression ratio is inevitably low because of the width and area of the combustion chamber at piston top dead centre; but the valves can be made large.
(Ludvigsen Library)

An alternative to the T-head layout is the L-head, in which a single side camshaft operates all the valves set in-line on one side. The compression ratio could in this case be higher although the combustion chamber shape leads to pumping losses as gas is shuttled between the main chamber above the piston and the smaller one above the valves. The engine shown here is the Erskine Six of a slightly later period. Apart from clearly demonstrating the L-head principle, it has interesting details including the worm-drive off the camshaft for the oil pump, and the drain tap for collected debris from the bottom of each cylinder!
(Ludvigsen Library)

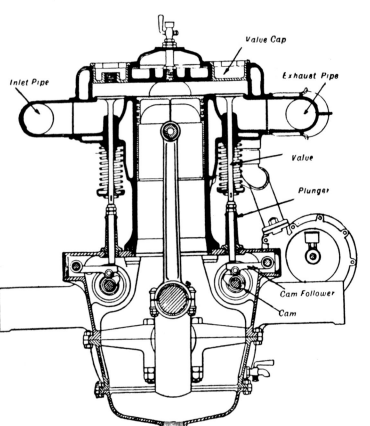

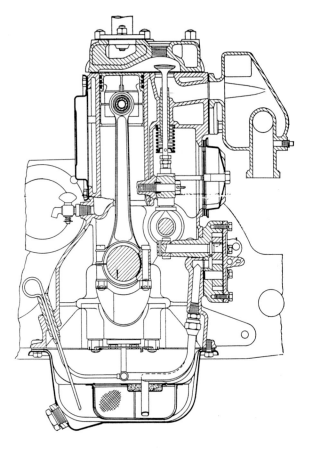

simply not occurred. The average engine ran a compression ratio of around 4:1, and you have to be up to around 8:1 before the limitation begins to bite. It was certainly appreciated by many engine designers that overhead valve layouts would make for better gas flow through the engine, but again, there was little point in achieving a high volume of gas flow unless engines could be made to run significantly faster than the 2,000rpm maximum of the day.

As to detail, the question of carburation had been more or less sorted, although many companies would enter that field during the 20th century, all with ideas of their own to improve the consistency of fuel-air mixture preparation in all circumstances. There was far less certainly over the question of fuel itself. The 19th century motorist was mainly accustomed to buying 'motor spirit' from the chemist or the hardware store. There were many producers, each with their own formulation and generally with a lack of understanding of the detailed chemistry of fuels. Standardisation there was not; that would all come much later.

The magneto had quickly become the standard ignition system, combining a strong spark and reliability with independence from an external electricity supply. From now on, engines would at least not be hamstrung by doubts about whether there would be enough energy to fire the mixture in the cylinder – so long as the mixture strength itself was about right, and the ignition timing was somewhere near the end of the compression stroke. Analytical souls had already taken a close look at the effect of varying the ignition timing, although it seems that serious thinking about the effect of valve timing, and especially of overlap (of having inlet and exhaust valves open simultaneously) took a little longer.

In effect, the first hurdles had been overcome. The passenger car engine was very much a going concern. The challenge from now on would be to improve it.

2 The 1900s

The coming of the multi-cylinder engine

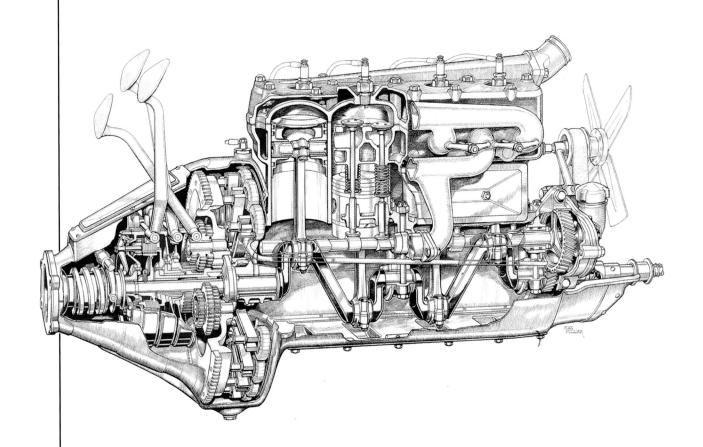

By the end of 1899, the internal combustion engine worked reasonably well and had already been refined in many respects. It was no longer a minor miracle that road-going vehicles could move under their own power. Thousands were already doing so. In the new century, customers did not regard it as an intriguing novelty, but as a tool. Those customers would take reasonable reliability for granted and be far more interested in performance and refinement. For the engine designer, that meant one thing: more cylinders.

The theory of mechanical balance in internal combustion engines had been fully laid out during the 1890s by Frederick Lanchester – even to the extent of suggesting the improvement that could be achieved by the addition of counterweighted balancer shafts. In fact, Lanchester had such faith in mechanical subtlety that the first cars sold by the company he founded, in 1901, had a flat-twin engine of massive proportions, with bore and stroke of 113.4 x 144.5mm for a capacity of 4,034cc. As explained in the previous chapter, each piston carried two connecting rods, driving crankshafts rotating in opposite directions, the result being well-nigh perfect mechanical balance – and a great deal of complication. Originally air-cooled – a system to which the opposed-cylinder layout more readily lends itself – Lanchester's engine was eventually given water cooling as its output rose with development, to a reputed 22hp.

Some by now well-established companies were at first slow to pick up on the multi-cylinder trend. De Dion-Bouton, encouraged by the number of pioneering vehicle manufacturers – even in the USA – who bought its tough, well-proven little single-cylinder engines, remained faithful to the configuration through the turn of the century and indeed, was still building and selling 6hp and 8hp versions until 1912. In 1902, the company filed its first patent for a 2-cylinder engine, an interesting device which appeared to consist of two single-cylinder engines, complete with their flywheels, back-to-back on either side of a central cylinder in which a third piston formed a balancing mass, moving in the opposite sense to the two 'real' pistons which moved in unison. The company claimed that this engine's use of full pressure lubrication, with feeds through the crankshaft and up the connecting rods to the gudgeon pins, was a world-first, although as already mentioned, Mors appears to have beaten them to it in 1899. To some extent it is a question of how you define full pressure lubrication, and the De Dion-Bouton system was certainly comprehensive even by modern standards. As Count de Dion observed at the time, the system resulted in much reduced oil consumption (because early drip-feed systems were in effect total-loss in principle) and also allowed significantly higher engine speeds because the lubrication of highly stressed bearings was far more reliable.

De Dion began building two series of 2-cylinder water-cooled engines in 1902, both with a bore of 110mm and a stroke of 100mm, thus 1,901cc capacity, with outputs of 12hp and 15hp respectively, but it is not clear how the difference was achieved. Strangely, the company then began a process of reducing the bore and increasing the stroke so that by 1914, the last 2-cylinder to be offered had dimensions of 66 x 120mm for a capacity of only 821cc and a rated output of 6hp. The main reason was that from 1904, De Dion had concentrated on 4-cylinder engines. In that year it filed a patent showing such an engine with a remarkable mix of modern and archaic features. For example, it had a robust five-bearing crankshaft and a gear-type oil pump driven off the camshaft; yet it retained atmospheric inlet valves and its cylinders were separately manufactured and water-jacketed. This approach kept the engine fairly light but also made it physically bulky in relation to its modest bore and stroke of 90 x 100mm (2,545cc) and a rated output of 15hp. The following year it had been followed by a 4,417cc (104 x 130mm) unit of 24hp, and in 1907, De Dion at last abandoned the atmospheric inlet valve in favour of all mechanical operation in an 'L-head' layout. Its first engine with this feature was a 4,942cc (110 x 130mm) unit rated at 30hp; but lest it be thought De Dion's engines were growing inexorably bigger – like so many in this decade, as we shall see – the company also embarked on a process of 'shrinking' its 4-cylinder engines in parallel with the 2-cylinders. Thus by 1913, it was offering an engine

Opposite: The Ford Model T engine reflected the experience gained with several earlier models, none of them built in large numbers. Ford's design solution depended on simplicity, on the philosophy of 'the minimum necessary' but also on some advanced features including what was then the latest in iron foundry techniques for casting the block, and gasket materials for the detachable head which so eased the frequent task of maintenance. The engine was made almost entirely 'in-house' but Ford bought his carburettors from Holley. (LAT)

Through the early 1900s De Dion-Bouton expanded their engine range to include a series of neat two-cylinder units like the one seen here. Though better balanced and with a higher power-to-weight ratio, and with output better suited to the larger and heavier vehicles beginning to emerge, they still retained atmospheric inlet valves, and cylinders (in this case, cast as a pair) with integral rather than detachable heads. This caused no great problem so long as the valves were housed externally in separate 'initial combustion' chambers. (Ludvigsen Library)

Sections through a two-cylinder De Dion-Bouton engine show how the long connecting rods were now slender I-section beams. The two-throw, two-bearing crank itself is machined all over. Note the bolted attachments of both the main bearings (with oilways leading to them) and the surprisingly slender big-ends; also the way in which the crankcase is split along the crankshaft centre-line and forms a completely stressed barrel with no separate sump. (Ludvigsen Library)

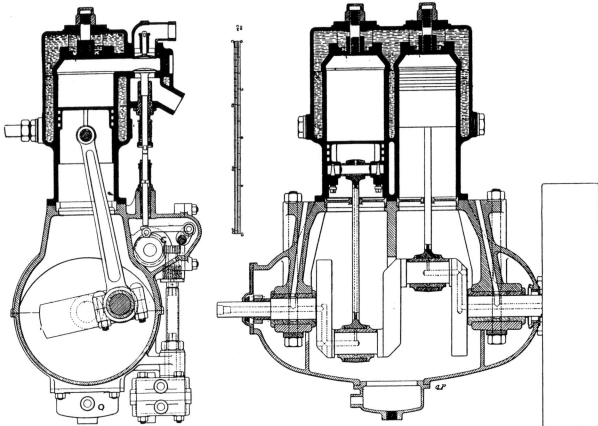

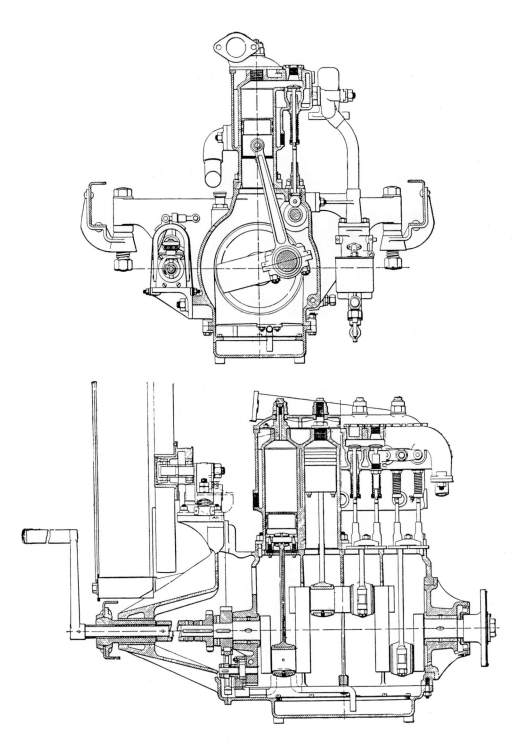

Later still in the 1900s, De Dion-Bouton – then one of the world's leading engine-makers with dozens of customers and licensed producers – extended its range to four-cylinder engines of the type seen here. Many of the principles seen in the two-cylinder engine are also evident, but there are important differences, most notably the final abandoning of atmospheric inlet valves in favour of mechanical actuation in an L-head layout, and the adoption of a conventional sump. Intriguingly, De Dion-Bouton also made some four-cylinder engines which resembled four single-cylinder engines on a common crank, and which therefore had a five-bearing crankshaft. (Ludvigsen Library)

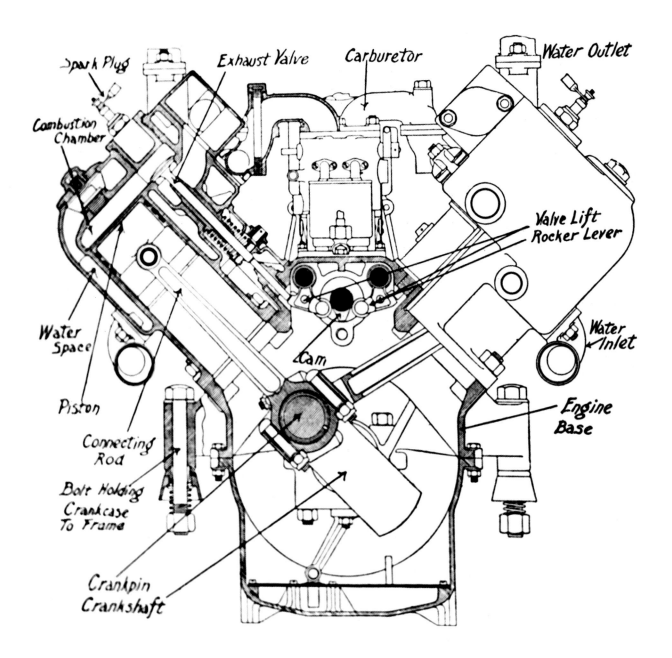

Spark Plug

Combustion Chamber

Exhaust Valve

Carburetor

Water Outlet

Valve Lift Rocker Lever

Water Space

Water Inlet

Piston

Cam

Connecting Rod

Engine Base

Bolt Holding Crankcase To Frame

Crankpin Crankshaft

Almost De Dion-Bouton's final throw as a leading-edge engine designer was this pioneering V8, with an L-head, side-valve layout that used a complicated bell-crank linkage to operate all the valves from a single shaft, and housed its updraught carburettor within the vee. Note that the cylinder heads are still integral rather than separate, with the cylinder castings bolted to the crankcase, a common practice in the 1900s. The crankshaft had only two main bearings, and the connecting-rod big ends were forked so that the cylinders could be directly opposite instead of offset. (Ludvigsen Library)

of only 1,008cc (54 x 110mm), rated at 8CV, to serve the light-car market with which it had always been closely associated.

De Dion-Bouton had one more ace up its sleeve, moreover. While others worked on 6-cylinder development, with Holland's Spyker exhibiting such an engine (with individual cylinders, a T-head side-valve layout, and a capacity of no less than 8,686cc) in 1902, and Britain's Napier becoming the first company to actually put a 6-cylinder engine into series production in 1903, the French company went straight for a V8, the first to be designed specifically for a car. The idea had its roots in the rash of V8s which had emerged in France, from 1904 onwards, for use in the earliest aircraft: examples came from Antoinette, Renault, Buchet and others, and some of these had been 'shoehorned' into high-performance and record-attempt cars. De Dion had a strong interest in aviation as well as cars, and by 1908 his company had developed a water-cooled 90° V8 aero engine of 100hp, quickly followed by a smaller air-cooled unit of 80hp. By 1910, the expertise thus gained had led to an automotive V8 with a bore of 94mm and stroke of 140mm, for a capacity of 7,773cc and a rated output of 35hp. Just as De Dion's 4-cylinder engines by this time resembled two 2-cylinder engines on a common crankshaft, so the V8 had the look of four such units, with the valve gear pushrods operated from a single camshaft in the centre of the vee.

The De Dion history modestly records that the V8 was exhibited at the New York Motor Show of 1912, and that an example was bought by Charles Kettering of Delco. Two years later, the first V8 Cadillac engine emerged . . .

Towards **more cylinders . . .**

The activities of De Dion-Bouton through the 1900s, starting with single-cylinder engines only and ending with the pioneering V8, showed how quickly the idea gained ground that engines with less than four cylinders were strictly for cheap, light cars. It had become widely appreciated that an in-line 4-cylinder engine would deliver acceptable refinement for most needs and that an in-line 6-cylinder would – in theory -come close to perfection. So the questions in the minds of engine designers changed. It was no longer a case of how to make the engine work, but much more one of how best and most economically to make a multi-cylinder in-line engine, which came down to the question of how you designed the cylinder block and head.

The most obvious approach was to make a crankcase – literally, a case surrounding the crankshaft and housing the main bearings – and attach individual cylinders to it. In this way a great deal of existing technology could be carried across, and engineers could feel reasonably confident about such things as cylinder roundness and cooling. It was not that they were unaware of the alternative of a single-cylinder

block containing four or six bores: more a case that they were worried about the way expansion of the block would turn those bores slightly oval, possibly with serious consequences. Also of concern was whether the flow of coolant through such a block would lead to some parts of the engine becoming much hotter than others, setting up thermal stresses and allied problems of distortion. The crankcase on the other hand had to be in one piece, and this is why the idea of considering at least the upper half of the crankcase and the cylinder block as a single cast-in-one unit took some time to evolve.

The safe approach at that time was to make cylinders individually – and most likely in one piece, with no separate and detachable cylinder head – and provide them with flanges via which they were bolted to the one-piece crankcase. The drawback of this layout was that the engine tended to be very long by modern standards because of the need to leave space to attach each cylinder individually. This in turn encouraged the 'modern' feature of a main bearing between every crankshaft throw: without being so well supported, the crankshaft would need to be massively heavy, or run the serious mechanical risk of 'whipping' itself to severe wear and early failure. It is almost entirely for this reason that the decade saw many 4-cylinder engines with five-bearing crankshafts, something which would not return to fashion, and for rather different reasons, until the 1960s. Some advanced ideas about cylinder block construction did emerge in this decade, most remarkable of all the 6-cylinder Napier already referred to, which used an aluminium block into which the steel cylinders were pressed, a concept several decades ahead of its time. The Napier certainly made a contrast with the much lauded Rolls-Royce 40/50 Silver Ghost, whose engine employed two blocks of three cylinders secured to a massive crankcase built around a seven-bearing crankshaft – very much an example, as so often with Rolls-Royce, of adopting a highly conservative design approach, but with painstaking attention to every small detail.

A halfway house to a fully integral cylinder block was to cast the cylinders in pairs, a move quickly undertaken by most engine designers. This made the engine potentially more compact, and cheaper to make, without running too many risks of distortion or local overheating. It also meant that some of the main bearings could be taken out, leaving an intermediate bearing only between each pair of cylinders. What was more, the idea lent itself to a 'modular' design

approach: two pairs of cylinders for a 4-cylinder engine, three pairs for a 6-cylinder. Ultimately, the integral block would take over, but that was really something for the next decade. For reasons of lightness and good cooling, many of the aero engines of the First World War, often emerging from pre-war car factories, retained individually fabricated steel cylinders with water jackets welded into place.

Refining the
cylinder head

The question of cylinder head design was something else. This was the decade which saw the rift open up between the side valve, sitting alongside the piston, moving in parallel and in the same sense, and the overhead valve. Eventually, as we know, the overhead valve won the day, but this was not at all obvious in 1900 and not dreadfully obvious until around 1930. The side valve had simplicity in its favour. As we saw in the previous chapter, before 1900 it had been realised that the best way to operate a valve was via a

Already pre-eminent among British manufacturers was Rolls-Royce, its reputation established by the 40/50hp Silver Ghost seen here. The cylinders for the straight-six engine were cast in two blocks of three; the single updraught carburettor, the inlet manifold and the cooling arrangements can all be seen in this installation view. Both then and later, the Rolls-Royce reputation depended on faultless workmanship and high-grade materials rather than advanced design. (Ludvigsen Library)

camshaft driven at half-speed off the crankshaft. With a side valve, all that was needed was to site the camshaft slightly above and to one side of the crankshaft, and use short pushrods to bridge the gap between the cams and the stems of the valves. If the valve was overhead, then the pushrod needed to be longer and therefore heavier, and somewhere above the cylinder head something like a fulcrum shaft and a rocker were needed to reverse the motion. The difficulty and expense of doing this encouraged the retention of atmospheric inlet valves for a remarkably long time – as we have seen, De Dion used nothing else until 1907. Yet, in the midst of this apparent

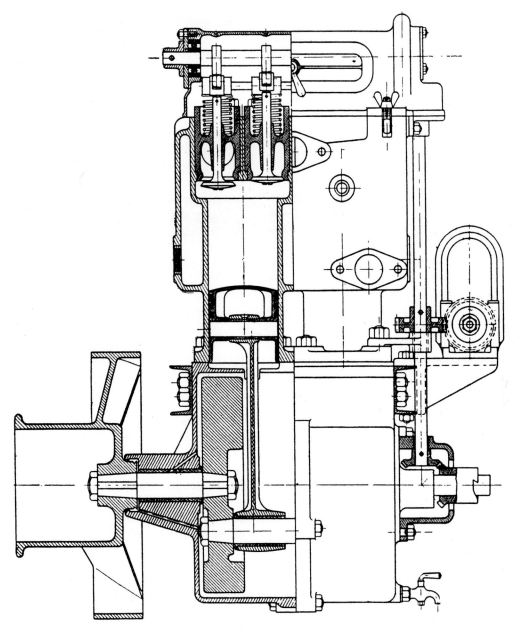

groping towards the idea of what we would call a modern engine with modern valve gear, some concepts appeared remarkably early, in fact well before their time – witness the 1907 Bollée Type E, which was equipped with hydraulic tappets pumped by oil from the engine pressure supply.

What was less immediately obvious was the best way of driving the camshaft(s). Most of the earliest engines used a gear drive, easy enough as long as the camshaft was sufficiently close to the crankshaft. But it was quickly discovered that gear drives could be noisy and subject to wear, and it took little time for

Even in the 1900s some manufacturers were experimenting not just with overhead valves, but with overhead camshafts. This is the two-cylinder engine offered by SK Simplex who built cars in Newcastle-upon-Tyne from 1908 to 1910. Note the use of a bevel-geared vertical shaft to carry the drive from crankshaft to

camshaft – a popular feature until decent chain-drive tensioners became available. The camshaft sprocket is twice the diameter of the crankshaft sprocket, to produce the required half-speed drive. Note also the roller cam followers – and the separate valve housings clamped into an integral cylinder head!
(Ludvigsen Library)

many designers to conclude that chain drives could be quieter, more compact and easier to install regardless of camshaft position – so long as chain tension could be maintained and any tendency of the chain's longest run to 'whip' could be damped out, which posed a new set of problems especially for the materials specialists. Opinion was not unanimous, however. For example, both Renault and Mercedes continued to use gear-driven camshafts right up until the outbreak of the Second World War.

It occurred to some engineers very early in the century that there was no reason not to sit the camshaft directly above a set of overhead valves, to create the overhead camshaft layout which we now find much more familiar. Arguably the first company to choose this option was Coventry-based Maudslay, founded by three brothers of that name in 1901 (their cousin Reginald was instrumental in the founding of Standard at about the same time). Apart from the overhead camshaft, the original 1901 Maudslay engine, designed by Alexander Craig, was odd in having only three cylinders – but in those days it was still rather a case of three cylinders being better than two, and the niceties of secondary balance which would worry the designer of a modern engine peaking at 6,000rpm were of no real concern at that time. Maudslay built a whole series of 3, 4 and 6-cylinder engines through the 1900s, always remaining faithful to its OHC layout. At one point, the company seriously studied an alternative slide-valve layout but took it no further than the drawing-board. Having pioneered engine design in this particular respect, Maudslay sadly petered out as a car manufacturer after the First World War, finding commercial vehicles a better business to pursue. Other engineers were quick to follow this lead, although generally only in specialised racing cars. Maybach was certainly aware of the theoretical advantages of the overhead camshaft and used the technology in his Mercedes racing cars from 1906, but clearly he felt it was too early to apply it to series-production cars.

The overhead camshaft **challenge**

The basic advantages and problems of overhead camshaft valve operation have not changed, needless to say; it was simply that in the 1900s they were being confronted for the first time. Inevitably, an overhead camshaft makes the engine much taller than a side-valve unit, although that was no real problem given the tall build of most cars of that era. Much more serious was the question of how to drive the camshaft from the crankshaft, given the separation involved. Gear drive was not exactly out of the question, but called for a whole train of gears rather than just a pair – more expense, more noise (but to this day it remains the method of choice for out-and-out racing engines). A possible alternative was a vertical shaft with a bevel gear at each end, driven by the crankshaft and driving the camshaft; but the bevel gears themselves threatened problems, calling at the very least for extremely careful and precise assembly. Some designers, then and later, used what amounted to a set of three long, slim connecting rods joining two 'mini-crankshafts', one driven from the actual crankshaft, the other driving the camshaft. This solution was used by Bentley among others. In the end, however, the chain drive proved the most satisfactory solution, cheaper, quieter and easy to lubricate, and requiring only that the chain be carefully tensioned. It was possible to use a single very long chain, or to split the drive part-way, with a primary chain to a jackshaft (which could usefully be used to drive accessories) and a secondary chain from there to the camshaft sprocket itself. Over the years, many subtle variations of the chain layout would be devised.

The decade saw a steady evolution in the quality of engine components and accessories – sparking plugs, magnetos, and most of all perhaps carburettors. In 1907, the SU carburettor, possibly the best-known of all such instruments, made its first appearance. Its potential was quickly exploited, but there is less evidence at this stage of any real care or understanding devoted to the scientific design of the inlet and exhaust manifolds. While racing engine designers might have been groping towards the fundamentals, simplicity and minimum cost reigned among production car engines with no attempt whatever to minimising intake flow resistance, avoiding the problems of 'wall wetting' with petrol evaporating out of the mixture before reaching the cylinder, still less of taking any account of flow interference between cylinders. But then, multi-cylinder engines were in their infancy and their subtler requirements could hardly be taken aboard all at once, even by Doctor Lanchester.

The decade did however see the first primitive work on engine supercharging, carried out in the USA by Chadwick, who was trying to coax a 6-cylinder side-valve engine with restricted breathing to produce the required output. It also saw the Swiss engineer Buch essay the idea of turbocharging, for a diesel engine – although it would be many years before the diesel became a practical power unit for any kind of road transport, let alone a passenger car.

The rise of **the Americans**

This was a decade in which the Europeans, having pioneered car engine technology thus far, found themselves being matched if not actually eclipsed, by the Americans. It was above all perhaps the decade during which Henry Ford, having worked his way through a whole series of car designs – the Models A, C and F with 2-cylinder in-line engines, the B and N with 4-cylinder units and even the Model K with a 6-cylinder power unit – finally pulled all his ideas together and rolled out the Model T in 1908. Not that the Model T engine was – in most respects – advanced even by the standards of its age: a tough 4-cylinder side-valve unit with bore and stroke of 95 x 101mm for a capacity of 2,864cc, it was eventually persuaded to deliver 22bhp at extremely modest speed (but a good deal of torque at even more modest speed, naturally). It was certainly notable for its detachable cylinder head, at a time when few manufacturers would have dared take the risk: but Ford was confident in the new technology of copper-and-asbestos head gaskets, following extensive trials. Also, despite a policy of making almost the entire car 'in house' (literally; freighters delivered iron ore to the Red River plant and complete cars emerged from the other end), Ford bought carburettors from Holley, having discovered just how difficult it was to develop a satisfactory instrument from scratch. It was good business for Holley, who eventually supplied the carburettor for every US-built Model T. But in so far as the engine helped the Model T to succeed, it was by being tough and easily maintained – thanks in no small part to that detachable head – rather than technically advanced or being unduly powerful.

Ford was by no means alone, although the success of the Model T left him outselling other manufacturers by some margin. While they worried about how they could possibly compete with Ford, they generally set out to appeal to customers who could afford to spend more than the Model T cost. Among these rivals were three of the companies which were eventually drawn into the General Motors empire – Buick, Cadillac and Oldsmobile – plus other respected names like Packard, Studebaker and Pierce-Arrow. Perhaps strangely – with the benefit of hindsight – only Pierce-Arrow actually concentrated on 6-cylinder engines prior to 1910, its range topped off by the huge 66, a T-head side-valve which began life in 1909 with a capacity of 10,619cc and was progressively enlarged to 13,514cc (127 x 177.8mm) early in the next decade. None of its American rivals had offered an engine with more than four cylinders by 1910, although they made up for it very soon afterwards. Some of their 4-cylinder engines were large, with Buick going as high as 5.5-litre capacity. In this, however, they still lagged well behind some of the monsters which were emerging in Europe, for which only Pierce-Arrow was a match at the time.

European engines: **bigger is better?**

Europe was splitting into two camps so far as car design was concerned. On the one hand there were engineers who ideally saw cars as being light, compact and easily handled – the 'runabout' idea. On the other, there were designers who saw no problem in making cars ever bigger and heavier, if that was the only way to achieve high performance and to make them suitable for long journeys.

The contrast was perhaps most evident in France. De Dion-Bouton, as we have seen, confined itself to relatively small engines; so did Panhard. Renault on the other hand worked its way steadily upwards, never kicking over the technical traces, always with side valves, seeking power and performance through increasing capacity, its first 6-cylinder engine of 1908 (for the massive Type AR, fiscally rated at 50CV) having a swept volume of 9,499cc (120 x 140mm). A year later, the Renault Type BH had a 6-cylinder engine with a more modest capacity of 7,536cc, notable among other things for its massively undersquare dimensions (100 x 160mm). Even Renault's 4-cylinder engines were becoming huge, the Type AT having dimensions of 130mm x 140mm for a capacity of 7,430cc.

Peugeot's engineering ran to similar extremes. The company entered the new century still building its rear-engined 2-cylinder models, such as the Type 30, on a modest scale, but in 1901 it began to create an ambitious range of front-engined cars including the

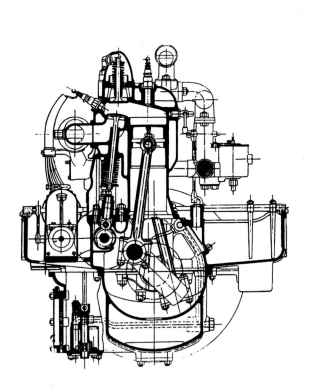

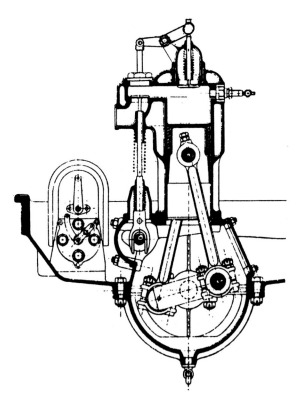

original single-cylinder 652cc (94 x 94mm) 'Bébé' (with a claim for operating costs of 'one sou per kilometre'), plus 2-cylinder and 4-cylinder models. By 1904, Peugeot's engine sizes ranged up to 7.1-litres, and with its introduction of 6-cylinder engines, there was more to come: by 1908 the largest Peugeot power unit was 11,150cc.

In Germany, a similar picture was emerging at the then rivals Benz and Daimler. At the turn of the century, the Benz Parsifal series offered one 4-cylinder engine of 3.1-litre capacity, but by 1903 the biggest Benz engine, a T-head with four cylinders arranged in-line as two blocks of two, had dimensions of 120 x 130mm for a capacity of 5,880cc. By 1906, Benz had moved up to an engine of similar configuration but with a capacity of 9,240cc (145 x 140mm). Technically of more interest in this decade were Benz's first engines with the four cylinders cast as a monobloc, with chain instead of geared camshaft drive and L-head instead of T-head valves. These engines, the 10/20 and 14/30 of 1909, were far more modest in size, with capacities of 2,610cc (85 x 115mm) and 3,560cc (90 x 140mm) respectively. Benz did not venture a 6-cylinder engine until well into the next decade.

An interesting split became evident at this time with the emergence of cars from the company which

Yet another alternative valve layout tried in the first decade of the last century was the 'F-head' with an overhead inlet and side exhaust valve. This layout was adopted by Audi for its 1909 four-cylinder engine (left), which shows how rapidly engine design advanced during the decade when compared with the 1904 *Horch four-cylinder unit (right) which used a similar layout but with the inlet valve in a housing in the roof of the main combustion chamber. In either case the valves can be made larger than in an L-head, side-valve layout. Note how the Audi's crankshaft centre is offset from the cylinder centre-line. (Ludvigsen Library)*

the former Benz engineer August Horch had founded, with ideas not too far removed from those of Henry Royce in that they called for achievement of the highest possible standards, almost regardless of cost. In Horch's case they also involved advanced thinking, because among the cars he developed in this decade was one with an OHV 4-cylinder 18/22hp engine, which was followed by the 7.8-litre, 6-cylinder 60hp. Disagreements over this model – which did not do well – led poor Horch to leave the company that bore his name; he went off to found Audi and begin yet another line of development.

Meanwhile at Benz's rivals Daimler, the decade had more or less commenced with the famous creation of the first Mercedes, designed by Maybach (Daimler himself having recently been laid to rest in the cemetery in Cannstatt) in accordance with an outline specification written by Emile Jellinek, and christened in honour of Jellinek's daughter.

The Mercedes was the first 'modern' car in Daimler's product line, and for it Maybach designed an engine which was a classic in many respects. In its original 35hp form it was big – two blocks of two cylinders with 116mm bore and 140mm stroke, for a capacity of 5,913cc. It had a T-head valve arrangement, with a camshaft at each side, gear-driven from the crankshaft, and originally included the oddity (although by no means unique at the time) of throttling the engine by varying the inlet valve lift. Having started large, Maybach next applied the formula to engines of more modest size, the 8/11 and 12/16 of 1,760cc and 2,860cc respectively. Thereafter, repeating the story spelled out elsewhere, it was a matter of growth in pursuit of power – all the way to 9,235cc 4-cylinder (140 x 150mm) and a 10,180cc 6-cylinder (120 x 150mm) engine. Along

the way, Maybach diversified his engineering approach to the extent of trying an overhead inlet and side exhaust valve layout (in the 15/20 of 1905 and the 14/30 of 1909) as well as moving to six cylinders laid out in three pairs. In the 6-cylinder engines he also resorted to the use of two sparking plugs per cylinder, an interesting and logical move.

There were yet other entrants in this 'capacity race'. In Italy, Fiat began the decade building modest little cars with 2-cylinder in-line engines laid on their sides for ease of rear-mounted installation. Then the company moved to L-head 4-cylinder engines of

This Fiat engine is in many ways typical of 1900s units, with four big cylinders cast in two pairs. Less usually, this particular example is a T-head design – note the four pushrods visible on this side – suggesting this is the 7.4-litre Series 3 24HP of 1905. The inlet manifold leading from the small updraught carburettor is simple in the extreme, and the geared accessory drive at the front is fully exposed. The steering column can be seen to the left, squeezing its way through the engine compartment. (Rinsey Mills)

Interest in horizontally-opposed engines was by no means restricted to Benz's flat-twin Velo units. From 1901 to 1907 Wilson-Pilcher built flat-four and flat-six engines for its cars, first in London and later in Newcastle-upon-Tyne. Illustrated is the 4-litre flat-six which powered the company's 18/24hp model. The advantages of low height and compact layout are easily appreciated. With engines like this being built so early, and both V4 and V8 engines appearing before 1910, one wonders why the V6 was such a late invention. (Rinsey Mills)

steadily increasing size, the massive 60hp of 1904 boasting 10,563cc (145 x 160mm) and its first 6-cylinder unit, the 50–60hp of 1907, at 11,039cc (125 x 150mm). Alfa Romeo was not formed until 1908, initially to take over and build on the foundation of Darracq's Italian operation, and up to the end of the decade it built only cars with that company's 1.5-litre, 2-cylinder side-valve engines. Its flowering of mechanical genius would come later. Lancia began serious operations in 1908 with the 4-cylinder engine for the Alfa, a relatively modest unit with its cylinders cast in two blocks of two, with dimensions of 90 x 100mm for a capacity of 2,453cc – but with the remarkably high claimed output of 53bhp at 1,800rpm. It was accompanied by the Dialfa, with a 6-cylinder engine which consisted in effect of three blocks of the same cylinders and hence a capacity of 3,815cc. By 1909 Lancia had already bored-out the

Alfa engine to 95mm for a capacity of 3,120cc for the Beta. It is perhaps significant that Vincenzo Lancia, a man of stubbornly held and usually sound engineering convictions, eschewed the rush to huge engines and was attracted to the idea of near 'square' bore and stroke dimensions.

Without ploughing through lists of similarly huge engines from many of the car manufacturers of the time – and there were plenty of them, especially in Europe – it becomes clear that the first decade of the 20th century was one in which most engine designers had given up on the idea of extracting high specific output from their passenger car power units. It was not that they didn't know how to do it: their racing engines, although again often huge, were far more sophisticated, with overhead camshafts and four valves per cylinder. For example, by 1908, Fiat had designed the 16-valve S61, a quasi-racing engine which delivered 115bhp at 1,800rpm, albeit from a capacity of just over 10 litres.

No doubt there were several factors which prevented them from going larger still, but one of them was fundamental to engine design and that was the speed with which the mixture burned. It had become clear that beyond a bore and stroke of about 150mm (or six inches in the then-current Imperial measure) the speed of piston movement could outrun the speed with which the flame front advanced through the mixture, leaving a residue still burning (or simply unburned) during the exhaust stroke. The result could be an exhaust-wrecking backfire – and with engines of this size, a backfire could indeed be a fairly serious explosion. This is why, even in this generation of monsters, one finds relatively few engines with a bore or stroke of more than 150mm – or, perhaps more accurately, with a combined bore and stroke of more than 300mm.

Had these engines run at more than around 1,300rpm which was all most of them could manage, the problem would have been even more serious. As it was, there were three possible approaches to a solution. One was to add more cylinders rather than to make each cylinder bigger – and this was certainly being done. The second was to employ internal aerodynamics to create rapid, turbulent movement within the cylinder, spreading the flame more quickly – although if this was done without sufficient understanding, it could do more harm than good, sapping power and (especially in the flat, inefficient combustion chamber of a T-head or L-head engine) creating pockets of weak mixture which would not burn properly. The third way was to light the fire in two places at once – in other words, to use twin sparking plugs, which is what Daimler (and Benz) eventually did. It is interesting to note, in passing, that the cylinder size limit was rarely exceeded by piston aero engines: for example, the Pratt & Whitney Wasp Major, possibly the 'ultimate' piston aero engine to see large-scale production, had a bore and stroke of 146 x 152.4mm – but 28 cylinders for a capacity of 71.5 litres!

Another *en passant* observation is that this decade perhaps understandably saw the steam car making a technical challenge. Two of the longer-lived companies in this area were in the USA. Stanley built cars mainly with flat-twin steam engines from 1897 through to 1927, while the White steamers, from a company founded in 1900, used compound engines, following practice already well established in ship engines, in which the energy remaining in the low-pressure steam emerging from one cylinder was extracted in a second, larger cylinder. White built its last car in 1918. In France, Serpollet persisted with a series of steam cars with flat-4 engines, but only until 1907. It should perhaps have drawn the logical conclusion from the fact that De Dion-Bouton, which had made increasingly successful steam-powered vehicles for nearly 20 years up to the mid-1890s, then switched its efforts to the internal combustion engine.

Modest beginnings

It must have been difficult for those working at the time to discern which of the then-new engine design features were truly significant and which were merely red herrings. At the turn of the century, new vehicle manufacturing companies were being created at the rate of up to 30 a year, in Europe and the USA. Many of them did not make their own engines, but bought them from other suppliers – which is where De Dion-Bouton did so well at this period – and others merely copied designs they had seen elsewhere. They did not always choose the best examples to copy; but ease and cheapness of manufacture was always a consideration and this certainly favoured either the side-valve configuration, or the already classic 'Daimler layout' of an atmospheric inlet valve over a mechanically operated exhaust.

There was particular confusion in Britain, or so it seemed. A great many companies, especially in the Coventry area, grew out of the then thriving bicycle

industry and to begin with were most interested in extremely light cars in which they could make best use of their existing expertise. This implied the use of simple, single-cylinder engines of a kind which were already falling out of favour in other countries. There may also have been some feeling that small, light vehicles chugging along at not much more than trotting pace would be less likely to excite the anger and opposition of those two great British vested interests, the horse and the railway. It is worth bearing in mind that the railways were already in trouble, having last paid a collective 4 per cent return on capital invested in 1891. Among the still-famous names that started off with light, single-cylinder products were Sunbeam, with a series of single-cylinder prototypes at the turn of the century; Wolseley, whose first (Austin-designed) production cars of 1901 had a transverse rear-mounted engine (114.3 x 127mm, 1,303cc); Humber, which was building the 5hp Humberette in 1903; and Rover, whose 8hp (114 x 130mm, 1,327cc) appeared in 1904. To these might be added Riley, which began by buying De Dion-Bouton engines, but made its own light vee-twin units from 1904.

In almost all cases, though, the ultra-light cars suffered two fundamental problems. Their performance when running properly was insufficient to compensate for the frequent occasions on which they did not; and (partly in consequence) they were incapable of commanding prices which would enable their manufacturers to operate profitably. The only way to go was up, towards 4-cylinder cars at least. Thus of the examples named – there were, of course, many others, some now almost lost in the mists of time – Sunbeam and Humber were building 4-cylinder models by 1902, and Rover by 1908, while Wolseley became for a while, part of the Wolseley-Siddeley operation whose largest engine was a ridiculous 4-cylinder unit of no less than 15.7-litre capacity! Austin had long since left Wolseley to found his own company which, by 1906, was building T-head side-valve 4-cylinder engines with individual, separately-cast cylinders.

This hasty change of approach did little to encourage truly original thinking where the principles of engine design were concerned. There were some honourable if, perhaps, premature exceptions: Maudslay's pioneering of the overhead camshaft layout has already been mentioned. A more consistent approach came from Daimler (of Britain, as distinct from the original Daimler in Germany).

The British operation began as a licence-builder of Daimler products but quickly became a manufacturer in its own right, with a series of high-quality but thoroughly conventional 4-cylinder and 6-cylinder cars which, during the 1900s, first gained the company its long-valued British royal patronage. In 1908, Daimler acquired the British rights to the Knight sleeve-valve principle and became its most dedicated and longest surviving user. In a very short time it had standardised on sleeve-valve engines, and retained them until the 1930s.

One of the more successful British companies, and much admired at the time, was Napier. It had been long famed for its expertise in machining, and was therefore well placed to solve some major problems confronting the engines of the 1900s. The first Napier engine, in 1900, was a vertical twin, but later that year the company produced a technical tour de force: an in-line 5-litre, 4-cylinder engine whose most interesting feature was a one-piece aluminium cylinder block into which cast-iron cylinder liners were pressed – a feature perhaps 20 years ahead of its time. Far less admirable was its use of no less than three atmospheric inlet valves for each of its big cylinders! By 1903, however, Napier had broken more new ground with the launch of the world's first series-production 6-cylinder engine, the 4.9-litre 18/30hp, and for the rest of the decade its engine range multiplied and its top-range engines became steadily larger. As already discussed at length, this was a time when more power was sought through ever larger swept volume rather than by increasing engine speed – an approach which had the benefit of increasing torque as well as power, which was why some cars of this era were not only remarkably flexible but capable of brisk acceleration from low speeds even by modern standards. This policy also ensured that engines became steadily heavier and bulkier. In the case of Napier's 6-cylinder engines this process proceeded through the 7,722cc (127 x 101.6mm, in other words 5 x 4in!) 60HP of 1907, and culminated in the 14,565cc 90HP, another 1907 model. These were all L-head side-valve engines notable for their high standard of build.

Napier had the arguable advantage of being London based and therefore away from the centre of motor industry activity in the Midlands, where all manner of ideas became fashionable, were tried and often discarded in favour of the next one. To be a pioneer car company in Coventry was to find it difficult to concentrate and maintain a clear design policy. The same geographical advantage applied to Vauxhall, which was founded in the London Borough of that name. The first Vauxhall appeared in 1903, and following a pattern already explained was powered by a relatively crude water-cooled single-cylinder engine of 978cc (101.6mm bore by 120.65mm stroke), sharing many features with the pioneering single-cylinder engines of the 1890s – integral block and head, a mechanically operated side inlet valve, and an atmospheric inlet valve, trembler coil ignition and a Vauxhall-designed spray carburettor. Power output was 5bhp at 900rpm, rising to 6bhp when the engine's stroke was increased the following year to 127mm, for a capacity of 1,029cc. The only really unusual features of this engine were the use of a control to change the tension of the spring on the inlet valve – tightening it increased the engine's maximum speed – and the fitting of a maximum speed governor in the drivetrain to the exhaust valve. This governor could be overridden by a pedal control. Neither feature was greeted with any great enthusiasm.

In 1904, Vauxhall took the unusual step of moving from a single cylinder to three; why not two or four is not revealed in Vauxhall's archive, but the balancing problems must have been interesting, although undoubtedly the engine was more refined than its single-cylinder contemporary, helped by its low maximum speed – it was governed to 1,300rpm – and its use of a four-bearing crankshaft. In keeping with the practice of the times, each cylinder (still with no separate head) was individually cast and water-jacketed before being assembled to the block. With a bore of 95mm and stroke of 115mm for a capacity of 2,445cc, the Vauxhall 3-cylinder, which powered the 12/14, had an output of 12hp (nominally at least). The valve arrangement in this engine was far more advanced, with a low-set camshaft on either side of the block to drive the side-mounted inlet valves on one side, and the exhausts on the other, in a T-head arrangement. Vauxhall quickly produced a similar but much smaller engine, with a capacity of 1,293cc (76.2 x 95.25mm) for the 7/9hp light two-seater, and by 1906 had added another of 1,669cc (81 x 108mm) for the Luton-manufactured 9hp; but after that, the 3-cylinder venture was ended.

As early as 1905, Vauxhall had moved on to its first 4-cylinder engine, a unit of 3,402cc capacity (95 x 120mm) for the 18HP. Apart from the addition of the extra cylinder and the consequent overcoming of many balance problems, the 4-cylinder engine broke little new ground, sadly. It retained the T-head layout of the 3-cylinder, and indeed the monobloc cast cylinder block and head bolted to a cast-iron crankcase. Light it was not. Nor was it powerful in relation to its size: 95mm bore and 120mm stroke meant a capacity of 3,402cc, yet the output was 18bhp at an extremely modest 950rpm. This was years after the German and French pioneers had realised the importance of engine speed in achieving a decent specific output, and sure enough the engine for the successor model, the 12/16HP of 1906, was substantially smaller (90 x 95mm for a capacity of 2,417cc) yet produced 23bhp, mainly by dint of its power peak coming at 1,800rpm. Early examples of this engine had what might be described as an interesting alternative to throttle control, in which wedges slid beneath the inlet valves (under the control of a hand lever) to vary the valve lift and thus the amount of mixture entering the engine. This system was fairly quickly abandoned in favour of a conventional throttle with an accelerator pedal.

Although the T-head layout did have one advantage in allowing the use of very large valves, its compensating drawbacks were by now becoming clearer, and for the A-type of 1908 Vauxhall moved to a new engine based on one which had first been developed for the car which won that year's RAC 2,000 Mile Trial. This engine had an L-head layout, with inlet and exhaust valves on the same side, pushrod driven from a single gear-driven camshaft. With dimensions of 90 x 120mm (3,054cc) and rated at 20hp under the taxation system, it actually produced 38bhp at 2,500rpm. Crucially for Vauxhall, it also proved to have a great deal of 'stretch' and development potential, when taken in hand by Vauxhall's famous technical director, Laurence Pomeroy. That, however, was mostly for the next decade.

In summary

If the 1890s was the decade in which the passenger car engine had been proved to work, the 1900s were the decade in which it was shown to work well and, with the aid of multiple cylinders, with a degree of refinement. Possibly the greatest achievement of the period was to convince those who could afford a car that to travel in this way was not necessarily to be vibrated and deafened en route. By the same token, it was the decade in which standards of reliability improved dramatically, no least through the efforts of the component suppliers, especially of carburettors and ignition systems but also of little appreciated but vital parts like valve springs. It would be a long time before reliability was taken almost for granted, but at least journeys could be undertaken without the near-certainty of immobilisation somewhere along the way.

Inevitably, it was in some ways a messy decade from an engineering point of view. By around 1905 the industry in each of the major developed nations comprised dozens of relatively small companies each with its own idea of what would make the perfect car – and the perfect engine with which to power it. The shrewdest soon perceived that the path to success was to avoid highly original and adventurous ideas and to concentrate on improving what was known to work. The shrewdest of all, like Ford, also realised that if the passenger car was ever to command a huge market, there was no point in developing 10-litre, 6-cylinder cars for sale by the handful to the wealthy. It was a lesson which took longer to penetrate in Europe.

It is easy, with the benefit of hindsight, to condemn many, in fact most of the volume production engines of the 1900s as unadventurous, with side-valves predominating. If racing cars could have overhead camshafts and multiple opposing valves, why were these ideas not reflected in everyday vehicles? The answer is that the market was not ready for them. Nor could it have withstood the cost, especially of the expensive materials which went into them.

The next decade might have, indeed did see further advances – but in most respects it was more like half a decade, in that war intervened, and the smooth course of engine development really only resumed in the 1920s.

3 The 1910s

The storm gathers, rages . . . and subsides

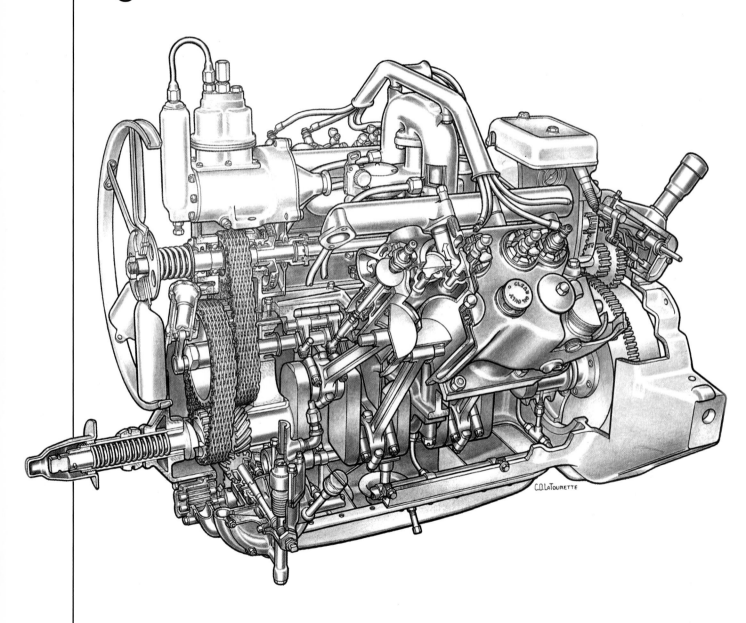

C.O. LaTourette

In many ways, the 1910s form half a decade in the orderly evolution of passenger car engine development. The latter half consists merely of war – although in this case, a war which contributed in its own way to continue and even to accelerate the process. It was a war in which the internal combustion engine played a crucial role, whether in the Paris taxis that rushed the French army eastwards, in supply trucks, in the first generation of tanks and of course in the rapidly evolving aeroplane. Just as important, it left behind a generation of men who had quickly become accustomed to living with and to maintaining cars and trucks. The motor car could never again be the preserve of a privileged upper class able to afford both the vehicle and the employees to keep it running (in the USA, of course, it had already ceased to be).

All this, however, is the story of the second half of the decade. Until 1914, the development of the motor car continued in an orderly way, extending the considerable achievements of the years up to 1910. Probably the great turning-point of that decade was the shift of the engineering balance from Europe to the USA. That was, perhaps, inevitable considering the size of market that the USA represented. Also, partly by chance, the USA saw a 'centre of excellence' for its industry form around Detroit, which had good facilities for materials supply and components manufacture, and a plentiful supply of people with the right skills. Most people are familiar with the story of Henry Ford and his application of the continuous-chain production line principle to car manufacture at the Red River plant, but in fact, the first dedicated car production plant in the USA was built in Detroit in 1899 to make the original Oldsmobile.

By 1910, people had become more accustomed to the idea of the motor car as a normal and useful, rather than an outlandish, form of transport. As observed in the previous chapter, engines in particular had begun to conform to a pattern – except in terms of sheer size. Multiple cylinders, most usually four but increasingly often six, had become the norm. Different valve arrangements had been studied but most engineers leaned towards the L-head side-valve layout, which reduced overall engine height and made for cheap and easy production – this was certainly Ford's view when designing the Model T, which was already well established by 1910 and easily the best-selling car in the world at the time. Others, like Buick as we have seen, preferred overhead valves despite their greater complication and cost, because more power could be achieved from an engine of given size. Some components, such as the carburettor, were already becoming the province of specialised companies, on both sides of the Atlantic.

Serving the first volume market: the USA

Ford, having launched the Model T, concentrated all its massive energy on this one model with few thoughts – at this time especially – of how it would ever be replaced. As previously pointed out, at the time of its introduction the Model T engine was a fairly advanced concept, for example in its provision of a detachable cylinder head which made overhaul, and especially the frequent decarbonising which was then necessary, much easier. It is worth noting that carbon deposits were partly the result of low (or variable) quality fuel with none of the detergent and other additives we now take for granted, and partly a consequence of considerable amounts of oil entering the combustion chamber. Piston ring technology was still advancing, and the concern in the 1910s was that any ring capable of keeping the oil down in the crankcase was probably creating a fair amount of friction and causing wear, either to itself or to the cylinder bore. People crept up on this problem with a combination of subtle shapes and better materials and surface treatments, but it was another 40 years or so before the dream of near-zero oil consumption, almost infinite piston ring and cylinder bore life, and no more carbon deposits was realised.

Engine speeds remained low for all manner of reasons, but mainly to avoid over-stressing the bottom end of the engine with the loads imposed by hefty cast-iron pistons. Everyone knew that light alloy

Opposite: The extent to which Cadillac may have cribbed the design of its first V8 from the pioneering De Dion-Bouton is debatable, although the inspiration was certainly there. This Cadillac cutaway shows the massive chain drive from crank to camshafts, with a second equally massive drive from camshaft to the upper jackshaft carrying the cooling fan and the carburettor. The crankshaft runs in three rather than two main bearings, and the big-ends are not forked as in the French engine, forcing the cylinders to be offset by half a crankpin width. (Ludvigsen Library)

pistons would greatly reduce loads on the big-end bearings and the crankshaft in general, to say nothing of improving operating refinement, but in 1910 the technical problems seemed formidable. In fact, the decade saw the first use of light alloy pistons, in the 1912 Aquila-Italiana, but it was a long time before the idea was widely adopted. In part it was a matter of aluminium casting alloys still needing improvement, but in the main it was fear of the aluminium pistons expanding more than the cast-iron block. The choice, it seemed, lay between a close fit at normal running temperature and a degree of 'slop' when cold, or the risk of piston contact and high wear – if not seizure – in normal running. Eventually, the piston specialists (this was another component which quickly became an industry sector of its own) found ways of designing alloy pistons with minimum expansion. Apart from the choice of material, the other aspect of piston design at this time which strikes the modern onlooker, is that the pistons were extremely deep, long and full-skirted. It was a surprisingly long time before designers learned the art – and, indeed, gained the confidence – to make pistons shallower than they were wide, and even then to cut away the skirt where the risk of contact with the cylinder wall is more or less non-existent. Thus apart from being made of cast iron, the typical piston of 1910 was shaped something like a miniature oil-drum, and a single piston from a 4-cylinder engine weighed rather more than a whole set of modern pistons for an engine of the same size.

General Motors – or the companies that became GM – certainly took a serious interest in alloy piston technology, as in almost everything which would make cars more powerful and refined, as well as easier and more convenient to use. The corporation had largely come together by 1910, already comprising Buick, Cadillac and Oldsmobile, with Chevrolet being added in 1918. The empire also extended into the components sector, since AC Spark Plug joined in 1909, and by 1911 GM had established its central testing and research laboratory, the Dayton Engineering Laboratory Company (Delco), headed by Charles Kettering, a highly influential, although not always successful figure in the history of engine development. One of Kettering's earliest developments was the electric self-starter, which was adopted in production by Cadillac as early as 1912.

In this decade, the corporation's engine design philosophy reflected the desire of then owner W. C. Durant, first to tie up the higher reaches of the American market – abdicated by Ford when it adopted its one-model policy with the T – and then to apply pressure on Ford from above, by increasing the volume and reducing the price of GM's 4-cylinder (and even its smaller 6-cylinder) cars. Buick and Cadillac were central to the first strand of this ambition, Chevrolet and Oldsmobile to the second.

By 1911, Buick had ceased building the 2-cylinder engines with which it had established itself, and concentrated on its range of 4-cylinder engines, of which it had three, from 2.7-litre to 5.5-litre capacity, all OHV of course. Then it turned to better things in the form of its first 6-cylinder engine, for the 1914 B55. In the spirit of the times, this was another big engine, with dimensions of 95.3 x 127mm for a capacity of 5,249cc, slightly smaller (and a lot smoother) than the superseded 4-cylinder.

V8 enters the fray

In the same year, 1914, Cadillac introduced its first V8 engine, possibly – as already related – drawing its inspiration from De Dion-Bouton's 1910 unit. Reflecting the De Dion layout, it was an L-head side-valve unit with dimensions of 79.4 x 130.2mm – a long way under-square, the stroke exactly two inches greater than the bore – for a capacity of 5,429cc. It may not have been the first automotive V8, but the Cadillac was certainly the first such unit to be produced in quantity – some 13,000 were made in its first year. Its output of 70bhp at 2,400bhp represented a step forward by the standards of the day, in both specific output and operating speed. Among other things, the engine featured thermostatic control for cooling. From this time on, Cadillac remained (and remains) a V8 company, its only excursions being higher up the market with a V12 and a V16 in the 1930s; and the Type 51 engine was good enough to continue with no more than running changes, into the 1920s.

Chevrolet was only founded in 1911 and did not become an integral part of GM until 1918, but its products were still crucial to Durant's planning. The company began by making 6-cylinder engines, and cars for the upper reaches of the market, but in 1914 it introduced the H-series OHV 4-cylinder and began to prepare its (lower) ground. In 1915, there appeared the 2.8-litre 490, a stripped-down 4-cylinder model (an electric starter was extra) so named because it was initially priced at $490. This was sufficient to apply pressure to Ford, but Ford responded with price cuts and retained its sales lead. Apparently by way of diversion, Chevrolet introduced a V8 in 1917, but this was really against the overall group policy and this engine died prematurely in 1919. Thereafter, as part of GM, it would concentrate entirely on 4-cylinder 'budget' models.

Oldsmobile entered the decade building the Limited, powered by the biggest engine in its history, a 6-cylinder side-valve monster of the old school, its cylinders cast in three separate pairs, with dimensions of 127 x 152mm for a capacity of no less than 11,581cc, reflecting one of the trends seen throughout the previous ten years. Under GM auspices, Oldsmobile abandoned such extravagance and developed engines which would appeal to a wider audience. By 1915, it had produced its own low-cost 4-cylinder engine, but this did not last long. In 1916, the division had a more suitable engine for Durant's aspirations, an efficient 4-litre V8 with aluminium pistons, which lasted into the 1920s.

Chrysler as a corporation did not exist until the 1920s – Walter Chrysler actually spent the period 1912 to 1920 as general manager of Buick – but Dodge, the earliest of the companies which eventually came together to form his company, started out in 1914 with a 4-cylinder, 3.5-litre engine technically notable only for its use of a dynastart combined starter motor/generator – an idea which has resurfaced at times throughout the history of engine development, but which seems to have reached fruition only in the 21st century with the advent of electronic means of reversing the electrical operation of an otherwise simple machine.

Packard pioneers the V12

Engine design ground was also broken in Detroit by Packard, which introduced its first 6-cylinder engine in 1912, a lumbering T-headed 8.6-litre unit, but by 1915 it had moved to the first automotive V12, the power unit for the Twin Six. Drawing its inspiration from early aero-engine practice, the 60° unit had a side-valve L-head layout and dimensions of 76.2 x 127mm for a capacity of 6,950cc. Strangely, considering that even then most 6-cylinder engines had four main bearings (very often as a consequence of having their cylinders cast in three pairs, with a main bearing between each pair) the Twin Six had only three bearings. That said, it apparently ran smoothly and reliably to its maximum design speed of

3,000rpm, producing 85bhp. The V12 engine continued into the 1920s when it was replaced by a straight-8, then the height of motoring fashion – but the formula had been established, and would return time and again. There were, and are, good reasons why it should. The V12 is, after all, two in-line 6-cylinder engines sharing a common crankcase and crankshaft, and even by 1910 it was well appreciated that the 6-cylinder engine had inherently excellent balance. Its only drawback, in the years before the First World War, was that many 'sixes' had grown huge, ran slowly both because of piston inertia and immensely high-gearing, and consequently suffered from poor refinement – the old joke about 'one bang per telegraph pole' was not far from the truth in some cases. A V12 enjoyed all the balance advantages of the 'six', but with twice as many firing strokes, thus less torque variation and an altogether smoother impression of power delivery. All this, of course, at the expense of almost twice as many components, a lot of complication and the risk of extra internal friction losses: it was an argument which would re-open fifty years later.

Blind alley: birth of the straight-8

As for the straight-8, its foundations were laid during this decade even if the formula only became truly fashionable in the 1920s. The brothers Duesenberg were certainly working on their ideas for an overhead-camshaft straight-8 from 1916, although their first production car only emerged in 1921. By this time they had been beaten to the post by Italy's Isotta-Fraschini, formerly best known for enormous overhead-camshaft 4-cylinder engines, which announced its own 5.9-litre (85 x 130mm, 5,898cc) OHV Tipo 8 in 1919, with first deliveries to customers in 1920. As the following chapter will show, these first examples were followed by a rush of imitators.

With the benefit of hindsight, it seems strange that the straight-8 became so popular when the V8 had already been invented, and moreover shown to work extremely well. To some extent it was a matter of pure fashion. Immensely long, tapering bonnets were seen as a visible expression of power and performance, and straight-8 engines justified their existence. If you opened such a bonnet, it really did seem full of engine – one of the later Duesenberg

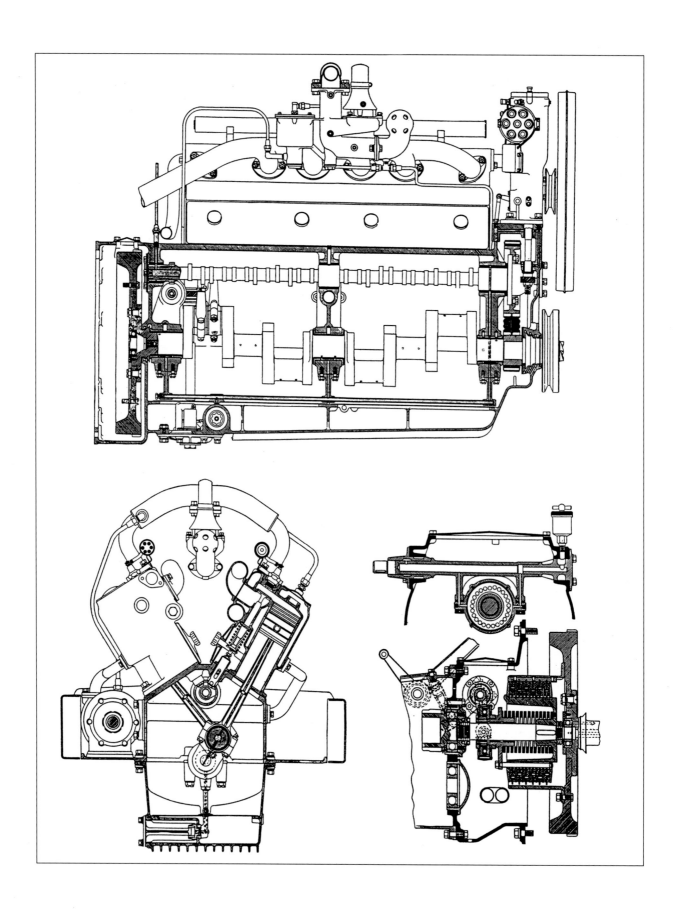

units was over four feet long. Certainly, engineers were encouraged by the thought that – for perfectly good aerodynamic reasons – some First World War aero engines had been straight-8s. It was surely also true that some designers, seeking the ultimate in refinement, shied away from the complication and slightly doubtful balance of the early V8 (until Cadillac solved the problem in the early 1920s with the two-plane crankshaft). Equally, a vee-engine crankshaft was more difficult and expensive to machine, and there was the challenge of fitting 16 cams on to a camshaft scarcely longer than that of a 4-cylinder – by no means insuperable, but a straight-8 camshaft provided more room.

Unfortunately, such long camshafts were subject to timing inaccuracy due to twisting, and the equally long crankshafts were susceptible to torsional vibration. Crankshaft vibration dampers were essential and maximum revs were limited. Racing engine designers often avoided such problems by taking the camshaft drive, and sometimes even the final drive, from between cylinders 4 and 5 but this was scarcely practical in a series production unit. The saving grace was that the straight-8 never sold in large numbers, and only in expensive cars. As a chapter in the history of engine design in general, it is really no more than a facinating example of how and why not to do it.

The European scene

While the American motor industry continued on its expansive way with no more than a brief interruption in 1916–18, things were very different in Europe, on both sides of the front lines in Flanders and France. That is not to say war did not act – as it so often does – as a spur to technology. It could be argued that the 1914–18 war was exceptional in that respect, bringing the tank, the submarine and above all aviation from the status of fringe activity (from nothing, in the case

of the tank) to a fully fledged aspect of conflict. Many European motor companies were heavily involved in designing aero engines too, even before 1914. De Dion-Bouton and Renault in France, Benz and Daimler in Germany, Napier, Sunbeam and Rolls-Royce in Britain all became deeply involved in aircraft engines and learned a great deal as a result, especially in the area of materials and weight-saving design, also in carburation and ignition systems. Not all of this knowledge could be read across directly to passenger car engines, on the grounds of cost if nothing else, but it added to the sum total of knowledge and the confidence these companies felt in tackling technical problems.

In Germany, both Benz and Daimler continued their development of car engines in parallel with their aero-engine activities. Between them, the two companies delivered around 34,000 aero engines during the years of conflict, and Benz was running a 675bhp V12 just before the Armistice. In vehicle engines Benz was arguably the less adventurous, since all its units of this period were L-head side-valve designs except for two 4-cylinder examples, one at each end of the decade: the 5.7-litre Prince Henry engine of 1910, and the 1.6-litre 6/18 of 1918. The Prince Henry unit, built mainly for competition, had a chain-driven camshaft on each side of the block, operating four opposed-vee valves per cylinder, with two plugs per cylinder. Obviously high-technology (and high-cost) for its time, it developed 80bhp at the fairly high peak of 2,200rpm. Eight years later, and clearly drawing on some aspects of aero-engine experience, the 6/18 had a single overhead camshaft, driven from the crankshaft by a vertical drive shaft and gears, and produced just 18bhp at 2,100rpm from its 1,570cc (68 x 108mm). In between times, Benz had concentrated mainly on 4-cylinder engines, and had failed to resist the European rush towards ever bigger power units in the period up to 1914. Its biggest 'proper' car engine was the 75bhp 33/75, with 130mm bore and 160mm stroke, for a capacity of 8,340cc – about as big as it was desirable to go with only four cylinders. Two even larger engines, including the monumental 200bhp 82/200 of 1912, with 185mm bore and 200mm stroke for a capacity of 21,495cc, were really intended for airships rather than cars. Benz's two 6-cylinder engines of the period, the 21/50 of 1914 and the 25/65 of 1915, with capacities of 5,340cc and 6,503cc respectively, were hardly state of the art, with their cylinders cast in three pairs with a main bearing between each pair.

Daimler likewise concentrated almost exclusively on 4-cylinder engines, including some monsters ranging up to the 9,850cc 38/70 of 1910, with bore and stroke of 140 x 160mm, a camshaft on each side of the block driving side valves in a T-head, and two plugs per cylinder, all to deliver 70bhp at 1,200rpm. At the other end of the size scale, the L-head 8/18 engine, also of 1910, produced 18bhp from a capacity of 1,846bhp (70 x 120mm). Certainly the most interesting of Daimler's car engines of this decade, from the development point of view, was its 6-cylinder 28/95 of 1914, with single overhead camshaft (a first for the company) driving vee-opposed valves via rockers. A geared vertical shaft carried the drive to the camshaft, and output was a respectable 90bhp from a capacity of 7,280cc (105 x 140mm). Originally, this engine owed a great deal to aeronautical practice, having spun-steel cylinders with a welded water jacket, but after the war it appeared with its cylinders cast in pairs, and with light alloy valve covers.

Daimler was one of several companies to be fascinated by the sleeve-valve concept, and took a licence for the Knight single-sleeve engine, which it began to produce in 1910. Eventually, the Mercedes-Knight engine was built in three different sizes (2,610cc, 4,080cc and 6,330cc) up to 1915, when work ceased. The great attraction of the sleeve valve, for Daimler and others, seems to have been quietness in operation, when compared with the noisy poppet valve gear (sometimes fully exposed) of conventional engines. In terms of actual performance there seems to have been little to choose, the Daimler sleeve-valve engines all delivering a specific output of just over 10bhp/litre, fairly well in line with the standards of the day, and running to a maximum 1,750rpm.

The scene **in France**

Another company to be won over by the apparent promise of the sleeve-valve was Panhard, which began building 4.4-litre engines under a licence from Knight in 1910. Unlike Daimler, Panhard obviously thought the sleeve-valve was worth persevering with, because they continued to broaden their range with both smaller (2,613cc) and much larger (7,363cc) 4-cylinder units plus a 6-cylinder, of 6.6-litre capacity, all prior to the outbreak of war. The company persisted after 1918, and indeed through the 1920s and into the early 1930s.

De Dion-Bouton, meanwhile, the great engine pioneer and purveyor of power units to many early vehicle builders, rather lost its way after the final triumph of the V8. Perhaps it spread its efforts too wide – it listed fourteen distinct models in 1914 – and consequently shallow: in the years up to 1914 it was still building cars with one, two, four, and ultimately eight cylinders. For no obvious reason, the company never built a 6-cylinder engine, except for commercial vehicles in the 1930s, when it had already abandoned car manufacture. Perhaps also, it clung too long to the formulae which had made it successful early on; for example, its 14CV 4-cylinder engine of 1912, with dimensions of 80 x 140mm for a capacity of 2,814cc, still had its cylinders cast in pairs with a huge centre main bearing between them, was still an L-head side-valve, and still did not have detachable cylinder heads. Access to the valves for assembly and maintenance was via screwed-in overhead caps – this was five years after Ford had launched the Model T. Sometimes, too, the company went for features which were elegant but impractical, at least for large-scale production. The 20CV V8 of 1912 (75 x 130mm, 4,595cc), like the larger original, had forked connecting rods which meant the opposing cylinders could be directly opposite one another instead of slightly staggered, as is necessary when big-ends are paired side-by-side on a single journal. Whether or not because of this piece of expensive elegance, De Dion then decided this big V8 needed only two main bearings!

This decade of course saw Peugeot's celebrated Grand Prix engine with its twin overhead camshafts and four valves per cylinder, but there were no such technical adventures in the company's production cars. Side-valve 4-cylinder engines were the order of the day, with modest capacities. Peugeot had briefly succumbed to the temptation of huge engines in the previous decade, including one 6-cylinder unit of 11,150cc, but it had established a strong reputation for light cars including its 'Bébé', and in the years leading up to the war Peugeot customers were offered the latest model to bear this affectionate name, with an 855cc (55 x 90mm) 4-cylinder engine designed by the young Bugatti, no less. Complementary Peugeot engines included one of 1,452cc, rated at 7CV, and a 2,613cc 12CV – competent, but not advanced.

Renault offered new car models in plenty up to 1914, but little in the way of advanced thinking where engines were concerned. All its power units of this time used the L-head side-valve arrangement, and represented a mix of 4-cylinder and 6-cylinder designs. The company seemed more enthusiastic than most about 'big-banger' engines and apart from the 10CV of 1910 (70 x 110mm, 1,693cc) designed nothing new of less than 2-litre capacity in the years 1910–14. Its biggest 4-cylinder offering was the 45CV DQ of 1913, whose 4-cylinder engine had dimensions of 130 x 160mm for a capacity of 8,495cc – proving yet again the point that there was a well defined upper limit to practical cylinder size. Of the 6-cylinder engines of this period, the smallest was 3,619cc (80 x 120mm) while the largest was 7,540cc (100 x 160mm). Apart from the fact that some of these engines – but not the bigger ones – had monobloc-cast cylinder blocks, Renault's approach of the time was rather formulaic, with no evidence either of originality or of concern for the lower end of the market. It was something of a missed opportunity, because almost as soon as the First World War came to an end, Renault would face a determined interloper with a shrewd eye for this market sector, in the form of one André Citroën. But that would be a story for the 1920s.

Fiat dominates in Italy

In Italy, Fiat already held sway, although like Renault, the Italian giant did not at this stage choose to venture too low in the market – or rather, it was by no means convinced that a profitable market for small, light cars existed. Thus in the run-up to 1914, Fiat's smallest engine was the 1,847cc (70 x 120mm) 4-cylinder L-head unit fitted to the Tipo 1 of 1910, and then in slightly developed form (with 19bhp at 2,000rpm instead of 15bhp at 1,700rpm) in the Zero of 1912, a model which would be built in larger numbers than any previous Fiat. In 1910, in fact, the Tipo 1 formed the bottom rung of a 'ladder' of five models of increasing engine size, with the Tipos 2 to 5 weighing in at 2,612cc, 3,967cc, 5,699cc and 9,017cc respectively – all with four cylinders, all using the L-head side-valve layout. At this stage, cylinder heads were still not detachable: the one-piece cylinder and head castings were bolted to the separate crankcase, as were so many contemporary European designs. One interesting feature seen in the Tipo 1 – and previously in Fiat's 1908 Taxi design – was the use of a large light-alloy casting which formed not only the engine sump, but also the lower half of the flywheel housing and of the gearbox casing, neatly tying the whole assembly together and enabling it to be mounted to the body as a unit.

Unlike Renault, Fiat was able to continue low-volume production of some of its models – notably the 2B and the 3A, larger-capacity developments of the Tipo 2 and Tipo 3 respectively, the first with a longer stroke, the second bored out – throughout the war, and to continue development programmes. Thus, in 1919, it was able to launch three new models, the 501, 505 and 510, as the basis for its post-war range into the 1920s. From the point of view of engine design, all three retained the L-head side-valve layout with single gear-driven camshaft which had characterised the pre-war production engines (as distinct from the several racing 'specials'). Only their specific output, well up on 1914 levels, revealed how much Fiat had learned in the war years, not least from its deep involvement in aero engine design. Thus the 1,460cc (65 x 110mm) unit in the 501, with 23bhp at 2,600rpm, managed nearly 16bhp/litre compared with the 10.3bhp/litre of the 1914 Zero. The 2,296cc engine in the 505 had a more modest specific output of 13bhp/litre, as did the 3,446cc 6-cylinder engine (with the same 75mm bore and 130mm stroke) in the 510. It is clear that this improved performance was achieved not least by running to higher speed, with improved manifolding and valve timing – moves very much in the right direction.

Alfa Romeo was not much of a power in the Italian scene in this decade – up to 1920 its total production barely exceeded 1,000 units – and it was in any case evolving into a company which would combine racing activities with the production of relatively small numbers of high-performance sports cars, in fact rather in the manner of the modern Ferrari. Lancia however was a more determined opponent for Fiat, although its presiding genius had yet to devise the narrow-vee layout which made his later engines such a remarkable combination of compactness and power, as related in the following chapter. In 1910, Lancia introduced a 4-cylinder monobloc engine of 3,460cc (100 x 110mm) for the Gamma, and in 1911 followed up with the longer-stroke (130mm, thus 4,080cc) version for the Delta and Epsilon. A further lengthening of stroke to 160mm produced the 5,030cc engine for the Eta, but it seems that Lancia was unhappy about the idea of going so 'under-square' and testing the sensible limit for the stroke dimension. In any event, in 1913 he produced the far more nearly 'square' (110 x 130mm, 4,941cc) engine for the Theta, delivering 70bhp at 2,200rpm, for a specific output of better than 14bhp/litre – good going for a pre-1914 unit, but then 2,200rpm was quite a daring speed for an

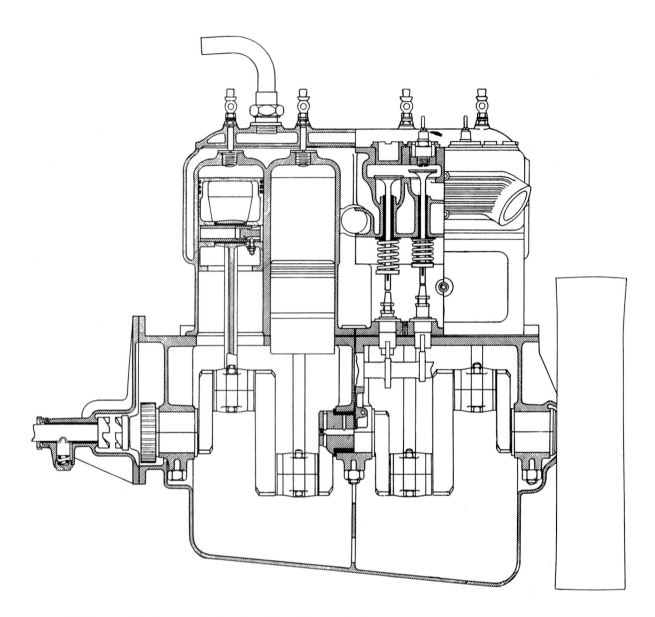

engine of this size, by the standards of its day. The Theta engine, which served the company well until the arrival of the narrow-vee engines in the early 1920s, was the first Lancia unit to use a Zenith carburettor – Lancia had previously made his own, but like Henry Ford, realised this was an area where the components specialists were now making the running. It was also the first European engine to be fitted with an electric starter, following the lead established by Cadillac in the USA.

Apart from Fiat, Alfa Romeo and Lancia, Italy was not without its small-scale operations, mainly producing large, luxurious cars in small numbers. One that has already been mentioned is Isotta-Fraschini, which managed to be the first car manufacturer to offer a straight-8 engine, and furthermore managed to do so, just, before the end of the decade.

In Britain: **the birth of an** idiocy

The year 1911 saw one of the most unfortunate episodes in the history of British production passenger car engine design, which cast a pall over the proceedings for the next thirty-odd years. This was the decision to adopt the RAC horsepower formula as the basis for annual motor taxation.

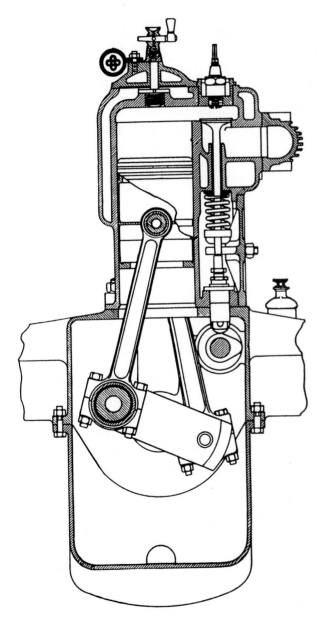

It is well worth a minor diversion into some basic mathematics to see how this came about. If, without worrying about actual units for the most part, we call the piston area A, the piston stroke L, the brake mean effective pressure (BMEP, the average pressure developed and exerted on the piston during the power stroke) P, and the operating speed of the engine (normally, in rpm) N, then the work per power stroke of the piston is:

(P x A x L)

and the rate of working in units per minute, in other words the power output, is:

(P x A x L x N)/2 (dividing by 2 because only every other stroke is a power stroke).

Now comes the remarkable reasoning which constrained British engine design for so long. The committee – of course it was committee – sought a way of turning this formula into an easily calculated number for the purposes of taxation. For this purpose, it needed to reduce the formula to one in which the only variables were the physical dimensions of the engine. It could have said, on the basis of established values at the time, that it was reasonable to assume a value (in the old money, so to speak) of 90lb/sq in for P, and of 2,000rpm for N, so that – with the insertion of a suitable additional constant to take care of the units – the rated horsepower would be:

90,000 x (A x L)

and of course, (A x L) was the swept capacity of the cylinder. Then multiply by the number of cylinders, and you have the 'official' horsepower.

However, this was too easy. The figure for P was indeed accepted, but in a fit of misguided mathematical elegance, the committee pointed out that (L x N x 2) was the average piston speed of the engine – the distance travelled per unit time, which we can call S. Thus the rate-of-working term could be written as:

(P x A x S)/4 . . . which seems commendably simpler.

Fatally, instead of saying that 2,000rpm was a fair average engine speed at peak power, the committee justified its elegance by deciding that 1,000 feet/minute was a fair average for the piston speed.

Now, therefore, the basic calculation becomes simply:

22,500 x A . . . and like magic, piston area has become the sole determinant of power output!

If this seems like nonsense to anyone who appreciates that power output depends on the rate of burning fuel, which in turn depends on the rate at which gas can be passed through the engine (air/fuel mixture in, burned exhaust gas out) which is in turn directly related to the swept capacity of the engine, then rest assured: it is a nonsense. But it was a nonsense which meant that from 1911 until 1947, British cars paid an annual tax based on engine piston area rather than capacity. It is interesting to note that the French adopted a very similar formula in 1911, and abandoned it for something more sensible (although more complicated to work out) in 1913! Eventually, to complete the story, the RAC rating was abandoned almost immediately after the Second World War. At first there was an attempt to replace it with a rating based on swept volume, but in 1948 the Treasury decided to apply the ultimate in simplicity and charge all cars the same amount – at least, until very recently.

The effect on engine design was entirely predictable. To minimise the tax payable, engine designers tended to go for the smallest possible bore and the longest possible stroke despite the fact that this made for high piston speeds and relatively low maximum rpm – as well as reducing valve area and generally restricting breathing. The result was a generation of tall, heavy engines poorly placed to exploit the discoveries which were made in the next two decades about the importance of gas flow – engines which were increasingly difficult for the British industry to export. The only 'advantage' was that many European cars, with engines designed to more rational principles, were handicapped by higher RAC ratings and were more difficult to sell in Britain. In effect, the rating was what we would now call a 'non-tariff barrier' to car imports.

Naturally, attempts to 'cheat' the formula concentrated on beating those two constant-value assumptions, for BMEP and piston speed. Progress was rapid on both fronts, and before 1920 it had become common practice among car manufacturers (and not just in Britain) to quote the rated or taxable horsepower of an engine followed by the actual output, hence (say) 12/30, an engine with a rating of 12hp but a demonstrated output of 30bhp. Both of the figures assumed in 1911 are now totally archaic. To optimise BMEP – without resorting to supercharging – it is necessary to ensure that the cylinder is filled with 'clean' mixture of exactly the right strength before ignition, and to have an efficient combustion chamber shape which ensures that as little energy as possible is rejected to the coolant. The 1911 figure of 90lb/sq in (620 kiloNewtons per square metre in modern units) was the average at a time when so little was known about the engine's internal aerodynamics, including inlet and exhaust pulse effects, that the gas in the cylinder would never have been close to an optimum mixture. That apart, the L-head side-valve combustion chamber, which was the norm at the time, was a long way from being efficient in modern terms. Today, we regularly see BMEP figures of 160lb/sq in (1,100kN/m2) in the best production engines. As for piston speeds, they have effectively gone through the roof: a modern production engine with a stroke of (say) 85mm will peak at up to 6,000rpm, which yields a mean piston speed of 3,350ft/min rather than the 1,000 of the formula. The reasons are to be found in ultra-light pistons, extremely strong and stiff crankshafts with a main bearing between each throw, strong yet light connecting rods, and last but no least, much improved lubrication of the big-ends.

A final factor is that the RAC formula also threw in, generously, an assumption that the average mechanical efficiency of an engine – its BMEP-generated output less its internal losses through friction and windage – was 75 per cent. Today, in a good engine, it is nearer 90 per cent in most circumstances.

So what effect did all this have on British engine design in the first ten years after the formula's introduction? It is difficult to say. Up to 1912 or 1913 there was clearly some degree of 'design inertia' from the days before it was clear what was going to happen. Then, in 1914, the process of development effectively came to a stop. So it is only in 1919 that engines began to emerge which showed clearly what the formula was doing – and the picture only became completely clear during the 1920s, as the next chapter will show.

Of the 'big names' in British motoring, Austin was building three 4-cylinder models in the run up to 1914, the smallest of 1.6-litre capacity, the largest of nearly 6 litres; no effect there. Post-war, of course, the dimensions of the tiny engine for the Seven reflect the long-stroke approach. Morris only began operations in 1913, using engines bought-in from White & Poppe, a Coventry-based specialist who supplied several other firms as well. Their 1,017cc engine went into the original Morris Oxford, and Morris was enterprising enough, even after 1914, to launch the Cowley with a 1,496cc engine imported from the USA, where it was made by Continental. Import restrictions brought this arrangement to an

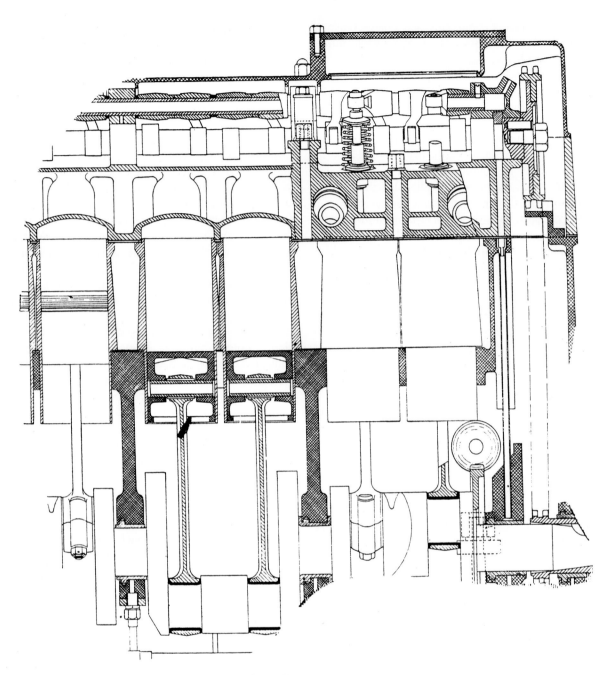

end in 1916. Wolseley and Riley were already old-stagers, founded before the turn of the century, but Riley produced no new engine of significance in the immediate pre-war years, and Wolseley was more concerned with rescuing a situation left behind by an ill-starred relationship with Siddeley. True, by 1913 it offered a range of three models, the 16/20, 24/30 and 30/40HP, but even these numbers suggest the company had yet to concern itself with combatting the effects of the rating. After the war, Wolseley was

In 1919 the British company AC introduced an overhead-camshaft engine which really stood the test of time, lasting in production until the 1960s. Among the features which were then considered advanced was the use of 'wet' cylinder liners (in three pairs) beneath a separate cylinder head, and above all the use of a long chain drive to the overhead camshaft, made possible by the development of an effective blade-type tensioner. See also the indirect operation of the valves via rockers, allowing easy adjustment of valve clearance. (Ludvigsen Library)

quick to introduce a completely new engine range of advanced (but long-stroke) design, with single overhead camshafts.

Of the one-day-to-be Rootes companies, Hillman launched a 9hp, 1,357cc 4-cylinder engine in 1913 – a sound design which in 6-cylinder form, as 'one and a half' of the 4-cylinder, lasted until the mid-1920s. This engine appears to represent a step down the long-stroke road, as does Singer's 10HP, the company's first 'in house' engine and again, a highly successful one that lasted well into the 1920s. Sunbeam went through the decade, before and after the war, mainly with the help of two unimaginative side-valve engines, the 12/16 and the 14/18HP.

A strange case was Rover, which in its early days, was deeply interested in small but refined cars with a selection of 2-cylinder engines. In 1911, Rover was yet another company to be seduced by the appeal of the Knight sleeve-valve concept, which it applied to a single-cylinder, 1,041cc engine rated at 8hp, and a 2-cylinder unit of 1,882cc rated at 12hp. These engines were not unduly successful, and Rover turned instead to a very straightforward side-valve 4-cylinder power unit designed by Owen Clegg, and rated at 12hp. This engine had dimensions of 75 x 130mm for a capacity of 2,297cc, and was therefore very much an RAC formula design which actually delivered 28bhp. It proved highly successful and returned to production after the war, joined not by the sleeve-valve engines but by a new air-cooled, side-valve flat-twin with a capacity of 998cc. This however was anything but a 'formula car' since the engine had near-square dimensions of 85 x 88mm, and it was rated at 8hp for an actual output of 14bhp. Although a sound design, it was effectively doomed from the start by the taxation system.

One British engine of the immediate post-war period which deserves attention is the unit designed by AC for introduction in 1919. The 6-cylinder engine had typical long-stroke dimensions of 65 x 100mm (1,991cc) but was equipped with a chain-driven overhead camshaft, the valvetrain including what seems to have been the first reliable chain tensioner. This quietly outstanding engine, never built in large volume, lasted until 1963, no less, possibly creating a record for sheer longevity of essentially the same design. In the AC sports cars of the 1950s and early 1960s, thanks to continuous steady development including, naturally, a huge rise in compression ratio, it was delivering well over twice the power with which it first appeared.

Perhaps, however, one of the best commentaries on the 'British situation' in this decade is provided by the early history of Vauxhall, at that time of course still entirely British and independent. It was a decade which saw the company secure the services of one of the great engineers of motoring history – Laurence Pomeroy – and yet it continued to make engines which were becoming almost archaic in some respects, with cylinder blocks and heads cast all of a piece, and side valves in an L-head layout.

The 4-cylinder engines continued the 1900s tradition and established something of a high-class sporting reputation – first in the Prince Henry series and then in the even more renowned 30-98. At first, the engine continued from the previous decade with dimensions of 90 x 120mm (3,054cc), developing 48hp at 2,500rpm for the A11/A12 series, compared with 38hp at the same speed in the A09 of 1908. Lessons were being learned . . . and the process of 'stretch' was still to come. The 3-litre engine powered the first Prince Henry tourers, but soon it was bored-out to 95mm, taking the capacity to 3,402cc and the power to 60bhp at 2,700rpm. Then its stroke was increased to 140mm and the capacity therefore to 3,969cc (without, note, increasing its RAC rated horsepower one iota). This enabled the output to be maintained at 60bhp, but at only 2,000rpm, for the big D-type and to no less than 86bhp at 3,300rpm – with a compression ratio of 5:1 and substantially different valve timing – for the 25hp Prince Henry. This was followed by the E-type engine, with dimensions 98 x 150mm (4,525cc) which powered the 30-98. This unit remained faithful to the basic Vauxhall layout – although it moved to a chain-driven camshaft, and indeed to roller cam followers – but in 1913 it produced 90hp at 2,800rpm, rising to 98bhp at 2,750rpm when production resumed at the end of the war.

Meanwhile, Vauxhall also produced its first 6-cylinder engines, beginning with a 3.5-litre unit (85 x 102mm, 3,473cc, rated at 27hp) which delivered 45bhp at 2,500rpm for the B10. This engine shared its basic layout with the 4-cylinders, with all six cylinders and heads cast in one, and secured to the crankcase surrounding the 7-bearing crankshaft. Sadly, the long cylinder block proved difficult to manufacture and the company switched to a layout with the cylinders in two blocks of three, on a new crankcase. This engine initially shared the 90 x 120mm dimensions of the A-series 4-cylinder and thus a capacity of 4,579cc; then it was bored-out to 95mm (again like the 4-cylinder) for full 5-litre capacity and an output of 60bhp at 2,500rpm. This engine was more successful but never achieved the reputation of the 4-cylinder engines of similar layout. None of these engines, it must be said, was particularly long-stroke in its design – but they were certainly better than average for their time.

In **summary**

What is there to say of engine design in this turbulent decade? It was a period which saw the general lines of development even more firmly laid down. There were to be few real oddities from now on, at least, very few that reached production. By 1920 it was clear that 'monster' engines were finished, except for racing and record-breaking purposes – sufficient output for all normal needs could be achieved with units of no more than 4-litre capacity, or a little more for the heaviest luxury cars. The V8 had become established and the sheer quality of the V12

satisfactorily demonstrated, even if the long-bonnet fashion of the 'Roaring Twenties' led the industry into an ill-considered enthusiasm for straight-8s. Partly with the help of the First World War, designers could call on better components – decent carburettors and reliable ignition systems – and engines were being made of better materials. Nobody cast cylinders in pairs any more. Very few designers persisted with the idea of one-piece cylinders and heads, and then not for very long. Light alloy pistons had made their appearance and were slowly growing in popularity. The L-head side-valve layout was still the most popular, and in general would remain so until the need for higher compression ratios, created by a rise in fuel quality underlined its limitations. But already there were plenty of engines – and not just competition engines – which demonstrated the advantages of overhead valves and even of overhead camshafts. During the 1920s, such arguments would become steadily more insistent.

4 The 1920s

Responding to the needs of a mass market

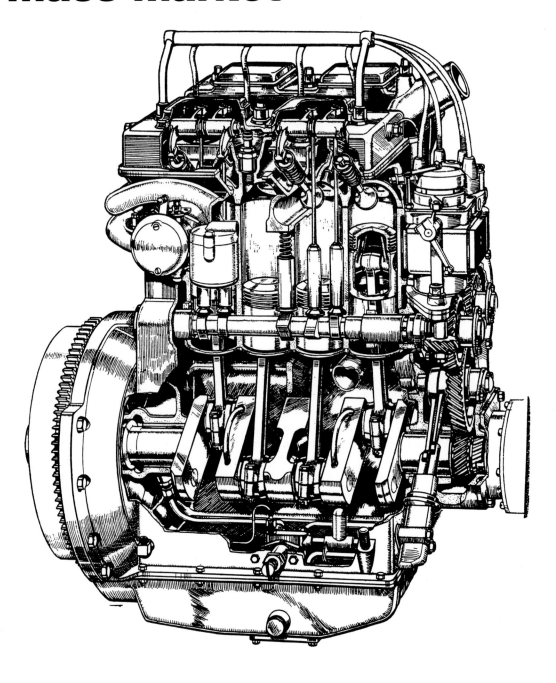

This was a decade which began with hopes of a fast recovery from the depths of the First World War, and which ended, in October 1929, in the first stirrings of the Great Depression which would make life a misery for so many in the first half of the 1930s. Almost inevitably, since engine design follows fashion and demand rather than anticipating them, many manufacturers had worked up to their most ambitious and advanced power units, intended for their most expensive new models, just as the bottom dropped out of the market, especially for luxury vehicles.

In an overall technical sense, this was a decade in which improvement was led by advances in chemistry and in materials technology. Among those advances were the introduction of ethylene glycol as a coolant additive, mainly for anti-freeze protection, but also to raise the boiling point, enabling systems to be run hotter and more efficiently; and in another area altogether, the development of austenitic nickel-chrome alloy steels which greatly improved the temperature resistance and life of valves. By 1922, S. D. Heron had proposed the sodium-cooled valve, which despite its effectiveness, has never achieved widespread use in volume production engines, on the grounds of cost.

The demands of air combat in the First World War had led to a far better understanding of what made a good petrol – good in the sense of resisting the tendency for detonation (knock) and also to providing better protection against corrosion of the fuel system and the engine as a whole. Harry Ricardo's research work in Britain was instrumental in pinning down the engine design features which made detonation more or less likely, while the 1920s was above all, perhaps, the decade in which fuel quality was both improved and standardised, thanks largely to research carried out by Thomas Midgley and Charles Kettering at Delco.

In previous decades, reputable fuel suppliers had maintained their own standards, usually helped by the fact that their supplies came from one particular source or area. There was however no guarantee that an engine carefully set up to work with one make of fuel would run happily on another. Midgley's work, starting with the empirical knowledge that some poorly regarded 'dirty' fuels exhibited greater detonation resistance than clear, 'clean' fuels, led to the conclusion that resistance could be improved with the aid of various additives, and that additives containing lead were the most effective of all. Midgley himself moved on from Delco to become president of the Ethyl Corporation, which specialised among other things in the development and supply of effective fuel additives. Meanwhile, Kettering worked on and by 1927 had established an industry-wide standard built around octane numbers, with fuel performance rated against that of mixtures of heptane (low knock resistance, zero-rated) and iso-octane (high knock resistance, 100-rated). This meant a procedure had been established to measure the quality of any fuel, regardless of its crude oil source and the refining methods used in its making. Eventually it became clear that with careful blending and a high additive level, fuels of more than 100 octane (strictly, Research Octane Number or RON) could be produced, although such improvements did not really appear until the 1930s.

In 1920, most of this work was still in the future, even if it was the near future. Vehicle manufacturers and their engine designers had other things on their minds. As the First World War slowly receded into history, there was a strong feeling, especially in Europe, that the motor car deserved a mass market. In the USA, thanks to Henry Ford and all those who followed in his tracks, the market was well on the road to reality. To create a mass market, prices needed to be brought down but also, engines needed to be made simpler and more reliable. Up to 1914 the majority of car-buyers had probably employed someone both to drive the vehicle and to maintain it: the chauffeur-mechanic had taken over from the coachman, the groom and the stable-hand. From 1920 onwards, the target audience consisted of people – in those days, almost entirely men – who would do their own driving and either perform their own maintenance or entrust the car to one of the thousands of garages established, in the main, by those who had learned their vehicle engineering in the services during the war.

Opposite: A classic British engine layout from the 1920s through to the 1950s was that adopted by Riley, which had hemispherical combustion chambers and used vee-opposed valves operated by pushrods and rockers from twin camshafts, one on either side of the block. The layout might be regarded either as an OHV conversion of the T-head, or as an elegant way to achieve good breathing on a low-built engine with a relatively uncluttered front end. In early Rileys, such as the Nine seen here, the camshafts were gear-driven. In later models they were driven by a short, tensioned chain. (Ludvigsen Library)

Unadventurous inclinations

Where cost did not matter, in the world of motoring competition, engineers were entirely prepared (and had been even before the war) to go for such advanced design principles as twin overhead camshafts and even four valves per cylinder – although for the sake of good cooling and durability, they tended to stick with one-piece (monobloc) cylinders and cylinder heads. There was of course another area in which low cost was not an imperative, and that was the true luxury car. But during the 1920s, such cars tended to become ever larger, heavier, more luxurious and better equipped rather than actually faster. The design emphasis was on smooth, quiet and effortless progress, thus on low-speed flexibility which also reduced the need for gearchanging in an era when clutches were heavy and gearboxes needed skilled manipulation. So in the luxury class there was a trend – a repeat of that seen before the First World War – to ever bigger engines with more cylinders, run at distinctly modest speeds. These requirements were entirely commensurate with side-valve engines – fuel consumption was no kind of consideration – and the 1920s even saw a shift back towards side valves among manufacturers who had begun to lean towards OHV layouts.

Thus the situation at both ends of the market placed a brake on technical innovation, at least in most respects. It favoured the side-valve engine which was both cheap to make and easy to service – easy, at least, so long as the cylinder head was detachable. Some engines survived into the 1920s with the cylinder block and head cast as one, but not for long. Despite the fears which some still felt about the integrity of gaskets, and the nuisance of having to allow for the insertion of bolts to hold everything together, the detachable head was a near-essential in an age where – thanks to still-doubtful fuel quality – it was necessary to decarbonise an engine every few thousand miles. With a monobloc design, this was a major exercise: with side valves and a detachable head, it became no more than a case of lifting the head, scraping out all the visible carbon from the head itself and the now exposed piston and valves, and possibly of removing the valves themselves (not so easy) and regrinding the seats.

In some respects, such maintenance was easier still with an overhead valve design in which the valves could be removed and the seats reground with the head on a workbench – and in which it was also easier to reset valve clearances when setting up the engine after reassembly. With a large handful of exceptions, however, the OHV layout was out of favour mainly on the grounds of cost. A side-valve block was a relatively straightforward casting, and the head an even more simple one: one straight skim across the mating face of each was the only essential machining operation apart from the preparation of the cylinder bores and the valve seats and guide housings in the block, and the drilling and tapping of the spark plug housing in the head. An OHV head called for a great deal more intricate machining, and there was little in the way of compensating savings in the block.

Reasons for survival

It is worth remembering, before passing on, why the monobloc approach had survived for so long. Apart from doing away with the need for a cylinder head gasket, it helped cooling because water passages could be run generously all around the combustion chamber and the upper cylinder, without the considerable interference of at least four, and preferably six through-bolts per cylinder needed to hold down a separate cylinder head. Bear in mind that up to 1920 if not beyond, peak temperatures needed to be held down if components (made of then-available materials) were to be properly durable. Remember also that cooling systems were still crude in the sense that the medium was more or less pure water – this was long before the days of glycol, let alone of pressurised systems which would eventually allow higher coolant temperatures without boiling and thus a greater rate of heat removal. It was also a time when aluminium alloy was almost unknown as a cylinder head, let alone a cylinder block material – and cast iron did not conduct heat away anything like so fast. The only answer, therefore, was to pass water through the system at a high rate, and the larger the coolant passages, the easier it was to do that. Many engineers must have begrudged the space given over to the cylinder head bolts, and the need to retain enough 'land' around the water passages where they passed through the cylinder head joint, to ensure reasonable gasket integrity. Anything less than around 5mm of joint width between cylinder bore and water passage was asking for trouble with the gasket materials and manufacturing techniques of those days, and many stout-hearted motorists carried complete spare gasket sets with them as routinely as they carried the spare wheel; a complete tool kit capable of effecting a cylinder head removal was of course taken for granted.

It is also worth thinking about the technical pressures which were already being exerted on the side-valve principle, even if it needed another thirty years for those pressures to take full effect. The T-head layout, with the intake valves on one side and the exhaust on the other, was already being consigned to limbo in favour of the L-head with both valves on the same side. There were two main reasons for this. The obvious one was that the L-head created a more compact combustion chamber. Engine design had already come a long way from the days when Daimler and Maybach had created and fired their mixture in a 'prechamber' remote from the main combustion chamber and joined to it by a passage which created significant pumping losses. By 1920, the L-head combustion chamber was a single space, although an oddly shaped one with, by modern standards, an appalling ratio of surface-to-volume (but as we have already noted, cooling was a headache and while this ratio did nothing for engine thermal efficiency, it certainly increased the heat rejection rate and provided better cooling performance).

The real drawback of the side-valve was, and would remain, a serious limitation on both compression ratio and valve lift. Because the area of the combustion chamber, viewed from the top, was getting on for twice the area of the piston, it meant that high compression ratio could only be achieved by making the chamber extremely shallow. To achieve a seriously high compression ratio (anything much over 8:1) with a side valve layout is more or less impossible. In addition, the shallowness of the chamber means that the valves can only open a short distance, limiting the gas flow and throttling the engine. To some extent this can be overcome by making the combustion chamber even shallower over the piston and deeper over the valves, so that the mixture is 'squished' towards the valves before being fired. Squishing can be a useful technique by encouraging a more thorough mixing of air and fuel in its aerodynamic turbulence but on the other hand creating the turbulence saps a certain amount of energy, as does the sideways shuttling of the mixture and of the burning gas between the area opposite the valves and the piston crown. Also, the careful shaping of the combustion chamber for this purpose called for close control of cylinder head casting – it was very easy to induce different compression ratios in different cylinders, and post-casting measurement and hand-balancing by 'shaving' was (and still is) very expensive.

Mechanical caution – **with reason**

To some extent all this could be lived with, in the context of the 1920s. Compression ratios started out the decade at around 4–4.5:1 and only slowly rose as designers gained confidence in fuel quality. The Americans, notably Chrysler, were among the first to offer 'hot-rod' high-compression alternatives where users were sure they could reliably obtain fuel of (say) 72RON or better. The cooling situation slowly eased as the decade progressed with the widespread, and eventual total adoption of aluminium alloy instead of cast-iron pistons. Not only did these dissipate heat more quickly, but because they were no more than half the weight of their iron equivalents, they greatly reduced mechanical stresses in the reciprocating and rotating components and allowed engines to run substantially faster. This was again, something which, to begin with, was exploited with caution by most, even though lubricant quality and journal bearing technology were also improving steadily with the adoption of a more scientific approach. Naturally, higher operating speeds threw the breathing shortcomings of the side-valve engine into sharper focus.

More seriously in many ways, higher operating speeds opened up the Pandora's Box of torsional vibration. Both crankshafts and camshafts, but especially crankshafts, could suddenly fail because under the successive impulses from the pistons, they had begun not only to twist from end to end, but first one way and then the other, setting up a vibration which in some circumstances, could enter a resonant period in which the vibration amplitude diverged. In other words, it became larger and larger until the shaft failed in shear, with disastrous results. Essentially, there are three answers to this problem. One is to make the crankshaft sufficiently stiff to ensure its resonant speed in torsion is so high that it is never reached in practice. Another, rarely adopted for obvious reasons, is to make it so weak that the resonant frequency is actually below the normal operating speed range. The third is to add some kind of device which damps down the vibration and prevents it diverging. A favourite technique of the 1920s, first applied to some big American engines of the previous decade, was to add a small second flywheel to the crankshaft nose, with a friction coupling to the shaft so that any sudden change in crankshaft speed – the symptom of torsional vibration – would jerk the wheel around the coupling, absorbing a small amount of energy in the process. It was crude, but it worked.

In any event, fear of torsional vibration became another very good reason not to run engines too fast. Fashion also made life difficult for engineers because for a while, in this decade and the next, the ultra-long bonnet became an admired up-market feature – the kind of bonnet which, if it was not purely for show (some were), covered a straight-8 engine. This trend was well underway during the 1920s and turned into a veritable flood during the following decade. With the best will in the world, it was extremely difficult to design an in-line 8-cylinder engine with a crankshaft proof against any danger of torsional vibration, simply because the crankshaft was so long. Simply to make it stiff enough would have made it prohibitively heavy. Restricted speed and torsion damping had to be used – unless, as in some cases, the designer adopted the more radical approach of treating the unit as two 4-cylinder engines 'tail-to-tail', taking the drive from between cylinders 4 and 5.

American
developments

In any event, what kind of engines did the decade bring? In the USA, there was a stark contrast between the companies which had combined to form General Motors, and Ford. At GM, in alphabetical order, there was variety. Buick continued through the decade building OHV 6-cylinder engines (the division has never built a side-valve engine, remember); it dropped its 4-cylinder engines in 1924 to concentrate on the mid-upper market. Cadillac had been building V8s since 1914, and simply continued doing so, in the process conceiving the two-plane crankshaft which improved the operating refinement of the 90° V8 through better secondary balancing, and also positive crankcase ventilation, to the benefit of oil consumption.

Chevrolet, GM's mass-market contender, by contrast began the decade with an unmitigated disaster. Charles 'Doc' Kettering, running the Delco components operation but increasingly seen as a technical guru, conducted research into air-cooling and decided this was the key to fulfilling GM's ambition to match the Ford Model T in the low-cost mass market. The result was the 'copper-cooled' 4-cylinder and any reference to 'air cooling' was avoided because the contemporary Franklin already used it with some success – and quite remarkably – in its technically

advanced OHC 7-bearing 6-cylinder engines. The air-cooled Chevrolet 4 had some odd features, including monobloc cylinders and heads, an OHV layout with largely exposed valve gear, and a cooling flow which drew air from the bottom of the cylinders, past vertical copper fins, and out at the top, drawn by a massive fan running at one and a half times crankshaft speed. The engine's dimension were exactly square with 3.5-inch (88.9mm) bore and stroke for a capacity of 2,207cc. Kettering also prepared an in-line 6-cylinder version which was supposed to be used by Oakland, then part of the GM group.

Chevrolet actually stopped building water-cooled cars and switched to manufacture of the copper-cooled four, but it quickly became a major disaster and the company was swamped by complaints from dissatisfied customers – not just some, but virtually all of them. The main complaint was of local overheating leading to detonation and generally poor performance, but there were plenty of other problems to add fuel to the fire. GM bit the bullet, stopped production and recalled all 759 which had found their way into customers' hands. The recall was highly effective and very few cars or engines escaped scrapping, but one that did, oddly or perhaps significantly enough, now stands in the Ford Museum at Greenfield Village! Chevrolet then concentrated on building relatively unadventurous 4-cylinder and 6-cylinder models and ended the decade with an equally marked success, the Series AC International Six whose tough OHV all-iron 6-cylinder engine of 3.2-litre capacity, had enough development potential to see it remain in production, in much modified form, until 1953. It was 40 years before Chevrolet tried again with the concept of air cooling.

Rounding off the diverse GM effort, Oldsmobile began the decade with an OHV 4-cylinder engine which was shared with Chevrolet to help the latter out of the copper-cooled mess, and in 1924 followed up with a 2.8-litre 6-cylinder engine. Technically, the division stayed well out of harm's way and concentrated on producing its well-respected but conventional products. Pontiac did not even begin life until 1926, when it was created as a low-cost marque which would 'shadow' the more expensive Oakland models. To help keep down the price, the first Pontiac was launched with a staid but workmanlike 3.1-litre side-valve 6-cylinder engine, designed by a former Cadillac chief engineer. The car's combination of low price and acceptable performance struck a chord – proving that advanced technology is by no means always the quickest route to market success – to the extent that by the early 1930s the child had swallowed the parent: Oakland was no more, but Pontiac continued to grow in strength.

Charles 'Doc' Kettering was one of the heroes in the development of engines and associated systems, but he made a serious misjudgement in seeking to bring the 'copper-cooled' Chevrolet engine to production. Kettering's idea was to air cool the engine via vertical rather than horizontal fins cast into the cylinder walls, *the flow pulled through by a massive radial-flow fan, belt driven from the crankshaft. In service, the results were so disastrous that the mechanical layout of the four-cylinder engine mattered little: General Motors tried to buy back and destroy every extant example, and almost succeeded.* (Ludvigsen Library)

While GM was sorting itself out in sometimes bizarre but eventually successful fashion, Ford kept plodding along with the Model T. At least, it did until 1927, when it became clear that the near 20-year-old design had outlived its appeal to the market. At this stage there occurred the famous hiaitus in production when the Model T line stopped and nothing happened until the new Model A appeared towards the end of the year. It was not that Ford had never thought about a replacement for the old car. Prototype engines of the early and mid-1920s, including a remarkable air-cooled X-8 (in effect, two 4-cylinder radial engines one behind the other), and 4-cylinder units with overhead camshafts and horizontally opposed engines, show that the company, and Henry himself, were undertaking intense research. What seems to have happened was that the

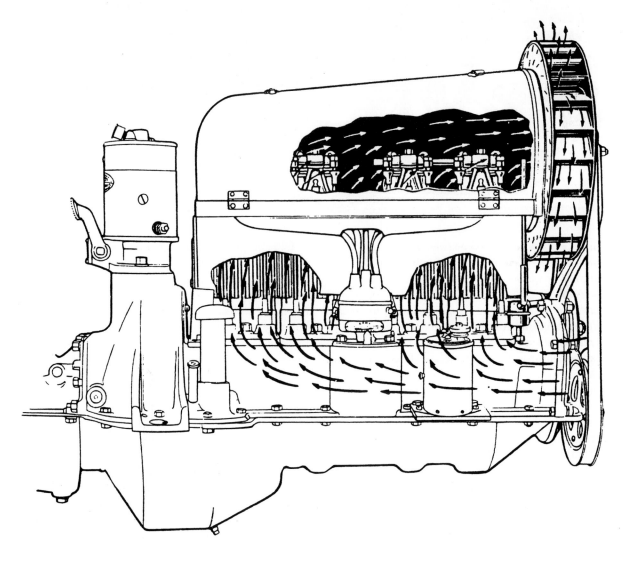

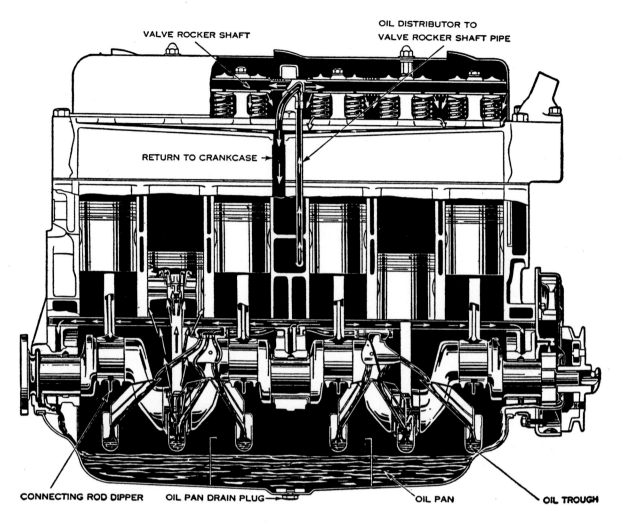

VALVE ROCKER SHAFT

OIL DISTRIBUTOR TO
VALVE ROCKER SHAFT PIPE

RETURN TO CRANKCASE →

CONNECTING ROD DIPPER   OIL PAN DRAIN PLUG →   OIL PAN   OIL TROUGH

The engine which rescued Chevrolet after the 'copper-cooled' disaster was the International Six, an uncomplicated six-cylinder OHV design which, as seen in this sectioned view, had a generously dimensioned cylinder block with coolant passages between the bores, and an extra-large gap to accommodate the wide centre bearing of the three-bearing crankshaft. The drawing was prepared to show details of the engine's lubricating oil circuits via large galleries, with carefully organised flow to all main components.
(Ludvigsen Library)

sudden collapse in demand for the Model T caught everyone by surprise. Ford's response was to make the Model A a much more modern-looking car with an extremely conservative engine design – a 3.3-litre (98.4 x 108mm, 3,285cc) side-valve 4-cylinder delivering 40bhp compared with the Model T's 22bhp. This became Ford's new standard engine: there was no other prior to 1932.

Chrysler, which had only come into existence as a group in 1924, concentrated mainly on 6-cylinder engines, starting with a specially created 3.3-litre side-valve unit. Dodge, the longest established group marque, had its own 6-cylinder engine in 1927. It was left to Plymouth, deliberately created as a low-cost marque to rival Ford and Chevrolet, to carve out a slice of the mass market. This it did to some effect, since demand for the Plymouth Model Q launched in 1928 with its 2,793cc (92.1 x 104.8mm) L-head engine initially outstripped demand, and its low price and economy stood the Chrysler group in good stead as the Depression forced buyers down market.

There were still plenty of minor-league (in terms of production numbers) American manufacturers during the 1920s. Most of them concluded that there was no competing with Ford and GM, and looked for a small slice of the luxury market. Some of them

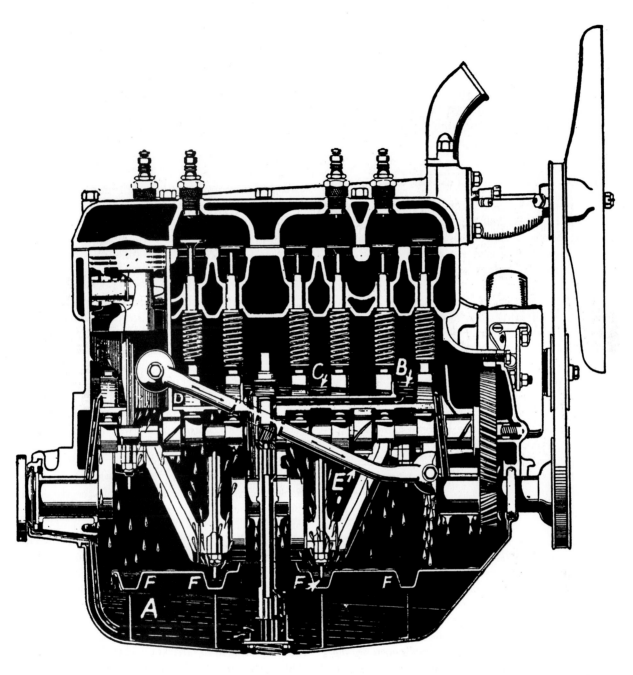

Ford eventually replaced the Model T with the Model A, which resembled its predecessor in having an L-head, side-valve engine. The crankshaft has three main bearings and the camshaft is gear driven. The sparking plugs, in the combustion chamber roofs, are well offset from the centre. Coolant passages around the valves and head are generous, and once again the cylinder block is an extreme example of what was, by 1920s standards, precision casting to save valuable amounts of weight. (Ludvigsen Library)

were at least partly responsible for creating the craze for straight-8 engines. Principal among them was Packard, which in 1923, replaced its pioneering V12 with a 5.7-litre straight-8 in the Single 8 model. Hudson, in this decade a marque to be reckoned with and very much a 6-cylinder specialist, was offering a straight-8 by the end of the decade. Many such engines came not from the smaller marques themselves but from specialist engine manufacturers, the most notable being Lycoming – subsequently better known as an aero-engine maker – who claimed at one time to be providing engines for 200 distinct vehicle models from 57 manufacturers. Among the companies it supplied were Auburn, Cord and Duesenberg, and in an earlier telling of a story which ran much later, Mr Cord liked the product so much that, in 1929, he bought the company, adding it to his luxury car and engineering empire.

Meanwhile, **in Europe...**

Europe was by no means immune to the lure of large-capacity engines and of the straight-8 under the long bonnet, but to begin with the Continent had to climb out of a much deeper economic pit than did the Americans at the end of the First World War.

However, the promise of a mass market beckoned and one of the first to see its potential was the dynamic André Citroën, who had built a major industrial facility to make munitions during the war and decided the best thing to do with it afterwards was to turn it over to car production. Citroën had not been one of the motoring pioneers although he undoubtedly took a strong interest in events prior to 1914. He would eventually become famous as an engineering innovator, but there was little sign of it in his first production engine, for the Type A. This was a well under-square 4-cylinder unit (65mm x 100mm for 1,327cc) with side valves and only two main bearings, at a time when most designers were using three. In theory, two bearings were perfectly acceptable as long as certain mechanical limits were observed, and had the advantage not only of reducing cost but also of lowering friction and increasing overall efficiency. Yet in practice, except for engines of less than 1-litre capacity, the mechanical limits were irksome, as Citroën discovered. The cylinder heads of Citroën's engines were detachable, and for the sake of weight-saving, a light alloy crankcase (as distinct from cylinder block) was cast in two halves. By 1921, Citroën had bored-out this engine to 68mm, taking the capacity to 1,452cc, with an output of 20bhp at 2,100rpm for the B2. There was also a Sport version, with alloy instead of cast-iron pistons, producing 22bhp! An OHV version was also developed for the Caddy, but built only in small numbers.

Citroën's next venture, in 1922, was into the world of the small car – his thinking must have paralleled that of Herbert Austin and the end result was a neat little 4-cylinder side-valve engine with dimensions of 55 x 90mm for a capacity of 856cc. The C-type car was equally neat, to the point where it was licensed for manufacture elsewhere and was also fairly unashamedly copied, not least by Opel.

The C-series was abruptly withdrawn from production in 1926, the year in which Citroën offered a further enlarged engine, of 1,539cc (70 x 100mm) in the B14. An all-new 4-cylinder engine, designed by Michelat, came in 1928. This had dimensions of 72 x 100mm for a capacity of 1,628cc. It was still side-valve, but most importantly it had a third main bearing. As a result it was able safely to run much faster, and its peak power of 30bhp came at 3,000rpm, while the two-bearing engines had been limited to 2,400rpm maximum. A 6-cylinder derivative followed, in effect one-and-a-half four cylinders, hence of 2,442cc, capable of being machined on the 4-cylinder line.

Peugeot spent the 1920s moving slowly and deliberately, making no significant technical moves, even introducing a new 4-cylinder, 1,122cc side-valve engine (for the much respected 201) in 1929. Renault, on the other hand, was still thinking in what had been conventional terms in the previous decade – bigger must be better. True, it soon ditched the huge and archaic 6-cylinder 40CV engine from the GX (100 x 160mm, with a capacity of 7,536cc) with its cylinders cast in two blocks of three, and it made nothing quite as large again. But by 1925 it had engineered the 4,767cc (85 x 140mm) 6-cylinder engine for the LZ, and rounded off the decade by following the path of the straight-8, with an engine of rather peculiar design – a block of four cylinders with additional blocks of two at either end – and dimensions of 90 x 140mm (7,125cc) for the Reinastella – just in time for the Depression. In the opposite direction, so to speak, Renault also caught the European enthusiasm for the 'little six' with the 1,476cc engine (58 x 93mm) power unit for the Monasix and Monastella. These 6-cylinder engines did at least have detachable cylinder heads, a feature which Renault was tardy in adopting. They were also the first Renaults with coil-and-distributor rather than magneto ignition. The only truly small engine offered by Renault in the 1920s was the 951cc (58 x 90mm) 4-cylinder seen in the 6CV KJ and in later form in the 1925 NN. Perhaps the most depressing thing about Renault engines in this decade, however, was their unswerving devotion to the side-valve layout, with geared camshaft drive. There was little evidence of engineering imagination, and much to suggest that planning was marketing-driven.

In Europe, some manufacturers of higher-performance cars were already investigating the practicality of twin overhead camshafts, which had been used in competition since before the First World War. Here are two views of the neat four-cylinder engine for the Ballot 2LS, showing one avenue of thinking. The front view shows a bevel-geared shaft drive to a geartrain in the head, splitting the drive to each camshaft. The side view shows an engine with the camshaft covers – missing in the front view – installed. Note the ring-gear round the flywheel – the electric starter was invented surprisingly early and was in widespread use by the 1920s. (Rinsey Mills/Ludvigsen Library)

Elsewhere in France, among the 'tiddlers', things were remarkably different. As early as 1921, Ballot had been making its DOHC 2LS, although in very small numbers. Two years later Salmson began making the first true series-production DOHC engine anywhere in the world, the 1,194cc Type D, the forerunner of a distinguished series of models all with the same engine configuration. The clear promise of the layout, with Salmson wringing 40bhp out of a 1,086cc engine in the St Sebastien model, was not necessarily lost on the rest of the world – it was simply that few of the volume manufacturers of that era thought they could ever afford the cost. Meanwhile, a sad footnote to French history came late in the decade with the demise of the once pioneering De Dion-Bouton concern, at least as a car manufacturer, its commercial vehicle side continuing rather longer. The company's final car engine was the 10CV of 1927, an odd unit of 70 x 120mm (1,847cc) with only two main bearings. Even more peculiar, the engine was offered in alternative side-valve and OHV layouts, which must have imposed some interesting engineering constraints.

In Germany, naturally, the interest centred on Daimler and Benz, both before and after their momentous merger of 1926. Apart from their 'bread and butter' side-valve engines, with four or six cylinders, ranging up to the 4,160cc unit for the 16/50, Benz's great work lay in the development of the massive (6,800cc initially, 7,065cc eventually) SOHC 6-cylinder supercharged engine for the Type S sports car series, whose appearance more or less coincided with the merger. With the overhead camshaft driven by a vertical geared shaft, and two plugs per cylinder, this engine began life with a naturally aspirated output of 120bhp at 3,000rpm – in other words, a specific output of less than 18bhp/litre – but finished up with twice that, in the SSKL. It is interesting to note that the engine survived with only four main bearings, and

At all times a work of art as well as an engineering statement, the massive straight-six supercharged Daimler-Benz engine as used in the SS/SSK/SSKL series. In particular, note the vertically installed Roots compressor at the engine's nose, in a finned housing and blowing through the updraught carburettors via a passage which also carries cooling fins. Intercooling had yet to be contemplated, but Mercedes knew the importance of delivering the compressed charge as cool as possible. Most details, including the shaft drive to the overhead camshaft, are neatly encased. (Ludvigsen Library)

that (according to the published figures) the supercharger always added 60bhp to the naturally aspirated output. It is also intriguing to see that the SSKL engine ran a compression ratio of 7:1, very high for those days, but one suspects it was not normally run on 'pump' fuel . . .

Daimler meanwhile, brought a more varied assortment of engines into the marriage, mainly SOHC units with vee-opposed valves, developed by Ferdinand Porsche, who succeeded Paul Daimler as technical director in the early 1920s. These engines ranged in size from the 1,499cc (65 x 113mm) 4-cylinder for the 6/40, to the 6,240cc (94 x 150mm) 6-cylinder for the 24/110. Porsche engineered all these engines to accept supercharging, although he was said to accept that the technique would only be acceptable in 'sports and luxury cars'. After the merger, however, new Mercedes engines mainly had side valves, with low-set gear-driven camshafts. Mainly they had six cylinders, although a straight-8 of 4,622cc, producing a modest 80bhp at 3,400rpm, was developed for the big new Nurburg range. There would be more straight-8s from Mercedes in the decade to come – but also a renewed interest in smaller engines with four cylinders.

There were many other manufacturers in Germany in the later 1920s, naturally. When Paul Daimler left the company that bore his (or rather his father's) name he joined Horch, for whom he developed first an SOHC 4-cylinder engine and then an admired DOHC straight-8. Meanwhile, Wilhelm Maybach's son Karl was the technical driving force behind the Maybach company, which specialised in large, powerful cars which, in accordance with Karl's engineering principles, were notably easy to drive by 1920s standards. A 7-litre, 6-cylinder engine was felt not to be sufficiently impressive, even with SOHC, and a 6.9-litre OHV V12 was duly developed, making its debut in 1929. Audi was another company with up-market ambitions, its 1924 Type M having an SOHC 6-cylinder engine of 4,655cc, its advanced features extending to an alloy block with steel liners. The company followed this in 1928 with the Type R, with a 4,872cc side-valve straight-8 engine. One begins to appreciate, perhaps, how besotted the top end of the 1920s was with long, slim engines, and never mind the problems implicit in designing a stiff enough crankshaft. At the other end of the market, buyers could choose from a range of 4-cylinder and 6-cylinder Opels of no great mechanical interest. By 1928 they also had the option of DKW's first light 2-

stroke car – a new venture for a company which had long been in the motorcycle business. As it turned out, the 2-stroke was a technical blind alley, but it took a long time before this was universally accepted.

In Italy, volume car production in the 1920s was the province of Fiat and to some extent of Lancia. Alfa Romeo was building quality sports cars, mainly spun off the back of pure racers, in very small numbers and could hardly be reckoned a technical force at this time – although things began quickly to improve once Vittorio Jano had moved from Turin to Milan. The full benefit of his work really only began to become evident in the production car range in the 1930s, however.

Fiat was lucky to begin the decade with three solid, workmanlike cars with side-valve engines, the 4-cylinder 1,460cc 501 and 2,296cc 505, and the 6-cylinder 510, whose engine was in effect a 505 with two extra cylinders, hence with a capacity of 3,446cc. An early, and effectively stillborn project was the 60° V12 520, whose 6.8-litre engine was to be rated at 90bhp at 2,000rpm. Slightly more modest, but far more successful was the 519 of 1922, whose 4,766cc (85 x 140mm) engine delivered 75bhp. The 519, like the V12 520, was an OHV engine; there followed Fiat's only SOHC production engine of the decade, unaccountably in the little 4-cylinder, 990cc 509. This engine was typical of many rival small units in having well under-square dimensions – in this case 57 x 97mm. It delivered its respectable 22bhp at the notably high peak, for 1925, of 3,400rpm. After that, however, it was a case of returning to the side-valve, partly it seems because many Europeans thought that was the direction in which American engine design was moving. For the rest of the 1920s, Fiat concentrated on keeping its existing model range up-to-date, but without any technical adventurism. One point of interest, however, is that Fiat like so many others planned a straight-8 model, the 520, but killed the project with the onset of the Depression. In engineering terms, though, the 1930s would tell a rather different story where Fiat was concerned.

If Fiat was unadventurous, Lancia was anything but. He (and the redoubtable Professor Fessia) devised a highly original engine layout with the cylinders arranged in a narrow vee, and staggered. Extra bottom-end clearance was achieved by having the cylinder centre-lines intersect in a line well below the centre-line of the crankshaft. The crankshaft itself was designed with crankpin angles that ensured that despite this apparently peculiar geometry, the

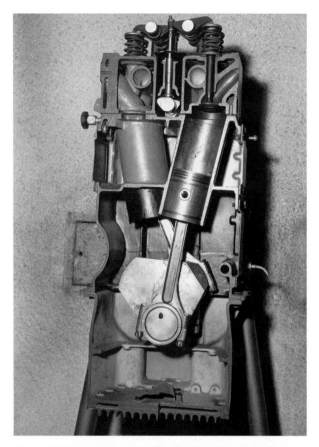

firing intervals would be equally spaced. The most important drawback of this idea, in some eyes, was that it needed very patient and careful calculation on the part of the designers. The geometry was far from 'natural' and the optimum angle between cylinder banks for tight cylinder packing was unlikely to emerge as a nice round figure. The fact that the centre lines of the cylinders did not pass through the centre line of the crankshaft did not greatly matter, within reason, so long as the connecting rod remained clear of the cylinder's bottom end: it simply meant the side thrust on the pistons would not be symmetrical. What it did mean was that the cylinders could be formed within a single block, which for the sake of being slightly wider, could also be a lot shorter, and therefore both lighter and stiffer (as could the crankshaft). The layout did however mean that if the valve gear was not to be a complete mess of pushrods from at least two low-set camshafts (for where would you put a single one, with no vacant centre to the vee?) then the only reasonable answer was a single overhead camshaft operating multiple rockers.

Incredibly, Lancia began the ball rolling with a narrow-angle V12 of 6,032cc capacity which was actually shown at the Paris Salon in 1919. This engine can still be seen in the Lancia Museum in Turin: it is certainly compact by V12 standards, and for an engine of that size, although one fails to see how its overhead camshaft, hardly thicker than a knitting-needle, could have operated 24 valves without twisting badly. However, the V12 went no further and the next move was a narrow-angle (14°) V8 for the Trikappa, in 1922. With well under-square dimensions of 75 x 130mm for a capacity of 4,594cc, the Trikappa had 98bhp at 2,500rpm, a highly

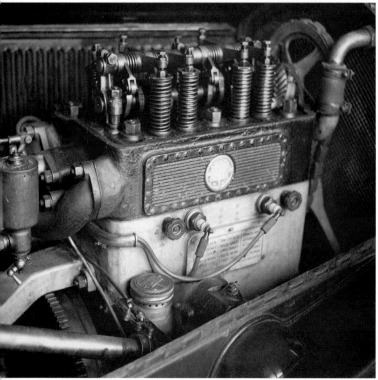

Two views of the highly original engine devised for the Lancia Lambda. The front view in particular shows how setting the cylinders in a narrow vee, and dropping the crankshaft centre below the intersection line of the cylinder centres, enabled the four cylinders to be staggered in a way which saved a great deal of engine length, making the block stiffer and lighter. The result was a challenge to the casting and machining experts, but it was overcome. Interesting is the way the water jacket is formed around the upper sections of the cylinders; also the way the single high-set camshaft operates the valves via short pushrods and rockers. The general view shows just how compact this narrow-vee engine was. (Ludvigsen Library)

respectable output for the time. It looked as though the narrow-vee formula worked.

There followed, in 1923, the narrow V4 for the celebrated Lambda, this time with dimensions 75 x 120mm for a capacity of 2,120cc. The shorter, consequently much stiffer crankshaft, and the slightly shorter stroke enabled Lancia to run the engine at far higher speed than was customary for road cars at that time, with maximum power (49bhp) coming at 3,250rpm. Mainly for this reason, the Lambda actually had a higher specific power output (23bhp/litre) than did the Trikappa (21bhp/litre). So good was the Lambda engine that as the decade progressed, it was bored-out twice, ending up with 82.55mm diameter cylinders – as far as it could safely be taken – for a capacity of 2,570cc and an output of 69bhp at 3,500rpm for the Lambda 223 of 1928. That year also saw a new narrow V8 of smaller dimensions, 79.37 x 100mm, delivering a full 100bhp at 3,800rpm, for the Dilambda. These two engines left Lancia well placed for the coming decade, but there was far more yet to be done with the narrow-vee layout.

Far less originality was evident in the UK, and a lot of dispersion of effort. As already mentioned, British designers suffered because their home market laboured under the stupidity of the RAC rating taxation formula whose main parameter was piston area. Since the name of the game was to make your engine produce more actual power than the formula result, the obvious approach was to design units which were well under-square, with extremely long stroke, to increase the capacity while retaining the same piston area. The problem here was that such engines suffered extremely high piston speeds (which could be why several UK companies were among the pioneers of advanced lightweight alloy piston design and manufacture), so they could not run to high revs without imposing high loads throughout the rotating assembly. In addition, the small bore size limited the engine's breathing – although to some extent, this matched up with the lower operating speed.

The real drawback, in the overall sense, was that British-market engines were very difficult to sell overseas, in European countries with more enlightened ways of calculating fiscal power, or in the USA where such considerations did not arise. It also meant that for the entire period up to the Second World War and for some time afterwards, the British car buyer tended to class cars according to their RAC rating. Thus a 'Seven' was a minimum practical car, an

'Eight' was a small family runabout, a 'Ten' was a step up from this, 'Twelve' was distinctly middle-class, 'Fourteen' was for the professional – the doctor or the lawyer, perhaps – and anything rated higher was really aimed at the gentry, who at that time still existed in some numbers, if in more straitened circumstances than before 1914. Within these classifications, the technical specification – even such factors as swept capacity – mattered less.

The bottom end of this layered market was established in 1922 by Herbert Austin, with the introduction of his Seven, one of the legendary cars of British motoring. This is not to say the engine was particularly admirable, except to the extent that it proved able to survive its minimalism in a remarkable way. It was a conventional – for the time – L-head side-valve unit with an iron cylinder block secured to an alloy crankcase to save weight, as in so small a car, this was important. The cylinder head was detachable, because this was a car which would be maintained mainly by its owner. It was originally designed with 54mm bore and 76mm stroke for a capacity of 732cc, but in this form it mustered less than 10bhp which was really not enough. So it was bored-out to 56mm (remember the need to stay within the 7hp RAC limit) and the stroke was increased to 76.2mm – in reality, to exactly three inches – to yield the familiar capacity of 747cc, and 10.5bhp at 2,400rpm. Certainly, 2,400rpm was quite enough, because the engine had only two main bearings, and even these were roller bearings rather than journals – with an additional ball-bearing to take axial thrust. By these means Austin reduced internal friction and improved economy, but it meant he was able to make the lubrication system minimal as well, and it was no surprise to find thermo-siphon cooling rather than a water pump.

Austin should not be thought of as a minimalist, despite the Seven which was a highly successful attempt to make four-wheeled motoring accessible to a wider public. Its competition was the motorcycle and sidecar combination, commonplace on the roads of the 1920s. But from 1921, Austin also offered a Twelve, which lasted, with improvements, until 1936, and in 1927 he added a 6-cylinder 3.4-litre Twenty, which was later scaled-down to make the 2.3-litre Sixteen. All these were L-head side-valve engines of no great technical interest.

Austin's great rival Morris, had no intention of slugging it out in the 7hp market where margins were whisker-thin. Morris did consistently well with its

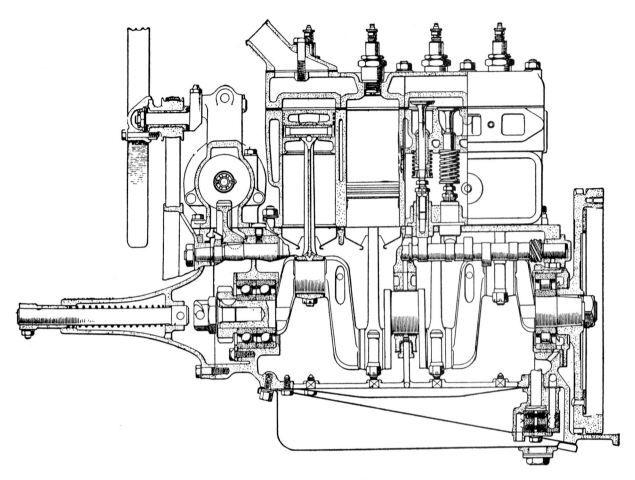

two long-running models, the 1,548cc Cowley and the 1,802cc Oxford, in effect sharing a single side-valve 4-cylinder engine of 102mm stroke but with a bore of 69.5mm for the Cowley and 75mm for the Oxford. Morris bought inspiration rather than seeking it, for in 1927 he acquired Wolseley, which following its aero-engine experience gained up to 1918 had developed a respected range of SOHC engines rated at 10, 12 and 15hp. Soon after the merger, Morris was offering an SOHC 6-cylinder of 2,468cc capacity (69 x 110mm) producing 60bhp at 3,200rpm; this engine was important in providing the foundation for the early MG 18/80, which followed on from the Oxford-derived 14/40. Meanwhile, Morris executed a minor technical tour de force with the introduction of the SOHC 847cc (57 x 83mm) Minor – at last, a small British car with something like an advanced engine. Sadly, as the next chapter will show, it was not to last, although fortunately the engine was taken up and fully exploited by MG.

Further evidence of good British intentions was seen in Riley, when in 1926, the company introduced the classic Nine with its opposed valves operated by a camshaft and pushrods on either side of the block, delivering 25bhp from a capacity of 1,087cc (60.3 x 95.2mm). 'One and a half' of these engines produced the 6-cylinder Fourteen of 1,631cc, and the basic layout was so sound that it survived, in larger 4-cylinder engines, well beyond the conflict of 1939–45. Singer also provided evidence of advanced thinking, most of all in its 848cc (56 x 86mm) SOHC engine for the Junior, with 15bhp. Of the other companies which would eventually form part of the Rootes Group, Hillman followed a rather staid technical course except for an astonishing flirtation with the fashionable straight-8, showing a 2.6-litre OHV engine in 1928, while Humber had a related range of engines with an unusual overhead inlet/side exhaust layout (sometimes referred to as F-head) which powered such models as the 985cc 8/18 of 1923, and the larger 4-cylinder 9/20 and 14/40. It was common practice in

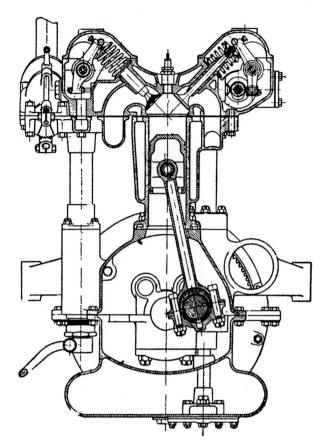

In the late 1920s Rover briefly used the engine shown here, designed by Poppe of the former White & Poppe company, in the 14/45hp. The combustion chamber layout resembles that of the Riley Nine, but valve operation was by a single head-mounted, shaft-driven camshaft which operated one set of valves via rockers and the other set by means of pushrods running horizontally through the head, and then a second set of rockers. This bizarre arrangement apart, the engine was also notable for the huge centre bearing which necessitated a big gap between cylinders 2 and 3. (Ludvigsen Library)

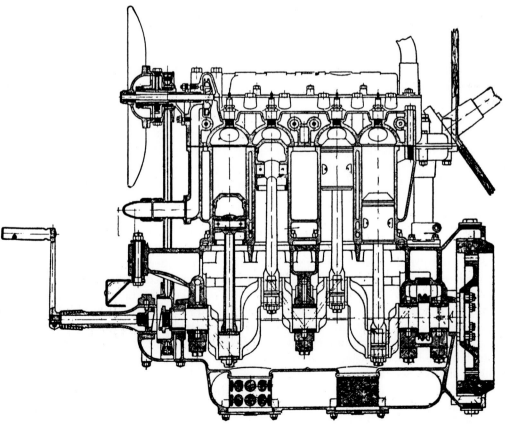

the 1920s especially, to quote the fiscal horsepower first, and then the actual horsepower, the ratio being up to 3:1 and sometimes more – and the 6-cylinder 20/55. Sunbeam, meanwhile, had converted its former side-valve engines to OHV operation, and introduced a new 6-cylinder 16/50, but above all in the eyes of the enthusiast had engineered the splendid DOHC 3-litre sports car.

Triumph meanwhile, was not to be left out of the small-car action, since in 1928, it launched the cheekily named Super Seven, which was actually an 8hp with a side-valve engine of 832cc (56.5 x 83mm) with an output of 14bhp. Certainly it represented a step up from the Austin Seven, but so did many others. What nobody did was to try to repeat the success of, or rival the Seven itself. Certainly Rover, after an early 1920s flirtation with a side-valve flat-twin 'Eight' of 998cc, made nothing smaller than the sturdy but unadventurous Nine from 1924 onwards – and even the Nine was an early attempt at niche marketing; better than an Eight, not as expensive as a Ten – and in 1925 came out with its own 6-cylinder, 2,413cc OHV 16/50. The company took on Poppe (of the former engine specialist White & Poppe) as its chief engineer. He designed one SOHC engine, for the 14/45, with a rather strange and complex way of operating vee-opposed valves, but then reverted to OHV for Rover's 2-litre 'Light Six' of 1928, an engine which would serve well in the coming decade.

Then there were the up-market British cars, with Rolls-Royce at the pinnacle, even though its vehicles were powered by engines which, however beautifully made, were anything but advanced even by the standards of the day. Daimler – by then part of BSA – was another matter, since it was firmly wedded to the sleeve-valve engine, with 6-cylinder 30HP and 45HP models, followed in 1926, by the Laurence Pomeroy-designed Double Six V12, rated at 50hp, with 73.55mm stroke and 104mm bore for a capacity of 6,511cc. Of all the car companies that used sleeve valves, Daimler persisted the longest and most successfully, although in the end (during the 1930s), Pomeroy decided he could achieve similar results far more economically with poppet valves. Lanchester, which would become part of Daimler just as the decade ended, remained a respected upper-class manufacturer with advanced SOHC engines, as in the big 6-cylinder 40HP of 1925, with bore and stroke of 101.6mm x 127mm (or four by five inches!) for a capacity of no less than 6,178cc – a lot for an output of 95bhp, but relaxation was more the name of this

game. Sadly, perhaps, Lanchester then succumbed to straight-8 fever, with a new 4,436cc (78.7 x 114mm) SOHC engine delivering 90bhp.

Then there was Vauxhall, an independent manufacturer until its takeover by GM at the end of the decade, and one whose products were distinctly more up-market than today's average customer would credit. Not that Vauxhall's thinking in the engine department was always advanced; not until 1921 did it build an engine with a detachable cylinder head. Even the celebrated original 30/98, designed by Laurence Pomeroy, had its cylinder block and head cast in one piece, subsequently attached to the crankcase. The engine for the 4-cylinder M-type broke new ground in many ways so far as Vauxhall was concerned, yet in its detail it underlined some of the problems and hard choices which faced designers in the years following the First World War when manufacturers were looking to sell cars to more people – but consequently, to people with less money.

The M-type engine's cylinder head was not only detachable, but made of aluminium. It was attached to a cast-iron cylinder block, which was in turn attached to an aluminium crankcase! The point was that the only way to make the block aluminium would have been to go to the expense and complication of fitting cast-iron cylinder liners (as Vauxhall did, at almost the same time, in the DOHC 1922 TT car). For a mainstream production car, the cost could not be justified. What was more, side valves were retained, and the crankshaft was reduced to three main bearings. Even for Vauxhall, who were then distinctly up-market, engineering down to a price had arrived. In other ways the M-type engine was far from exceptional. Well under-square dimensions of 75mm bore by 130mm stroke gave a capacity of 2,297cc, and with a compression ratio of 4.8:1 its power output was quoted as 43bhp at 2,400rpm.

Meanwhile, Clarence King, who had taken over from Pomeroy when the latter departed to Daimler (and who remained with the Vauxhall until the 1950s) reworked the old-fashioned D-type engine. By the time King had finished, the cylinder head was not only detachable but carried a set of overhead valves. In fact, very little of the original remained other than the dimensions – still 95 x 140mm, hence 3,969cc – plus the five-bearing crankshaft and the chain-driven side camshaft. King also added a Lanchester-type harmonic balancer in a quest for 6-cylinder refinement – a story which would be repeated many years later. With the relatively low compression ratio of 4.2:1, the OD-type produced 60bhp at just 2,000rpm. In other words the change to OHV layout may have done something to improve efficiency, but it certainly hadn't turned the big Vauxhall 'four' into a high-speed engine. When the same techniques were applied to the E-type for the final 30-98 series, however, the result was no less than 120bhp at 3,500rpm, sufficient to enhance the car's reputation as a genuine performer – in fact, the fastest car catalogued in Britain at the time. To achieve this, King had followed one of Pomeroy's dictums and made the valves as large as possible – so large, in fact, that the valve seats ran all the way to the edge of the combustion chamber. To cope with the high engine speeds (by the standards of the day) double valve springs were fitted and the connecting rods were reinforced, with four bolts per big-end.

In renewing its 6-cylinder range – one of the last things Vauxhall did before it was taken over by General Motors – the company committed a major aberration, an extremely complicated power unit designed by Harry Ricardo (who already had long associations with Vauxhall) and employing a single sleeve-valve system developed by the Glasgow consortium of Burr & McCollum (the latter was actually Canadian). As we have seen, the sleeve-valve concept already had by this time a relatively long and decidedly chequered history, but the Vauxhall management was sold on the idea and Ricardo's 6-cylinder engine amounted to two 3-cylinder units nose to nose, with a central flywheel. If you are going to be original, be really original . . . Bore and stroke were 81.5 x 124mm (typical horribly under-square dimensions to achieve an RAC horsepower rating of 'only' 25hp) for a capacity of 3,881cc and an actual output of 70bhp at 2,700rpm. The engine was offered in the 25-70hp S-type of 1925, but regardless of the merits or otherwise of the engine, the car was expensive and no more than around 50 were ever made. It was indeed one of the nails in the coffin of the independent Vauxhall, and the takeover came later in 1925. The new management quickly canned the S-type and instead built the R-type, with a thoroughly conventional, and equally undistinguished 6-cylinder engine with overhead valves, cast-iron head, seven-bearing crankshaft and single side camshaft. It did, however, adopt Delco-Remy coil ignition in place of the HT magneto of all immediately preceding models (and the car moved to 12-volt electrics). It may not have been a technically exciting engine but it was built in its thousands, and lasted GM/Vauxhall into the next decade.

Surveying the 1920s with the benefit of hindsight, it seems clear that engine designers were floundering – perhaps they were receiving too little clear-sighted guidance from their boards of management. As had happened ten years earlier, there was a tendency for engines to grow massive at the top end of the market, and several companies were badly caught out with freshly prepared straight-8 and V12 designs just as the Depression struck. It is easy to see, at this distance, how somebody like Lancia could be so outstanding in the 1920s context – and how companies like Ford, for all the Model T/Model A changeover debacle, could survive more comfortably (as did Chevrolet) by not allowing its horizons to expand too far, by ignoring the siren-song of the high-class market and sticking to what it could do best. What engine designers needed to do during the 1920s was to take stock of the opportunities being offered to them by the metallurgists, the fuel specialists and the systems developers. For the most part they failed to do so, although the 1930s would prove rather different.

5 The 1930s

Frying pan to fire -
a last flash of glory

The 1930s opened in the depths of the Depression and finished with the outbreak of the Second World War. Between those two low-points, some remarkable highs were achieved. In many ways the stage had already been set. As we have seen, the 1920s produced considerable advances in fuel and materials technology. By 1930, most of the knowledge required to design and build a truly 'modern' engine either existed or could be foreseen, and in 1936, for example, 100-octane (RON) fuel was available in the USA.

By the same token, some of the most ambitious cars conceived during the 'Roaring Twenties' actually emerged into the cold light of the Great Depression. Possibly the best example of all is provided by the V16 Cadillac Type 452, the first and almost the only time an engine of this configuration had been designed for installation in a car. The V16 Cadillac was actually announced at the end of 1929 and offered for sale in 1930. Almost at the same time, Bugatti was proposing his V16 Type 47, but that never made it into anything like series production. A year later, Marmon in the USA also offered a V16, but that only lasted two years, dying with the firm itself in 1933, yet another distinguished victim of the Depression. The Cadillac soldiered on however, selling by no means well in its early days but doing better as time went on and confidence was restored to the market. In the late 1930s, the division substantially reworked the engine but the range included a V16 until 1940, substantially outlasting all its rivals and being built in far greater numbers – although scarcely large in absolute terms.

V16: Top of the heap

History explains why Cadillac felt impelled to develop the V16. Already the pre-eminent American luxury car, at least in the eyes of owners General Motors, the marque's status had been under severe pressure ever since Packard had begun building its V12s well before 1920. Thus the top Cadillac ideally needed more than 12 cylinders, and the only real option was the V16. An engineer might argue that in some respects a refined V12 would have been a better choice: from the point of view of balance the V16 more nearly resembles two straight-8 engines sharing a single block and crankshaft, and thus lacking the near perfect natural balance of the in-line 6-cylinder, therefore also of the V12. But it was the

number of cylinders that mattered in the eyes of the salesman, so a V16 it was – a narrow vee with just 45° between the cylinder banks, mechanically a perfectly acceptable angle for an engine with this number of cylinders. This made the engine relatively tall but narrow, which fitted well with Cadillac's styling ideas. The era of grotesquely wide American cars had yet to come.

In 1930 (and for years afterwards), American engineers still thought in inches, and there was nothing complicated about the choice of dimensions for the V16, which had a bore of three inches and a stroke of four inches – or, as Europeans might say, 76.2 x 101.6mm for a capacity of 7,412cc. Remarkably, the engine had only five main bearings, yet there was never any suggestion of weakness or lack of refinement – and this in an engine running to speeds which would have been unthinkable ten years previously. The overhead valves were installed in-line, all 32 of them operated from a single camshaft in the vee of the cylinder block. For the sake of refinement, a form of hydraulic zero-lash tappet was used. Everything but the valve gear was outboard of the cylinder banks, so the narrow angle was not really a design constraint. One big updraught carburettor fed each bank of eight cylinders and the exhaust pipes emerged to transfer some of their heat to the incoming mixture, in accordance with then-common practice. The compression ratio was relatively modest at 5.5:1; it could have been higher given the OHV layout and the improving quality of fuel, but the maximum power output was in any case quoted as 165bhp at 3,400rpm, and the torque was prodigious – as well as being delivered very smoothly.

The Cadillac V16 became a classic but was outsold ten-to-one by the V12 derivative which the division revealed only a few months later, sharing many of the same features but bored-out to 79.4mm for a capacity of 6,037cc. Then, in 1937, the V16 was

Opposite: Ford's first V8, when it appeared in the early 1930s, might well have been viewed as two four-cylinder, L-head, side-valve engines mounted at 90° and sharing a single crankshaft and central gear-driven camshaft. Yet again, however, both block and cylinder heads represented a step forward in cast-iron foundry technology. To modern eyes the block looks over-cooled, but this was well before the era of pressurised cooling systems and high-efficiency radiators. The engine was so compact that the carburettors and induction system could be raised high, well clear of the exhausts. (Rinsey Mills)

replaced by a completely new engine, still a V16 but far more remarkable in its way, with an angle of no less than 135° between the cylinder banks, side valves instead of overhead – a truly retrograde step by any standards – and nine main bearings instead of just five. It was generally more compact (although inevitably wider) than its predecessor, and also lighter and cheaper to make (and easier to maintain). Yet it lasted only three years before being abandoned. Customers even at the top end of the market had become price-conscious and less concerned about having as many cylinders as possible beneath a long, graceful bonnet.

Other divisions of General Motors in the 1930s may not have stretched to a V16 or even a V12, but they had great enthusiasm for the straight-8. From 1931 onwards, Buick offered no less than three such engines in different sizes, with 3.6, 4.5 and 5.7-litre

capacity – all OHV, naturally, in line with the division's long-held policy. Chevrolet, as the 'budget brand' continued with its 6-cylinder models but Oldsmobile had a 3.9-litre straight-8 from 1932 onwards – replacing a V8! Pontiac's 1930s history was slightly more chequered. In 1930 it replaced its former 6-cylinder side-valve engine with an OHV unit, and in 1931 gained a 4.1-litre V8 originally intended for Oakland. However, Oakland effectively became Pontiac in 1932, and the V8 in turn was quickly, and possibly foolishly supplanted by a straight-8 of 3,654cc. The new engine marked the height (or maybe the depth) of straight-8 passion by being offered in cars that cost less than $600.

While the General Motors divisions – except for Chevrolet – were becoming firmly wedded to the idea not only of eight cylinders but of straight-8s at that, Ford chose a different route. Having established the 4-cylinder Model A (although not to the extent of regaining market leadership from Chevrolet) Ford announced its own V8 in 1932. In many ways this was as epoch-making event as the original Model T launch, and for many of the same reasons. The V8 was ruthlessly optimised for cheap and efficient production, it was light and compact, it was tough, and it avoided advanced technology except where it was absolutely necessary – hence its side-valve layout. It was also fairly modest in size, with bore and stroke of 77.8 x 95.25mm for a capacity of 3,622cc. With an output of only 65bhp it did not rate highly in terms of power per litre, but its power-to-weight ratio was rather better by the standards of the day. Such were the engine's merits that it remained in production for 21 years, its final withdrawal coming in 1953.

Ford – staying unadventurous

The Ford V8 – or rather, the Model 18 in which it was launched – was intended to become the company's new standard product, replacing the Model A which was seen as a stop-gap, rushed into production when the writing appeared on the wall for the Model T. In fact, Ford did offer a 4-cylinder version, the Model B, but priced it only $10 lower than the V8, quite enough to ensure in a land of cheap petrol – then as now – the V8 took most of the sales. Compared with the technical adventurism of General Motors, Ford took it as steadily through the 1930s as it did through the 1920s – except that it was building its presence in Europe, with independent engineering of smaller models to suit the very different market. Meanwhile, General Motors had done effectively the same thing in the late 1920s by acquiring Vauxhall in Great Britain and Opel in Germany. This is not to say that Ford did not compete at a higher level in the market, as it did so through Lincoln, which it had acquired in 1922 and turned into its luxury marque. In 1932 the Lincoln V8 was supplemented by a hefty side-valve V12 with a capacity of 7,238cc (82 x 114mm), producing a modest (in relation to its size) 150bhp. Among other things, this helped maintain Lincoln's superior status now that almost every new Ford would have a V8 engine.

Altogether there were three Lincoln V12s; the first was the 1932 original, followed two years later by a smaller 6.3-litre, 125bhp unit – designed from scratch, not merely downsized – which replaced the lingering V8s of the range. The following year the larger V12 was dropped after only two years of existence, and replaced by a slightly enlarged (6.8-litre, 150bhp) version of the smaller unit. Finally in 1935 a much smaller V12, of 'only' 4.4-litre capacity, was developed for the new Lincoln Zephyr range. This engine had many features in common with the Ford V8, making it far more economical to produce and contributing to the Zephyr's low pricing, far below that of the 'traditional' Lincoln K-series. It was also rather more efficient, at least in terms of specific power, since with 110bhp it produced 25bhp/litre

compared with the 22bhp/litre of the 6.8 V12.

By the end of the decade all but the smallest Lincoln V12 had been dropped and the first era of the automotive V12 was virtually over. When the first Lincoln V12 was launched in 1932, American buyers could choose from no less than six different V12 models (Auburn, Cadillac, Franklin, Lincoln, Packard and Pierce-Arrow); by 1939 three of those companies had ceased independent existence and interest was moving back towards the V8, which was destined to become the predominant force in American motoring for many years hence.

The other great force in the American industry, Chrysler, opted out of the top-level fashion for 12 or 16 cylinders. It could not, however, ignore the much stronger fashion for the straight-8. In 1931 Chrysler itself introduced two new engines of this configuration, of 3.9 and 6.2-litre capacity. At that time De Soto – another Chrysler group company – and Dodge, already had straight-8s, the Dodge engine itself only launched in 1930. The De Soto was stopped with the launch of the Chryslers, and production of the Dodge engine ceased in 1933. Plymouth never offered anything more than a 6-cylinder, fulfilling its role as Chrysler's highly successful budget marque.

Packard, still a powerful American name in the 1930s and renowned for its introduction of the first-ever automotive V12 many years before, came back into the top-level fray in 1931 with a new V12, a 7.3-litre unit with a strange 76° angle between the cylinder banks, and four main bearings. After several years of concentrating on its straight-8s, Packard clearly felt it had to have a V12 in order to compete at the top level.

As already noted, this decade saw a brief flowering in the USA of some names which are now looked back upon with reverence, although at the time they failed to command sufficient markets to enable them to survive. Among them were Auburn, which briefly (1932–34) offered a V12 with a 6.4-litre engine from proprietary engine supplier Lycoming, which later and famously devoted itself to aero-engine manufacture. Pierce-Arrow had its 7-litre L-head V12, another 1932 launch, and in the same year Franklin unwisely tried its hand at a V12, air-cooled like every other engine the company had ever made.

A more lasting impression was made by the very fast straight-8 sports cars offered by Auburn, Cord and Duesenberg, all of which eventually formed part of the Cord empire, which failed disastrously in

The straight-eight engine of the Duesenberg Model J makes an interesting comparison with the 1920s Mercedes supercharged six-cylinder, likewise as much a work of architecture as an engine pure and simple. Points of interest include the massive inlet manifold extending from the single carburettor, and the centrally mounted eight-point distributor, as well as the central drive to the twin overhead camshafts, avoiding the risk of torsional vibration in a long, thin shaft driven from one end.
(Ludvigsen Library)

1937. Up to that time the Duesenberg Model SJ with its DOHC straight-8 supercharged engine of 6.9-litre capacity, delivering a claimed 320bhp, bore comparison with any car of its type in the world – and was as expensive! The Cord 810/812 by contrast depended on Lycoming engines, although the 812 was also supercharged, and the Auburn Speedster (with V8 engine replacing the former straight-8) sought to continue the tradition of its name; but it all came to nothing, and from the point of view of engine design they collectively represent a blind alley leading away from the main path of progress.

The European scene

Europe had felt the weight of the Depression just as severely as the USA, and its motoring scene reflected a similar pattern. Again, there were companies which had spent the last years of the 1920s preparing new, technically advanced, large and powerful designs with which to skim the cream off the growing market for luxury cars – and suddenly, that market collapsed. Companies caught in this position had to fight to survive, and survival often depended on painful decisions to ditch treasured and prestigious projects and concentrate on products for those markets which remained strongest.

Two of the three major French companies had pursued relatively conservative policies which should have left them in good shape to withstand the storm. Citroën entered the 1930s building just three types of engine, all conventional side-valve units: two with 4 cylinders, of 1,452cc and 1,628cc respectively, plus the C-series 6-cylinder of 2,442cc. These engines were enlarged and further developed until 1934, when the 'clean break' came: the switch not only to a new range of OHV engines with wet-lined cylinder blocks, but also to front-wheel drive, and a number of other technical innovations – including a disastrous early attempt at automatic transmission. Any one of these might have proved a strain, but taken together they were too much, and Citroën collapsed financially and had to be rescued by Michelin.

From the point of view of engine design this was a shame, because the new units were of real merit and one of them, the long-stroke (78 x 100mm) 1,911cc, became an industry classic, remaining in production well into the 1960s. The choice of an 'open deck' block with wet liners meant the block itself could be an extremely simple casting, although Citroën noted even at the time that care had to be taken to make the cylinder head sufficiently stiff to contribute the strength that would normally have been provided by a closed-deck block; this was especially important to ensure good sealing at the head gasket. The cylinder liners – also of cast iron – were clamped in place by the head, and sealing at the bottom end seems never to have been a serious problem. The engine installation also featured 'floating power' soft rubber engine mounts which the company had already adopted with enthusiasm, following the pioneering of the concept by Chrysler in the USA – André Citroën had always been keen on gleaning technical ideas from the other side of the Atlantic.

Citroën's problem, encouraged by the relative ease with which the size of the cylinder liners could be altered, was that it could not resist creating in one go a whole family of related engines to replace all its existing production models – the 8, 10 and 15CV – so that by the end of 1934, the Traction Avant family was already being offered with engines of 1,303cc, 1,628cc and 1,911cc, with outputs of 32, 36 and 42bhp respectively, matched to French fiscal rating classes (7CV, 9CV and 11CV). Still to come, and in the event not until 1938, was the 6-cylinder which was in almost every respect one-and-a-half of the 1,911cc 4-cylinder, hence with a capacity of 2,867cc and an output of 77bhp at 3,800rpm. Meanwhile there was also a stillborn project for a 3,822cc V8, in effect two 1,911cc 'fours' sharing a common block and crankshaft and delivering 100bhp for a proposed 22CV model – but this was understandably a casualty of Citroën's travails and existed in prototype form only.

Two other things are worth noting about Citroën after the Michelin takeover. One is the instigation, in 1936, of studies which eventually led to the 'mobile tin shed' 2CV with its air-cooled flat-twin engine –

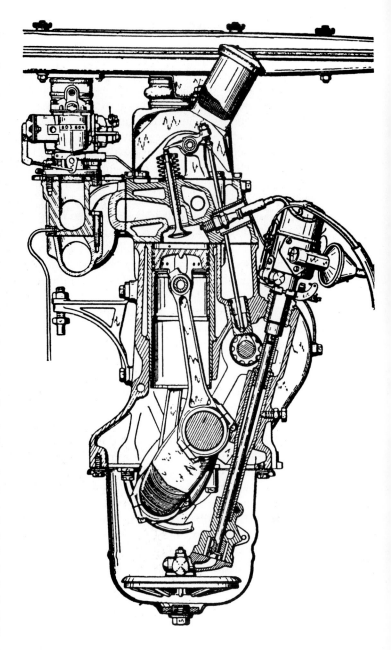

Light, simple and efficient, the Citroën engine for the front-wheel-drive 11D 'Traction' has a simple cylinder block casting housing 'wet' cylinder liners clamped into place by the cylinder head itself, and a camshaft positioned so that the pushrods are parallel to the inclined valves in the wedge-shaped combustion chamber with the sparking plug in its short side. While everyone was astonished at the car, fewer people realised this was an engine which would enjoy a 30-year production life and a great deal of progressive development. (Ludvigsen Library)

but this eventually came to fruition in the 1940s. The other is the company's introduction in 1936 of very early high-speed, light-duty diesel engines, following a development programme carried through with Ricardo Engineering in Britain. Citroën's diesels were offered only in light commercial vehicles, but consideration was certainly given to fitting the 1,767cc 4-cylinder engine, delivering 40bhp at 3,650rpm, in a large car, or at least a taxi.

While Citroën lurched through crisis, Peugeot worked on slowly and steadily, following a financial policy of never getting into debt – which acted as a brake on technical developments, but kept the company clear of trouble in some turbulent times. It began the 1930s with a series of profoundly unadventurous side-valve engines that went into the cars which began the now-famous numbering sequence: the 1,122cc 201, the 1,465cc 301, the 1,720cc 401 and its only 6-cylinder engine of the decade, in the short-lived 2,150cc 601. At that point, apparently stung by the technical admiration heaped on the Citroën Traction Avant, Peugeot decided it must be a little more daring – but only a little. It developed a new range of OHV engines for a series of much more modern-looking cars, beginning with the 1,991cc 402 launched in 1935. The 1,758cc 302 followed in 1937, and the 1,133cc 202 in 1938. None of these cars, let alone their engines, broke any radical new ground – but they built a reputation for value and reliability, and the 202 in particular was a strong enough design to continue after the Second World War.

What of Renault meanwhile? During the 1930s, Renault spread its technical effort widely – probably too widely – in developing everything from small cars like the Monaquatre of 1932 (1,300cc, 66 x 99mm) and the Juvaquatre of 1938 (1,003cc, 58 x 95mm, astonishingly under-square by most standards) to models with straight-8 engines to match the fashion of the decade, something Citroën was in no position to do and Peugeot could not be bothered with. Only Renault, along with smaller companies bearing great names but with slim hopes of survival, sought to compete at the top level. Renault's efforts included the 1930/32 Nervastella, Nervahuit and Nervasport, all using the same engine of 4,240cc (75 x 120mm), and culminating in the Suprastella with its 5,448cc engine (85 x 120mm). In a masterpiece of mistiming, the Suprastella was launched in 1939 . . . In between these extremes Renault managed also to produce a string of medium-sized 4-cylinder and 6-cylinder models. All had features in common: they were all

side-valve, and they still used gear rather than chain drive to the crankshaft. Advanced engineering they were not. Renault, it seemed, was too busy playing the numbers game with cylinders and engine capacities to take any major technical steps forward.

The 'junior ranks' of the French industry in the 1930s included several famous names: Delage, Delahaye, Hispano-Suiza, Hotchkiss and Salmson among them. Hispano-Suiza more or less ignored the Depression and greeted the decade with a huge V12, the 9,425cc Type 68, following it with the Type 68bis whose engine was enlarged to 11,310cc. It did however also offer more modest 6-cylinder versions of the same car. Delage entered the 1930s with a 4.1-litre straight-8 as its main product, but was absorbed into Delahaye in 1935. Delahaye itself had concentrated on lively OHV 6-cylinder engines up to 3.5-litre capacity, but in 1937 it ventured a V12, just as the companies who had been building such engines since early in the decade had decided there was no future in it. Hotchkiss was another company whose prime products used OHV 6-cylinder engines: it did well in production car competition, winning the Monte Carlo Rally several times in the 1930s (and again after the Second Word War). Salmson continued with its policy of building light cars with exquisite DOHC 4-cylinder engines. Ballot had been absorbed by Hispano-Suiza in 1930. Sadly, none of these manufacturers left any significant mark on the mainstream of engine development.

Mercedes leading the way

During the 1930s, Germany turned into a technical powerhouse where the motor industry was concerned. Naturally enough, the way was led by Mercedes-Benz, now very much a single company following the 1926 merger of the two pioneers. For the most part, the engine range as the company entered the decade was Daimler rather than Benz, with the important exception of the big, supercharged 6-cylinder engine series in the S/SS/SS27/SSKL high-performance sports car range. These engines represented an excellent example of progressive development. The basic design used a single overhead camshaft, driven by a geared vertical shaft; two valves and two sparking plugs per cylinder, twin carburettors of Benz's own design (when most of the lesser engines used Zenith instruments by this time), and of course the all-important positive displacement supercharger. Intriguingly, the crankshaft ran in only four main bearings – remarkable, considering the loads imposed on it. However, it was not over-long, because the engine was well under-square. The engine started life with dimensions of 98 x 150mm, for a capacity of 6,789cc, but was soon bored out to 100mm and 7,065cc. Progressive improvements in materials and in fuels allowed the compression ratio to be raised from 4.7:1 in the original 6.8-litre to 7.0:1 in the ultimate SSKL, which famously developed 240bhp naturally aspirated, and 300bhp with the blower engaged.

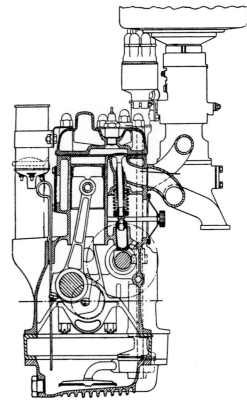

Despite the advanced technology of its sports car engines, Mercedes's bread-and-butter power units stuck to the side-valve, L-head formula. For its mid-range cars the company developed this new 2.3-litre six-cylinder engine with four main bearings, the centre bearings opposite wide spaces between the pairs of cylinders, already a somewhat old-fashioned feature. The shape of the combustion chamber, with its strong squish-effect towards the valves and spark plug, is an interesting feature, as is the lack of coolant passages between adjacent cylinder bores.
(Ludvigsen Library)

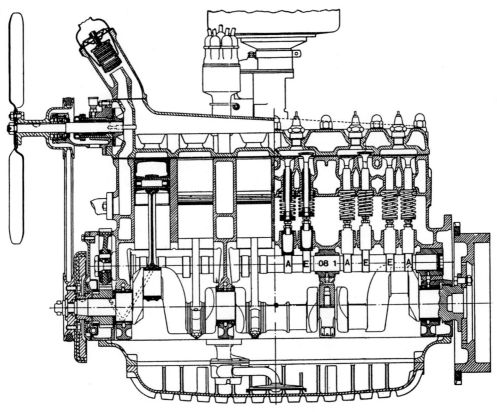

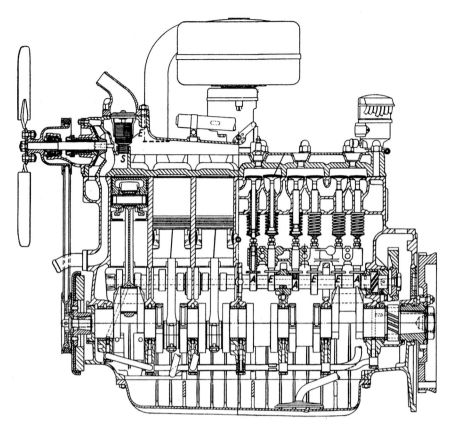

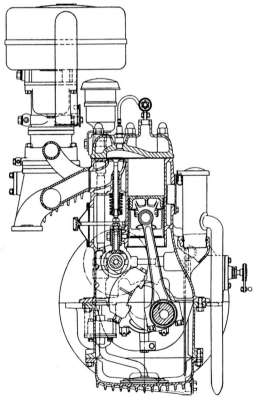

Superficially similar to the engine in the preceding illustration, this is the 3.4-litre six-cylinder engine developed for Mercedes's larger volume-production cars. Differences from the smaller unit begin with seven rather than four main bearings, with the cylinders spaced in two 'siamesed' sets of three – the centre main bearing being wider than the others, and opposite the only coolant passage between the cylinders. The valve gear is very similar in detail, both engines using geared camshaft drive, but the shape of the combustion chamber in the larger engine is subtly different. (Ludvigsen Library)

In no way, however, did the big sports car engine define the company's mainstream technical agenda, which was more accurately reflected by the other Daimler-Benz engines which spanned the turn of the decade, and which had been developed either by Ferdinand Porsche or Hans Nibel. They were all side-valve, L-head engines: for no apparently good reason, the merged company abandoned the more technically advanced Daimler units of the earlier 1920s with their single overhead camshafts and vee-opposed valves.

Small these 'bread and butter' engines were not, in modern terms. Two had six cylinders, and there was a straight-8 for the 18/80 Nurburg. The smallest was the 2,581cc (74 x 100mm) unit in the 10/50 Stuttgart; much larger was the 82.5 x 115mm (3,689cc) unit in the 15/75 Mannheim, while the Nurburg engine had dimensions of 80 x 115mm for a capacity of 4,622cc. These three engines had outputs of 50bhp at 3,400rpm, 75bhp at 3,200rpm and 80bhp at 3,400rpm, suggesting (on the basis of output per litre) that the 8-cylinder's valve timing favoured mid-range torque. All three engines, like their immediate predecessors, had gear-driven camshafts. Their compression ratios, in the range 5.0–5.2, were dictated as much as anything by the side-valve combustion chamber shape. All three engines had the maximum number of main bearings (seven for the 6-cylinders, nine for the straight-8). All had electric starters, and were equipped with mainly Zenith, or Solex carburettors.

For the 1930s, Daimler-Benz developed its engines along three lines. It evolved a new series of 4-cylinder engines for smaller cars, announced from 1934 onwards. It developed new series of 6-cylinders units, more compact, with only four main bearings; and it enlarged and extended its straight-8 range. The one thing it did not do was follow the fashion of the decade and add a V12, although it could have done so easily; after all, another division of the concern spent the time developing one of the classic V12 aero engines, which proved its quality in the Messerschmitt Bf109 and other Second World War aircraft.

The 4-cylinder engines were by no means exceptional, their interest being mainly that they represented a move downmarket. They retained an L-head side-valve layout for the sake of compactness and low production cost, they had only three main bearings, and at least to begin with, they were designed for rear-engined vehicles – the 130 (1,308cc), 150 (1,498cc) and 170H. However, the company quickly decided the conventional front-engine layout was preferable, and its final two 4-cylinder engines of the decade (with one important exception) were the 1,697cc (73.5 x 100mm) unit in the 170V and the completely new – but still side-valve, with the remarkably high compression ratio of 7.5:1 – 2,007cc (82 x 95mm) 53bhp engine for the 200V. It was the smaller engine, however, which was destined to spark Mercedes' revival after the coming war. It is worth noting, in passing, that the 1930s saw the establishment of the Mercedes engine series numbering system, with M-numbers for petrol engines and, eventually, OM-numbers for diesels. The numbers quickly multiplied: the first small 4-cylinder

was the M23, the 150 unit was the M30, and the 200V engine was the M149!

The new Mercedes 6-cylinder engines emerged from 1931 onwards, and reflected the brief passion for 'small sixes'. The engine for the 170 had dimensions of 65 x 85mm, for a capacity of 1,692cc and a modest power output of 32bhp at 3,200rpm. This engine was soon bored-out to 70mm for a capacity of 1,961cc for the original Mercedes 200, which was succeeded in 1936 by the 230 with a larger but mechanically similar 4-bearing, side-valve L-head unit, of 2,229cc (72.5 x 90mm). This engine continued in production into the early war years, seeing only a slight enlargement – bored-out by 1mm to 73.5mm with a capacity of 2,289cc – and being joined by a much larger seven-bearing engine (82.5 x 100mm, 3,208cc) for the 320 which appeared in 1937.

In a parallel move, the company developed a smaller, more compact, five-bearing straight-8 (M22) for the 380 of 1933. But this OHV engine, initially of 3,923cc (78 x 100mm) and soon 4,019cc (80 x 100mm) was short-lived. The emphasis was more on the larger, nine-bearing units, initially with side valves and evolving from the Nurburg unit (M08) which was also 'shrunk' for top-range versions of the smaller Mannheim (M19). Completely separate were two more nine-bearing OHV straight-8s, the M24 for the 1934 500K, which was quickly enlarged to 5.4-litres for the 540K. But for the intervention of the war, it would have been followed by the 5.8-litre M124, with near-square (95 x 100mm) dimensions. And, of course, there was the even larger 7.7-litre (95 x 135mm, 7,655mm) supercharged OHV twin-plug unit for the Grosser Mercedes series, initially as the M07 with a compression ratio of only 4.7:1 and an output of 150bhp naturally aspirated and 200bhp blown, and eventually as the M150 with 6.1:1 compression, but still only with a claimed 155bhp naturally aspirated and 230bhp blown. Outright power was not the issue with this engine; torque was far more important.

The Mercedes range in the 1930s also included one 4-cylinder, five-bearing, OHV engine of outstanding interest. This was the OM138, the first diesel engine actually to be installed in a series-production passenger car. This 2.5-litre (90 x 100mm, 2,545cc) engine was, naturally, an indirect-injection unit working on the swirl-chamber principle: its output was a healthy 45bhp at 3,000rpm, underlining the way in which the early diesels were more nearly a match in output for their petrol contemporaries, especially the side-valve

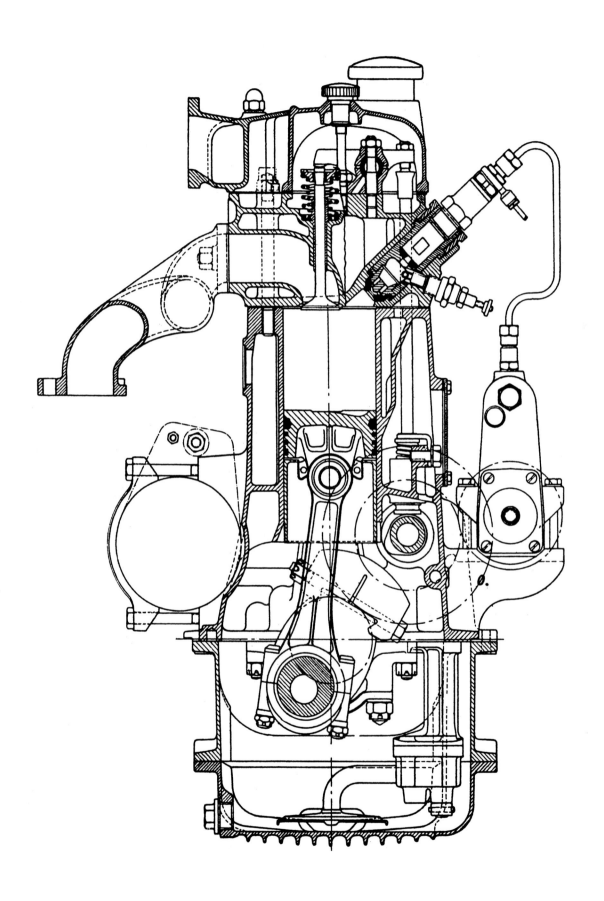

units. It is pretty well impossible to conceive of a side-valve diesel; the required compression ratio simply could not be achieved. It was only in the 1950s that new generations of petrol engines with better breathing and higher compression ratios began to widen the gap.

Other German **efforts**

While Mercedes led the way, BMW was starting more or less from scratch as a car manufacturer, having taken over the Dixi concern towards the end of the 1920s, and began serious development of its own ideas in 1931 with its conversion of the Dixi's Austin 7-based side-valve engine into a slightly larger OHV engine, for the 3/20. The physical limitations of the tiny Austin cylinder block meant that the extra capacity had to be achieved by lengthening the stroke of the two-bearing crankshaft, from 76.2 to 80mm. With the bore left at its minuscule 56mm, the capacity went up to 788cc – but it was the better breathing of the OHV cylinder head which mainly contributed to lifting the power output from 15 to 20bhp.

BMW's next move was to add two more cylinders to the 3/20 engine, although by the time the design had been finalised it did little more than retain the same bore and stroke. The block was completely revised, with the cylinder bore spacing further apart (a move which more than any other, perhaps, creates a different engine) to allow the installation of a four-bearing crankshaft: the two-bearing shaft was marginal with four cylinders, and unthinkable with six. The resulting 1,173cc engine, fitted to the BMW 303, produced the required 30bhp at 4,000rpm, but more importantly it was extremely smooth, setting the standard by which future BMW 'sixes' would be judged. The engine was substantially enlarged by boring and stroking to 58 x 94mm, making it considerably more under-square,

increasing the capacity to 1,490cc but raising the power output only to 34bhp, although with substantially higher torque, for the BMW 315. Then it was found possible to stretch the engine still further, all the way to 65mm bore by 96mm stroke, yielding a capacity of 1,911cc, and delivering either 45bhp or 55bhp depending on its state of tune – essentially the compression ratio and the number of carburettors. This larger engine powered the BMW 319 and 329, but an all-BMW engine had yet to emerge: in theory, the lineage of this 1.9-litre engine could still be traced back to the Austin 7 original, although with a much revised cylinder block, two extra cylinders and a completely new OHV cylinder head, there was about as much left of the Austin as of George Washington's legendary axe. The only arguable carry-over was the retention of cast iron for both block and head.

There was still one more extension of capacity left, a further boring-out by 1mm to take the capacity to 1,971cc. In this form, still with modest output, the engine powered the 320/326 series; but the radical change came with the modification of the engine for the 328. This engine had a completely new alloy head, designed to incorporate vee-opposed valves in a hemispherical combustion chamber. To do this without going to an overhead camshaft – which might be thought the more obvious option, since the head was all-new anyway – BMW devised a way of driving the opposed valves via the existing pushrods from the low-set camshaft. The inlet valves were operated in the normal way while the exhaust valves were operated via an extra pushrod linkage which took the movement across the top of the head to the other side. To avoid threading the inlet ports through the side pushrods, they descended into the combustion chamber from above. When the inlet manifolds were added, the engine was about as tall as it would have been with an overhead camshaft. However, this odd adaptation not only worked, it worked extremely well, raising the power output from 50 to 80bhp and helping to make the 328 into a classic.

In the late 1930s, BMW also developed a much larger 6-cylinder engine, of 3,485cc (82 x 110mm), another OHC unit with a four-bearing crankshaft, and developing a modest (in relation to its size) 90bhp when fitted with a single carburettor. This engine went into the BMW 335, but production had barely begun when the war intervened.

Of the smaller-volume German manufacturers, Maybach had introduced an OHV 60° V12 (a technically advanced unit with a cast-iron linered alloy block and eight main bearings) in 1929, and enlarged it to 7,977cc (92 x 100mm) in 1931 for its Zeppelin luxury car – so much for the Depression! Horch also produced a V12 in 1931, but it was technically far more conservative, with side valves and a capacity of 'only' 6,032cc. However, most of Maybach's exquisitely crafted but modest production through the 1930s was of SOHC 6-cylinder models, while Horch almost unbelievably spread its later efforts across a range of side-valve V8s and a 4.9-litre SOHC straight-8! Amidst all these efforts, Horch also became one of the constituent parts, in 1932, of the Auto Union combine, joining Audi, DKW and Wanderer in a concern which had to contend with a bewildering array of engines including the little DKW 2-strokes.

A more serious proposition in many ways was Opel under General Motors ownership. Opel was put to work to capture a major share of the popular car market in Germany and its succeeded, to the extent of taking 40 per cent of the national market in 1937, while also exporting strongly. It did this with a new range of competent but unadventurous 4-cylinder and 6-cylinder engines, of which the most notable was the over-square OHV 1,488cc (80 x 74mm) unit for the Olympia, an engine which survived the war and

became a foundation for Opel's renewed efforts in the late 1940s.

The other momentous German development in the later 1930s was the creation of the programme, under Ferdinand Porsche's direction, to produce the ultra-cheap popular car which became the Volkswagen. Porsche's technical decisions were in many ways almost deliberately contrary, although in most cases logical. The flat-4 configuration was certainly not the obvious choice if one was looking for low cost, since every engineer of the era (and later) who compared it with the conventional in-line layout concluded that the flat-4 was bound to cost more. On the other hand, the flat-4 lent itself very well to air cooling, which Porsche wanted to use for the sake of overall simplicity (including simplicity of operation). To help the cooling as well as for the sake of production technology, the cylinder half-blocks were light alloy with cast-iron liners, and the heads were light alloy, with overhead valves. The engine began life with a capacity of 985cc but this was increased to 1,131cc (75 x 64mm) for all serious production, which began of course in the 1940s. The over-square dimensions kept down the piston speed, for reliability, and made it rather easier for Porsche to 'throttle' the unit by using small valves and ports, so that it ran out of breath before encountering any kind of mechanical limit, hence its apparently low output of 25bhp achieved at only 3,300rpm. It had naturally occurred to Porsche, with his long experience of motorsport, that far more power might be available by reworking the cylinder heads to improve the breathing, but that was very much a post-war exercise.

Left and opposite: Ferdinand Porsche's flat-four engine for the Beetle seems not to have been designed to be cheap to make. The apparent bulk of the complete engine ready for installation is largely accounted for by the air-cooling fan and the ducting needed to direct the airflow to the areas where it is most needed. The exhaust system with its cross-mounted silencer and twin exhaust pipes, so much a Beetle feature, is also clearly seen.

With the air-cooling ducts removed, the essential simplicity of the design, with its vertically split crankcase and air-cooled cylinders pressed into place, becomes much clearer. The third view looks into one half of the crankcase with the crankshaft and camshaft in place; note the gear drive to the camshaft – beneath the engine as installed – also the two 'loose' connecting rods which belong to the removed half of the engine. (Graham Robson)

The Italian scene

Italy's 'big three' – Alfa Romeo, Fiat and Lancia – very nearly became two in the 1930s, when Alfa Romeo ran into terminal financial problems and could only be rescued by nationalisation. Whether this was despite, or because of a wholehearted concentration on high-performance sporting models with some of the world's most advanced engines – all DOHC 'hemispherical head' cross-flow units – is arguable, but the policy can hardly have helped through the years of recession, neither can the amount spent on works competition, even when it yielded so many successes. Through the 1930s, before and after nationalisation, Alfa Romeo built only 6-cylinder and straight-8 engines, the foundation for its power unit range having been laid by Vittorio Jano after he moved from Fiat. The 8-cylinder engines, like the 2,336cc (65 x 88mm) engine for the 1931 8C2300, were designed almost as two 4-cylinder engines one behind the other, with the geared camshaft drive taken from between cylinders 4 and 5, greatly reducing the risk of camshaft twisting and torsional vibration. The 8C2300 produced 142bhp at 5,000rpm in its original form, but eventually achieved 180bhp at 5,400rpm. The Alfa 6-cylinder engines, although still DOHC, were somewhat more conventional.

However, Alfa Romeo's unit output in the 1930s was minuscule compared with that of Fiat. As we have seen, the giant of Turin entered the decade with a fairly mundane range of side-valve engines, 4-cylinder and 6-cylinder. Neither did the company do very much to break out of its technical straitjacket until, having launched yet another side-valve engine, the 1.0-litre (65 x 75mm, 995cc) 4-cylinder unit for the 508 Balilla, it converted it to OHV configuration for the 508 Sport in 1934. Even then, two more side-valve engines followed, a bigger 4-cylinder for the 518 Ardita and the 6-cylinder for the 527, which was in essence a version of the Ardita anyway. In fact, two versions of this 4-cylinder engine were prepared, with a stroke of 92mm in common, but with bores of 78 and 82mm respectively, yielding capacities of 1,758cc and 1,944cc. The 6-cylinder was slightly more of an oddity in having well under-square dimensions of 72mm bore by 103mm stroke, for a capacity of 2,516cc. One might almost have called this a 'British' engine with its small piston area, and consequently low rating under the RAC system, which was already becoming discredited.

It was only when the 1500 appeared in 1935 that things took a turn for the better. The obsession with side valves was overcome and the new car had a small 6-cylinder engine whose mildly under-square dimensions were exactly the same as those of the 4-cylinder 508, thus giving a capacity of 1,493cc; but it had overhead valves and delivered an adequate, although hardly sensational 45bhp at 4,400rpm. One might have expected such an engine to have real development potential, but it was only ever developed in detail, ending its production days as late as 1950 in the 1500E, and still only delivering 47bhp. In truth, the age of the 'little six' was past, even though there was some post-war attempts to revive the fashion. The problem was (and is) that while the 6-cylinder enjoys the advantage of operating refinement, it suffers more friction losses than a 4-cylinder engine of similar size, with 50 per cent more piston rings sliding and bearings rotating. Add to this the thermal inefficiency of a swept volume as small as 250cc/cylinder (because the ratio of surface to volume goes up as the size comes down, enabling a greater share of energy to be rejected to the coolant) and it becomes clear that the minimum practicable size for a 6-cylinder engine in a road car – not necessarily a racing car – is around the 2-litre mark.

The Fiat engine which followed in 1936 reverted to side valves but was in its way still remarkable. This was the tiny (52 x 67mm, 569cc) 4-cylinder unit for the original 500, the Topolino. In many ways, a 2-cylinder engine would have made more sense, but Fiat's Dante Giacosa insisted when the 500 was in its planning phase, that the car should be 'markedly superior in terms of comfort, performance and appearance' to any of the ultra-light cars then being made in Germany and France, and now mercifully almost forgotten. These devices all had one or two cylinders; therefore a 4-cylinder unit, even with an individual cylinder capacity of 142cc, would inevitably be superior in terms of refinement and probably also of power output, given the extra piston area. Whether it would be as economical was another matter, but here Fiat had the advantage of being able to optimise components in a way denied to small-volume manufacturers. It is also worth noting that Fiat had been studying the idea of a small, cheap, low-powered car for some time. Another of its engineers, Oreste Lardone, had prepared plans for a front-driven car in 1931; a drawing published in Dante Giacosa's account of his career at Fiat (1) appears to show it with two alternative power units, a flat-twin and a 3-cylinder radial! In the event, the 500 emerged with a

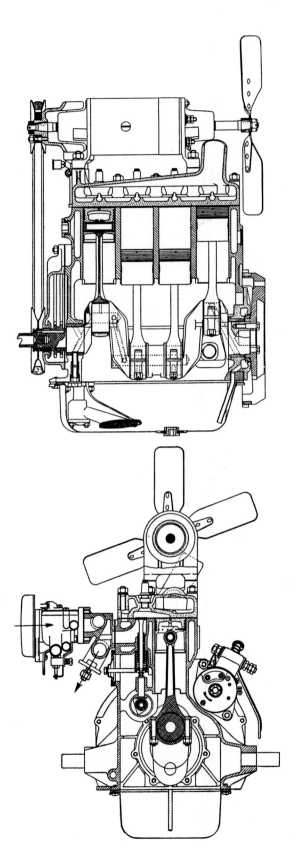

conventional drivetrain to the rear wheels. Even with four cylinders, with a bore of only 52mm and no water between the cylinders, the engine was so compact – and with side valves, fairly wide but extremely low – that it could be installed ahead of the front axle line with the drive belt for its generator and cooling fan (the radiator was above and behind the engine) overhanging by no more than a few inches.

Giacosa also makes the interesting point that at the time, Fiat's view was that a low-cost engine should be restricted to 4,000rpm. This, as it was seen, enabled it to be made without any need for expensive materials or for tricky and costly manufacturing techniques. With such a limit, the piston area became an even more important factor. As launched, the 500 offered 13bhp at 4,000rpm, not a lot in terms of specific power – larger Fiat engines were delivering a good deal more than 26bhp/litre – but quite enough to give the 500 a maximum speed of 85km/h (53mph), enabling it to outrun anything which might have been thought competitive. In its production form, having gone through several iterations, it had a remarkably hefty crankshaft running in only two main bearings, the elimination of the centre bearing helping to reduce friction losses. There were no counterweights, but in an engine of this size that hardly mattered. Even so, Giacosa says the engine suffered from unacceptable noise until the original crankshaft design had been substantially modified.

The 500 engine was the last side-valve unit produced by Fiat, being followed by the 508C. To power this compact car, Giacosa explains that he took the 508 Sport engine – itself in effect a conversion of the standard 508 side-valve unit – and bored it out by 3mm for dimensions of 68 x 75mm and a capacity of 1,089cc. The combustion chamber, says Giacosa, had 'a very compact shape and the spark plug was in a position which would favour rapid progressive combustion . . . the combustion chamber of the 508C is still used today whenever simplicity, economy and efficiency are sought in combination.' Certainly, this engine was destined for a long future, being fitted to the 1100 of 1939 and to a whole series of Fiat models after the Second World War. Fiat rounded off the decade with one more very state-of-the-art OHV engine, a 2,852cc (82 x 90mm) 6-cylinder for the 2800 – the biggest engine the company had produced for a decade.

Lancia, while following Fiat's policy of not becoming too involved in motoring extremes, either of massive luxury or of high performance and top-level motorsport, still pursued a fairly adventurous policy where engines were concerned. Through the 1930s it was completely wedded to Vincenzo Lancia's narrow-vee configuration which certainly resulted in units which were outstandingly compact and efficient. These engines were either 4-cylinder, in which case they were almost 'square' in their installed length and width, or they were narrow V8s which were generally shorter than the average in-line 6-cylinder, without being unduly wide. The geometry of these units was always carefully studied, and the angle between the two cylinder banks was never chosen arbitrarily, but always to pack the cylinders efficiently while retaining adequate cooling. Consequently, the angle was usually measured not merely in degrees, but in minutes and even seconds of arc.

Lancia engines had always been capable of running faster than most of their contemporaries, and the Astura V8 (2,604cc, 69.85 x 85mm) and the Artena V4 (1,925cc, 82.55 x 90mm) of 1931 produced their maximum power – 73bhp and 55bhp respectively – at 4,000rpm, a very high peak at that time. Then came the much smaller Augusta V4, with its capacity of only 1,196cc (69.85 x 78mm) and an output of 35bhp. The biggest Lancia V8 was the 82bhp Astura 233 of 1934, with its capacity of 2,972cc (74.61 x 85mm), while the later 1930s saw a new 1.4-litre (later 1.5-litre) V4 for the Aprilia. The smallest V4 came with the 1939 Ardea, a little jewel of 993cc (65 x 68mm), providing 29bhp at 4,600rpm.

Fragmentation **and** **stagnation** in Britain

Even where Britain's car manufacturers were slowly coalescing into the groups which would become familiar after the war – MG and Wolseley were already under the Morris wing, Riley was destined to become part of the Nuffield (Austin) empire, and the component parts of the Rootes Group were already drawing together in Coventry – there was no real sign of standardisation. Worse, the dead hand of the RAC taxable horsepower formula, which placed such pre-eminence on piston area, meant that in order to succeed on the British market, engines had to be drastically under-square, with very small bore and very long stroke.

From the point of view of installation, this tended to mean engines were fairly tall, because of the long stroke, but short in overall length, because of the narrow bore. Among other things, this positively encouraged some designers to think in terms of six cylinders where four would have done well enough for the purpose. Britain was not alone in having a fashion for 'small sixes' but it probably had more of them, the smallest apparently being the MG SOHC engine in the K-type Magnette and other models, with a bore and stroke of 57 x 71mm for a capacity of 1,087cc! More to the point, however, the 'RAC influence' meant high piston speeds and therefore low-revving engines. Even this had its silver lining: if they could not use sheer speed to draw a lot of gas through their engines, British designers had to look to combustion chamber, valve and inlet port design to achieve the best possible breathing with whatever speed they were mechanically limited to.

This should, and in some cases did, lead to thoughts of vee-opposed valves and overhead camshafts, but it did not always happen. Austin, for example, produced no OHV engine until after the Second World War. On the other hand Riley, which only became part of Nuffield in 1938, came through the 1930s with its cross-flow 'hemi-headed' engines, with one camshaft each side of the block (and a complicated and sometimes troublesome 'hot spot' arrangement to warm the incoming charge, the exhaust being on the other side) carried on from where it had started with the 1,087cc Riley Nine engine to produce two larger 4-cylinder engines in the same mould, one of 1,496cc (69 x 100mm) in 1934 and the other of 2,445cc (80.3 x 120mm) in 1937. Both engines survived the war, lasting into the late 1940s in the highly regarded RMA/RME and RMB/RMF series respectively; the larger engine lasting even longer than that, being carried over into the Nuffield-engineered Riley Pathfinder.

The Morris Eight L-head, side-valve engine seen externally and in cutaway form. This engine was something of a retrograde step even when it appeared in 1931, since many previous Morris engines had been OHV or even OHC. But it was extremely cheap to make and very tough, despite its weak-looking two-bearing crankshaft. Both the distributor and the oil pump were driven off a single shaft, gear-driven from the crankshaft nose, and the belt-driven dynamo shaft also carried the fan – an important component in an engine which still depended on thermo-siphon cooling. As is clearly seen, the carburettor was the inevitable – and very efficient – SU. With a capacity of 918cc, this engine remained a familiar part of the British motoring scene after World War Two, since it powered early examples of the Morris Minor until replaced by the new BMC A-series.
(Herridge & Sons Collection/ Ludvigsen Library)

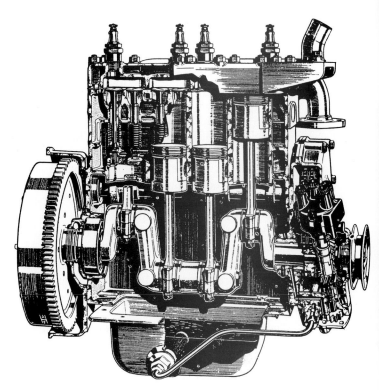

Morris was more adventurous than Austin, although it was happy to use simple side-valve engines where price mattered more than performance. Hence, in 1931, the neat little SOHC 847cc engine was heaved out of the Minor – but left, thank goodness for the MG Midget and later light sports cars, while in 1935, there appeared the Morris Eight, with a side-valve engine of 918cc which survived into the first series of the (Issigonis-designed) Morris Minor at the end of the 1940s. Yet other models in the Morris range, from the Ten to the 25, carried OHV engines, even if none of them were of special merit. Meanwhile, Wolseley continued into the 1930s with its range of praiseworthy SOHC engines, in the Hornet and the Viper among others, but by 1936 had switched entirely to using Morris OHV engines. The era of common componentry, if not yet of badge engineering, was drawing closer.

The member companies of the Rootes Group had a fairly undistinguished decade from the point of view of engine design. This was especially true of Hillman, which invented the popular Minx and stuck to it, complete with side-valve engine (the first OHV Minx arrived in 1955!), while Humber came into 1930 – the year it became part of Rootes – still using its intriguing overhead inlet/side exhaust engines but later standardising on side-valve 6-cylinders of no outstanding interest. Sunbeam, once it had fallen to Rootes in 1935, was a shadow of the technical strength it had been in the 1920s. Singer was different, fighting its way through a period in which it had the oddest mix of side-valve, OHV and SOHC engines, to standardise on a tidy range of SOHC units by 1935, the Nine (especially as the Le Mans) being the best-known model with its 30bhp, 972cc (60 x 86mm) SOHC engine. But Singer did not become part of Rootes until 1956 . . .

Standard was another company which remained almost entirely faithful to the side-valve layout: it was also another of the 'small six' enthusiasts, while Triumph, then a rival (their merger came in 1945) similarly offered the 1931 Scorpion with a 1.2-litre 6-cylinder engine. In the mid-1930s, Triumph bought many of its engines from Coventry Climax, most of them using the briefly popular overhead inlet/side exhaust valve layout. By the late 1930s Triumph had settled down to a range of fairly ordinary OHV 4-cylinder and 6-cylinder engines, for the Gloria and the Dolomite. The company did, however, provide the technical foundation on which Weslake developed the highly impressive SS100 OHV engine for Jaguar,

showing what could be achieved – at relatively low cost – by an engineer who knew the importance of gas flow through the cylinder head and, indeed, the entire inlet and exhaust system.

Rover, that once-adventurous company, eased its way through the 1930s mainly on the back of one 2-litre OHV 6-cylinder power unit, the 'Light Six'. Only after the war did the company show more imagination. Ford's designers were not really paid to use imagination, but to produce quite a lot of value for relatively little money – which in this decade still meant the side-valve. The Model Y appeared in 1932 with a 933cc engine, while in 1934 came the Ford Ten, with an engine whose capacity (1,172cc) and appearance were destined to remain familiar into the 1960s!

Vauxhall, meanwhile, followed a completely independent engineering path from Opel even though both were part of General Motors. Vauxhall moved into the 1930s under pressure from its masters in Detroit to widen its range, although not yet to move towards a small car for the mass market. The company did not, in fact, offer a 4-cylinder engine until 1937, when the H-type Ten-Four appeared. Intriguingly, every one of its 1930s engines was OHV; it disdained the side-valve as down-market, which indicated just as clearly as its concentration on six cylinders where its intentions lay. It also tended to develop two versions of the same basic engine, one with a narrow bore for the British market and one bored-out (therefore with a substantially higher RAC rating) for export. For example, the 1933 Light Six was a 12hp model, with a capacity of 1,531cc (57 x 100mm) for the British market, but was bored-out to 61.5mm, for a capacity of 1,782cc, for other markets. The change made it a 14hp under the British system, which meant not only that it paid more tax but also that it competed, in the eyes of the market, in a completely different segment.

If in the 1930s, Britain's volume car manufacturers provided a rather motley picture of bright spots against a rather dull background where engines were concerned, one could always point to the upper-crust. Daimler began the decade in its stately sleeve-valved way, its range including the Double Six which was actually a 1920s design – but Laurence Pomeroy abandoned sleeve valves as more trouble than they were worth in the mid-1930s, and launched instead, a series of refined 6-cylinder and straight-8 engines. But the uppermost crust was of course Rolls-Royce, which in 1936 produced a V12, the Phantom III, to top its range. The V12 Phantom was everything the

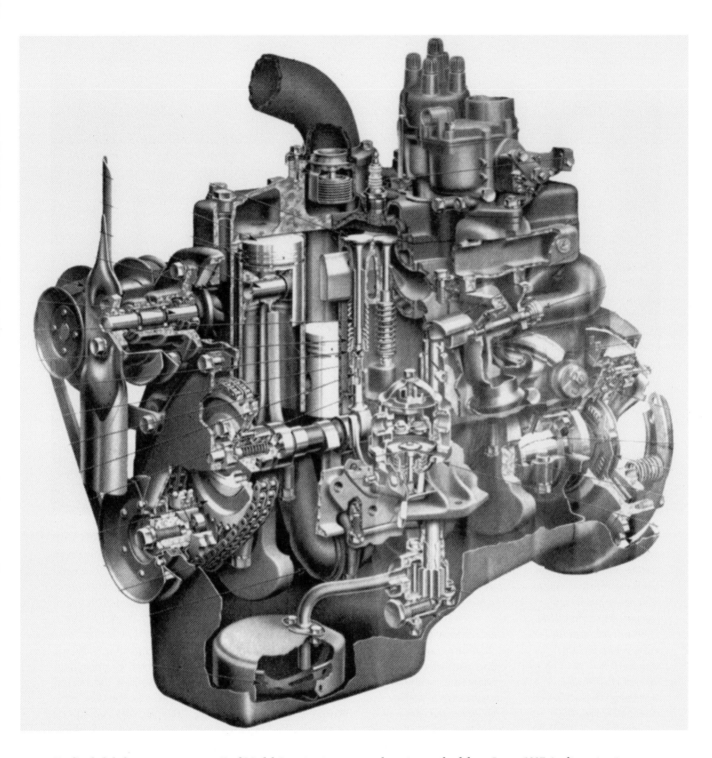

Ford's slightly larger answer to the Morris side-valve engine was the 1,172cc side-valve unit fitted to the Ford Ten – although it might also have been seen as a Ford Model A engine in miniature. This extremely simple engine was not only cheap to make but extremely tough, pulling well, though unwilling to run fast, at least in standard form. Its virtues were sufficiently strong for it to survive well beyond the end of World War Two, powering the once familiar Ford E93 and 100E Anglia series, into the 1960s when it ended its life in the 100E Popular after the 105E Anglia had been introduced. (Ford Sidevalve Owners' Club)

6-cylinder Rolls-Royce models – 1920s engines in every way – were not. It was advanced and efficient, with overhead instead of side valves (Rolls-Royce apparently considered but rejected various overhead camshaft layouts) and it had a one-piece light alloy block, clearly owing much to the lessons the company had learned with its aero engines, with wet cast-iron cylinder liners and (naturally) seven main bearings.

Like the aero engines, it had two plugs per cylinder, in fact two completely independent ignition systems. With a bore and stroke of 82.55 x 114.3mm – or, as they would certainly have put it then, $3\frac{1}{4}$ x $4\frac{1}{2}$in – it had a capacity of 7,340cc, placing it firmly among the 1930s giants. It delivered 165bhp (this was before Rolls-Royce became coy about the output of its car engines) which meant it was scarcely over-stressed at 22.5bhp/litre, despite its advanced features. The engineering fundamentals of Rolls-Royce were not to be transgressed, whether the power unit was an elderly side-valve 'six' or a state-of-the-art V12. Alas, the Phantom died a premature death upon the outbreak of war in 1939. That applied even more to the Lagonda V12, which only appeared in 1939. It is worth comparing the performance of the 4,453cc (78 x 90mm) Lagonda with that of the much larger Rolls-Royce engine: the Lagonda delivered 180bhp, or just over 40bhp/litre!

In conclusion

Thus ended a decade in which the motor industry, and in particular its engine designers, had agreed on only one thing – that there was no future in the idea of a simplified, ultra-light car with only one or two cylinders. The most successful very small car of the 1930s, Fiat's 500 Topolino, was praised precisely because it was 'a proper car' on a small scale and not a flimsy little 2-cylinder banger. At the other extreme, by 1939 most of the steam had gone out of the notion of huge cars with straight-8, V12 or even V16 engines. Perhaps the one real surprise of the decade was that the V8, a concept dating back to 1910, its technology well sorted (especially by Cadillac) in the 1920s, had not made a better showing – but its day would come.

Probably, the majority of volume-produced cars in 1939 still had side-valve engines, although the OHV layout was steadily advancing. This was rather astonishing considering that fuel quality had improved so much and engines could easily have exploited the higher compression ratios which OHVs made possible. There was no lack of examples to drive home these advantages; it was just that cost, both of manufacture and of re-tooling, was beginning to frighten managers. In a way, perhaps it was as well that the years 1939–45 saw so much of the old tooling either destroyed, or worn out supporting the war effort. Things would look rather different in the mid-1940s.

6 The 1940s
The aftermath of the storm – clearing up, sorting out

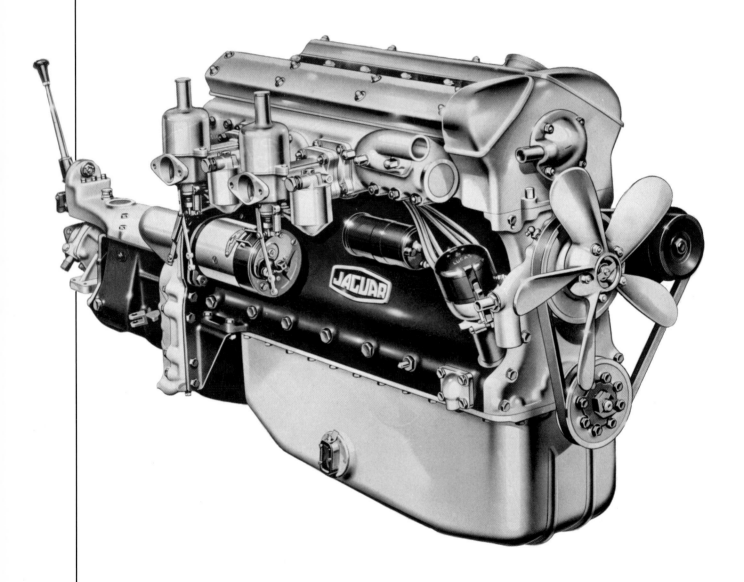

For the purposes of this history, this decade really starts in 1945. In the immediate post-war era, things were difficult for everyone. Those on one side of the former conflict, especially Germany, but also Italy and occupied France, had factories mainly in ruins. On the other side, there were factories, which for several years (six years in Britain, four years in the USA) had devoted their production and the inventiveness of their engineering staff to the development and building of products other than passenger cars. It is not easy, in retrospect, to say which was the more difficult – to rebuild a ruined factory from scratch, or to re-convert an existing plant to the purpose it was serving in 1939 or 1941. The latter may have looked the preferable option, but brought with it the temptation – almost the compulsion – to dust off the old tooling and recommence manufacture of the same product. Rebuilding from scratch gave the freedom to develop new products better suited to the post-war world.

On the purely technical side, the war brought fewer benefits than one might have expected, so far as passenger car engines were concerned. The advances had mainly been in materials, for instance in sparking plug insulators (plug quality was much better after 1945), in high-temperature alloys developed for the new gas turbine aero engines, but also suitable for poppet valves, in lubricants, and in vital although seldom appreciated side-issues such as filtration media for both oil and air. But aero engines, which might have been expected to provide a technical spin-off for the motor industry, had gone the way of high-pressure multi-stage supercharging and exotic fuels (the near-standard octane rating for military aviation fuel by 1945 was 115) which could never be reflected in the passenger car. Then, towards the end of the war, there came the switch to gas turbine technology which, it might be argued, formed a technical side-track up a blind alley that formed something of a distraction for post-war engineers. Never mind the gas turbine, indeed: a scientist told *The Autocar* in 1946 that he doubted if there would be an atomic car for 'at least 20 years'.

Thus the passenger car manufacturers faced the latter half of the 1940s armed mainly with elderly designs, and a market which was slow to recover its late-1930s volumes, even in the USA, let alone a rationed, restricted and reconstructing Europe. There was a fear in Europe that the Americans would cash in on their ability, through economy of scale, to build engines and cars cheaply and flood the European market. It never happened, because the American products which were dusted off in 1945 and put back into production had been largely unsuitable for Europe even before the war, and were even less so afterwards.

In America, the last days of the straight-8

In the late-1940s USA, in fact, you could still buy a car with a straight-8 engine from no fewer than five marques (Buick, Chrysler, Hudson, Packard and Pontiac). Of these engines, only the Buick was OHV – Buick never built a side-valve engine, remember. The rest of them were relics of a bygone age. The largest of them came from Packard, which was still building a range of three engines with a common 89mm bore, including one with a stroke of 117mm for a capacity of 5,840cc and an output of 160bhp at 3,600rpm. Elsewhere in the world, the tradition was continued only by Daimler with its 5.5-litre straight-8. But there was a clear recognition that the way forward was the more compact, potentially lighter and faster-running V8, and of course the OHV combustion chamber layout which, by enabling higher compression ratios, would allow much better use to be made of the higher-quality fuels now readily available in the USA. So far as the layout was concerned, one might say that Ford had been right in 1932 (as had Cadillac in 1914). What the American market now needed was for Chrysler to develop a V8 of any kind, for Ford to update its ancient side-valve engine, and for General Motors to follow where Cadillac had been leading the corporation for several decades already.

Opposite: Simplicity could be combined with performance. Jaguar's DOHC six-cylinder XK engine, was famously sketched during World War Two by a small team otherwise engaged in fire-watching. This view shows the general tidiness of the unit with its characteristic twin SU carburettors and exceptionally deep sump. Reaching the distributor for service was never easy, however . . . (Herridge & Sons Collection)

In the event, GM was the only one of the three to make the move within the 1940s. By 1949, two of its divisions had armed themselves with essentially modern OHV V8 engines. Cadillac had developed an over-square (96.8 x 92mm, 5,420cc) engine to

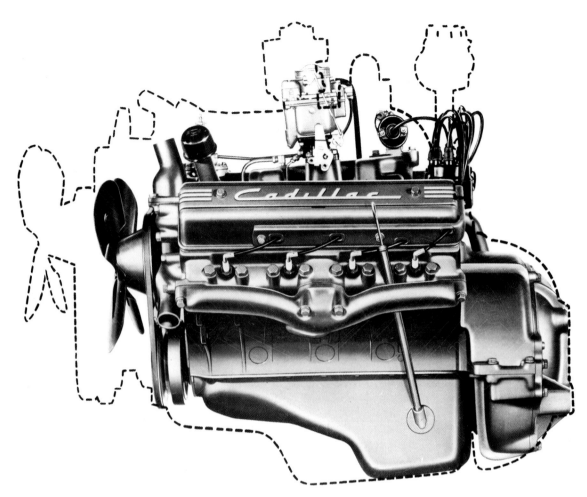

Better materials, better lubricants, and more efficient cooling techniques developed during the conflict enabled post-war engines to be made smaller and lighter for the same output. When Cadillac launched its new over-square V8 in 1949, the division issued this visual comparison of the engine with its predecessor. It typifies what became the American V8 of the post-war era, with pushrod OHV from a single camshaft in the vee. Details, which look crude by later standards, include the very simple manifold and the vee-belt drive to the cooling fan.
(Ludvigsen Library)

replace its older units and provide all its models with 160bhp at 3,800rpm; a reflection of true progress, the new engine was more compact, lighter, more powerful and more economical than its side-valve predecessor. Meanwhile, Oldsmobile had developed the 'Rocket' V8, similarly oversquare, slightly smaller (95.3 x 87.3mm, 4,970cc), delivering 135bhp at 3,600rpm. This engine proved to have a lot of inherent potential and would eventually deliver

almost twice this output. The choice of oversquare dimensions in both cases had little to do with any ability to run engines at much higher speeds: after all, both units peaked at comfortably below 4,000rpm. It was more a matter of shaping the engine package. In a 90° V8, width can become a limiting factor especially with an OHV layout – it had been less of a problem for Ford with its side-valve unit. Even though American cars were by this time well along the road to full-width, all-enveloping bodywork, the available width between the front wheel arches still imposed an engineering constraint. One way to make an OHV engine narrower – although slightly longer – was to make it over-square, reducing the stroke and increasing the cylinder bore, and this was duly done.

For most of the decade there was also one surviving American V12, in the Lincoln Continental. The car had been launched in 1940 with the carried-over Zephyr V12 engine, which proved to be embarrassingly under-cooled and under-lubricated. For the 1942 model year – and thus in effect for 1946

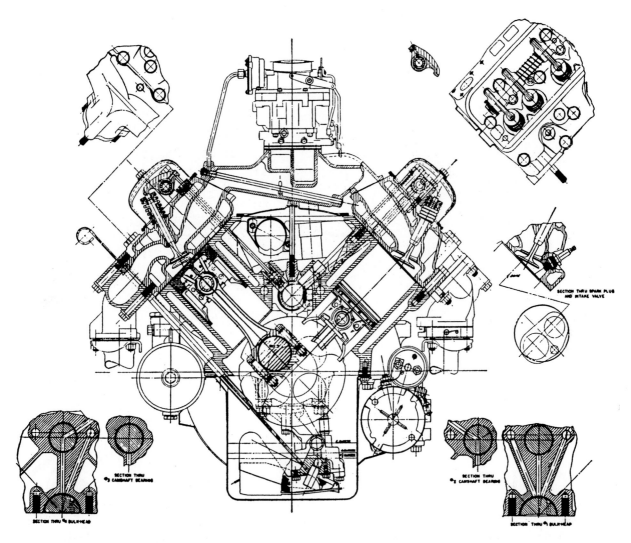

SECTION THRU
#2 CAMSHAFT BEARING

SECTION THRU #4 BULKHEAD

SECTION THRU SPARK PLUG
AND INTAKE VALVE

SECTION THRU
#3 CAMSHAFT BEARING

SECTION THRU #4 BULKHEAD

– this engine was replaced by a tougher, larger 5-litre side-valve V12, still producing only 120bhp, that was built in small numbers from 1946 onwards. In 1948, this engine in turn was replaced by a new L-head side-valve V8 of even larger capacity and greater output (89 x 110mm for 5,530cc, 152bhp at 3,600rpm). Arguably, this was one of the last side-valve engines to be designed from scratch for a major passenger car application. Eventually it would deliver 205bhp, but its outdated design made it a candidate for replacement almost as soon as it appeared.

Lesser Ford models continued to use evolved versions of the 1930s side-valve V8s. By 1949 its latest models, the Tudor and Fordor, were thus powered by an engine which had hardly changed since 1932, with dimensions of 81 x 95.4mm for a capacity of 3,920cc and an output of 100bhp at 3,800rpm. For the 1949 Mercury, this engine was given a longer

Cross-section through the Oldsmobile Rocket V8, showing the new American design approach in more detail. Apart from the central camshaft sitting in the vee, and the pushrods operating the overhead valves, details of this classic engine include a cross-flow cylinder head with induction in the vee and exhausts outboard,

and wedge-shaped combustion chambers with slightly inclined valves and the sparking plugs in the angle of the 'roof'. The pistons are flat-crowned. With the help of consistently high fuel quality, late-1940s engines like this were developed to produce far more power through the 1950s. (Ludvigsen Library)

stroke (of 102mm) to take its capacity to 4,190cc and its output to 110bhp at 3,600rpm – scarcely competitive in the face of the new generation of over-square OHV units.

Alongside the long-serving V8, Ford also offered an

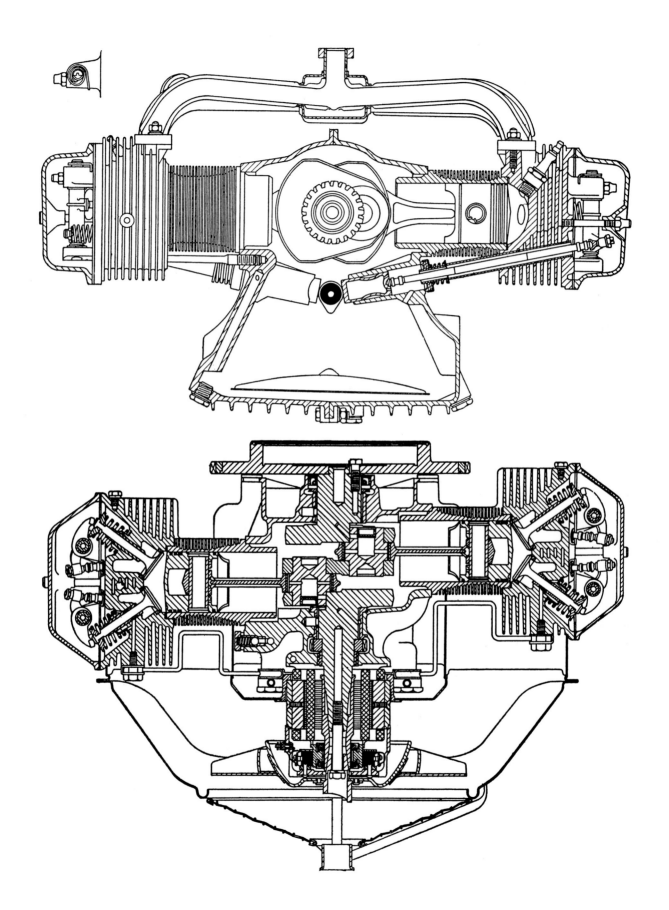

in-line 6-cylinder engine, the first such production unit in its history, introduced in 1940. By this time Ford had realised that in the American market, a 4-cylinder engine simply would not do even for the more basic versions in its range and that it needed a 'six'. The new engine could hardly be called ground-breaking in any other respect, with its side-valve layout and modest output of 95bhp from a capacity of 3,700cc (83.8 x 112mm), but it began a new line of Ford evolution which would, among other things, eventually provide the 'base' engine for the Mustang in the mid-1960s. Meanwhile, it enabled Ford to compete at the lower end of the American mass market with the 6-cylinder models offered by Chevrolet – as always – plus Oldsmobile and Pontiac for General Motors, and by Chrysler, Dodge and Plymouth (the latter two using effectively the same engine) for Chrysler. Of these, only the Chevrolet engine was OHV. The only 4-cylinder engines offered by domestic manufacturers in the USA during the 1940s were the strange little 720cc Crosley, which died a predictable death without making any kind of sales impact, and the basic 2.2-litre side-valve unit produced by Willys and installed in early-series Jeeps, creating the original civilian off-road market. But even Willys also offered a 6-cylinder engine as an alternative, frequently preferred.

France struggles **back to life** – economically

Post-war France, struggling to rebuild itself, saw its motor industry as one of the keys to ultimate prosperity, and its government acknowledged – unlike its British counterpart – that a healthy domestic industry had to be built on a strong home market, with the anticipation of exports to follow. The one thing the French set their faces against was large luxury cars, which they discouraged by taxing them heavily, both to buy and to operate. The French system of reckoning fiscal horsepower (CV) was very different from the old British RAC rating, and was worked to a complicated formula which took many things, even the overall gearing, into account: for many years, French manufacturers found it worth offering special versions of many models with 'long' gearing – generally a raised top gear – which knocked one point off the CV rating! It was (and is) however a fairer way of reckoning engine tax-worthiness, and less of a technical straitjacket. What really hurt the larger cars was that the government could, and did, choose a sliding scale of taxation which meant that anything over around 12CV paid disproportionately higher tax, and above around 17CV the rate verged on the penal.

It just so happened, or so some would have you believe, that the already-classic 4-cylinder, 1,911cc Citroën Traction Avant, the 'Maigret car', was rated at 11CV; but the result was really bad – in fact, terminally bad news for the likes of Delage with its 3-litre 6-cylinder OHV engine, the Delahaye range with OHV 6-cylinder engines either of 3.6-litre or 4.5-litre capacity, the Mathis with its 2.8-litre engine of similar configuration, and even Ford France with its 'small', 2.2-litre (66 x 78.8mm, 2,158cc) side-valve V8. In the end, it even doomed the 2.9-litre, 6-cylinder Citroën 15CV version of the Traction, apart from actively discouraging French engineers from developing new car models for the large luxury sector. In France, it had ceased to exist.

There were two ways in which French manufacturers might react to this situation. One was to go for ultra-economy with an extremely small but efficient engine in a very light car. The other was to maintain a sense of proportion and reckon that whatever the attraction of cars rated at 2, 3 or 4CV, there would still be a healthy market for 'sensible' cars in the 6CV-10CV range.

Perhaps mercifully, only 25 years had passed since the horrors of the cyclecar era following the First World War, and many retained memories of that time and were aware that it would take an exceptional design to make a success of the entry level of a market which was in straitened circumstances overall. Thus the one exceptional design which already

Opposite: Cross-sections of the Citroën flat-twin A-series engine, launched in the 2CV in the late 1940s. The front view shows many superficial similarities with the VW Beetle, including the vertically split crankcase with separately inserted air-cooled cylinders, and a camshaft beneath the crankshaft. The long pushrods are threaded through the cooling fins on their way to the valve-operating rockers. Top view shows the vee-opposed valves in the hemispherical combustion chamber, and the remarkable built-up crankshaft with throws and webs separately manufactured and then shrink-pressed together. The view emphasises that flat-twin engines are far from perfectly balanced laterally because of the cylinder offset. (Ludvigsen Library)

existed, clandestinely developed through the war and almost ready for production, had little serious opposition when it appeared in the form of the Citroën 2CV.

The 2CV was not, in fact, a product of post-war austerity but had been designed to a specification written by the company's chief executive, Georges Boulanger, in the mid-1930s, once the fuss surrounding Michelin's takeover had calmed down. Boulanger looked at what might rudely be termed the French-peasant market and wrote the outline description of a kind of mobile platform with four seats and an umbrella, capable of carrying its load in comfort and economy, although not of necessity, terribly fast. This was translated by the technical team into a 'mobile tin shed' in the nose of which was fitted an air-cooled, mainly light-alloy, OHV flat-twin with some fairly strange features, including a crankshaft which was built-up rather than formed all of a piece and then machined, and a nose-mounted contact-breaker ignition system lacking a conventional distributor (the generator was nose-mounted too). This engine, designed by Walter Becchia, actually replaced the water-cooled original of the pre-war prototypes, which proved very difficult to start at low temperatures.

Compared with some possible alternatives, the 2CV power unit was an expensive engine to build, but it had its own rationale. It was very light. Its shape meant it could be installed ahead of the front axle line, leaving the body interior free from intrusion. As a 'boxer' flat-twin, it was tolerably well balanced. None of its components was very large, nor did they need expensive machinery for their manufacture. Assembly was a matter of manpower; and Citroën cherished its reputation for doing things 'differently'. Even so, had the design team known that the company would end up building over 5 million examples of this engine and its derivatives, some decisions might have gone another way; although by way of consolation, the little A-series proved capable of being stretched to almost twice its original size and several times its original output. As things were, this strange little engine, with 'square' dimensions of 62 x 62mm for a capacity of 375cc and an output of just 9bhp at 3,500rpm, was fitted in the extreme nose of the 2CV, driving the front wheels, when the car was officially launched in 1948 after its furtive wartime development. It was an instant success, and from then on, for a decade or more, Citroën's main concern was to build enough of them,

without worrying too much about progressive development or about filling the yawning product gap between the 2CV and the Traction Avant 11CV.

In a sense, this product gap reflected the influence of France's fiscal policy towards cars. The French market – and embryo export markets – still needed engines of around 2-litre capacity, because a fair number of customers could afford the higher tax rates applied to cars with double-digit CV ratings. This need was fulfilled by developments of pre-war engines, in some cases simply by continuing to make them almost unchanged, like the Citroën 11CV. But any 'fresh engineering' had to be devoted to smaller, lighter cars which would command volume sales in the France of 1948 and beyond.

Nobody – at least, nobody of any substance – challenged Citroën for the 2CV market. True, there was the single-cylinder, 310cc Julien which actually matched the Citroën on power although little else, but for most designers, 4CV was the minimum practical target.

This was certainly the case at Renault, with a political background of nationalisation and industrial unrest, and the ability to do little more than prepare to resume, on a small scale, where it had left off in 1939. Its first move was therefore to reinstate production of two pre-war models, the 1-litre Juvaquatre and the 2.4-litre Primaquatre, both with side-valve engines. However, the 'little more' involved the preparation of one new engine, a small 4-cylinder water-cooled OHV unit with some unusual features. Although it was all cast iron, it nonetheless used 'wet' cylinder liners, stepped at the bottom and flanged at the top, and squeezed into place by the cylinder head. This meant the cylinder block casting was relatively simple, easy and cheap to make, although it placed something of a premium on accuracy of machining, for the sake of liner sealing. It also meant that potentially, the engine could be 'stretched' until the liners began too closely to approach the block. In its initial form this engine had well under-square dimensions of 55 x 80mm, for a capacity of 760cc, although it became more familiar with the bore reduced by 0.5mm, taking the capacity to 747cc. With different cylinder liners, it could even be shrunk to only 603cc to create cars with a 3CV rating. Citroën installed the A-series in the nose of the 2CV: Renault's engine, by contrast, was installed in the extreme rear of the 4CV – overhung aft of the rear axle line in the manner of the Volkswagen, whose choice of layout had undoubtedly exerted an

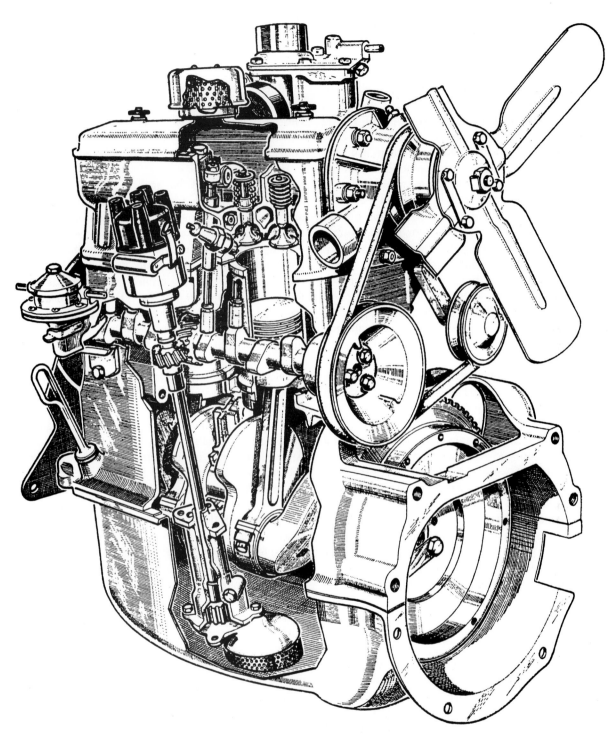

Renault's small post-war
four-cylinder engine is seen
in its original 'back to front'
configuration as developed
for the rear-engined 4CV and
later Dauphine, with the rear

face ready to receive not just
the gearbox but the entire
transaxle. This was a
pushrod OHV engine with a
cylinder block of linered
construction, making it easier

to alter the swept volume by
varying the bore size. Note
the way in which the
camshaft has become a key
component, not only driving
the distributor and oil pump

at opposite ends of a worm-
driven shaft, but even
carrying the drive pulley for
the cooling fan and (behind
the fan) the water pump.
(Ludvigsen Library)

influence (but nobody influenced Citroën!). As it happened, both engines were destined for a long life, and in Renault's case especially, for very substantial development – to say nothing of a 1960s move to the front end of the car.

Peugeot meanwhile quietly entered the market as a one-model company, continuing production of the pre-war 202 until it was ready to switch to the 203, whose OHV 4-cylinder engine was notable not only for its oversquare dimensions (75 x 73mm for a capacity of 1,290cc) but also for a cylinder head with opposed valves, all operated by inclined pushrods from a single side-mounted camshaft. This quietly successful engine lasted in production, as did the 203 itself, from 1947 until 1960; Peugeot did not introduce a companion model until 1955!

It should not be forgotten that the post-war French industry was certainly not just a matter of Citroën, Peugeot and Renault. There was also Simca, building light 4-cylinder OHV engines of no great distinction (except that one of them was extremely small, with dimensions of 52 x 67mm for a capacity of 570cc and an output of 16bhp); and as already mentioned, several great names fighting vainly for survival: Delage, Delahaye, Gregoire, Hotchkiss, Mathis and Salmson among them, the last still building its nice but expensive DOHC engines driving through Cotal transmissions. In one way and another, all retired from the scene or were absorbed by stages into the 'big three', without managing to carry their power unit technology any further forward – if one excepts Panhard, which by 1950, was offering the remarkable Dyna with its new flat-twin engine (72 x 75mm, 610cc, 24bhp) which was developed by small but determined stages into a 1960s Monte Carlo Rally winner – if only by dint of a 'formula' which ensured it would win, provided only that it finished!

German **travails**

Germany took its time emerging from the chaos, although some companies were affected more than others by the partition into East and West. BMW for example found many of its 1930s facilities now in the East, and preparing to operate independently. Mercedes on the other hand retained its grip on most of its pre-war infrastructure around Stuttgart, and by dint of much effort began producing its 170S, with side-valve 1.8-litre 4-cylinder engine, and its diesel derivative with reduced cylinder bore and OHV head. Nothing else very much happened in the engine

department prior to 1950, although of course the following decade would see an explosion of Mercedes engine technology. Cars with BMW badges (but red and white, rather than blue and white) were produced – under the auspices of the occupying Soviet forces – by the old Eisenach factory, but the product plans of BMW in the West, with their accompanying engines, took a long time to come to fruition and nothing of substance happened in the 1940s.

The same could be said in many respects of Mercedes, except that here there was a plan behind it all. The company's handful of production engines, in the 170V and later the 170S, were carry-overs of pre-war technology, L-head side-valve engines (M136), well under-square – the 170S at 75 x 100mm for a capacity of 1,767cc and a power output of 52bhp at 4,000rpm. Alongside was the OM636 diesel engine for the 170D, from 1949 onwards, which was a 1.7-litre OHV unit delivering 38bhp at 3,200rpm. It all looked far from impressive – unless one was aware what was happening in the research, design and development offices in Stuttgart, where things were happening that would make the world see Mercedes in a different light from the 1950s onwards.

As for Volkswagen, it started slowly. The tale has been often enough told of how British (and American) motor industry representatives looked at the product and wrote it off as an oddball design with no long-term prospects; and indeed of how the post-war factory was goaded back into business almost single-handedly by a British officer in the Army of Occupation, Ivan Hirst, now remembered as one of VW's founding fathers. From the point of view of engine design, VW had a number of strengths which could be exploited in the post-war German situation. Air cooling – as VW subsequently pointed out in so many of their advertisements – meant no problems with coolant freezing (and antifreeze was one of the many things in short supply). Its 'unburstable' character, thanks to deliberately restricted breathing, meant reliability and reasonable economy. Also – rather like the Citroën 2CV, but on a larger scale – none of its engine components was very large. The cast cylinder pairs were pressed into the central crankcase, itself formed in two halves which were physically the largest parts. Much of the apparent bulk of the engine, when the rear bonnet was opened, was formed by the cooling fan and the ducting which ensured that the air reached all the right places in sufficient quantity. The single camshaft sat directly

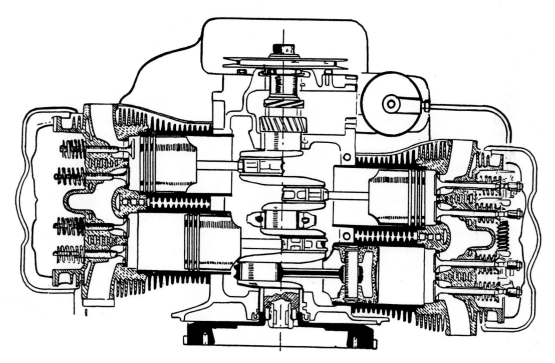

beneath the crankshaft, gear-driven from it, both being clamped within the vertical split of the crankcase. Because the engine was installed aft of the rear axle line, it could fairly easily be removed for major work – not that much was needed.

What was needed, as 1950 neared, was a little more performance, most easily achieved by increasing capacity. This was where the separately cast cylinders were a boon. The engine could be bored-out without a major redesign, and without touching the machining of the rest of the unit. As a first stage, in 1949, 5mm was added to the bore dimension, taking the engine to 1,131cc (75 x 64mm) from the pre-war 985cc (70 x 64mm). Power was increased only from 22bhp to 25bhp, an 11 per cent lift for 13 per cent greater capacity, but that was due to the restricted breathing. Torque was increased rather more, and more usefully in the circumstances of the day.

It had long since occurred to Dr Porsche that the breathing restriction in the VW engine could be readily removed. Indeed, in 1939 there had been prepared a small batch of the VW Type 64, intended for a Berlin–Rome–Berlin road race (scheduled to take place in September of that year!) in which the standard heads had been replaced by new ones with bigger valves and a higher compression ratio, and fed by one carburettor per cylinder pair. Through the 1940s and beyond the Porsches, father Ferdinand and son Ferry, extended this concept into a series of

The Volkswagen Beetle engine had to be grown to meet post-war performance standards while retaining the artificially restricted breathing which rendered it so 'unburstable'. This lengthwise cross-section shows more clearly how the cylinder heads were cast in pairs with shared inlet ports. Differences from the Citroën 2CV engine include not only (and obviously) the centre main bearing, but also the simple combustion chamber shape with the small, in-line valves whose limited permeability restricted maximum speed. For his own purposes, Porsche quickly adopted a new and much more efficient cylinder head and combustion chamber layout! (Ludvigsen Library)

sports cars, the 356 series, which ended up (in 1955) with what was still fundamentally a Beetle engine but with DOHC cylinder heads and an output of 100bhp at 6,200rpm. Mainstream Volkswagen development, however, was headed in other directions.

In Italy, the emphasis was likewise on recovery from a disastrous war which had left many facilities in ruins. Alfa Romeo, which had hardly been a major player before the war was now state-owned and with ambitions to success in larger volume, and began a study and development programme which came to fruition in the 1950s. Fiat continued to develop its most recent pre-war OHV engine designs, for the 1100 and the 6-cylinder 1500, and had in the little 500 a unit well suited to getting the nation mobile once more, at minimum cost and with low fuel consumption. The major undertaking at Fiat in the 1940s was to modernise the 500 concept into the 500B, converting the little engine (still with the same 569cc capacity and only two main bearings) to OHV configuration with its output raised from 13 to 16.5bhp. As Dante Giacosa, who oversaw these post-war programmes observed, the 1100 engine was already OHV, and greater output was achieved by improving the inlet and exhaust manifolds and fitting a larger carburettor. However, the majority of the work in the late 1940s was devoted to making ready a brand-new 1400 engine, which would appear early in the next decade.

Lancia took up production of its pre-war models, the 1.5-litre Aprilia and the 900cc Ardea, and carried through a programme of development, especially on the Ardea. As at Fiat, the most serious work was devoted to a new project – in this case a replacement for the Aprilia, which would emerge in 1950 as the Aurelia, with an engine that would represent a complete break with Lancia's narrow-vee engine tradition.

In Britain, a struggle seemingly against the odds

In Britain, most of the pre-war factories still existed, although they had long been turned over to producing military vehicles or aeroplanes. In theory at least they could dust-off their pre-war designs and resume production, while developing new vehicles and power units for the post-war world. That was the theory. In practice the economic position was desperate.

It was not that people did not want to own and run cars, far from it. It was not even that they could not afford to – a million or more of them, at least could. It was more that the country *thought* it could not afford them. For the sake of the overseas trading balance of payments, petrol was severely rationed, especially in Britain, and was also of generally low quality. 'Pool' petrol became a standing joke, with its low octane rating causing some of the better-performing, and carefully preserved pre-war cars to 'pink'. Further grist was provided for the UK music-hall comedians' mill with the dyeing of petrol, yellow for the meagre all-purpose ration and red for the heavily restricted 'commercial' fuel – practically a hanging offence if you were caught using it when you shouldn't have been. Add to this the requirement that

the British motor industry should export at least half of its production – already low because of restriction on steel sheet supply for body-building – and the result was that the pressure to develop new power units was not great. It was also subject to contrary pressures. Did you develop for a home market that was heavily restricted, but hopefully would become less so as time went on, or for export to countries (notably the USA) with very different requirements? Did you try to do both, as for instance did Standard when it developed and introduced the 4-cylinder, 2.1-litre OHV engine installed in the Vanguard?

The 1940s did bring one welcome note of relief, however. In January 1947 the RAC horsepower rating as a basis for annual car taxation, that bane of British engine designers for many years, was abandoned (for newly registered vehicles – it continued for those already on the road!) in favour of a far more logical one based on engine cubic capacity. A year later, in a remarkable piece of rationalisation, the Treasury scrapped the whole rating system in favour of a flat rate of £10 for any new car regardless of engine size. It was in effect being recognised that the buyers of larger cars were paying extra tax on their fuel – and, in the 1940s, in a high rate of purchase tax. In any event, no longer would British design offices be forced to look at their overseas rivals developing far more efficient engines, knowing that they could not do the same because they would be taxed out of their home market. Naturally, the RAC rating had also to some extent formed a non-tariff barrier against imported cars, in the year before the war. It is interesting for example to note how little chance the VW Beetle would have stood in a British market had the RAC formula been retained. Even in its original 985cc form it would have carried a rating of 13hp, putting it into competition – in the eyes of the market – with British cars with engines of 1.5-litre capacity or even more. And the market really did think like that: it took several years after the 1947 change before British buyers stopped thinking in terms of an 'Eight' or a 'Twelve'. (Another point against the Volkswagen: apart from the basic 'Seven', even numbers were favoured, for some reason.)

For the most part, the British approach was indeed to begin building the pre-war engines all over again, which often meant side-valve units which, had the war not taken six years out of the normal course of engineering events, would have been well past their sell-by date. British side-valve engines which lasted until the end of the 1940s, and in some cases well

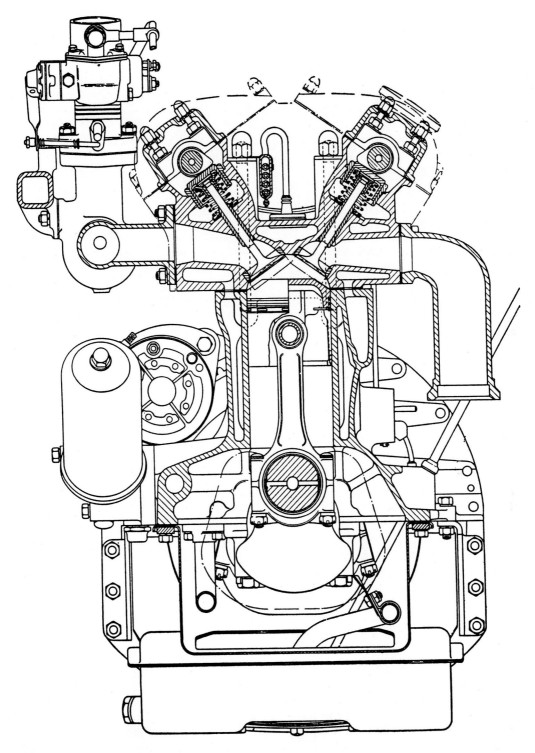

Jaguar's DOHC six-cylinder XK engine combines a simple cylinder block featuring integral liners, with a virtually symmetrical cylinder head in which the valves are angled far apart to encourage breathing through the cross-flow gas system. The angling of the valves, and the use of direct-acting camshafts with bucket tappets, helps to reduce the engine height. Valve clearance is adjusted by selected shims within the tappet buckets. (Ludvigsen Library)

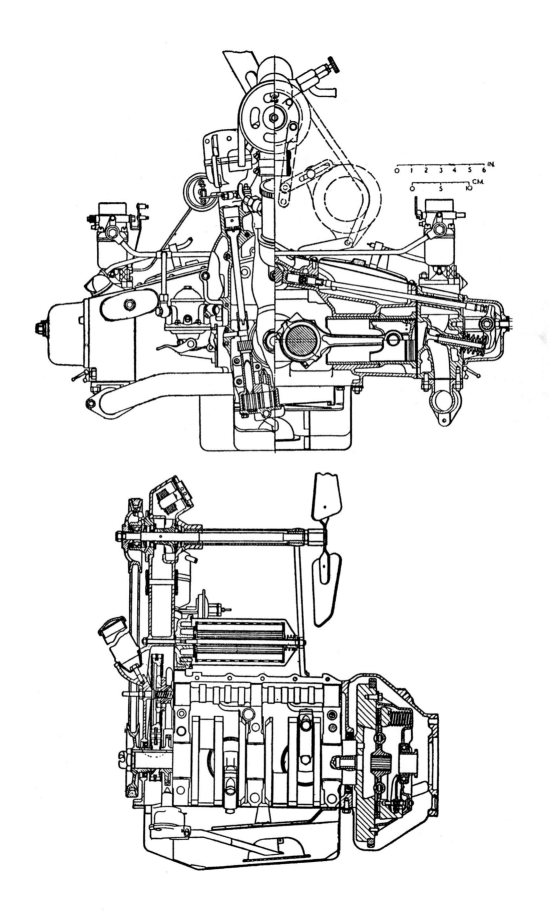

Opposite and above: An interesting comparison with the Volkswagen flat-four engine is provided by the Jowett Javelin 1.5-litre power unit which, as the under-bonnet shot shows, was housed in the car's nose rather than its tail, and which was, almost as evidently, liquid rather than air-cooled. In this case the camshaft, chain-driven despite its closeness to the crankshaft, sits above rather than below so that the pushrods also pass above the block, which is of wet-linered construction, unusual in a British engine of the period. The combustion chambers are wedge-shaped and the heads cross-flow. The Javelin engine performed well and mutterings about its 'killing' are part of British motoring folklore. (Ludvigsen Library/Giles Chapman Library)

beyond, included all of Ford's products (indeed, Ford at this stage was producing only side-valve engines worldwide, including the USA). The Morris Minor and Oxford continued with pre-war engines; so did the Hillman Minx, and the big Humbers, the 4-cylinder, 2-litre Hawk and the 6-cylinder, 4.1-litre Super Snipe. Vauxhall did no more than mildly update their pre-war, long-stroke OHV 4-cylinder and 6-cylinder engines.

Yet at the same time, the sheer variety of British engine design before the war, and the number of companies still in business, meant that the technical range was wide: Morris might be side-valve, but Austin (1.2-litre A40, 2.2-litre A70/A90, and 6-cylinder 4-litre A135) was OHV. The Singers, still independent, and the Wolseleys, already part of the Morris empire even retained their overhead-camshaft engines – but not for much longer, with rationalisation looming over the horizon.

Undoubtedly the two most technically interesting British engines of the immediate post-war era were the DOHC Jaguar XK, prepared in moments of quiet spare time during the war, powering the XK120 and eventually every model in the Jaguar range, and the 1.5-litre Jowett flat-4 which had hydraulic tappets, even, to avoid the need for resetting valve clearances in an engine which was difficult to access: the first move in changing a sparking plug was to remove a front wheel and access panel! This engine powered the Javelin and the Jupiter until the company folded, amid dark mutterings that it had been killed off by powerful rivals because its products were just too good. True, the Jowetts of the 1940s and later were much admired and praised by owners, but it still needs to be said that – the example of the Volkswagen (and later of others) notwithstanding – most of the industry's engineers who looked at the flat-four layout came to the conclusion that output for output, it would always be more expensive to make.

Below: Two 1940s British ways of making an engine for a reasonably large luxury car. On the left, the 2.7-litre Austin OHV six-cylinder engine which became the BMC C-series, with applications from the Westminster to the Healey 3000. On the right, Rover's 2.3-litre engine for the 75 and several subsequent 'Auntie' Rovers. The C-type is very straight up-and-down with extremely straightforward pushrod valve gear. The Rover uses a remarkable overhead inlet, side exhaust arrangement with pushrods passing through the head to reach the upper, inlet rockers. This created a strange wedge-shaped combustion chamber – requiring pistons with oddly shaped crowns – which clearly worked well enough, but whose efficiency may have left something to be desired by later standards. (Ludvigsen Library)

Rover also created a mild sensation after the war by introducing a brand-new engine range in 1948, to power the P3 and eventually also the P4 range. The 'F-head' design – for which there had been some precedents, not least the contemporary Rolls-Royce 6-cylinder engine – employed a strange wedge-shaped combustion chamber in which one side was formed by the side exhaust valve, and another by one face of a piston with a decidedly asymmetric crown, while the upper (and longest) side formed the roof, and housed the sparking plug. The overhead exhaust valve was effectively covered by the piston at top dead centre, limiting the scope for valve overlap. A single camshaft operated the exhaust valve via a rocker, and the inlet valve via a pushrod and rocker. An advanced

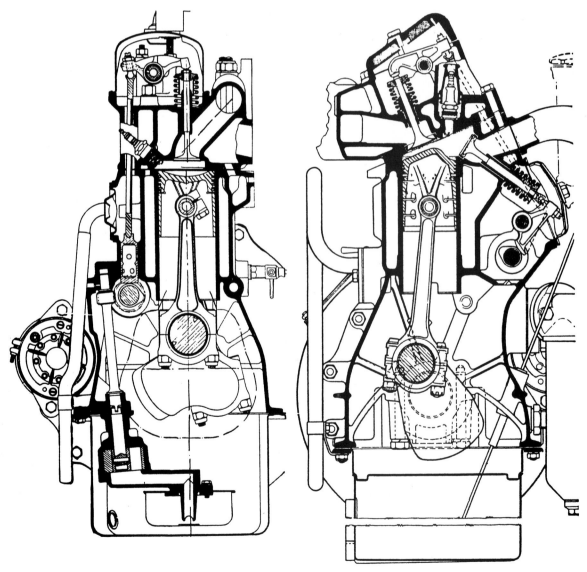

feature for the time was the use of roller cam followers to reduce sliding friction and valve train loads. In 4-cylinder and 6-cylinder form, this basic design, in the 60 and 75, later also in the 90 and the 105, lasted Rover until the 1960s, when it moved in other directions altogether.

During the war, Rover had also been closely involved with the early British aircraft jet engine programme, a substantial part of the British motor industry transforming itself into an aircraft industry for the duration. Rover thought the potential existed for a gas turbine power unit for cars and during the late 1940s, it conducted a development programme which led to the successful demonstration, in 1950, of the JET1 prototype which was followed by several others. Nor was the company alone in its efforts. In the 1950s there was a positive scramble to exhibit gas turbine-powered cars, by the likes of Fiat Turbina (1954), the Renault Etoile Filante (1956) and various American projects, notably from Chrysler and GM. But it all came to nothing . . . at least, so far. Nobody was able to solve the twin problems of the gas turbine when it came to cars: poor response to the accelerator, and extremely high cost. Unless the 21st century comes up with some radical solutions, it looks as though the gas turbine was a technical cul-de-sac where automotive power unit development is concerned.

In summary

What is there to say about the 1940s? While the motor industries of different countries resumed operations at different speeds and from different starting points, the one overwhelming impression was that most engineers had spent several years putting their inventive talents to other uses. To that extent, the first half of the 1940s were largely 'lost' to passenger car engine development. It stopped in 1939–41, and only restarted in 1945. True, there were examples of continued development through the war, in one form or other. Jaguar's small but gifted design team famously sketched the XK engine while factory fire-watching at night. Citroën managed to conceal the 2CV project from the occupying Germans. Renault employed all kinds of stratagem to keep a development programme alive, and paid a heavy price for some of those efforts post-war, with accusations of collaboration which led to nationalisation. Volkswagen undoubtedly learned valuable lessons from the military vehicles it built in substantial numbers up to 1945.

There was also the problem that in 1945, the two halves of the developed world were set to move in different directions: the Americans towards big, 'lazy' engines and never mind about the fuel consumption, and the Europeans towards smaller vehicles and higher levels of efficiency. The post-war years would see very few examples of 'crossover' at the technical level, although European cars found a ready market in the USA.

The technical improvements of the Second World War were gratefully taken aboard, but as explained earlier, they mainly concerned materials of all kinds – metals, fuels and lubricants. It took time to assimilate such advances into car engine design. It was never a case of applying them to existing units. The industry would have to wait until a new generation of engines was developed, and for the most part, that meant waiting until the 1950s.

7 The 1950s
A farewell to **side-valves** – and a **race for power** in the USA

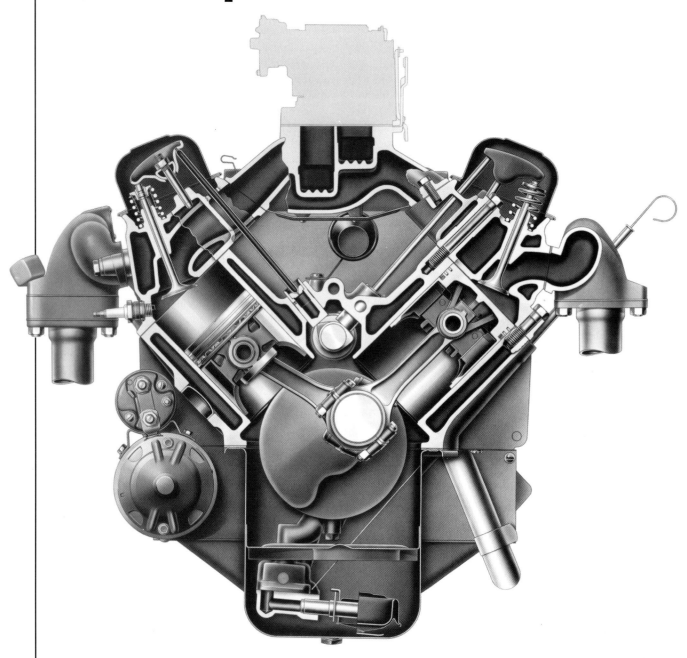

For forty years, engine designers had been coming to terms with the fact that while side-valve engines were mechanically simple and cheap to make and to maintain, overhead valves created a far more efficient combustion chamber shape with a lower ratio of surface to volume, and consequently less heat rejection to coolant during the power stroke. Also, with overhead valves, the compression ratio could, within limits, be made as high as necessary – and with the fuels becoming available, it was now possible to contemplate ratios of 9:1 or even more. To achieve this kind of ratio in an L-head side-valve engine (let alone the old-fashioned T-head) was next to impossible. It implied an extremely shallow combustion chamber with a dreadful surface-to-volume ratio and, almost certainly, limited space for valve lift. In the OHV layout, valve lift could be whatever was necessary, so long as care was taken, through choice of valve timing, to avoid valves and piston trying to be in the same place at the same time.

Indeed there was more to the OHV layout than that. It actually offered a choice of combustion chamber shapes. It was possible, for instance, to form the chamber entirely within the piston crown and have a completely flat cylinder head – the so-called 'Heron' head. This made for easier and cheaper machining of the head, and arguably for better cooling around the valves. It also meant that, because pistons could be cast to a high degree of accuracy, compression ratio would be consistent from cylinder to cylinder, with little variation. This was useful, since the knock limit of any engine is determined by the cylinder with the highest compression ratio – or at least, it was until 1980s when electronics made it possible to vary the ignition timing from cylinder to cylinder. Against that, the Heron layout more or less required the use of upright in-line rather than vee-opposed valves, and a high degree of 'squish' as the flat part of the piston crown came almost within touching distance of the flat cylinder head at the top of the compression stroke. At one time squish was seen as a desirable characteristic, since it forced the air-fuel mixture to spill into the bowl-in-piston combustion chamber with high turbulence, ensuring that the mixture stayed mixed, so to speak, until ignition took place.

On the other hand, many designers didn't like being confined to more or less upright, in-line valves. Most of them were drawn, at least in theory, to the 'hemispherical' combustion chamber layout which called for a piston whose crown was either flat or more

likely, dome-shaped to whatever extent was necessary to create the desired compression ratio. Given the extra complication and expense of a suitable cylinder head design, the interest may have been no more than theoretical, but there were many designers who at least wanted to be able to incline their in-line valves to one side to form a wedge-shaped 'pent-roof' chamber which would, among other things, gently squeeze the mixture towards a sparking plug housed in the opposite face; in the Heron head, the sparking plug tip had to be closer to the cylinder centre and consequently found itself in potential conflict with the valves. The pent-roof chamber also slightly increased the width available to accept larger valves, for better breathing. Much later, when exhaust emissions became a concern, it was clear that the almost-but-not-quite-contact squish area between the Heron-head piston and head created a monster 'crevice' in which hydrocarbons could lurk largely unburned, to the detriment of emissions performance. By that time also, squish itself had become a discredited technique, except in small and carefully controlled quantities.

Opposite: A far more conventional American V8 of the 1950s, but also designed for efficient operation at very high compression ratios, was the 'small block' Chevrolet unit. Compared with the Chrysler 'hemi', differences of approach seen here include not only the tight wedge-shaped combustion chamber with considerable squish effect towards the outboard sparking plugs, and inclined valves, but also the alternative approach to porting and manifold arrangements, with the exhaust taken out through the top of the cylinder head to manifolds well away from the engine. (Ludvigsen Library)

Thus once the side-valve had been consigned to history, the choice lay between the cheap but somewhat constrained flat-faced Heron head with bowl-in-piston combustion, and a variety of layouts in which the chamber was formed in the cylinder head. As pointed out in the previous chapter, the L-head Lincoln V8 of 1948 was probably the last such side-valve unit to be designed from scratch, and by the time it appeared the writing was already on the wall, in letters several feet high.

America **goes V8, and the** power struggle **begins**

In the USA, strangely enough in view of its industry's belief in cubic inches rather than clever engineering,

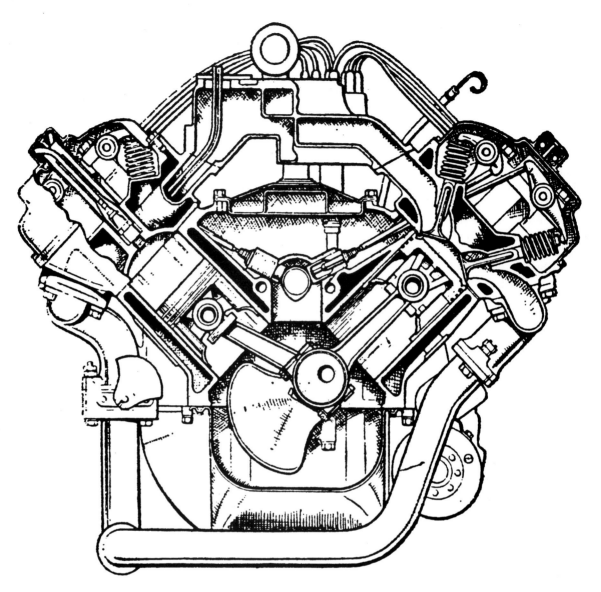

one of the early moves of the decade was towards the hemispherical combustion chamber. In 1951, Chrysler introduced its celebrated Firepower V8, with over-square dimensions of 97 x 92mm for a capacity of 5,440cc (331cu in) and an output of 180bhp at 4,000rpm – at a time when the 1949 OHV Cadillac engine of similar size was producing only 160bhp, although that situation would not last for long. Chrysler used its new engine in the New Yorker and luxury Imperial, but it also developed a smaller 'hemi' V8 for Dodge – this from a company which had not produced a single V8 up to the end of the 1940s. The Dodge engine, with bore and stroke of 87.3 x 82.6mm for a capacity of 'only' 3,950cc (241cu in), developed 140bhp at 4,400rpm. In both

Chrysler's 'hemi' V8 was typically modern American in its layout until you reached the crossflow cylinder heads. These housed quasi-hemispherical combustion chambers (not truly so, because the high compression ratio forced them to be made shallower) and vee-opposed valves operated by different length, differently angled pushrods and rockers from the centre camshaft. The result was exceptionally free breathing by American standards, and allowed high power outputs to be achieved without resorting to high engine speeds.
(Ludvigsen Library)

cases, the valves were operated in the same way as in the Peugeot 203 – by running pushrods at different angles from a single camshaft.

At the beginning of the decade, Chrysler made all the running in the USA with these new engines, with the Oldsmobile Rocket V8 forming the only serious opposition – although it is worth noting that in 1950, the Rocket appeared in 'Quadrijet' form with the first of the huge four-barrel carburettors which would later become so much a part of the American scene. However, GM soon piled on the pressure with one new engine after another. In 1953, it launched the 322 cubic-inch (5.3-litre) OHV V8 with 188bhp for the Buick Roadmaster (but the Buick Special retained its 4.3-litre straight-8 for a while longer). Meanwhile the still-recent 5.4-litre Cadillac was constantly upgraded in terms of power output. By 1952 it had gained an extra 30bhp with the aid of a new four-barrel carburettor and an improved exhaust system. Increases in compression ratio and breathing saw output at 250bhp by 1955, and 270bhp for the Eldorado with twin four-barrel carburettors – one choke per cylinder. Then, in 1956, the capacity was increased to a full 6 litres (365cu in), and the following year a further increase in compression ratio, to no less than 10.1:1. This move, unthinkable in a production car only ten years previously, saw the SAE gross power rise to 300bhp. By the end of the decade there had been a further capacity increase to 6.4 litres (390cu in) with power rising to 325bhp for most Cadillac models, and 345bhp for the Eldorado.

The point is that this was not an exceptional development history for American V8s during the 1950s, although some companies started later than others. By 1957 Chrysler had not only introduced its 300 series but taken it as far as the 300C, with a claimed 375bhp from 6.4 litres (392cu in). The following year it tried a further increase to 390bhp with the aid of fuel injection, but this was a technical failure. Back at GM, and at Chevrolet in particular, 1955 saw the announcement of the first 'small block' V8, designed by Ed Cole, a masterpiece of compactness and relative simplicity, with a capacity of 4.3 litres (265cu in), weighing less than the old straight-6 it replaced, and as much admired for its reliability and ease of repair as for its initial power output of 162bhp at 4,400rpm. But the small block would go on to become one of the most successful engines of all time in American motor racing. Among other claims to fame, it provided the basis for all early Corvette sports car engines. Confusingly, the small block would end up not all that small, being opened out to an eventual 5.7 litres (350cu in), slightly larger

than the almost equally celebrated GM 'big block' V8 family which began life at 348cu in capacity.

Ford stuck to its trusty side-valve V8s – dating back to the 1930s – until 1954, when it launched its first OHV V8 power unit, a relatively modest 3.9-litre (239cu in) engine of 130bhp for the Victoria. From then on Ford added new V8s, or versions, in a steady stream and developed its technology so that by 1958 it could offer the ill-fated Edsel with a choice of 303bhp 5.9-litre (361cu in) or 345bhp 6.7-litre (410cu in) units. Its biggest V8 of the decade was the 7-litre (430cu in) engine producing 375bhp in the Lincoln Continental Mark III.

Even the 'tiddlers' of the American scene were forced to join the V8 fray, to gain themselves a few more years of existence. Studebaker had its own 3.8-litre (233cu in) V8, producing 120bhp, as early as 1951. Packard soldiered on into the 1950s with its range of straight-8 engines, the largest of which was a 5.9-litre (359cu in) unit producing 212bhp. At last, in 1956, Packard announced its own OHV V8, of 5.2-litre (320cu in) capacity and producing a highly respectable 225bhp, but it was already too late . . .

It would need a book in itself to detail the development of the American V8, and the emergence of the 'muscle car' during this decade and the next – and such books exist. Yet it has to be said that all this development did little to further the cause of engine technology. The Americans were very good at building engines that were bigger, stronger, able to exploit the potential of the very high-octane fuels which were by then available. But they built to a formula, and that formula was the pushrod OHV V8, with minor variations. The big corporations still built 6-cylinder engines for the 'base' versions of their smaller models (4-cylinder units had pretty well died out), but by the late 1980s, V8s accounted for 80 per cent of all new car sales in the USA.

Against this background, the designers of the day, and the product planners who guided their work, had no real incentive to do anything else. They were building engines – and cars – for consumers to whom the cost of petrol (gasoline) meant very little. True, in the 1960s many American consumers began to worry about 'conspicuous consumption' and whether all that metal and all that burning of fuel was justifiable (let alone necessary) – but that is a story for the next chapter. The lesson of history is that the 1950s saw American car engine design start up a technological blind alley from which, with a few honourable exceptions, it has never really extracted itself.

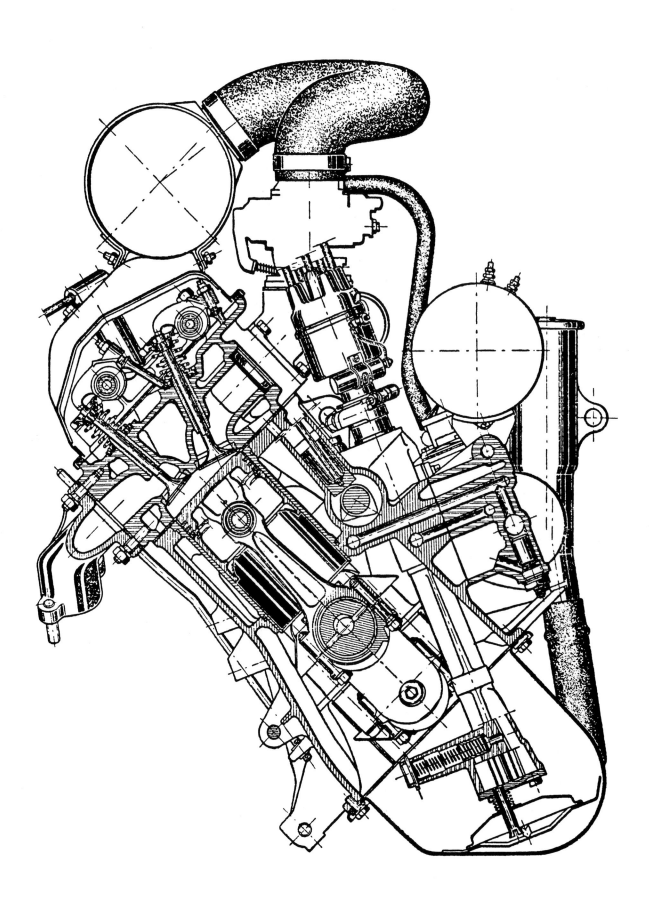

France: drawing breath

The 1950s was not a decade of high achievement in France, as far as engine design was concerned – although much would change in the 1960s. For Citroën, this was the decade of the technically sensational DS, launched in 1955 – yet beneath its smooth bonnet (and indeed, part-way into the cabin, beneath a pronounced bulge in the bulkhead) was mounted the long-stroke 1,911cc OHV 4-cylinder engine which had already served the Traction Avant well for 20 years. One might almost have attached more significance to the boring-out of the 2CV engine to 66mm, taking the capacity from 375cc to 425cc and increasing the power to a dizzy 12bhp. One achievement of the Citroën DS seems to have been the almost total eclipse of the near simultaneous launch of another important French model, the Peugeot 403. Citroën's devotion to publicity in those days was matched by Peugeot's tendency to shrink away from it. The 403 arrived to accompany the 203, which until then had been Peugeot's only post-war production model. To some extent, the 403 engine represented new thinking, since it was oversquare (80 x 73mm for a capacity of 1,468cc, compared with the 203's 75 x 80mm for a capacity of 1,290cc), although it retained a similar valve layout with opposed valves operated by different-angle pushrods from a single camshaft. The new engine produced 58bhp at 4,900rpm, and proved quietly successful – though in 1955, few onlookers would have accepted the notion that within 20 years Peugeot would have taken over Citroën, and that in 25 years it would also control what had once been Simca.

Renault was another company which spent the 1950s ditching the side-valve and replacing its old engines with new OHV units. It had begun with the 'Ventoux' engine for the 4CV, which proved an immediate success but which needed a little more power – and a roomier body – to achieve real volume in export markets, which was one of Renault's great ambitions. Consequently, exploiting the engine's wet-liner construction which meant it could easily be bored out, the company created the 845cc unit for the Dauphine, which involved no more than increasing the bore to 58mm. With all of 31bhp, and not weighing a great deal (partly because of clever but flimsy and rust-prone body construction which eventually proved its downfall) the Dauphine was lively enough to attract many European customers, and even did well in the USA, although only briefly – the fall from grace there was dramatic. Meanwhile, however, Renault next decided for whatever reason to create a new, modern 2-litre OHV engine – rather than the 1.5-litre which might have sat better in the late-1960s market. The original idea was, almost incredibly, to stretch the 4CV engine all the way to 2-litre capacity, bored-out as far as it would go and given a much longer stroke. Problems with this engine, including bending of the very long connecting rods at high speed, led to a complete redesign. The resulting unit had dimensions of 85 x 88mm for a capacity of 1,997cc, and a five-bearing rather than a three-bearing crankshaft. This was the engine which went into the Fregate, and was stretched to 2.1 litres (88mm square, 2,141cc) for the Caravelle. Sadly, all this effort proved, in the end, was that the market was not enthusiastic about big 2-litre Renaults, front-engined and rear-driven. The 1960s would see the company take a different and much more successful approach.

By the end of the 1950s, the number of companies in the French industry had reduced. Delahaye had died in 1954, its assets taken over by Hotchkiss who by now were building only commercial vehicles. Salmson quit car production in 1957, to concentrate on components. Talbot-Lago lasted until 1959, but for years previously had been building big cars (with 4-litre, 6-cylinder OHV engines, in over-taxed France!) on a very small scale. All that were left, in fact, apart from the 'big three', were Simca – formerly Ford France – whose most promising new product was the 1,221cc OHV Aronde, and Panhard, whose flat-twin Dyna engine resembled a scaled-up and more sophisticated Citroën 2CV unit. Panhard was destined eventually to become part of Citroën, and Simca, after passing through the hands of Chrysler Europe and spending a brief period under the revived Talbot name, would be subsumed into the PSA group. All that, however, was for the future.

Like most of its French rivals, Peugeot wet-lined its cylinder block for the 404, but inclined the cylinders at 45 degrees to reduce the engine height beneath the bonnet. The asymmetric combustion chamber layout, with narrow vee-angled valves operated by inclined pushrods and rockers from the single camshaft, is unusual. For the sake of accessibility, only the exhaust manifold is attached 'beneath' the engine, the carburettor and distributor being easily reached. (Ludvigsen Library)

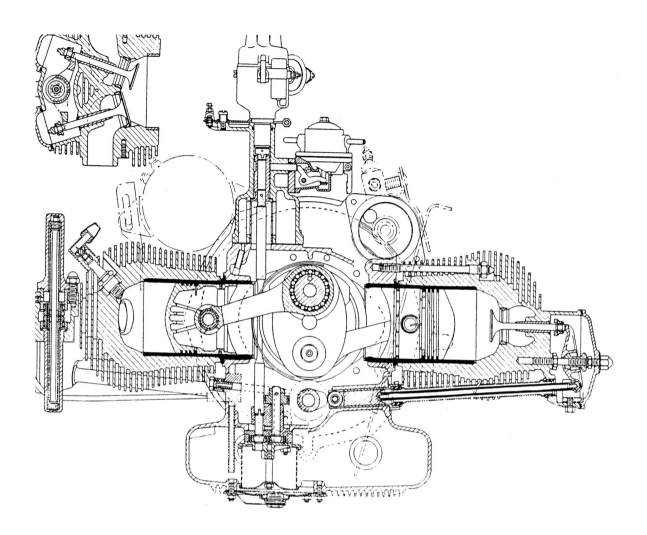

German **energy**

In Germany, there was a clear will to forge ahead both technically and in volume of production, although different companies went about it in different ways. BMW was still far from certain of its position, and spread its efforts to the two extremes of the market. On the one hand, in 1952 it began building the 501 powered by the pre-war 1,971cc 6-cylinder engine, then in 1954 introduced a remarkable wet-linered, alloy-block, 90° OHV V8, with a single central camshaft, with near-square dimensions of 74 x 75mm for a capacity of 2,580cc and a power output of 105bhp. This engine went into the 502, and was followed up a year later by a second, larger unit bored all the way out to 82mm (showing what capacity for 'stretch' can be afforded by wet liners, so long as sufficient care is taken with the cooling) to make the V8 well over-square and bring its capacity to 3,168cc, with a power output of 140bhp at 4,800rpm.

This unit was fitted to the 502 Super, the 503 coupé and convertible, and the beautiful 507 roadster (and lasted into the early 1960s in the 3200 L, S and CS), but the market simply was not big enough to make such a product sustainable on its own. So from the mid-1950s, BMW also embarked on production of the Isetta series of 'bubble cars', culminating in the 2-cylinder, 582cc 600. An earlier project to create a true economy car by fitting a 600cc BMW motorcycle engine into a light but 'real' car along the lines of the pre-war Fiat 500 had been vetoed by the board, but towards the end of the decade BMW developed the much more respectable 700 series – still with two air-cooled cylinders, but now with 697cc and 30bhp (40bhp in the final series), in a car with a wheel at each corner . . .

Mercedes had a great deal more self-confidence. Having carefully consolidated its position up to 1950, the company achieved so much during the next ten years that it more or less regained the technical preeminence it had enjoyed in the late pre-war era. In effect, the revolution was built around three basic engines: a 'small' OHC 6-cylinder with four main bearings, which first appeared, as the M180, in the 220 of 1951; a 'big' OHC 6-cylinder with seven main bearings, the M186, for the 300, again in 1951; and a three-bearing 4-cylinder OHC, the M121, launched in the 180 in 1957. All these were very much 'new wave' engines, two of them over-square – the M180 was 80 x 72.8mm for a capacity of 2,195cc, the M121 85 x 83.6mm for a capacity of 1,897cc – and the 'big six' M186 just undersquare (85 x 88mm for 2,996cc). In addition, the M121 gave rise to a new OHC diesel, the OM 621, which had the same dimensions – saying something for the strength of the basic engine – but an output of 50bhp compared with the 65bhp of the original petrol engine, which in any case, had been developed to produce 80bhp by the end of the decade, and 90bhp with twin carburettors in the 190SL sports coupé, first seen in 1955.

The 190SL was of course junior partner to the celebrated 300SL of 1954, powered by the 'big six' engine developed to produce no less than 215bhp (and these were European, not American, horses) at 5,800rpm with the aid of Bosch direct petrol

injection. In fact, Mercedes worked steadily at petrol injection, always with Bosch, through the latter half of the 1950s, following the experience gained with the 300SLR competition coupé and in the Formula 1 programme. Thus, apart from the 300SL itself (with its engine redesignated M198), 1956 saw the M199, the same basic engine but delivering only 175bhp, offered in the 300SC, but only for one model year. Alongside these frankly ambitious programmes (considering that direct injection for volume-manufactured passenger car engines really became practical only during the 1990s) the 1950s also saw the first two Mercedes with indirect petrol injection,

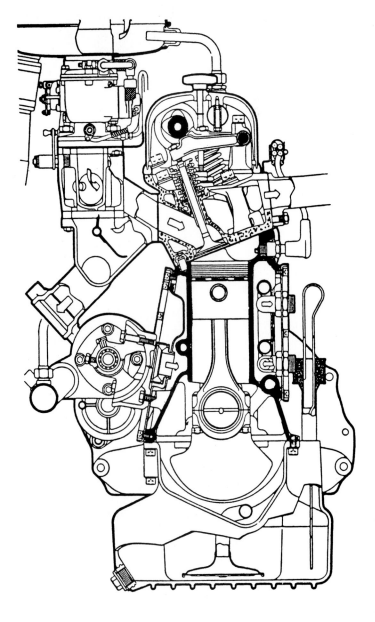

By the 1950s Mercedes was well into developing its first post-war passenger car engine range, including the six-cylinder M186, with its single overhead camshaft operating the inclined valves via finger-type cam followers, allowing for easy valve clearance adjustment. The combustion chamber shape is unusual, with the humped piston sweeping the charge across towards the shaped cavity containing the side-mounted sparking plug. The tall build of the engine was not a serious consideration at the time. (Ludvigsen Library)

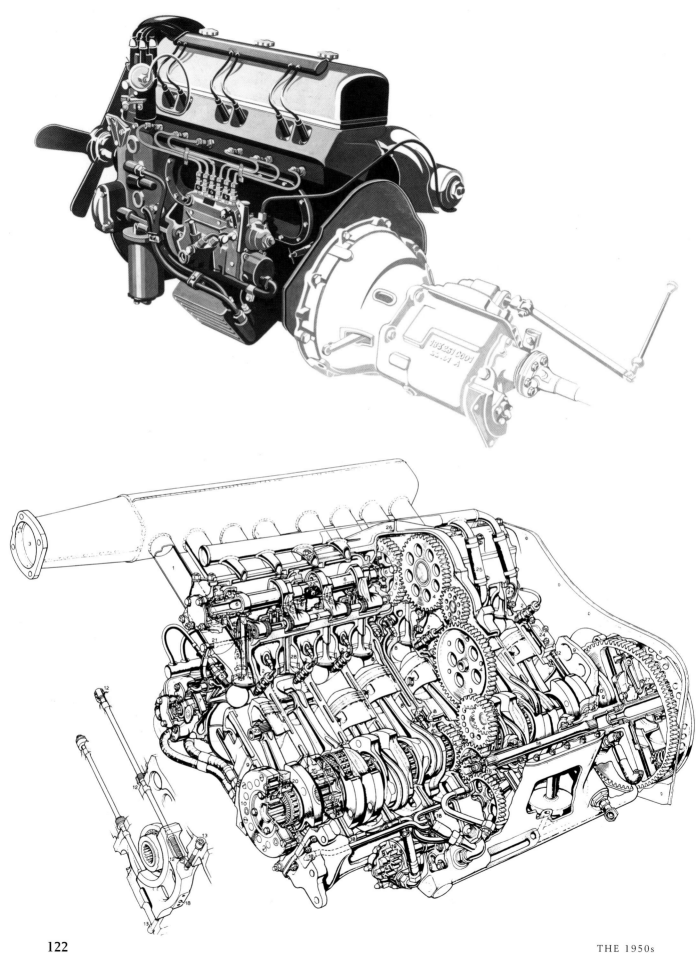

the 300 saloon of 1957 (again the 'big six' but redesignated M189, with 160bhp) and the 220SE of 1958 (the 'small six', M127), with 115bhp, rising to 120bhp by the end of the decade.

If Mercedes was the technical powerhouse, Volkswagen was the generator of sheer quantity. The 'Beetle' was no longer a joke: the validity of Porsche's philosophy had been proven, although there was only a single major change to the power unit during the whole decade, a boring-out from 75 to 77mm to raise the capacity of the flat-four to perhaps its most familiar figure, 1,192cc, with an output of 30bhp. That was in 1954: eventually, towards the end of the decade, increases in compression ratio had taken it to 40bhp. Reliability and reasonable economy were sufficient to ensure that Volkswagen's only problem was meeting demand, although it kept an engineering team busy studying alternatives, and Ferry Porsche, son of Ferdinand, demonstrated the potential of the unit by taking the 356 series of engines to 100bhp, with the aid of a capacity increase, twin-overhead camshafts per bank and unrestricted breathing of the kind which VW wanted to avoid!

Elsewhere in Germany, relatively little of technical significance was happening, if one excepts the efforts of Borgward, which was achieving excellent results from a 1.5-litre OHV 4-cylinder engine in the Isabella, and DKW, which by 1957, was trying to re-

establish a market for light 2-stroke engines. On the other side of the Iron Curtain, of course, the top-level planning decision had been taken that the East German industry would develop 2-stroke cars – hence, eventually, the Wartburg and the now legendary Trabant – while Czechoslovakia would do the 4-strokes, in the form of the Skoda range and the big rear-engined Tatra, the latter an astonishing device with an air-cooled, overhead-camshaft 3-litre V8, rear-mounted. In fact, during the 1950s, Skoda was producing some competent front-engined, rear-driven cars with OHV 4-cylinder engines of its own design, but this was also the decade in which the company decided that the Renault Dauphine pointed the way to the future, and produced its own interpretation of the idea which led to a series of rear-engined cars that persisted well beyond their sell-by date. Back in West Germany, meanwhile, Ford and Opel were still struggling to establish meaningful programmes with modern products, which would not come properly on stream until the 1960s.

Italian flair to the fore

Italy was another matter. Alfa Romeo, before the war essentially a small-scale manufacturer of high quality sports cars and a racing specialist, had fallen into public ownership and was now determined to broaden its range. It did so, remarkably, with a series of models powered by 4-cylinder twin overhead camshaft engines, first the 1900 and then in 1954, the brilliant Giulietta unit, originally of only 1.3-litre capacity (74 x 75mm, 1,290cc). This engine, with its classical hemispherical combustion chambers, in a cross-flow cylinder head which made the most of the potential of its Weber carburettors, formed the first stage in the development of a whole series of much admired units extending over several decades.

From Fiat came a whole series of new engines, again much admired by commentators of the day. In 1950 came the 1400, still an OHV 4-cylinder with only three main bearings, but with extremely over-square dimensions (82 x 66mm for a capacity of 1,395cc) and considerable potential for development from its initial output of 44bhp at 4,400rpm. Forming part of the same team, so to speak, was the 1900 of broadly similar layout which appeared two years later, with the same 82mm bore but the much longer stroke of 90mm for a capacity of 1,901cc. This engine was used not only in Fiat's larger cars but also, for a very long time, in the Campagnola off-road vehicle, in

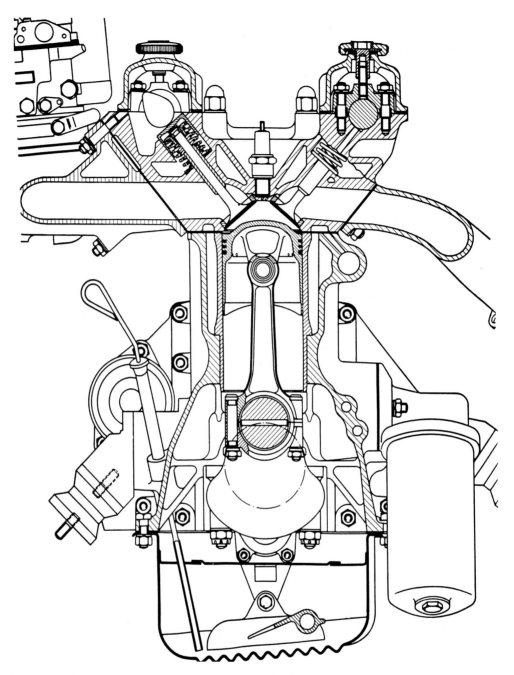

Another simple engine, and in some ways an interesting comparison with the Jaguar DOHC unit. This is the first of the classic Alfa Romeo twin-cam engines, launched in the Giulietta in the 1950s and destined for a long and successful life. The cylinder head arrangement adopts the same geometry with wide-set valves and central sparking plug. The cylinder block is about as different from Jaguar's as could be, with 'wet' cylinder liners and the block walls extending downwards well below the crankshaft centre-line for extra stiffness. (Ludvigsen Library)

which it remained until 1973 and for which it was also converted to diesel operation. This diesel unit, launched in 1953 in the 1400D (despite the fact that the engine's capacity was 1.9-litres) produced only 40bhp and lacked any appeal except to the ultra-frugal.

In between times, Fiat's engineers had fun with a high-output OHV V8, oddly laid out with a 70° angle between the cylinder banks, with over-square dimensions of 72 x 61.3mm for a capacity of 1,996cc

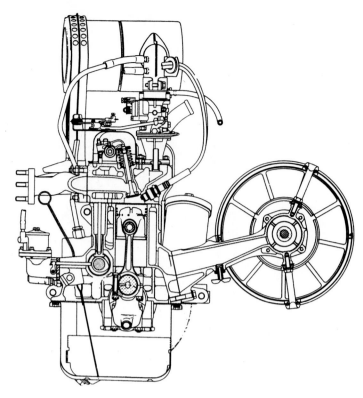

– very much on the small side for a V8 and indicative of its quasi-competition status. The 8V sports car in which it was fitted was made only in small numbers.

Very much at the other extreme were Fiat's two new small cars of the 1950s, first the 600, launched in 1955, and then the Nuova 500 of 1957. Both of these cars were rear-engined, Fiat's design team having decided this was the most effective packaging arrangement for four seats and an engine in a minimum-size vehicle. The 600 engine was a 4-cylinder OHV unit with a bore and stroke of only 60 x 56mm, for a capacity of 633cc, and an output of 22bhp at 4,600rpm. Small though the engine was, its over-square dimensions meant that a three-bearing crankshaft was essential if it was not to suffer a speed limitation. Dante Giacosa described how early studies for the 600 included an air-cooled 150° vee-twin engine with an extremely unusual valve and combustion chamber arrangement, but ultimately, and despite the problems of packaging (the engine was mounted in-line with the radiator and cooling fan

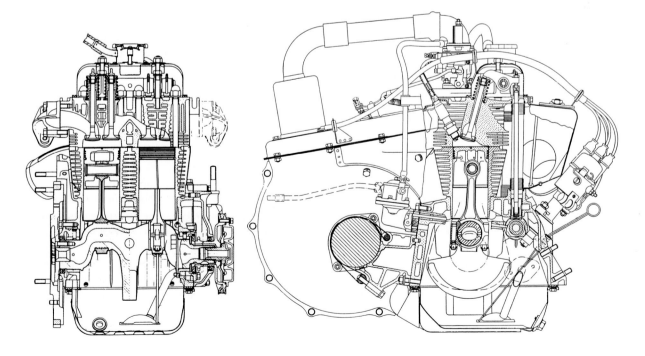

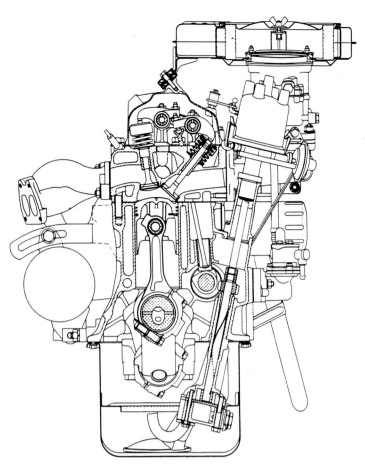

it was found possible to ease out the bore dimension to 67.4mm, bringing the capacity to a precise 499.5cc. With a higher compression ratio, the power output then became 17.5bhp (the 0.5bhp was clearly seen as important) at 4,600rpm.

As if all this work was not enough, Fiat ended the decade with another new engine, this time a 6-cylinder OHV unit with vee-opposed valves, which appeared in 1959 as the 1800 (72 x 73.5mm, 1,795cc) and as the 2100 (with the bore increased by 5mm to 77mm, for a capacity of 2,054cc). This engine, designed by Aurelio Lampredi, had slightly strange 'polyspherical' combustion chambers in which the valve layout was not symmetrical, the exhaust valves being nearer to upright than the inlets. It did mean however that with the use of two rocker shafts, all the valves could be operated by a single set of parallel pushrods. The engines proved perfectly satisfactory, but the layout was not repeated.

At Lancia, production was concentrated on three models: the Aurelia, launched at the beginning of the decade, the little Appia, introduced in 1953 as a replacement for the Ardea, and the big Flaminia which was announced in 1957. The Appia followed Lancia tradition in having a narrow-vee 4-cylinder engine with 68mm bore and 75mm stroke, for a capacity of 1,090cc and an output of 38bhp at 4,800rpm. The Aurelia, on the other hand, had one of the earliest 'conventional' V6 engines with the ideal 60° angle between cylinder banks. Launched as the B10 with a capacity of 1,754cc (70 x 75mm), this was an engine

alongside), the small but conventional 4-cylinder was chosen. It was probably just as well, because in enlarged and developed form it went on to enjoy an extremely long life in Fiat's smaller cars, right up to the 1990s.

Giacosa pointed out that the 600 was seen as the replacement for the 500C, while the Nuova 500 was a completely new 'minimum car' for the Italian, and European, entry-level market. Consequently, when the 500 emerged in 1957, there was nothing wrong with it having a 2-cylinder engine, even though the original 500 Topolino of the 1930s had used a 4-cylinder engine of similar capacity. The Nuova 500 outwardly somewhat resembled a shrunken 600, but the engine was an in-line air-cooled 2-cylinder with the two pistons moving in unison, balanced by a massive counterweight between them, at the centre of the two-bearing crankshaft. Alternative flat-twin boxer engines (as in the Citroën 2CV) were studied but rejected, mainly it seems on the grounds of cost. Air cooling was chosen even though it had been rejected for the 600 on the grounds of interior noise: in the 'minimum car' this did not matter so much. The 500 had a bore and stroke of 66 x 70mm (considerably more than the 600, therefore) for a capacity of 479cc and an output of 13bhp at 4,000rpm; but before long

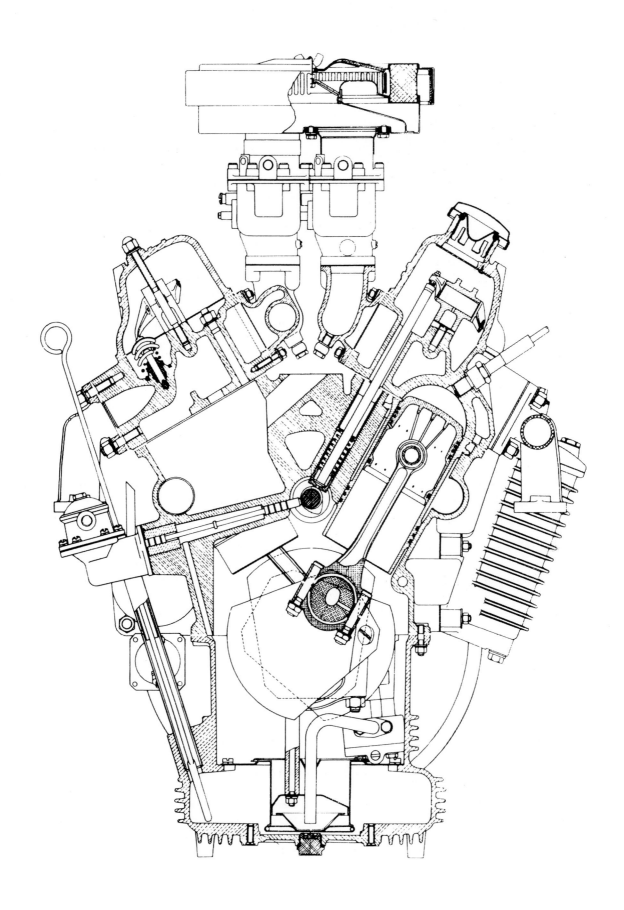

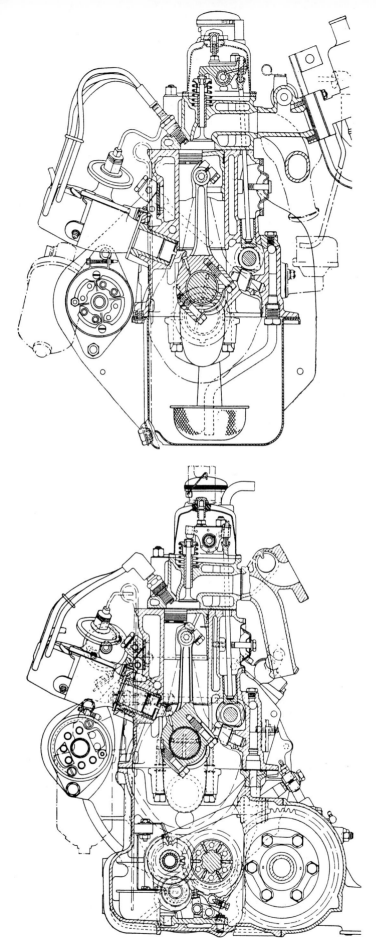

which in some ways was conventional by Lancia standards, with a single camshaft in the vee and pushrods operating the in-line overhead valves. But as the first series-production V6, it is remarkable, looking back, to realise that over 60 years elapsed between the first car and the emergence of this configuration which is now almost the most popular engine. In any event, the Aurelia engine proved amenable to 'stretch', and towards the end of the decade, when the Aurelia itself was replaced by the Flaminia, it grew to no less than 2,451cc (78 x 85.5mm) delivering 118bhp for the 2500GT versions of the car.

Although of similar configuration, the Flaminia engine was new and basically larger, to suit the heavier car. It was launched at 2,548cc (80 x 81.5mm) with 102bhp, but was bored out to 85mm, for a capacity of 2,775cc and a power output of 146bhp (with three Weber carburettors) for the final 2.8GT versions of the big car.

Updates in **Britain**

The 1950s equally saw rapid moves in Britain to get rid of ancient side-valve engines and replace them with OHV units which could more easily achieve the high compression ratios that would enable the potential of high-octane fuel to be properly exploited.

Pre-eminent in this respect, at least in terms of volume, were the three engines in effect launched by BMC as part of the great Austin-Morris merger (although they were primarily of Austin, that is, Longbridge as opposed to Cowley, origin). These were the small 4-cylinder A-series, the larger 4-cylinder B-series, and the 6-cylinder C-series. In terms of what

None too well appreciated at the time it appeared, the BMC A-series engine went on to an exceptionally long production life and great success. In essence it was a simple unit first conceived quite literally as a scaled-down B-series with a capacity of 800cc instead of 1,200cc. Part of the secret of its success was the research work carried out by Harry Weslake into combustion chamber design, which resulted in the A-series 'bathtub' with in-line valves and moderate squish. The two versions of the engine shown here well illustrate the extent of the changes needed to adapt the A-series from its original in-line, rear-drive installation, to transverse installation with 'gearbox in sump' for the Mini and 1100/1300 series. The one arguable weakness of the A-series, less evident in these transverse cross-sections, was its inability to be opened out beyond 1,300cc. (Ludvigsen Library)

was happening elsewhere in the world, none of them was terribly adventurous in their engineering, but they represented a big step forward for Britain, and the A and B-series turned out to possess a huge amount of development potential, and remained in production for decades in their advancing forms, fitted to many different cars.

The A-series appeared before the BMC merger, in the Austin A30 which attracted much interest at the time as being the 'spiritual successor' to the Austin Seven (this of course was in 1951, when the Seven itself was less than thirty years old). Thus it was observed by *The Motor* at the time that 'the stroke happens to coincide exactly with that of the old Seven, but the bore is larger by 2mm'. Comparisons were actually fairly pointless, because this was an all-new design with a three-bearing crankshaft and enough room within the block – unlike the Seven – for boring-out from its initial 58mm to an eventual 70.6mm for the 1,275cc version of the 1960s and beyond – and slightly more than that, for the 1,293cc competition engines, but only with blocks carefully

selected from the foundry! The stroke, initially 76mm, was likewise pushed out to 81.3mm for the largest production version. It needs to be said, however, that by comparison with contemporary European engines the A-series began life with substantially under-square dimensions: the old British approach to engine design had yet to be abandoned. In its initial form the A-series displaced a modest 803cc and delivered 30bhp at 4,800rpm; as *The Motor* observed, this output was 'actually 25 per cent

A general cutaway view of the A-series in its epoch-making transverse front-drive form, in this case for the original Mini. Because the Mini was so small and the A-series was an adapted engine, the alternative transmission arrangement of an 'end-on' gearbox rather than one in the sump was never really examined. Below the lower level of the A-series cylinder block (at the crankshaft centre-line) everything was newly designed, with the added awkwardness of a common lubricant for engine and transmission. (Herridge & Sons Collection)

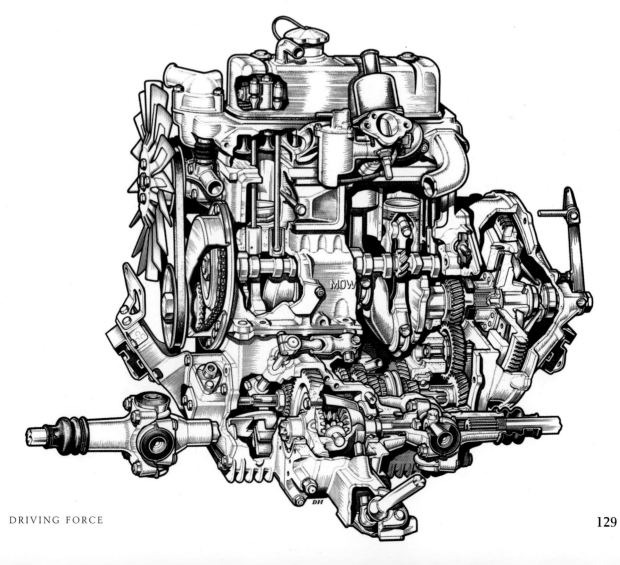

greater than that of the 900cc post-war Austin Eight.' One of the first moves by the new BMC was to throw out the pre-war Morris-designed 918cc side-valve engine and replace it with the A-series, which became by degrees the corporation's standard small engine for all purposes including, when it emerged, the Austin-Healey Sprite and MG Midget series of sports cars. Towards the end of the decade, of course, the A-series was turned sideways, re-engineered as a package with a remarkable gearbox-in-sump transmission, and installed in the Mini.

The BMC B-series appeared in 1953, immediately after the BMC merger, and first saw the light of day in the MG Magnette. Again, it rapidly became standard, across the corporation's mid-range, not only in a whole series of 'badge engineered' saloons but also in the MGA sports car and its successors. As launched, the B-series had dimensions of 73 x 89mm for a capacity of 1,489cc and an output of 60bhp at 4,600rpm, with the aid of a pair of SU carburettors. This was yet another under-square design or, as *The Motor* kindly put it, 'a compromise between traditional long-stroke and fashionable 'square' ideas concerning engine proportions'. In general appearance, the B-series understandably looked like a scaled-up A-series, again with three main bearings, and it proved likewise suitable to 'stretch' although in this case only by boring-out, in two stages to capacities of 1,622cc and then 1,789cc, with cylinder diameters of 76.2 and 80.3mm respectively. However, the latter move, which included other important changes, did not come until the 1960s.

The C-series was less successful, partly because it was intended for a range of large cars – the Austin Westminster and its luxury badge-engineered Wolseley sister, as well as the Austin-Healey 100 sports car. As launched in 1954, the C-series was a four-bearing 2.6-litre engine, with dimensions of 76.4 x 88.9mm for a capacity of 2,639cc. Its stroke, therefore, was identical with the B-series but it was certainly not one-and-a-half of the 4-cylinder engine. For one thing, the cylinder head, developed by Harry Weslake, had 12 separate ports, where previous practice had been to 'siamese' the adjacent ports within the head, simplifying the design of the manifolds and leaving space to run the valve operating pushrods. In the C-series, the camshaft was transferred to the other side of the head (to the right rather than the left, as seen by the driver) where the pushrods and their guides could be installed without interference. As launched in the A90 Westminster,

the 2.6-litre C-series produced 85bhp at 4,000rpm, yet again well down on the kind of specific output (bhp per litre) then being achieved elsewhere in Europe. Like the B-series however, it could be bored-out, to 83.4mm for a capacity of 2,912cc for cars which were marketed as '3-litre'. Like the B-series engine, but less wisely in terms of the use of corporate resources, the C-series was also heavily redesigned in the next decade.

With these three engines, by no means advanced in

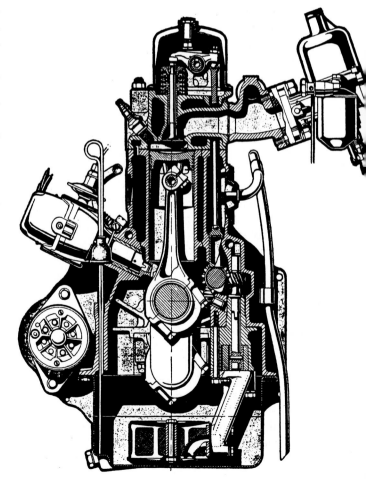

The BMC B-series, seen here in its 1,489cc form, came before the A-series but inevitably bears a striking physical resemblance to its smaller cousin, not only in valve gear and cylinder head design, but also in the detailing of the block casting. Yet unlike the A-series, the B-series proved capable of being 'stretched' all the way to 1.8-litre capacity for cars like the Austin 1800 and the MGB – and even formed the original design basis for an OHC adaptation which became the British Leyland O-series. (Ludvigsen Library)

absolute terms, BMC prepared to face its opposition for at least the next ten years. It may have been further put off the idea of advanced technology by its brief experience with the MGA Twin Cam, a derivative of the standard OHV MGA powered by a DOHC adaptation of the B-series engine launched in 1958, offering 108bhp at no less than 6,700rpm. Although mildly successful in competition – at a time when the specialised sports-racing car was becoming a breed apart – the Twin Cam was quickly withdrawn from production when it became clear that its need for high-grade petrol, and for skilled and regular service – to say nothing of sympathetic driving on the right side of the red line – was not always being fulfilled.

BMC's potential – and eventually, very real – competitor for market leadership in Britain was Ford. Through the 1950s its smaller cars continued to be powered by the faithful 1,172cc side-valve engine of pre-war origins, but the larger 4-cylinder Consul and 6-cylinder Zephyr appeared in 1950 with new OHV engines, and the old V8 Pilot vanished from the scene soon afterwards. In effect, the two engines were a single design, with identical bore and stroke 79.4 x 76.2mm (so over-square, a British market revolution) so that the 68bhp, 2,262cc Zephyr engine amounted to one-and-a-half 47bhp, 1,508cc Consul engines. The 6-cylinder had more gentle valve timing for stronger mid-range torque, and its peak power came at 4,000rpm compared with 4,600rpm for the Consul unit. It is interesting, looking back to 1951, to see *The Motor* unable to resist earnestly explaining that these engines had RAC horsepower ratings of 16 and 24hp respectively, even though the rating as a basis for British taxation had been dropped at the beginning of 1947 – it took a long time for people to stop thinking in terms of strictly nominal 'horsepower'. It was more of a comment of Ford's technical outlook up to that time that the magazine was able to comment that 'overhead valvegear is a novelty on a Ford car . . .' By 1956, the engines had been revised and enlarged for the Consul, Zephyr and Zodiac Mark 2, most notably with the adoption of cast-iron crankshafts with hollow webs to reduce weight and inertia without sacrificing stiffness.

These engines established a strong reputation and the market spent most of the rest of the decade wondering when the smaller cars would see an equivalent improvement. It did not come until 1959, but when it arrived it was something of a technical eye-opener. The replacement for the old E93/100E side-valve was radically new, to the point of having dimensions so over-square that they seemed to belong to the world of racing. The new unit, the 105E first seen in the Anglia, actually had dimensions of 81 x 48.4mm for a capacity of 997cc. It was still, however, a pushrod OHV engine and it had three main bearings when five might have been better, given the considerable crankshaft length forced by the big bore (on the other hand, of course, the throws of the cast-iron crankshaft were very short). What nobody outside Ford knew at the time was that the 105E would be handsomely stretched via a series of increases in stroke – but that was for the 1960s. As it was, the high-revving nature of the 105E was a revelation even if it had its down-side. 'When accelerating below 20mph in top gear,' strictured *The Autocar* road test, 'the engine is decidedly lumpy, to such an extent that a driver who has forgotten to change down is promptly reminded to do so.' In a strange postscript to the saga of the RAC horsepower formula, Ford discovered that the Anglia was unsaleable in the island of Mauritius, apparently the final corner of the Empire to have retained the formula for taxation purposes. The little 997cc engine, by virtue of its large cylinder bore and piston area, had a rating of 16hp . . .

Competition for the small BMC cars was provided through the 1950s by the Standard Eight, and later the Ten, with a neat three-bearing 4-cylinder OHV engine, launched in 1953 with dimensions identical to the original BMC A-series (58 x 76mm, 803cc) but down on power, with 26bhp rather than 30bhp. This engine was bored-out to 63mm (for 948cc) for the Ten, and proved remarkably stretchworthy, its later versions seeing service in the Triumph Herald series and then opened up all the way to 1,493cc for the final-series Spitfire 1500 sports car. Alongside this new small engine, the 2,088cc 4-cylinder Vanguard unit continued on its stolid way until the advent of the Vanguard Six. However, the 2,088cc engine was sleeved-down to 1,991cc, and its breathing considerably improved, for fitting to the TR2 sports car, in which the 2-litre unit was rated at 90bhp.

Vauxhall's range already had all-OHV engines, and the company might have been slightly miffed to see everyone else catching up. Its only move to maintain its position, though, came with a new range of engines with slightly over-square rather than grossly under-square dimensions, 79.4mm bore by 76.2mm stroke for a 4-cylinder capacity of 1,508cc. These appeared in the Wyvern from 1952 onwards, and the first of the Victors

At the end of the 1950s, Ford astonished the British motoring world by introducing the 105E engine for the new Anglia. This massively over-square engine had a piston area which would have qualified it as a 16hp under the old RAC classification, yet its capacity was less than 1 litre and its power output was moderate. Its then-unusual dimensions gave the engine an unusual appearance in cross-section, with an extremely shallow block. The bathtub-type combustion chamber may look small in this view, but bear in mind the large area and short stroke of the piston . . . (Ludvigsen Library)

from 1957 – and a 6-cylinder capacity of 2,262cc, for the big Velox and Cresta, also from 1952. Although they were all-new, there was nothing outstanding about these engines: the 4-cylinder was a three-bearing unit, the 6-cylinder had four main bearings.

The Rootes Group also moved to abandon side-valve engines during the 1950s, offering new OHV units first in the big 6-cylinder Super Snipe, then in the 4-cylinder Hawk and Minx. Rover retained its basic engine design with the odd inlet-over-exhaust valve layout, gradually expanding into a range of 4-cylinder

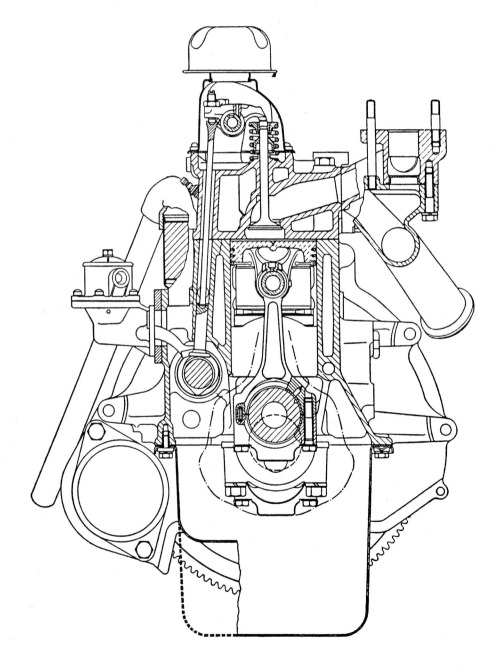

and 6-cylinder engines for its somewhat heavyweight cars – but the company was also preparing a major surprise for the new decade. In fact, the only engine in volume production in Britain which might be thought state of the art in, say, the mid-1950s was Jaguar's DOHC XK engine, which was beginning to serve a multitude of roles, delivering high power for the XK120 sports car and its successors, while at the same time being shrunk from its original 3.4-litre capacity all the way down to 2.4 litres, through a drastic shortening of the stroke from 106mm to 76.5mm, for a capacity of 2,483cc instead of 3,442cc. In doing so, Jaguar shortened the connecting rods and lowered the height of the cylinder block by no less than 67mm, saving a good deal of weight and gaining stiffness. In this smaller form the engine – retaining the existing 83mm bore – was slightly over-square and felt extremely lively, as indeed it should, considering that it was still delivering 112bhp, at the very high peak (for the time) of 5,750rpm.

Another simple and strong British engine of the 1950s was the 2-litre Triumph engine which found its way, among other models, into the early TR sports cars. Unusual among British engines in being linered, it has a three-bearing crankshaft which looks precariously spindly – and short of counterweights – by any modern standard. Yet it performed well and reliably, emphasising the extent to which well-balanced bottom ends have as much to do with refinement as with durability. (Ludvigsen Library)

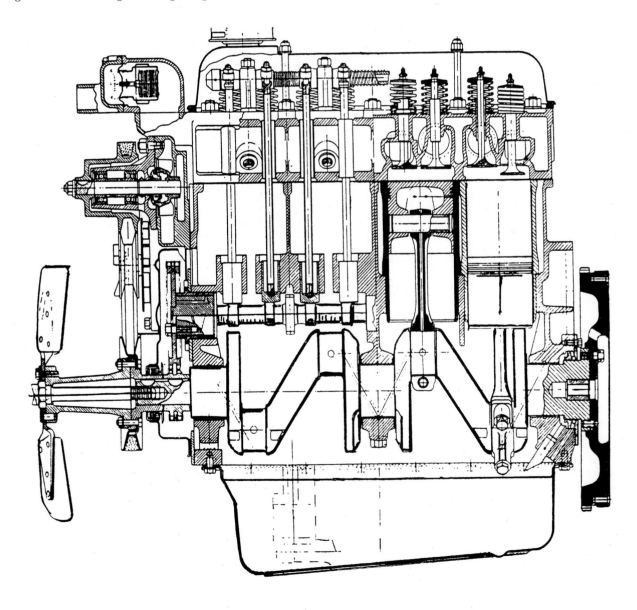

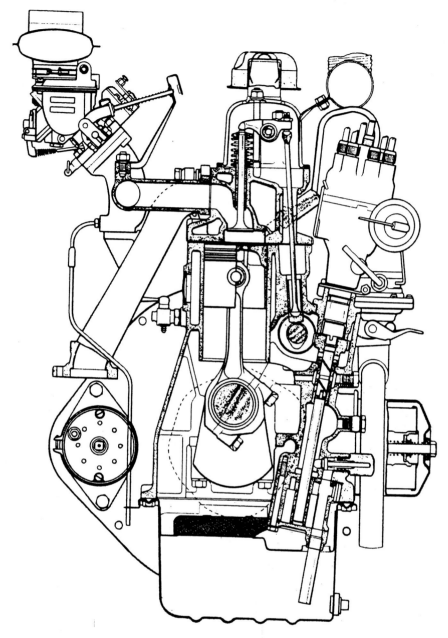

Eventually Triumph felt the need for a more refined six-cylinder engine, seen here in its original form for the Standard Vanguard Six. It became much better known in the Triumph 2000 and in the later TR sports cars, was enlarged to 2.5-litre capacity and offered (with mixed results) with fuel injection.

Unlike its four-cylinder predecessor, the six-cylinder did not have a linered block. Its valve gear is in every sense conventional, and its single-sided gas flow, with carburettor and exhaust on the same side, is typical of much 1950s practice but promises no great efficiency. (Ludvigsen Library)

In **summary**

The 1950s was above all the decade in which the side-valve engine died. A few examples lingered on into the 1960s but in truth, there was little justification for the layout. Even the improvements achieved in the chemistry of fuels and lubricants played their part. It had long been a justification of the side-valve that the process of decarbonising the engine was utter simplicity. You drained the engine, lifted the head, and there exposed were the piston crowns and the valve heads. You removed as much of the carbon deposit as was practicable, then bolted the head back into position with a new gasket. There was no need to touch the valve timing, whereas with an OHV engine, everything had to be reset afterwards (and with an OHC engine, an expert touch and deep understanding was often called for). But by the 1950s, carbon deposits were no longer forming with the same speed or determination. Better sealing, both around the valve stems and in the piston ring package where chromed top rings and other measures were becoming commonplace, was keeping oil out of the combustion chamber. The better engines of the 1950s no longer measured their oil consumption in terms of a few hundred miles per pint or less than a thousand kilometres per litre. The ceremony of lifting the head became a thing of the past, and with it went the last lingering reason (apart from minimal manufacturing cost) for the side-valve layout.

It was not just the side-valve that died. So did the long-stroke engine, although many British engineers found it difficult to kick the habit. Over-square, big-bore engines called for longer crankshafts, but also provided the space in which to fit additional main bearings (although this would be more widely exploited during the 1960s). Even more to the point, they had the space for bigger valves, which meant better breathing, which meant higher specific power. Nobody any longer worried too much about the once-assumed piston speed 'limit' of 2,500 feet per minute for production engines, although *The Motor* yearbooks of the 1950s still included, as a preface to the Road Test Summary, pronouncements such as 'two bhp per square inch of piston area may be considered normal' and that a maximum piston speed of '2,500 feet/minute is a normal figure, less being proof of a low-revving engine or one of unusually short stroke.' By the end of the 1950s, such yardsticks belonged to history. Advances in materials and detail design, lighter pistons and stronger connecting rods, plus a growing understanding of in-cylinder gas flow had rendered them archaic. By 1959, it was much more indicative to compare the

specific outputs of engines in terms of bhp per litre – the kilowatt as a unit of power was still somewhere in the future! An engine might produce high power from a small capacity either by running very fast, or by ensuring the minimum resistance to the passage of gas from intake to exhaust (or both).

Did it matter how fast an engine ran, or how high its maximum piston speed might be? So long as it achieves good durability, and doesn't squander too much energy in overcoming internal friction (which can rise steeply at very high revs), and is quiet, clearly it does not matter. With those provisos, high specific output simply means a smaller, lighter engine for whatever purpose it was designed. The 1950s marked that period in engineering history when designers returned to these basics, rather than adhering to a set of arbitrary yardsticks which no longer had much meaning.

The 1950s will also be remembered as the decade in which motorists became aware of fuel quality. British motorists, after a long period in which they had nothing but 'pool' petrol of doubtful quality (branded fuels finally appeared on the market in 1953), began to appreciate the subtleties of octane rating. Compression ratios which had started the decade at around 7:1 ended it at 8:1 or higher – and there was no question that a side-valve engine with a compression ratio of more than 8:1 needed a combustion chamber of extremely strange shape and dubious thermal efficiency.

This was also a decade in which there came the first stirrings of interest in fuel injection, at Mercedes and in some of the big American V8s, as the struggle to claim the title of 'most powerful' intensified. Diesel engines, purpose-developed for passenger cars, could still be numbered on the fingers of two hands, perhaps of just one.

Above all, beyond doubt, this was a decade in which European and American interests in the area of engine design diverged almost completely. Engineers in both markets knew what they wanted, and how to get it. It was simply that they – or rather their customers and their product planners – wanted different things. It was a story that would be continued unbroken through the 1960s.

8 The 1960s
Power and efficiency

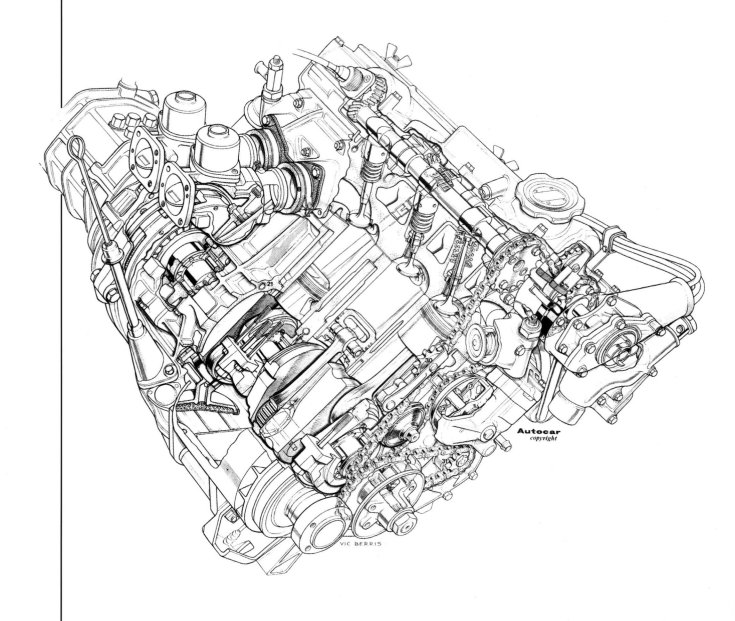

VIC BERRIS

Autocar
copyright

Although the world was not without its travails, the 1960s were generally an excellent decade for the motor industry. In the developed markets, the emphasis had now shifted from building volume to competing for it. Motoring consumers, even in Europe, were no longer grateful – as they had been at least until the early 1950s – to lay hands on any kind of modern car. They were more prepared to assess, to compare, and to demand better. Not for nothing did this decade see the rise of the major consumer organisations, Consumers' Union in the USA, the Consumers' Association in Britain, and their equivalents in many other countries. The decade also brought to prominence the first great 'consumer advocate', Ralph Nader, who began to dissect some of the less praiseworthy aspects of the motor industry, especially in the USA.

What was the effect of this background on the engine designers? It depended where they were. In the USA, the 1960s was the decade of the power struggle. Power output, as high as could be advertised, sold cars. In the USA, this process was made easier because the manufacturers measured output according to the SAE (Society of Automotive Engineers) method, which basically involved removing anything which might result in a parasitic power loss. The Europeans really did not approve of this approach and more often measured output using the German DIN method, which gave a figure much more representative of an engine's output when installed in a car. Some Europeans quoted both SAE and DIN outputs, which indicated just how much the American method exaggerated the power actually available under the bonnet. They might almost have come to blows, except that there was no market overlap to speak of. American cars no longer sold in Europe in any numbers worth talking about, and the validity of SAE ratings was of serious concern only to those European enthusiasts and journalists who still had access to a range of American products. Meanwhile, European – and, as the decade wore on, Japanese – manufacturers exporting to the USA either quoted an SAE figure for their products, or were selling to enthusiasts of one kind or another (enthusiasts for perceived European sophistication, or for economy of operation) who either knew the score or did not care.

This proviso has to be stated because, in a world which has become used to 'honest' power outputs, some of the American figures claimed during the 1960s were truly astonishing. To quote 400bhp, even from a monster 7-litre (427cu in) V8 in 1968 was seriously to try the patience of European manufacturers who were getting half that (but DIN) from 3.8-litre engines of considerably more advanced design. The harping on power diverted attention from torque, where the big American V8s were inevitably superior and highly impressive. They were also, on the whole, refined, durable and – helped by economy of scale – remarkably cheap to make. Generally though, the American V8 engines of the 1960s were not advanced in their engineering. They ran to a pushrod OHV formula in which strong output was achieved with the aid of high compression ratio and generous carburation. This was the decade not only of the 'muscle car' but also of the monster four-barrel carburettor, from Carter, Holley or Rochester, names hardly known, except by reputation, in a Europe where Stromberg, SU, Weber and Zenith still ruled, even if Bosch fuel injection was beginning to write the story of their eventual demise. It was also the decade in which the traditional ignition system of coil and distributor began to give way, by stages, to the potential of the transistor.

One thing all these 1960s American engines had in common was thirst. Petrol – gasoline – cost very little, and the general standard of living was high. Few customers cared if their cars failed ever to achieve 20mpg – those that did bought 'cute little imports'. It was not simply that these engines operated almost all the time at speeds and loads far remote from the point at which their efficiency was highest, first accelerating along the freeway entry ramps and then dawdling along using less than 10 per cent of their potential output. The engineers knew that one certain way to prevent overheating at high load was to add extra fuel, which would not burn but would reduce the combustion temperature through evaporation. Eventually this helped to create a new problem for the American industry, and then the industry worldwide: exhaust emissions. Ultra-rich mixtures, even if held for no

Opposite: The 1960s saw the Japanese manufacturers coming to the fore in terms of engine design. Honda drew heavily on its motorcycle manufacturing background, by then already considerable, when designing its early small sports cars. The four-cylinder S800 engine seen here was water-cooled – unlike the engines of the first Honda minicars – and excited great admiration for its specific power output, though this was achieved at very high revs and with the aid of features such as a roller-bearing camshaft. (LAT)

more than a second or so, resulted in a big increase in unburned hydrocarbons emerging from the tailpipe, and an unhealthy output of carbon monoxide into the bargain. By the end of the 1960s, the city of Los Angeles had had enough. On bad days, the onshore wind from the Pacific prevented traffic fumes from escaping out to sea, instead pinning them against the half-circle of mountains behind; and an atmospheric temperature inversion clamped a lid on the whole cauldron, so that the 'smog' built up and anyone with a breathing problem really suffered. Thus it was, against the kicking and screaming of Detroit, that the State of California enacted the first emission control regulations as 1970 approached. A whole new era was about to come into being.

Not all American cars were behemoths, although all-too-many of them were. But in the early 1960s there emerged a new class of 'compact' cars for buyers whose means (or inclination) prevented them from buying a 'full-size' V8. The class was supposedly created by the short-lived Studebaker Lark but it came to be typified by entries from the 'big three': the Plymouth Valiant from Chrysler Corporation, the Ford Falcon – and the Chevrolet Corvair, launched for the 1960 model year. All these cars had 6-cylinder engines, shared in most cases with the 'base' versions of the full-size models. The Corvair however was completely different. In a fit of rampant inventiveness which carried uncanny echoes of the 1923 'copper-cooled' fiasco, Chevrolet decided that its compact would not be a mildly scaled-down derivative of a full-size model, but a completely new concept powered by a rear-mounted air-cooled flat-6 engine. Admittedly, this decision came at a time when Volkswagen was making rapid inroads into the 'entry level' American market but it sought to carry the principle much too far.

The comparison with the 'copper-cooled' Chevrolet should not be taken too far. In terms purely of engine design, the Corvair power unit, developed by a team under Henry Barr, who had cut his engineering teeth on the Cadillac V16, was by no means a disaster. In fact it was almost the only American attempt at a truly 'modern' design in the whole of the 1960s, and it has among other things been widely used in homebuilt light aircraft in which it is valued for its toughness and refinement as much as for its light weight and air cooling. Among its advanced features for the time were a torsional vibration damper, hydraulic valve lifters (partly to compensate for awkward access for maintenance) and a decent oil cooler – always advisable on an air-cooled engine.

However, the problems of the Corvair chassis apart, the engine was simply too small and lacking in power even for the compact market. With its initial 2.3-litre capacity (with well over-square dimensions of 85.7 x 66mm, 2,287cc) and 80bhp at 4,000rpm, the Corvair engine could not be compared with the tough 6-cylinder in-line unit in the Ford Falcon, for example, which may only have produced 101bhp but delivered substantially more torque. Subsequently Chevrolet enlarged the engine – eventually right out to 94 x 75mm (3,122cc) – and even offered versions with turbocharging, but the real interest lies in why the decision was taken to proceed with such a radical unit.

Undoubtedly the Volkswagen was a strong influence. VW itself makes the point that in 1958, while car production in the USA was falling by 29 per cent, in Germany it rose by 23 per cent and VW's own production handsomely exceeded half a million for the first time, with many of those cars exported to America. The urge to reply with a domestic rear-engined, air-cooled car was therefore strong. For the mainstream market, however, a 4-cylinder engine was out of the question. It had to have six cylinders, and the only practical configuration if the engine was to be rear-mounted was a flat-6, despite all that was known about this being an expensive solution. Also, if the car was not to be grossly tail-heavy, the engine would have to be made largely of aluminium, which at least dovetailed neatly with the air-cooling: high rates of heat transfer, easily and accurately cast cooling fins. But it could still not be made too large. In the end, all of the purely engineering problems were solved, and the cooling in particular seems to have been well worked out. Yet the Corvair power unit spawned no imitators. It was very much a case of nice engine, shame about the application. The only engine of similar 6-cylinder configuration to emerge – six years later, bear in mind – went into the Porsche 911, and that drew on what was already nearly 20 years' experience in building ever more heavily modified and powerful Volkswagen derivatives, apart from being aimed at a very different market, and built in a different kind of way.

However, the Corvair was not the only example of GM's fascination with aluminium as an engine manufacturing material. Its other divisions (except for Cadillac) entered the 'compact' market but with far more conventional cars, the Buick Skylark, Oldsmobile F85 and Pontiac Tempest, all built off the same front-engine, rear-drive platform. It was intended that these cars should have a V8 engine, but

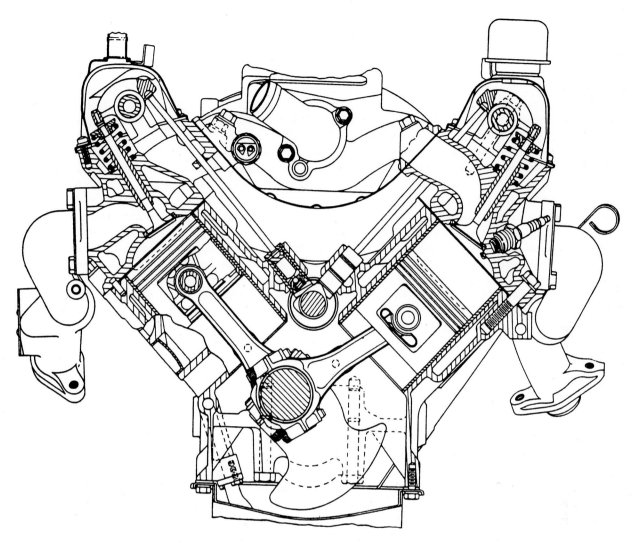

It may look like a conventional American 90-degree V8, but this is actually the all-alloy V8 3.5-litre engine for the 1961 Pontiac Tempest, one of a family of 'compact' GM models from different divisions. The problem of running aluminium pistons in aluminium bores is overcome by casting in a thin cast-iron liner, visible here. In most respects the engine reflects then-current GM design practice, in its valve gear and manifolding for instance. Abandoned by GM because of service problems associated with its aluminium construction, the engine was taken over by Rover, which developed it into a huge family of applications continuing to this day. (Ludvigsen Library)

the fear was that an existing all-iron V8 would be too heavy, leading to more understeer than even Americans would be prepared to countenance. Thus the decision was taken to develop an all-aluminium V8. After a series of experiments with wet-lined blocks, the definitive engine emerged with dry cast-iron liners inserted into the mould before the block was pressure die-cast – in itself a major undertaking and one of the earliest examples of the process for a component of this size.

Apart from the use of aluminium alloy, the engine was totally conventional in its layout, with dimensions of 88.9 x 71.1mm for a capacity of 3,529cc (215cu in in American parlance). It produced 150bhp at 4,400rpm, or 155bhp at 4,800rpm for Oldsmobile, who modified it in several respects, principally concerning the cylinder head and piston design. In its lightest form it weighed only 144kg (317.5lb), so it clearly achieved its targets. Its only problem – but it turned out to be a serious one – was that the alloy block needed more care in the maintenance of the cooling system, and in particular the use of the right coolant additives, than American motorists were prepared to give it. Thus although it performed well – to the extent that Oldsmobile offered a turbocharged version, in the Jetfire, which produced 215bhp – the all-alloy engine lasted only three years in US production, being withdrawn in 1963. The ingenious alternative for the 'compact' class cars was to retain the machine tooling, chop two cylinders from the block and cast it in iron instead of light alloy, enlarging the cylinder dimensions to create an engine initially of 3,244cc (198cu in) capacity. At the same time, the extremely sound basic design and the inherent 'stretch' created by the original need to leave room for the insertion of iron liners in an alloy block meant it could also be continued in cast iron form as a V8, eventually enlarged by Buick to as much as 340cu in (5,572cc). The iron V6 also led a chequered history, being enlarged to 95.2 x 86.4mm, 3,687cc (225cu in), and was then sold to Jeep. Later it was bought back again for use in SUVs. Because it had been derived in this way from a V8, the angle between the V6's cylinder banks was 90° rather than the theoretically ideal 60° as seen in the Lancia Aurelia engine (previous chapter) for example, but with suitable mountings – and a degree of forgiveness – this was not a major problem, as various other 90° V6 engines subsequently proved.

The alloy V8 saga might nonetheless have been a historical blind-alley but for the fact that Spencer Wilks, the chairman of Rover Cars, literally stumbled over a discarded example of the engine in a boathouse belonging to a GM executive while on a visit to the USA. He promptly decided it was just what his company needed and bought the manufacturing rights – although the process of 'Roverising' it was by no means simple, involving for example, a sand-cast rather than pressure die-cast block, pressed-in instead of cast-in-place cylinder liners, cast instead of machined combustion chambers, and of course a switch from the Rochester carburettor to twin SUs on a new manifold. In much developed form, this engine is still in production in 2002, making it now one of the longest-lived engine designs of all time. That, however, is jumping well ahead in the story.

Elsewhere in America, there seemed to be only two paths of development: rugged in-line 6-cylinder engines for 'entry level' models, and bigger V8 engines with ever more power. Well before the end of the 1960s the compact cars had become rather less compact, as the 'full-size' cars had grown even bigger, and the V6 was abandoned in its turn. Basic they

might have been in American terms, but such straight-6 engines were still large in European eyes. By 1967 for example, the Pontiac Tempest was powered by an engine with dimensions 98.4 x 82.4mm for a capacity of 3,769cc (230cu in), delivering 215bhp (SAE) at 5,200rpm with a compression ratio of 10.5:1. This, however, was the highly tuned Le Mans version; more typical was the Chevrolet version used in cars like the Biscayne, actually with a longer stroke of 89.6mm for a capacity of 4,097cc (250cu in) but with a compression ratio of only 8.5:1 and an output of 155bhp at 4,200rpm, a very conservative figure which shows how much stress was placed on robustness and on 'lazy' performance when teamed with a three-speed automatic transmission, which by this time was virtually standard in American cars.

This decade, and especially its latter half, was the period of extreme growth for the post-war V8. For anyone but a dedicated American specialist, the engines came in a bewildering number of variations, although some of the most widely used units became known simply by their capacity in cubic inches, hence the Ford 289 (101.6 x 72.9mm, 4,727cc) as used in the Mustang and others, and the 428 (104.9 x 101.2mm, 7,016cc) in the company's larger high-performance models. It is worth noting in passing that for the most part, the Americans at this time were still designing in inches and fractions rather than in metric units, and – especially in the biggest engines – it can be frustrating trying to match up the last few units when converting from one system to the other!

However, although enthusiasts concern themselves with the differences between these V8s, they all used the same basic layout, a 90° vee with a single camshaft at its centre and pushrod operated valves. Despite the widespread admiration for Chrysler's 'Hemi', most of these engines used wedge-shaped combustion chambers with in-line valves, with side inlet ports from the vee-mounted multi-barrel carburettor, and overhead exhaust ports sweeping downwards to outboard manifolds. The cylinder blocks were cast iron, partly because this was a time when the US industry was becoming expert at casting such components with a high degree of consistency and accuracy, with thinner walls that saved both weight and cost, making it very difficult for aluminium to compete. In cylinder heads, where thermal characteristics were more important, aluminium made some headway but many of the big V8s were all-iron.

Large they certainly were: by the end of the decade, the Cadillac engine in the front-driven Fleetwood Eldorado had grown to 'square' dimensions of 4.3 inches, (109.2 x 109.2mm) for a capacity of 8,195cc or 500cu in, making it the largest engine to be used in a production passenger car in the post-war era. Ford's biggest was the 7,538cc (460cu in) engine in the Lincoln Continental, while Chrysler restrained itself to a mere 6,981cc (426cu in) for the highest-performance versions of models like the Dodge Charger and Plymouth Barracuda. These, it must be emphasised, were the biggest: the average American was happy enough with an engine of up to 5-litre (say 300cu in) capacity. In defence of the top-range units, it must be said that many low-volume 'prestige' manufacturers in Europe, unable to afford the cost of developing their own high-output units, were very happy to exploit their huge torque, excellent reliability and remarkably low cost. The roll-call includes AC, Bristol (407 onwards), Gordon-Keeble and Jensen in Britain, Facel Vega in France, and Iso and de Tomaso in Italy . . . all such manufacturers had to do was install the V8s as delivered, and resist the temptation to 'develop' them.

Europe: a scene of contrast

While this scramble for sheer size and output was taking place in the USA, what was happening in Europe? In the 1960s, a great deal. Perhaps the most notable feature of the 1960s in Germany was the resurgence of BMW following a period of severe financial embarrassment which very nearly led to the company being bought by Daimler-Benz. In the event, BMW was able to remain independent due to some brave financial backing and one brilliant new product, the 1500. As related in the previous chapter, through the 1950s, BMW – rather like Citroën, but even more so – had followed a strange and precarious policy of building large cars and very small cars, but with a great gulf between them and no cohesion whatever. The 1500 changed all that by adding to the range a well-judged medium-sized model, light, roomy and reasonably powerful. Not only did it plug the gap in the company's model range, it provided the foundation from which a whole new range of 4 and 6-cylinder models was developed, eventually at the exclusion of all else. To power the newcomer, at the very beginning of the 1960s, Alex von Falkenhausen designed a 4-cylinder SOHC engine which determined the formula on which the company's subsequent fortunes were largely founded.

This was a comfortably over-square (82 x 71mm, 1,499cc) engine which, for the sake of lower installation height, was designed to be installed leaning over at a 30° angle. Its single overhead camshaft was chain-driven, and operated the valves, vee-opposed but also staggered, via rockers. The not-quite-opposite valves sat in hemispherical combustion chambers formed in the die-cast aluminium head, while the block was cast iron and very simple, thanks to the absence of pushrods. The crankshaft was very strong, of forged steel and with five main bearings. The only real problem with the chosen layout was where to position the sparking plugs, but they were inserted at a shallow angle into each combustion chamber more or less between the two valves. The combustion chamber itself was not circular but had a fair amount of squish, and the piston crowns needed recesses to ensure valve clearance.

Once this simple masterpiece had entered production, BMW set about developing it through both tuning and a complex process of enlargement. First, it was both bored and stroked to 84 x 80mm taking it to 1,773cc for the 1800 of 1963. Then the new 84mm bore was combined with the original 71mm stroke to yield a capacity of 1,573cc for the 1600. Both these engines were then given a higher compression ratio and twin Solex carburettors to produce TI versions, the 1800TI producing 110bhp at 5,800rpm. Next, the 1800 was bored-out again to 89mm, for a capacity of 1,990cc – and to confuse the issue, this new larger bore combined with the original 71mm stroke produced a new 1,766cc capacity, which became the new 1800. Meanwhile, the 2000 was given the TI treatment, to deliver 120bhp, and then (by 1969) developed with an early Kugelfischer fuel injection system, offering 130bhp at 5,800rpm as the 2000tii.

By the later 1960s, it had been decided to develop a 6-cylinder engine series which would to all intents and purposes be one-and-a-half of the 4-cylinders. These engines emerged in 1968 in two sizes, 2,494cc (2500) and 2,788cc (2800), with the same 86mm bore but with strokes of 71.6 and 80mm respectively, and delivering 150 and 170bhp. They quickly established a reputation for outstanding smoothness and operating refinement, and their success probably discouraged BMW (at that stage) from proceeding with a project to create a 3.6-litre V8 by combining two 1800 cylinder blocks into a single 90° crankcase, although prototypes were tested in 1969.

While all this was going on, not far down the road from Munich, in Dingolfing, Hans Glas had moved on from early production of the Goggomobil 'bubble car' to produce a series of larger and more adventurous projects. The first, the S1004 of 1961, had a 4-cylinder single overhead camshaft engine in which the camshaft was driven by a carefully tensioned toothed belt running from the crankshaft to the camshaft sprocket. The belt needed no lubrication and was hidden only by a pressed steel cover to prevent the ingress of debris (and fingers). It was greeted with considerable suspicion but proved to work perfectly well, eventually creating a situation in which the designers of OHC engines faced a straight choice between chain and toothed belt drive. Examples of both continue to emerge in 2002. While it simplifies lubrication requirements and is easy to replace when necessary, the belt needs slightly more room – a consideration especially in transversely mounted engines – and can be noisier. None of this did Hans Glas much good: a financial crisis led to a BMW takeover, leaving behind two toothed-belt engines, the original 4-cylinder (in 1.3-litre and 1.7-litre form) and a V8 which consisted of two 1.3s spliced together. BMW carried on building them for a short time but stopped before 1970. Paradoxically, no BMW engine had ever used a toothed belt camshaft drive, its team consistently preferring single or duplex chains.

Steady progress at Mercedes

The 1960s saw Mercedes move steadily forward. The 1950s had seem the company move into grand prix racing, purely as a demonstration of its technical superiority, and leave again once that superiority had been proved beyond doubt. There was no inclination to go that way again. Mercedes' technical and racing guru, Rudolf Uhlenhaut, interviewed by the author in 1968, stated flatly that the company's production engine programme was too diverse and complex to spare the hundred-odd top engineers who would have been needed for a new foray into grands prix.

It was true that Mercedes, like BMW, seemed to have found a formula for engine design and was sticking to it. Indeed, there were similarities, in that both engineering teams then favoured a single chain-driven overhead camshaft, although Mercedes preferred directly operated in-line valves rather than opposed valves and a train that included rocker arms. But Mercedes had a wider range of requirements to fulfil. It had already established four basic needs: three petrol engines (a 4-cylinder, a small 6-cylinder and a larger 6-cylinder) and a diesel. When it entered the 1960s, these requirements were fulfilled by the 4-cylinder, three-bearing M121 series, the 6-cylinder, four-bearing M180, the 6-cylinder, seven-bearing M186 and its derivatives – some of them with alloy cylinder blocks – and the 4-cylinder, three-bearing OM621 diesel. First priority was given to a new and more refined 4-cylinder petrol engine with five main bearings, the M115, which appeared in the W115 series of cars (the 200 and upwards) in 1967. The 'small six' was replaced by a new seven-bearing design, M108/M114, which first appeared in the 250 in 1965 and had sufficient space to stretch to 2.8-litre capacity. As for the 'big six', it was slated for replacement by a 3.5-litre V8 (M116) in 1969, which it made its first appearance in the 280SE 3.5. Meanwhile in 1967, again for the launch of the W115 series, Mercedes prepared a new five-bearing, 4-cylinder diesel based on the M115 petrol engine, sharing the same principal dimensions in 2-litre form.

By the time the M116 V8 made its appearance, Mercedes already had a V8, but of a very different kind. This was the M100, with dimensions of 103 x 95mm for a capacity of 6,332cc, intended for the big Mercedes 600 series whose objective was to create a German alternative to the Rolls-Royce. It is probably best to note at this stage that Rolls-Royce had finally phased out its exquisite but rather quaint 6-cylinder engine from the Silver Cloud and replaced it with an equally exquisite pushrod OHV V8 of 6,230cc (104.1 x 91.4mm, or more precisely 4.1 x 3.6 inches), and in 1966 the Cloud itself gave way to the Silver Shadow which ushered in all kinds of new-fangled ideas like unitary construction and disc brakes. But for many years, Rolls-Royce would not quote any power or torque outputs for its V8, saying merely that they were 'satisfactory'. Mercedes had no such reservations, quoting 250bhp (DIN) at 4,000rpm for the M100, the low peak speed pointing to the fact that this was a conservatively tuned power unit, as the specific output of less than 40bhp/litre suggested. But unlike the Rolls-Royce engine, the M100 had a single overhead camshaft per bank, and Bosch fuel injection . . .

This last point underlines the fact that Mercedes spent much of the 1960s working mainly with Bosch

to introduce both fuel injection and transistorised or static ignition on an increasing number of engines and models. The process had actually begun during the 1950s, but it was the next decade which saw Bosch's D-Jetronic injection system adopted for the 2.5-litre, 6-cylinder engine in the 250CE coupé, and in the M116 V8 when it appeared. The programme would accelerate rapidly in the 1970s, not least under the impact of exhaust emission regulations.

NSU embraces the
Wankel rotary

While Mercedes spent the decade on a logical if complex path towards higher efficiency and the fearless deployment of technology, other German companies had different strategies. NSU for example spent the early 1960s building itself into a kind of small-scale rival for Volkswagen, with a series of small but rather smart cars with rear-mounted, air-cooled engines. By the mid-1960s it had a range of three cars, all with SOHC in-line engines. The Prinz 4 had a 2-cylinder engine which delivered a healthy 30bhp at 5,500rpm from only 598cc (76 x 66mm). The Prinz 1000, more of an incipient threat to the VW

A brave try which came to very little: the twin-rotor Wankel engine as fitted to NSU's Ro80 saloon. The three-faced deltoid rotors rotate within two-lobed epitrochoid housings, creating a geometry within which four-stroke combustion can take place. The smooth operation and compactness of the Wankel engine were extremely attractive, and its early problems of sealing the rotor tips could have been overcome, but the poor shape of the combustion chamber leading to thermal inefficiency was a more fundamental flaw. (Ludvigsen Library)

Beetle, had a 4-cylinder engine of 996cc (69 x 66.9mm) and 43bhp – more than the contemporary Beetle 1300 – while the top of the range was the NSU 1200C with a 1,177cc (75 x 66.6mm) engine delivering 55bhp, thus comfortably out-gunning the Beetle 1500. However, NSU's management was imaginative and ambitious. They had forged a very early understanding with Felix Wankel and held the primary rights to his rotary engine principle. Indeed, it was NSU's engineering director, Walter Froede, who was to Wankel almost what Maybach had been to Daimler in terms of turning the rotary engine into a practical, and ultimately a production proposition.

NSU began limited production of a Prinz Coupé with a single-rotor Wankel engine in 1963. Virtually all were sold within the motor industry, and one imagines most of them were quickly taken to pieces again to be studied in minute detail. Then, in 1967, NSU followed up with the admirable Ro80 saloon, with a twin-rotor Wankel engine delivering 113bhp at 5,500rpm from a nominal 1,990cc. Sadly, although it was produced in limited volume for almost a decade, the Ro80 was hamstrung by teething problems with the rotary engine and in particular its sealing system – the equivalent of piston rings in a conventional reciprocating engine. The NSU seals had behaved admirably in high-load, high-performance testing, but proved more fragile when the car was driven by ordinary customers in stop-start traffic conditions. To make matters worse, the combustion chamber shape in the Wankel was long and shallow, with a poor (that is, a high) ratio of surface to volume, bad for thermal efficiency and therefore fuel consumption. NSU's product planners did not help the situation by deciding only to offer the engine in combination with a semi-automatic transmission – a three-speed gearbox, torque converter and automatic clutch. The author had one chance to drive a development car with a five-speed manual gearbox, and it felt much better. Eventually, the whole issue of the Wankel engine was resolved, after a fashion, in the 1970s. A slightly smaller car, the K70, was developed in parallel with an all-alloy 1.7-litre 4-cylinder engine, but before it could be put into production NSU fell into financial difficulties and was taken over by Volkswagen.

Volkswagen itself, meanwhile, was sticking rigidly to its rear-engine, air-cooled flat-4 formula. The sensational rise of sales through the 1950s and early 1960s meant the company could hardly do anything else, yet it needed new product (other than the already popular Microbus) to broaden its range – as well as constantly improving the Beetle itself. But any new product would have to conform to the same general layout. Thus, through the 1960s, the Beetle engine was enlarged in stages, first with its stroke extended by 5mm to 69mm, bringing its capacity to 1,285cc, then by being bored-out 6mm to 83mm, for a capacity of 1,493cc.

Beyond this, a series of new, larger and more powerful models was prepared, starting with the 1500 of 1961 and progressing through the 1600TL, with the Beetle engine further bored-out to 85.5mm for a capacity of 1,584cc, to reach the large 411 which needed a substantially new engine but still with the same configuration, with well over-square

dimensions of 90 x 66mm for a capacity of 1,679cc. As the 411LE, this model was fitted with a very early Bosch electronic fuel injection system, with which it developed 80bhp, but some teething problems were encountered.

None of the new models achieved anything like the success of the Beetle and by the end of the 1960s it had become clear that a radical new approach was needed. To some extent, it must be said, the change of direction was probably eased by the death in 1968 of Heinrich Nordhoff, who had led Volkswagen through 20 years of rapid expansion and notable success. From then on, it was only a matter of time before the idea that the only good Volkswagen was one with a rear-mounted, air-cooled engine was abandoned, although the first serious moves came only with the dawn of the 1970s.

Other things too were happening in the technically fertile German industry. The 2-stroke engine had proved as much of a thirsty and polluting dead-end for DKW as it had for Saab, but you could not tell that to the East Germans with their Trabants and Wartburgs. By the end of the 1950s, the company's West German assets – its original home had been in the East – were bought by Mercedes with the object of creating a new 'sub-Mercedes' marque which would combine an efficient new 4-stroke engine, of Mercedes design, with DKW's front-wheel drive traditions and the light compactness of its last cars. Mercedes plucked Audi out of history as the revived name for the new marque. Production began in 1965 with the 70, powered by a very straightforward pushrod OHV 1.7-litre engine designed specifically to fit ahead of the front axle line within the body shell of the last DKW 2-stroke, the F102. This meant slightly under-square dimensions (80 x 84.4mm, 1,696cc) to make the engine short enough, but it turned out to be a highly efficient unit, helped in particular by a combustion chamber with strong swirl for good mixing. In combination with the car's light weight it established something of a reputation for economy, and the original 70 quickly evolved into the more powerful 90. By this time, though, Audi had already been sold on to VW, and its Ingolstadt facility was combined with the nearby NSU works in Neckarsulm to create a new manufacturing group in southern Germany.

The 1960s also saw the launch of the Porsche 911, a car which took the evolution of the VW Beetle formula into a sports car several stages further than the 356. Most notably, the 911 engine was a flat-6 rather than a flat-4, originally with dimensions 80 x 66mm for a capacity of 1,991cc, and with a single overhead camshaft per cylinder bank, driving the vee-opposed valves via rockers. There was little sign, when the 911 was launched (complete with a 4-cylinder sibling, the 912) of what an icon it would become, or the way in which the original engine

would evolve, through a long series of step-changes, into something 160 per cent bigger and 200 per cent more powerful. And while the 911 represents a milestone of sorts, it did not greatly influence the course of engine design elsewhere. The 'boxer' configuration was still seen as expensive, and with transverse engines and front-drive now coming into favour, in-line 4-cylinder or V6 units were (and still are) seen as preferable.

In the 1960s the Ford operations in Britain and Germany remained completely separate from an engineering point of view. Consequently, the German arm took an earlier interest in front-wheel-drive and needed a suitably compact engine to mount ahead of a

front transaxle. This extremely compact 1.2-litre pushrod OHV V4 was the result, used not only in the Taunus series of saloons, but also, in enlarged 1.5-litre form, sold to Saab to replace the two-stroke engine in the 96, thus creating the 96V4. (Herridge & Sons Collection)

The Americans in Europe

This was also a rather strange period in the histories of the Ford and GM operations in Europe, in which the British and German subsidiaries were allowed completely separate powertrain operations even

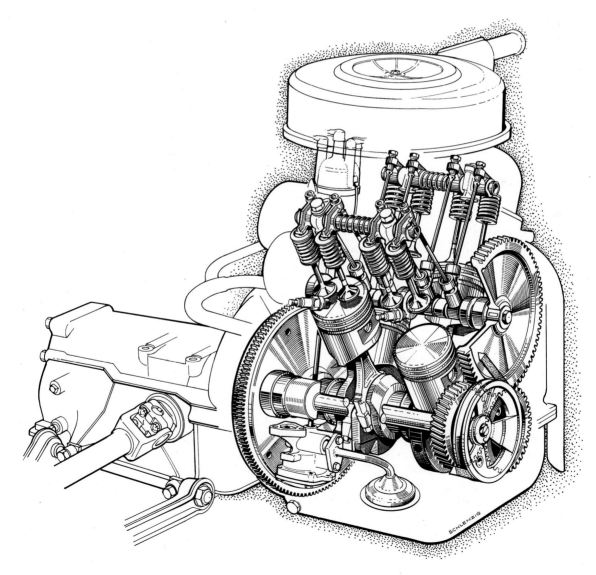

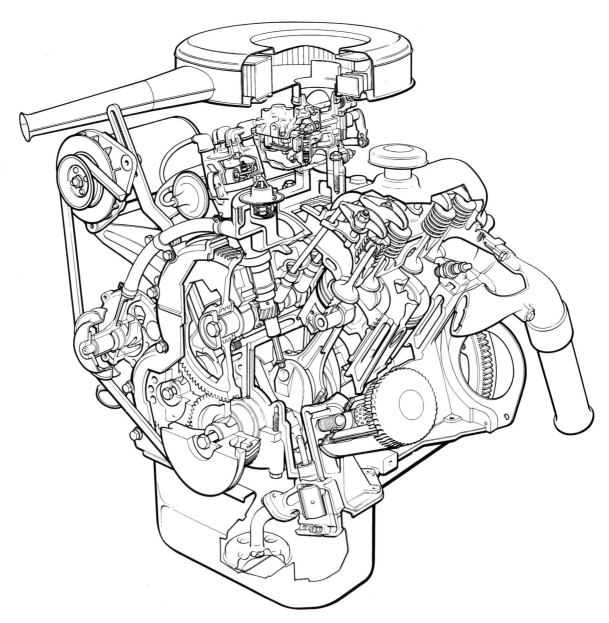

Ford of Britain also embraced the V4 engine for its compactness and produced this engine, larger (at 1.7 and 2.0 litres) and less compact than its German cousin, but admirably suited for some purposes, including the

earliest versions of the supremely successful Transit van in which its relative lack of refinement mattered little. The engine was also fitted to the Corsair saloon car series with satisfactory results.
(Herridge & Sons Collection)

though they were beginning, especially in Ford's case, to share platforms and body shells. Thus Ford in Germany developed an unusual series of vee-

configured engines, all with the same 60° angle between banks regardless of whether they were V4 or V6. It is of course the right angle for the V6 and consequently wrong for the V4, but in this case the V4 has to be regarded as two-thirds of the V6, with the virtue of being able to pass down the same machining transfer line. Cologne produced three intimately related V4s (1.3, 1.5 and 1.7) and three equivalent V6s (2.0, 2.3 and 2.55); the smaller V4s being set up for front-wheel drive in the Taunus 12M/15M series. It was never an engine noted for its refinement, but the V4 was tough and extremely compact, and was selected by Saab as a replacement

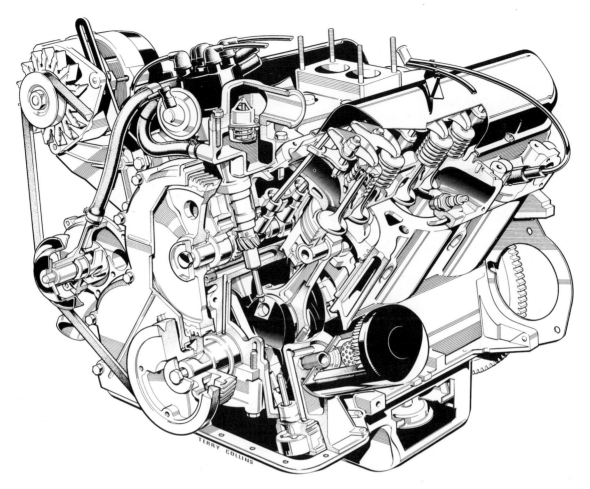

for the 2-stroke engine in the 96 when it became clear that more performance and a cleaner exhaust were needed.

In Britain meanwhile, Ford was busy exploiting the potential of the over-square 105E Anglia engine. It began quite simply by lengthening the stroke to just over 65mm, taking the capacity to 1,340cc for the car launched as the Consul Classic. Then came two more versions, again differing only in stroke, for the 'Consul Cortina'. With 58.2mm stroke the capacity was 1,198cc for the Cortina 1200; with 72.75mm stroke (and two additional main bearings) it grew to 1,498cc for the Cortina 1500. In this longest-stroked, but still comfortably over-square form the engine proved amenable to tuning and adaptation. First it received a conventional working-over – higher compression ratio, better carburation and valve timing for more overlap – to power the Cortina GT. Then, at the behest of Colin Chapman of Lotus, Harry Mundy (the author's predecessor-but-one as Technical Editor of *Autocar*) designed a completely new twin overhead

The 3-litre V6 equivalent of the British Ford V4, the 'Essex', makes an interesting comparison with the smaller unit. For the V6, the 60-degree angle between cylinder banks is correct, whereas for the V4 it is not, hence the latter's poor refinement. But the two engines share many features, including details of the valve gear and the 'Heron' combustion chambers formed in the piston crowns beneath an essentially flat cylinder head with upright valves. (Herridge & Sons Collection)

camshaft cylinder head, with chain-driven camshafts, to mate with the existing block. The result was an outstandingly successful engine which remained in production for several years, powering the Lotus Cortina, Escort Twin Cam, and Lotus Elan and Elan Plus 2. Mundy related that Chapman offered him £100 or £1 per engine; he considered for a split second and took the £100, thus bidding a premature farewell to about £10,000. In 1967, the standard Kent engines were still further improved, with the adoption of cross-flow cylinder heads and Heron-type bowl-in-piston combustion chambers. The two standard sizes were now 1,298cc (1300) and 1,598cc (1600) with stroke measurements of 63 and 77.6mm respectively: the original 105E bore dimension of just under 81mm still remained unchanged. Towards the very end of the decade, in this 1600 form the engine provided the foundation for yet another high performance adaptation, the Cosworth-developed BDA with 16-valve cylinder head and belt-driven camshafts.

While all this was going on, Ford of Britain was developing larger engines to replace the long-serving in-line units in the Zephyr and Zodiac. The result was a series of 60° vee engines (bearing no relationship whatever to their German counterparts), which in 1966 powered the new Mark 4 Zephyr/Zodiac series. Ironically, these compact units were housed beneath possibly the longest bonnet of any post-war British car, leaving plenty of room for the spare wheel in the extreme nose. The largest of these Essex engines had dimensions of 93.7 x 72.4mm for a capacity of 2,994cc, and with two cylinders lopped off, it became a 1,996cc V4 for the Zephyr 4 and eventually, also the Corsair 2000E. A shorter-stroke version (60.35mm for 1,663cc) was used in the Corsair V4, when it was decided the model needed more output to avoid being slower than the smaller Cortina whose 1.5-litre engine it originally shared.

Meanwhile, Opel and Vauxhall were treading equally separate though slightly less hectic paths. Opel spent the 1960s evolving an engine range with just two basic designs – a very ordinary little 1,078cc (75 x 61mm) pushrod OHV unit for the Kadett, and a range of 'cam in head' (c-i-h) engines for its larger and more powerful models. The cam-in-head arrangement was an interesting compromise in which the chain-driven camshaft was installed in the cylinder head, but alongside rather than above the valves, which it operated via rockers. The result was a useful reduction in engine height, and most of the advantages of an OHC layout, for a little added width – and, arguably, some constraints on the design of the ports and manifolding. Opel kept to this basic design, in 4-cylinder and 6-cylinder form, always with the same crankshaft stroke of 69.8mm, well into the 1970s and in some cases beyond. At the end of the 1960s, the 'king' of the Opel c-i-h units was the 2.8-litre 6-cylinder engine in the big Admiral, producing 165bhp (DIN) with the aid of Bosch electronic fuel injection.

Today, the idea of Vauxhall producing its own

1,057cc (74.6 x 61mm) engine for the new small Viva, launched in 1963, might seem absurd when Opel already had a unit of almost exactly the same size – but this was 1963 and Vauxhall did its own engineering. In other respects, Luton carried on developing the related family of square, or mildly over-square 4-cylinder and 6-cylinder engines introduced for the Victor and Cresta during the late 1950s. By 1965, the Cresta engine had been bored out to 3.3-litre capacity (96.1 x 82.55mm, 3,294cc) for the new PC series. However, the Vauxhall engineers then introduced an all-new engine series with single overhead camshafts driven by a toothed belt, principally for a new-series (FD) Victor, launched in 1967 to replace the little-loved FC-series Victor 101. Sadly, the new engines, with nominal capacities of 1600 and 2000cc (sharing a stroke of 69.2mm, but with 85.7 and 95.25mm bore respectively) proved something of a disappointment, partly it seemed because of the strange and complicated provision which had been made in the design of the direct-acting tappets to allow the clearance to be adjusted with the aid of an Allen key.

Renault: preparing new positions

In France, the biggest news of the 1960s was Renault's rapid conversion to front-wheel-drive, following in the steps of Citroën. Yet the conversion was not uniform: it began with the announcement of the utilitarian Renault 4 in 1961 and continued with the launch of the radical new Renault 16 in 1965, yet in between the company continued to plug away with the R8 and R10, its rear-engined successors to the Dauphine. For these two models, Renault developed a new small engine which appeared unadventurous but which was destined for a long production life. This was a five-bearing engine, wet-linered despite having an iron block, but an aluminium cylinder head, initially 65 x 72mm (956cc) for the R8 which was soon opened out to 70mm bore (1,108cc) for the R10. For the sake of low cost, the little R4 was launched with the old small engine, in three sizes up to 845cc. However, the new 'Iron Cleon' engine – so nicknamed after the huge factory on the River Seine where it was assembled – could not be stretched to the size Renault needed for its new mid-size family car, the R16.

When it emerged, the R16 engine was remarkable above all for its extensive use of aluminium. As we

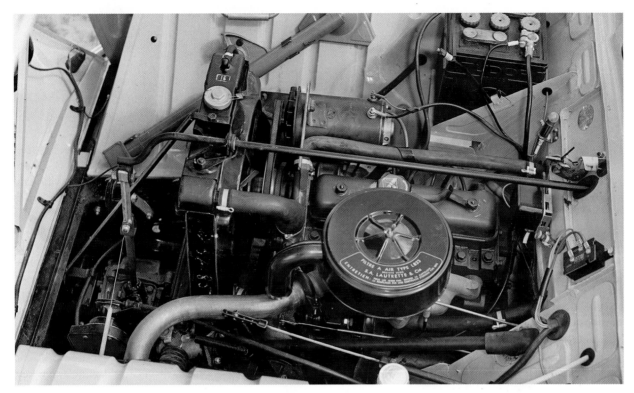

To create its first mass-produced front-wheel-drive car, the R4, Renault simply took the four-cylinder OHV engine package and transaxle, developed for its earlier small rear-wheel-drive models from the 4CV onwards, and moved it forwards, with the gearbox at the front and the rearmost cylinder next to the cabin bulkhead. This avoided overhanging the engine in an unduly long and heavy nose, but called for some hard thinking when it came to the gearshift linkage, seen here as the rod running forward above the engine from the 'umbrella handle' in the dashboard. (Giles Chapman Library)

have already seen, it was not exactly a pioneer in this respect but it represented the first European commitment to high-pressure die-casting for the manufacture of its wet-linered cylinder block. In other respects it was not unduly remarkable by the advancing standards of the 1960s – pushrod OHV, slightly under-square dimensions of 76 x 81mm for a capacity of 1,470cc and a modest power output of 59bhp at 5,000rpm, a specific output of almost exactly 40bhp/litre. But like so many wet-linered engines, there was space for an appreciable degree of 'stretch' even though the process did not begin until the 1970s.

By a process of parallel reasoning, Peugeot produced a new medium-sized front-driven car, the 204, almost at the same time as the Renault 16. In fact, the 204 engine was technically more advanced than the Renault in many ways. It had a single overhead camshaft and over-square dimensions of 75 x 64mm, for a capacity of only 1,130cc – despite which its output was only 6bhp less, at 53bhp. Its smaller size meant the 204 enjoyed a fiscal advantage in France, because its official CV rating was lower, and in most respects it was seen as a head-to-head competitor for the R16 with the advantage of lower running costs. But Peugeot's approach proved a distinct drawback in the British market where buyers were at last becoming used to classifying cars

primarily by engine size, and 1,130cc did not seem to be very much for the asking price. For Peugeot, the 204 was an expansion of the range, produced in parallel with the then recently launched 404, whose 1,618cc OHV engine was simply a larger-capacity version of the 403 unit, bored-out another 4mm but also increased in compression ratio and other details to deliver 80bhp instead of the previous 65bhp. Then, towards the end of the decade, the 404 was joined by the 504, the engine this time increased in size (to 1,796cc) by a stroke increase to 81mm, while the 204 was effectively supplanted by the 304, with the engine carefully enlarged to 76 x 71mm (1,288cc).

For Citroën, it was an odd decade, dominated on the engine design front by two events. In 1961, the 425cc

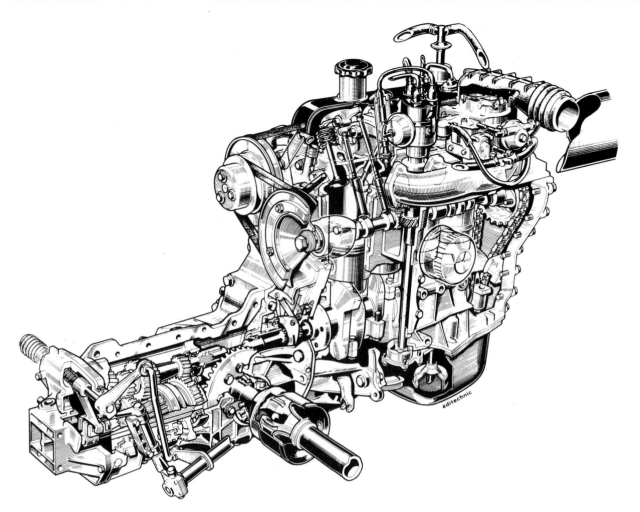

A far more ambitious Renault project for a medium-sized front-wheel-drive family car, the R16, was served by an all-new engine, of linered, all-alloy construction, with inclined pushrod-operated overhead valves. This engine used some of the largest pressure die-cast aluminium components seen up to that time. The original engine was of 1.5-litre capacity, but it was easily enlarged to the 1.6 litres of the 16TS version illustrated here. (Giles Chapman Library)

flat-twin 2CV engine was opened out all the way to 74 x 70mm – about as far as it could be taken – for a capacity of 602cc (which made it a 3CV in French fiscal terms). In this form it produced 20bhp at 4,500rpm and powered the odd-looking Ami 6. Later, since it retained the same overall dimensions, it was also offered in the 2CV itself (and in the 'intermediate' Dyane) to create the 2CV6. At the other end of the scale, Citroën at last brought the saga of the long-stroke 1,911cc engine to a close, replacing it in the DS series with a brand-new five-bearing unit, still pushrod OHV, but with the pushrods splayed to operate opposing valves from the single camshaft. The new engine first appeared in 1965 as a 2,175cc (90 x 85.5mm) unit for the top-range DS21, delivering a full 100bhp at 5,500rpm, but a smaller-bore (86mm, 1,985cc) version soon followed, to consign the old 1930s engine to a place in history – or to be strictly accurate, a place in a handful of Citroën light commercial vehicles. By the end of the decade, Citroën had begun to take fuel injection seriously and was offering a Bosch EFI version of the DS21 with 125bhp.

Throughout the decade Citroën's management seemed to be alone in failing to appreciate the huge product gap between the Ami 6 and the DS series. In private, naturally, this was not so. As early as 1960 the company was well advanced with the C60 project, which would have had a flat-4 air-cooled engine in two sizes, 1.1 and 1.4-litres. But the C60 gave way in turn to the Project F, which among other things, might have been powered by a Wankel rotary engine, in which Citroën was deeply interested. On the other hand, Wankel development was proving long drawn-out and the Project F was also prepared with the flat-4 engines from the C60. Vacillation over engine policy led to delays which allowed Renault's 16 in particular to occupy the ground for which the F-car had been planned, and in turn, it was shelved in favour of Project G, which eventually emerged as the GS – but not until 1970. It is worth noting in passing that Citroën had long been fascinated by the boxer configuration and in the 1950s had built prototypes, both water-cooled and air-cooled, of a 1,806cc (74 x 70mm) flat-6 engine intended for installation in the DS, but abandoned on grounds of cost. In a repetition of this history, during the 1960s, a water-cooled flat-4 engine was taken to prototype stage for what became the CX, but again abandoned in favour of turning the new DS engine sideways . . .

The Italian scene

This was a strong decade for Alfa Romeo, which continued on the course set in the 1950s, of turning itself into a medium-volume passenger car manufacturer notable for the quality of its twin overhead camshaft engines. To put the figures into context, as Alfa Romeo itself has pointed out, the company built fewer than 35,000 cars between 1910 and 1955, but the total figure had risen to around 500,000 by 1970. The technical pattern had been established in 1954 by the 1.3-litre Giulietta, but in 1962 there emerged the Giulia Super, with an outwardly similar but usefully larger engine (78 x 82mm, 1,570cc), delivering 98bhp at 5,500rpm, but with the potential for far more.

It is not widely appreciated that Alfa Romeo contemplated moving down in size, as well as up, from the Giulietta. Tucked away in the Alfa Romeo museum is a fascinating small, but still viable four-seater car, the Tipo 103. Beneath its bonnet is a DOHC engine which looks remarkably like a shrunken version of the Giulietta's (actually 66 x 66.5mm, 896cc), which produced 52bhp at 5,500rpm. Even more remarkably, the engine is installed transversely and drives the front wheels – this in a prototype which was running in 1960. The car itself equally resembles a scaled-down Giulia. Alfa Romeo old-stagers still refer darkly to pressures applied by Fiat on the Italian government (Alfa at that time still being nationalised) to stop the Tipo 103 in its tracks, before it spoiled everything for the Fiat 850 . . .

As it was, Alfa moved up rather than down. It had relatively little luck with its 6-cylinder 2600, but in

1967 enlarged the 1600 Giulia into the 1750, still with the same engine architecture but with bore and stroke now 80 x 88.5 for a capacity of 1,779cc.

The later 1960s were a period of revolution for Fiat

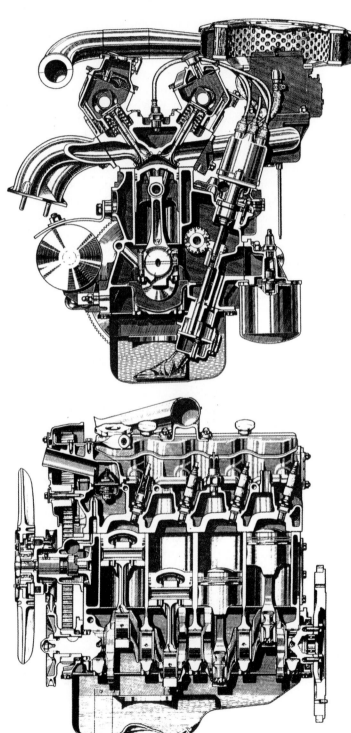

The Fiat Sport Spider was powered by an engine which superficially resembled Alfa Romeo's twin-cam series. However, the Fiat engine was a straightforward conversion of the pushrod OHV 124-series engine, fitted with a completely new crossflow, twin-cam cylinder head in which the camshafts were driven by toothed belt rather than chain; the advent of the toothed belt made such conversions much easier to carry out. (Ludvigsen Library)

in the engine department. In 1960, its range of power units was entirely pushrod OHV, and these evolved by stages until 1964, when the 850 was announced with a rear-mounted 843cc 4-cylinder engine produced simply by enlarging the 600 unit to 65 x 63.5mm. In time, this engine's stroke was further increased to 68mm, taking the capacity to 903cc, a figure which was to become one of the most familiar in Fiat's history. This was not revolution, however. Nor was the all-new but apparently conservative pushrod OHV engine which powered the 124 in 1966. Just over-square at 73 x 71.5mm (1,197cc), this simple 60bhp 4-cylinder engine had five main bearings and a block which had enough room to allow it to be bored-out to 80mm for a capacity of 1,438cc. The increase in capacity alone took the power to 70bhp, but more to the point, the engine had been designed to accept an alternative twin overhead camshaft cylinder head rather in the manner of Ford's Lotus-Cortina. The difference – apart from the use of toothed-belt instead of chain drive to the overhead camshafts – was that Fiat intended to produce this

version of the engine in significant quantity, first of all for the 124's sporting derivatives, the 124 Coupé and Spider, and eventually for a version of the saloon itself (the 124 Special T). With the new cylinder head, the power went to 90bhp at 6,000rpm.

Yet there was still more to come from Turin. Only a year after the 124, Fiat announced the 125 with a square, 80 x 80mm (1,608cc) engine equipped from the outset with belt-driven DOHC and delivering 90bhp at 5,600rpm. Then, in 1969, two more engines were announced, one a well over-square (96 x 66mm,

Another intriguing Fiat engine was the 1.1-litre SOHC unit developed for the 128, the camshaft again belt-driven, with the valves in-line and slightly inclined to achieve a 'classic' wedge-shaped combustion chamber form. The 128 engine was notable for its willingness to *run to high speeds, and was developed into a family of larger units not only for the 128 but also for its successors, and for the X1/9 sports car in which it was installed ahead of the rear axle line, driving the rear wheels. (Ludvigsen Library)*

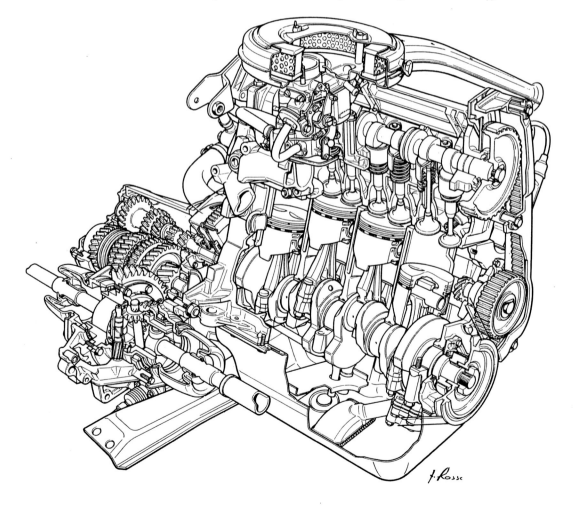

2,866cc) 2.9-litre SOHC 60° V6 with belt drive to the camshafts, and intended for the big 130 saloon. The other was far more significant, and again was well over-square and with belt-driven SOHC – but in this case it was a 4-cylinder engine, the dimensions being 80 x 55mm for a capacity of 1,116cc, and it was installed transversely in the 128, driving the front wheels. After years of testing the water with the Autobianchi A111 and A112 models – Autobianchi existing as a kind of 'junior Fiat' marque – Fiat itself had taken the plunge into front-wheel drive, and with an extremely good car powered by an outstanding engine which was destined to serve it well for many years.

By contrast with Fiat's improving fortunes, the 1960s was the terminal period for Lancia as an independent company. By 1970, having rejected a takeover offer from BMW, it had instead been bought – complete with its by then massive debts – by Fiat, for the extremely nominal sum of one lira. Yet, in 1960, Lancia had introduced the Flavia, a break with Lancia tradition in that it used a flat-4 engine, initially 82 x 71mm (1,500cc almost precisely), and in 1963 had

For the Flavia, successor to the Aurelia, Lancia moved to a 1.8-litre flat-four engine of largely alloy construction, shown here, mounted ahead of the front axle line and driving the front wheels via a transaxle. The flat-four configuration meant it could be made compact enough for this purpose, avoiding excessive overhang. It proved a successful if not outstanding engine, being enlarged to 2-litre capacity and offered with fuel injection. (Ludvigsen Library)

followed with the Fulvia, in principle a replacement for the Appia and powered by a 'traditional' Lancia narrow-vee 4-cylinder engine with dimensions 72 x 67mm for a capacity of 1,091cc. Both cars were recognised as being of high quality and both were continuously developed, the Flavia ending up as a Kugelfischer-injected 1.8-litre with 102hp, and the Fulvia – in its svelte coupé form – ultimately growing to 82 x 75mm (1,584cc) with 114bhp in standard form, and sufficient potential to become a Monte Carlo Rally winner. And yet, by the turn of the decade, Fiat was firmly in charge of Lancia's fortunes . . .

Fatal flaws **in BMC**

In Britain, the 1960s saw BMC soar to major success and then, through a combination of awful industrial relations and bungled product planning – both symptomatic of poor management quality – come crashing down again.

The last chapter told how the corporation ended up with a range of just three engines to power all its mainstream products: the small A-series, the medium-sized B-series, and the large 6-cylinder C-series. A series of factors conspired, admittedly with the benefit of hindsight, to upset calculations based on this philosophy. First, although the A-series now began at 845cc (62.9 x 68.3mm) in the Mini, it proved capable of enlargement to 1,275cc (70.6 x 81.3mm) for various purposes, and it existed also in 998cc and 1,098cc forms. The impetus for its development came from high-performance versions of the Mini – the 998cc Mini Cooper and the 1,275cc Mini Cooper S –

and from the new, larger transverse front-drive car introduced as the Austin and Morris 1100, with the 1,098cc A-series. This model series was eventually also 'up-gunned' to 1,275cc as the Austin/Morris/MG/Wolseley 1300 and the Riley Kestrel: badge-engineering at its height. From an engine point of view, the bad news was that the A-series was at the limit of its reliable stretch at 1,275cc – even to go to 1,297cc for works competition purposes, cylinder blocks had to be inspected as they left the foundry, and the ones with the thickest walls selected.

This would have been no problem if the B-series engine had remained where it started, at 1,489cc. But it had not: it had first been enlarged to 1,622cc for the mid-sized Farina cars, and then in 1962 – initially for the MGB sports car – it had been substantially redesigned with a five-bearing crankshaft and capacity increased to 1,798cc. This now became the 'standard' B-series (although the 1,622cc version continued as long as the Farina saloons did, which was

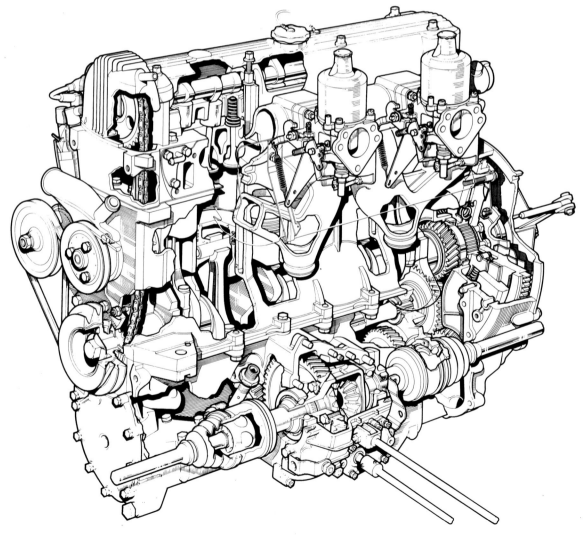

much too long). The size gap between the 1,275cc A-series and the 1,798cc B-series was not only too big, it was centred squarely on the engine size where, from the mid-1960s, the British market was showing its greatest potential: around 1,500cc where the Ford Cortina was beginning to reign supreme, its main challenges coming from Hillman and Vauxhall (and from a growing body of imports including the Renault 16). Yet BMC's step up from the 1100/1300 series was almost two steps up, in the form of the 1800 in which the B-series, physically too big for the smaller car, was installed transversely in a model which proved far too large and cumbersome to sell in the numbers which would have enabled the programme to make a profit.

What was needed was a new engine, preferably embodying more advanced technology, to plug the gap. Eventually, in 1969, this engine emerged in the form of the E-series, installed in the original Maxi. With dimensions of 76.2 x 81.28mm for a capacity of 1,485cc, and with a chain-driven SOHC, the engine – like the car – was anything but a success. It quickly transpired that its design had been hopelessly compromised by a requirement that it should be built also in 6-cylinder form, this version being just sufficiently compact for transverse installation in the 1800. As a result, the 4-cylinder was the right size but the wrong shape, with limited potential for development, although during the 1970s the new management – BMC having in effect been taken over by Leyland Motors to form British Leyland – explored what potential there was. Meanwhile, the transverse 6-cylinder cars, whether based on the 1800 or its successor the Princess, sold in very small numbers and failed to recoup the programme cost.

As for the C-series, it died a lingering death. For the 1960s it was expensively re-engineered with seven main bearings instead of the previous four, and was installed principally, and fairly disastrously, in the

MGC – in which the big engine was precariously substituted for the B-series in the MGB – and in the Austin 3-litre, an ill-fated adaptation of the 1800 with an extended bonnet and boot, and rear-wheel drive. By then, however, the ground had been cut from beneath the feet of such conventionally large engines by two newcomers, the Rover 2000 and Triumph 2000.

These two cars were introduced within weeks of each other in 1963, and had been designed on the premise that customers would be prepared to pay the same price for a well-appointed but medium-sized four-seat saloon with advanced engineering features, as for large, heavy and thirsty six-seaters like the Austin Westminster, Ford Zodiac or Vauxhall Cresta. The premise turned out to be amply justified. From an engine design point of view, the interest lay in the fact that the two new cars took substantially different approaches. Rover developed a completely new SOHC 4-cylinder engine for its 2000, with precisely 'square' dimensions of 85.7mm bore and stroke for a capacity of 1,978cc. Like several of its contemporaries, the Rover engine used a Heron combustion chamber, formed entirely in the piston crown, with a flat-faced head and upright in-line valves. Triumph on the other hand, simply carried over the pushrod OHV 6-cylinder engine of similar capacity (74.7 x 76mm, 1,998cc) from the existing Standard Vanguard Six. The two engines were astonishingly well matched. Both produced 90bhp; the Triumph had a slight edge in torque output. It is interesting to note that of the two, the Triumph proved to have the greater remaining potential for development, ending up with a much longer (95mm) stroke for a capacity of 2,498cc, and equipped with Lucas fuel injection to deliver 125bhp in the TR6 sports car and the 2.5PI saloon. The best the Rover could manage was a boring-out to 90.5mm, taking its capacity to 2,205cc and its best power output (as the 2200TC) to 115bhp. The important thing however was that between them, they helped establish a market in which medium-sized but high quality was better than big and otherwise rather ordinary, which helped bring British attitudes to engine and car design closer to those of Europe.

For the Rootes Group, the 1960s began with disaster and thereafter limped on to eventual demise, bought by Chrysler which subsequently sold the remaining operations on to what became PSA Peugeot-Citroën. The disaster lay in a decision to produce a small car to compete with the Mini, and indeed with a host of European designs with engines

The BMC E-series was supposed to be a family of engines for transverse front-wheel-drive applications, with a requirement that the top end of the family should be the 2.2-litre six-cylinder, chain-driven SOHC unit seen here, breathing through two SU carburettors. Sadly, the six-cylinder engine not only proved unattractive, but also hopelessly compromised the design of its 1.5-litre four-cylinder companion, which had to be machined on the same transfer lines. This left the Austin Maxi with an engine ill-suited to meet the needs of its customers. (Herridge & Sons Collection)

of (mainly) just below 1-litre capacity. At the time of initial decision-taking, almost all these cars were rear-engined, and that was accepted more or less 'on the nod'. It was then decided that the engine would be extremely advanced, built entirely of aluminium alloy to make it as light as possible and minimise handling problems, with a very high compression ratio for efficiency and economy, and with a single overhead camshaft. It represented a large challenge for a small development team, and the result was that the new car, the Imp, was not launched until 1963, by which time the Mini had been on sale for several years, and the 'centre of gravity' of the market was moving upwards. The 875cc (68 x 60.35mm) engine proved fragile in some respects – components like the water pump and even the throttle linkage gave endless trouble – provoking comments that it was just as well it had been installed in such a way that it could be removed easily as a unit for major servicing. It was also significantly lacking in development potential. Its capacity could be increased, but hardly enough to matter, and only at considerable cost. The little alloy engine soldiered on for as long as the Imp itself and then vanished, having effectively ruined Rootes in the process. Its greatest contribution to the state of the art was to provide a catechism in how not to proceed. Don't place your faith (and your development budget) in a comprehensive range of new technologies in which you have no existing expertise; leave some room in the design for 'stretch' and general development rather than needing to extract the absolute maximum from the outset simply to fulfil the specification; and preferably – not always an option open to engine design teams – ensure the engine is going into a vehicle for which the market peak is ahead rather than receding into history.

The warmth of the rising sun

Significantly, this was the decade which saw the Japanese motor industry first establish itself as a major force in the world. As an illustration of how suddenly that presence was achieved, consider that in 1959, Toyota produced 30,235 passenger cars. In the same year, Volkswagen's total was 605,301, from the same post-war standing start. Yet, in 1969, Toyota's car production for the year had climbed to 964,088 compared with Volkswagen's 1,531,651. There are, of course, lies, damned lies and statistics, especially when one statistic is starting from a very low base, but the fact remains that Toyota's car production in the 1960s multiplied some 32-fold while Volkswagen's rather less than tripled.

Even at this stage, the Japanese industry had in some respects divided itself in two, depending on how companies regarded the special taxation class created in Japan for 'minicars' with tightly specified maximum dimensions, and engines (at that time) of no more than 360cc. This was a specification which might almost have been written about the 'bubble cars' which had been a 1950s craze in Europe, but which had died under the impact of the Mini as much as anything. Toyota and Nissan had nothing to do with the minicar, and their product ranges began, originally, at around 800cc. All the remaining companies, notably including Honda, but also Daihatsu, Mazda (Toyo Kogyo), Mitsubishi, Subaru (Fuji Heavy Industry) and Suzuki, addressed the question of how much 'real car' you could create within the minicar constraints.

Most of the early minicars had 2-cylinder engines, but the only one to become familiar in Europe was the Honda N360, which was more or less typical of the breed at that time. Its air-cooled 2-cylinder in-line engine had dimensions of 62.5 x 57.8mm for a capacity of 354cc, out of which Honda persuaded 27bhp (net) at 8,000rpm – yes, *8,000*: Honda was able to draw on its already extensive motorcycle racing experience. This was equivalent to a specific output of 76bhp/litre and in many ways was indicative of what might (and eventually did) happen when the Japanese became inventive rather than derivative in mainstream passenger car engine design. In fact, there were other indications, because the N360 only emerged in 1967, by which time Honda had already developed a series of light sports cars up to and including the S800, whose 60 x 70mm (791cc) engine delivered 70bhp, again at 8,000rpm.

Honda exported the N360 and the identical but larger-engined 599cc N600 to the British market in the late 1970s, but failed to make an impression. It was not the engines which were at fault, however, but the cars. The other Japanese manufacturers, if they came, did so with their 'mainstream' cars, which usually comprised a small model with a 4-cylinder pushrod OHV engine in the 1-litre class – Datsun 1000, Mazda 1200, Toyota Corolla – and what the British were coming to regard as a 'Cortina class' car, again 4-cylinder, whose engine might have SOHC valve gear like the Datsun 1600 and Mazda 1800, or OHV like the Toyota Corona. The point was that during the 1960s, outside of the minicar class, the Japanese engine designers were playing technical catch-up – but the signs were already there that they had succeeded, and would in many respects move ahead during the 1970s.

Tailpiece: emissions

As mentioned earlier, the 1960s was also the decade in which the power-party began to come to an end as the first exhaust emission regulations began to bite, initially only in California but soon in the USA at large. Compared with the limits that exist today, those early requirements seem almost laughable, but they caused great consternation at the time. To begin with, the regulations concentrated on limiting unburned hydrocarbons (HC) and carbon monoxide (CO) because they were the obvious cause of the problems being suffered in Los Angeles and other places, although it was not long before oxides of nitrogen (NOx) were added to the list, making the task more difficult.

The earliest regulations were imposed in California, on 1966 model-year cars; the equivalent US Federal requirement coming two years later. All that was really required at the time was that engines should actually burn most of the fuel that was put into them. This caused engine development teams problems only because – as previously pointed out –

one of the easiest and most commonly employed techniques for overcoming the danger of overheating at temporary high load, or of avoiding hesitation during sudden acceleration, was to inject extra fuel (via an 'accelerator pump' forming part of the carburettor). Suddenly, this became a much more restricted option. One early idea was to inject extra air into the exhaust system to burn up any fuel emerging unburned from the cylinders and many American engines of the early 1970s were equipped with air pumps for this purpose. The requirements also acted as a spur to the development of high-energy electronic 'solid state' ignition systems, since misfiring had to be avoided at all costs, and there were emission control advantages in being able to control ignition timing more precisely than any mechanical-pneumatic distributor could achieve. But engine design still went through something of a sticky patch in which 'driveability' – consistently crisp throttle response with no flat-spots or jerkiness – undoubtedly suffered. Ultimately, a large part of the answer lay in electronic fuel injection, but few manufacturers (other than Mercedes) were then prepared to consider the cost, and in any case, it was not yet sufficiently developed for all purposes.

All this was bad enough, for people who had never even considered emissions before it became an issue in California in the mid-1960s. But by the end of the decade, the US government was talking in far tougher terms . . .

9 The 1970s

Fuel crises, downsizing and uncertainty

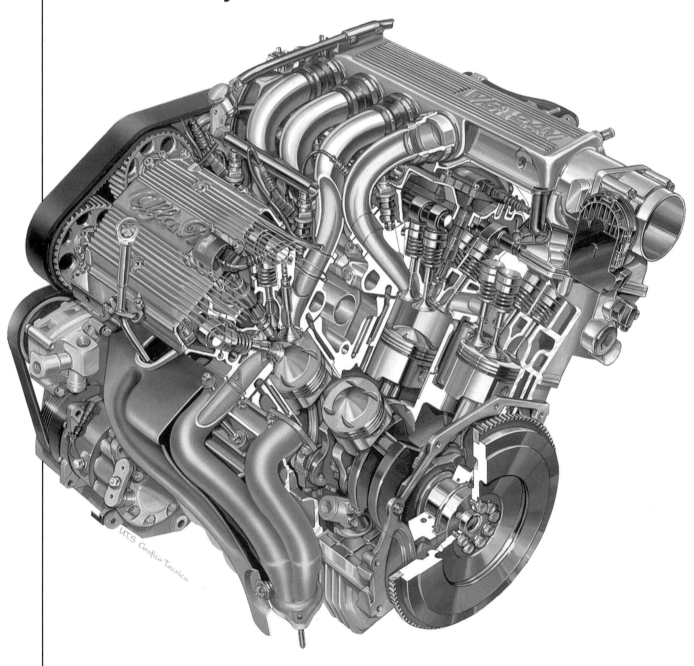

For the engine designer, this was a decade overshadowed by two things above all: exhaust emissions legislation, and violent fluctuations in oil prices which meant it was never clear how much car buyers would value economy.

The only thing in favour of emission control legislation, from the selfish point of view of the motor industry – at that time, primarily the US industry – was that it was a steadily ongoing process. It was predictable. To a degree, it could be slowed down by a combination of public argument and political pleading, but by 1970 it was already clear that it could not be stopped. This was the year in which the US Congress approved the first major Clean Air Act, and its provisions were startling at the time. To put it into context, typical new cars of the 1960s were emitting – for reasons already discussed – up to 13 grams per mile of unburned hydrocarbons (HC), 87 grams per mile of carbon monoxide (CO), and 3.6 grams per mile of oxides of nitrogen (NOx). The Clean Air Act demanded a reduction, for new cars, to 0.41 grams per mile HC and 3.4 grams per mile CO, by 1975, and 0.4 grams per mile of NOx by 1976.

This was not tinkering with the problem of emissions, it was wholesale slaughter. In the USA it would probably have been enough in itself to squeeze out any other kind of major development and innovation for the whole of the decade, but things were made worse by the oil price situation. Even when the 1970s began there were fears, largely in the aftermath of the 1967 Middle East War, that oil prices would rise steeply and big, thirsty engines would become less popular. These fears were greatly increased by the effects of the 'October War' in 1973, in which the threat of oil starvation was used as a political weapon. Then, towards the end of the decade further fears arose on the back of the Iran-Iraq conflict, and oil prices which had stabilised and begun to fall were subjected to a further shock. The evidence, at least in the USA, was that people still wanted the big cars to which they had become accustomed, but were inclined to retreat to buying smaller and more economical ones whenever oil prices rose sharply. It was a nightmare situation for product planners, and they had to tell the engine designers what kind of power unit was needed.

There was a further pressure on American designers to develop smaller engines, and that came from the growth of imports. Through the 1960s the increase in sales of the VW Beetle in the USA had been an embarrassment for the domestic producers, but things were made far worse when it became clear that the Japanese manufacturers were capable of doing even better. Thus, apart from coping with emissions controls and fluctuating oil prices, American designers found themselves saddled with a third task, that of fighting off the imports by designing cars which would appeal to the same kind of customer.

The impact of emissions

It quickly emerged that the requirements written into the 1970 Clean Air Act simply could not be met within the timescale it imposed. The Act itself had tacitly admitted there were multiple challenges, by setting different timescales to deal with HC/CO and NOx. In theory, all that was required for HC/CO was to ensure that every last atom of fuel was properly burned, preferably in the engine, but if not, then in the exhaust. The early approach, described in the last chapter, of avoiding operation with over-rich mixtures and injecting downstream air to oxidise remnants in the exhaust system had considerably reduced emissions but could not, in most cases, begin to approach the clean-up levels called for by the Clean Air Act. By the early 1970s, it was becoming clear that the only way to bring HC/CO down to those levels was to use a 'one-way' catalytic converter which would positively ensure the pollutants were oxidised. The motor industry argued its case that time was needed to develop catalytic converters – and that a whole new industry was needed to make them – and won its delay of execution. In 1974 the HC/CO standards were postponed to 1978; in 1977 the HC standard was again postponed to 1980 and the CO standard to 1981. The NOx standard was also postponed to 1981, and the proposed limit was relaxed to 1 gram per mile. People were beginning to realise what a challenge the control of NOx emissions would turn out to be.

In fact, the first one-way catalytic converters began to appear as early as 1975, but they threw up a whole new

Opposite: A much admired engine which first emerged during the late 1970s was the Alfa Romeo V6, originally of 2.5-litre capacity although it was subsequently enlarged to 3 litres and developed into 24-valve versions as seen here – not something its original design team would have contemplated. But the design was of such quality that when Fiat took over Alfa Romeo, it quickly dropped its own V6 in favour of the 'incomer'. (Alfa Romeo)

problem. The precious-metal catalyst layer which did the chemical work was quickly overlaid ('poisoned') by the lead additives in petrol and quickly lost efficiency. It was therefore essential, if converters were to provide an effective long-term answer to the emissions challenge (and there was no other means, at least at the levels set by the Clean Air Act) to make petrol without lead additives widely available. Yes, this would reduce petrol octane ratings and would require compression ratios to be reduced to the detriment of performance; tough.

Dealing with NOx was far more difficult. The first promising approach was to recycle part of the exhaust gas into the inlet manifold, to mix with the fresh incoming charge. This, it was found, lowered combustion temperatures and reduced NOx formation, which arises from the 'fixing' of normally almost inert atmospheric nitrogen in the combination of high pressure, and very high temperature in the combustion chamber. It proved an effective way of meeting interim limits in the 1970s, but was difficult to control accurately, and unable to reduce NOx, even to the relaxed Clean Air Act limit. The only other available and practicable solution was to move to 'three-way' catalytic conversion, in which the oxygen from the NOx would be used to oxidise the HC and CO to 'harmless' CO_2. This was the 1970s, and nobody had given much thought to 'greenhouse gas'. The biggest problem with this approach, apart from the obvious one of developing suitable catalyst units, was that the three-way approach would only work if the engine was running a very precisely controlled mixture containing just sufficient air to burn all the fuel – the so-called stoichiometric mixture strength of around 14:1 (air-to-fuel, by weight). This meant the fuel supply had to be metered exactly according to the amount of incoming air – no rich mixture for acceleration, no lean mixture for economical running on light load. If the mixture strength was not held precisely, the efficiency of the converter fell off sharply. Too strong a mixture would see HC/CO emissions shoot up: too weak a mixture would carry NOx through with very little conversion.

As an aside, such fears and complications led to an enthusiasm for impractical solutions. The 1970s saw great if short-lived interest in the revival of the steam car and for exploitation of the Stirling engine – both of these being external steady-state combustion devices whose emissions were potentially inherently smaller and more easily controlled. Bill Lear (of Learjet fame) tried very hard to develop an efficient modern steam car, using a specially developed working fluid in a closed circuit, but without success.

The Stirling engine simply lacked the 80-odd years of steady development which already lay behind the internal combustion engine. Prototypes were built and demonstrated, but it was clear that they were horribly uncompetitive in terms of power-to-weight or power-to-cost ratio, even when the cost of a catalytic converter system for the internal combustion engine was taken into account. It was also the decade in which enthusiasm for the battery-powered electric car suddenly increased. This idea lingered on until the late 1990s, when it finally became clear beyond question that the battery itself was always going to cost too much.

Equally, the 1970s saw the first burgeoning of interest in the deliberately lean-burn engine, exploiting the idea of a stratified charge – in which a rich mixture would be created close to the sparking plug, with progressively weaker outer layers. In this way, it was argued, consistent combustion could be achieved with weak mixtures of maybe 18:1 or even higher; and it was known that such lean-burn operation would reduce both fuel consumption and HC/CO emissions. The trouble was that trying to run such lean mixtures in conventional engines had always resulted in a degree of misfiring – of the occasional fire failing to light in the combustion chamber – which ruined both the fuel economy and the emissions. The additional snag was that NOx emissions were known to rise sharply with lean-burn.

The point of stratified charge was that in-cylinder aerodynamics, and in particular the use of a swirling motion to 'shape' the fuel charge, consistent combustion would overcome the first two objections. As for NOx, it was quite frankly hoped that levels could be contained to the point where they would scrape through the legal requirement.

While almost every car manufacturer experimented with the idea of lean-burn and stratified charge during the 1970s, only one – Honda – actually produced such an engine in quantity. This was the 1.5-litre CVCC (Compound Vortex Controlled Combustion) engine fitted to the Civic for the Japanese and US markets. The CVCC engine in some ways resembled the Ricardo diesel prechamber principle, except that a small additional valve admitted a rich mixture to the prechamber where ignition took place. The burning mixture then erupted into the main chamber where it was shaped by swirl induced by the port admitting additional air, before eventually being exhausted in the normal way. Honda had rightly decided that the task of achieving stratified charge in an open cylinder was simply too difficult with 1970s technology, and came up with an alternative that worked – to a point. Undoubtedly, the CVCC was the cleanest car engine

of the 1970s, but it could not achieve the Clean Air Act standards without a catalyst, and there was no point in combining the two principles, so eventually the CVCC vanished. It was never offered in Europe where the emission limits at the time were far higher; a simple 1.2-litre SOHC engine of conventional design was quite sufficient and gave comparable performance.

An ambition of many engine designers in the 1970s was to produce a 'stratified charge' engine which would allow lean-burn operation without misfiring, and thus with low exhaust emissions. The only company actually to produce such an engine – and in considerable numbers – was Honda with its CVCC, in which a rich mixture was ignited in a pre-chamber, diesel fashion, before expanding into the main chamber. The CVCC achieved its technical aims but was eventually overtaken by ever tightening emission regulations which called for other approaches.
(Ludvigsen Library)

Carburettors: **the beginning** of the end

The requirement for precise stoichiometric mixture control with three-way catalytic converters proved an almost impossible challenge for the carburettor

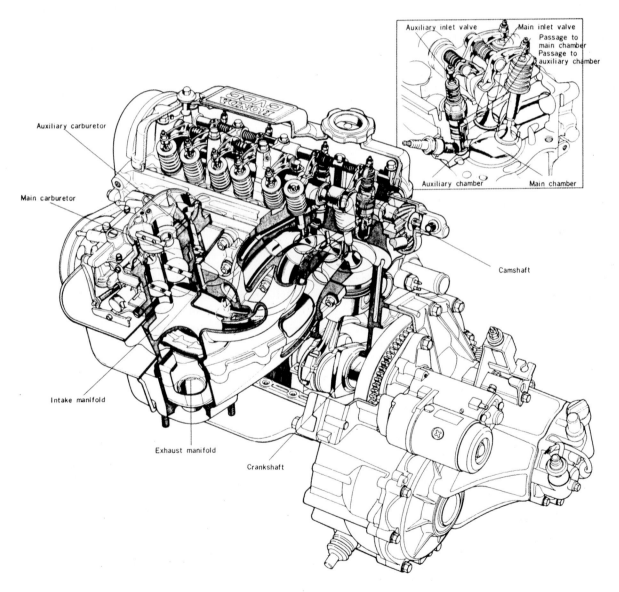

manufacturers. For years, carburettors had been getting more and more complex as their makers tried to achieve perfect fuel delivery in all circumstances, but most of their efforts involved devices – pumps, emulsion tubes and auxiliary jets – to 'trim' the basic characteristic of the main jet. The problem was that none of these devices reacted fast enough to provide the response now demanded. The situation was compounded by inaccuracy and slow reaction of the devices then available actually to measure the amount – the mass flow – of incoming air.

The answer lay in electronics, and in particular in a sensor devised in the mid-1970s by Bosch (and first used by Volvo) which actually measured the oxygen content of the exhaust gas. This device, called the lambda-probe because it switched state when the perfect mixture strength (lambda = 1) was departed from, meant that the fuel delivery could be trimmed always to achieve the right mixture without being directly dependent on accurate measurement of air mass-flow. If the content was not as it should be, the sensor could generate an instruction to weaken or richen the mixture: but how was the (electronic) instruction to be executed?

Some argued for 'electronic carburettors' in which either needle movement was controlled, or at least influenced, by a solenoid, or in which the shape of the venturi changed. In practice however, the late 1970s did see a number of variable venturi carburettors enter production, although the technology was moving beyond that. Electronic fuel injection, increasingly widely used among up-market cars in Europe and already a known quantity in America, was a much more practical solution. The signal from the lambda-probe could be fed directly to the electronic control unit, which could be programmed to react accordingly – and very fast. Once the emission control requirements really began to bite, the carburettor was as good as dead – but because the bite only came in 1981 in the USA (and in 1991 in Europe) most cars of the 1970s still used carburettors.

Downsizing and stagnation in the USA

It was in the USA that the 'three problems' really struck. The decade began with the launch of two cars intended as import-fighters, the Chevrolet Vega and the Ford Pinto. The Vega had an engine which was truly remarkable in some ways, yet another example of Chevrolet's tendency every now and again to exhibit a real burst of technical innovation. In the case of the Nova engine, this involved the design of a 4-cylinder SOHC engine with an alloy cylinder block – but a cast-iron head! Furthermore the block exploited the then-newly devised Nicasil process in which the cylinder bore was coated with an etched silicon-nickel layer which enables aluminium pistons to run directly in the alloy block. The engine had dimensions of 90 x 92mm for a capacity of 2,287cc but managed to produce only 90bhp (SAE) at 4,600rpm. As might have been predicted, not least in the light of some previous Chevrolet history, the venture was far from being a complete success and the compact 'H-body' platform on which the Vega and allied models were based knew more success with larger all-iron OHV engines. In 1974, an attempt was made to boost the image of the Vega engine with a DOHC 16-valve cylinder head conversion by Cosworth, with the stroke reduced to yield 2-litre capacity, but only a few thousand were produced. There had also been a plan to produce the Vega, from 1973 on, with a Wankel engine – GM having spent $50 million on a Wankel engine licence in 1970 – and the car's engine compartment and transmission tunnel had been sized accordingly. However, the Wankel's most serious drawback was poor fuel consumption, and 1973 was the worst possible time to launch a thirsty new engine, so the whole project died a sudden death.

Meanwhile, Ford began building its rival Pinto with a choice of imported engines, the 1.6 Kent engine (ex-Cortina/Capri) from Britain, or a new 2-litre SOHC engine (destined also for the Cortina 3) from Germany. The latter engine indeed become widely known as the Pinto engine although in 1974, Ford actually replaced it with an American-built 2.3-litre unit. As a model, the Pinto lasted until 1980, thus outliving its rival the Vega by three years, but neither succeeded in doing what they were supposed to do – fend off the growing tide of imports. It is significant that neither of them lasted until the full implementation of the Clean Air Act.

Among the larger and still mainstream American engines, the main feature of the 1970s was the reappearance of the V6, partly as a result of the safety legislation which was running in parallel with emission limits. A V6, being far more compact than a straight-6, allowed far more crush-length to be left under the bonnet to meet the frontal impact case. In addition, some engineers, seeing the trend in Europe and looking ahead, knew that it would be quite easy to fit a V6 transversely in the average mid-size American car body, driving the front wheels, while a straight-6 turned sideways simply would not fit. GM of course had a 90° V6 tucked away in its history (see previous chapter) and from 1975 reinstated it, to begin with, in Buick models, in modified form. This was now a 3.2-litre or 3.8-litre engine, the latter simply bored-out from 3.4 to 3.8in (88.9 to 95.2mm) for a capacity of 3,791cc. Even in this form it delivered only 110bhp at 3,600rpm – although it has to be said that by this time the SAE had rewritten its output measurement specification to bring it closely into line with the more 'honest' rule. Ford was able in the first instance to turn to its European arm for a supply of V6s, specifically in the form of the 2.8-litre Cologne engine which powered the Mustang II from 1974 onwards, but it also set about developing larger engines of the same configuration in the USA.

On top of all these developments, the V8 lumbered on, although no longer in its largest sizes – not least because with emissions measured in grams per mile, large engines suffered a built-in handicap. There was the further incentive in 1974, that the US Congress approved the first Corporate Average Fuel Economy requirement, for implementation in 1978. It wasn't much of a requirement by European standards, with the 1978 figure set at 18mpg (USA; 21.6mpg imperial, 13.1 litres/100km) rising to 20mpg by 1980, but it put a considerable brake on the enthusiasm of manufacturers to carry on producing 8.2-litre engines like those fitted to the Cadillac range in 1970. But with measures to improve economy wherever possible, V8s of up to 5.7-litre capacity remained common. The challenge was to produce and sell enough more economical cars to compensate for them in the corporate average – which was where models like the Vega and Pinto and their 4-cylinder engines really came in.

Invention in Germany

While engineers in the USA struggled with the challenges and wondered which way to turn, those in Germany were in a much better position. Their home market was keen to buy ever more powerful cars, and so was a substantial part of their export market.

BMW went from strength to strength, devoting most of the decade to development of their big 6-cylinder engine, opening it out by degrees to reach a capacity of 3,453cc (93.4 x 84mm) for the 635

coupé. At the same time, the company introduced a brand-new 'small' 6-cylinder unit (M60) of nominal 2.0 and 2.3-litre capacity. With a spacing between cylinder bore centres of 91mm and bores of 80mm, there was clearly no chance of enlarging this engine other than by increasing the stroke, but since it had been designed for a niche, that did not matter. An interesting sideline in the early 1970s was the offer of a rather crude 2002 Turbo, a highly specialised version made to legitimise the company's saloon car racing effort. The use of a big turbocharger with a high boost setting meant the compression ratio had to be reduced to 6.9:1, which did nothing for the fuel consumption, while the delayed-tripwire response to the accelerator called for anticipation and judgement of a high order on the part of the driver. Thirty years on, the author still has craven memories of being driven round the Salzburgring in a race-trim 2002 Turbo, courtesy of Diester Quester . . .

What was certainly not known at the time was that plans were well advanced for a range of BMW V8 engines and a V12. The V8, carrying the project office designation M36, would have come in four versions with capacities of 3.6, 4.0, 4.5 and 5.0 litres. The V12 would have consisted of two 323i engines mounted on a common crankcase at a 60° angle. Both the V8 and the V12 were built and tested in prototype form – and both died in the aftermath of the 1973 energy crisis, leaving the 'big six' to soldier on until eventually, the V12 project was revived. But that is for the next chapter.

The 1970s was to some extent a restrained decade for Mercedes, who perhaps felt a little more of the American-style pressure and worked hard to equip itself with suitable answers for the 1980s. This was especially so after the political-economic watershed of 1973. Before then, however, the company had announced two significant new engines, a 6-cylinder and a V8. The 2.8-litre 6-cylinder (M110) had chain-driven DOHC and vee-opposed valves, and in carburetted and fuel-injected form was fitted to the 280 and 280E members of the mid-range W114 family. The block was essentially the existing 250 bored out by 4mm (to 86 x 78.8mm, 2,746cc) but naturally the head was entirely new, and the output of 185bhp at 6,000rpm, in fuel injected form, set a high standard at over 67bhp/litre. The new V8, meanwhile, was an addition to the family begun with the 3.5-litre engine of 1969. With the same bore dimension but a much longer stroke (92 x 85mm, 4,520mm) and a new motor designation (M117

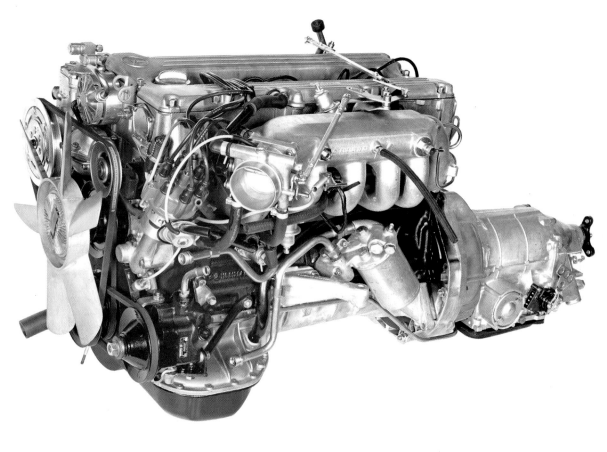

164

By 1972 Mercedes had decided the time was ripe to begin introducing twin overhead camshafts into its top-range six-cylinder production engines, with a substantial improvement in breathing and therefore in specific power output. At this stage, as the illustration shows, ignition systems were still based on mechanical distributors, but that would soon change. So far as this engine was concerned, the carburettor had already made way for fuel injection. (Ludvigsen Library)

instead of M116) the 4.5-litre was a relatively 'lazy' device with an output of 198bhp at 4,500rpm, and at first was fitted to a new 'Q-car' saloon, the 280SE 4.5. The only other petrol engine launched by Mercedes in this decade, almost in defiance of politics and economics in 1975, was a new version of the mighty M100 V8, bored-out from the original by 4mm to dimensions of 107 x 95mm (6,834cc). This huge engine delivered 286bhp at 4,250rpm with the aid of one of the earliest applications of the ingenious Bosch K-Jetronic 'mechanical balance' fuel injection system, almost certainly the most satisfactory non-electronic fuel injection system ever devised for passenger car use. Initially it was fitted to yet another 'Q-car', the 450SEL 6.9.

An interesting Mercedes sideline at the beginning of the decade came with a series of very advanced sports car prototypes, with the designation C111, powered by Mercedes-developed Wankel rotary engines – Mercedes having been among the many buyers of a Wankel development licence. Two engines were produced and demonstrated, one with three 600cc rotors, producing 280bhp at 7,000rpm, and the other with four rotors, delivering 350bhp at the same speed. The cars' appearance and performance had the look of serious motoring competition about them, but Mercedes was still foresworn from such ideas and besides, as already noted, interest in the Wankel engine waned rapidly once the world found itself in the midst of an energy crisis.

If petrol engines had gone on to the back burner in

Another Mercedes innovation for the 1970s was the five-cylinder diesel engine – count the plungers in the Bosch in-line injector pump. Eventually, the long supply lines from pump to injector would give way to the tidier and more advanced common-rail fuel delivery system, though not for some time. With careful balancing and engine mounting, five-cylinder engines were found to present fewer problems than earlier generations had feared. (Ludvigsen Library)

the Mercedes project office, diesels certainly had not. The energy crisis had made customers take the idea of diesel economy much more seriously, and the concern was to make the engines more acceptable in other respects – less noisy and more 'normal' to drive, without the abrupt operation of idling and high-speed governors. In 1973, Mercedes announced the 4-cylinder 240D unit, which was simply the existing 220D bored-out by 4mm to a capacity of 2,404cc with an extra 5bhp, but this was a stepping-stone to a more interesting engine, the OM617 5-cylinder, in effect one-and-a-quarter 240Ds with a capacity of 3,005cc and an output of 80bhp. Then, in 1978, this engine was turbocharged, and its bore ever so slightly reduced – according to Mercedes – to bring its capacity down to a tidy 2,998cc, while output rose to 120bhp at only 3,800rpm. European customers were distressed to discover that this engine was aimed primarily at the American market, which was beginning a short, intense, but stormy and ultimately doomed love affair with the diesel.

Still in Germany, there was the future of Volkswagen to attend to. By the early 1970s the last dregs were being wrung out of the rear-engined flat-4 air-cooled formula, in the shape of the 412LS with its 1,795cc (93 x 66mm) engine producing a modest 85bhp at 5,000rpm with Solex carburettors. There were also Audi and NSU, which had become part of the VW empire. The influence of Audi engineering was soon seen in the Passat with its in-line water-cooled 4-cylinder engines, originally of 1,296cc (75 x 73.4mm) and 1,470cc (76.5 x 80mm) driving the front wheels via a transaxle – both the engines and the drivelines happened to be identical with those of the contemporary Audi 80L and 80LS, and none the worse for that. However, the ex-NSU K70 had been rather cruelly re-engineered, its formerly alloy engine now cast iron and much heavier, but theoretically topping the range with its capacity of 1,807cc and output of 100bhp. It was never clear how VW management squared the idea of having two cars of very similar size and performance but diametrically opposite mechanical design, the 412 and the K70, in the range simultaneously, but in any event neither model lasted very long under the impact of the 'new wave'. It had also been decided that while production of the NSU Ro80 would continue at very low volume for the time being, nothing more would be spent on the Wankel engine's development.

When the decade began the Beetle was still in full-scale production at Wolfsburg, but with the aim, it

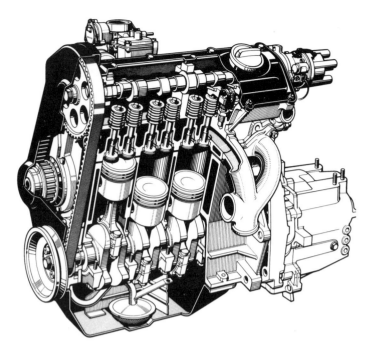

seemed, at least partly, of passing the production record established in 1927 by the Ford Model T. This milestone (for the record, 15,007,034 units) was duly passed early in 1972, and the last Beetle rolled off the Wolfsburg line little more than two years later. This meant that after years of agonising, a replacement project had finally been approved. There had been no shortage of such projects, and for some time the front-runner was a Porsche-developed concept with an engine flat-mounted beneath the centre floor. In the end, however, notice was taken of trends elsewhere in Europe, and the replacement emerged with a transverse-mounted 4-cylinder engine driving the front wheels. As though unable to resist one final decoy attempt, VW first launched this platform as a small sports coupé – the Scirocco – and only admitted to the existence of the chunky five-door hatchback counterpart, the Golf, a short time later in mid-1974.

One interesting aspect of the Golf was that from the outset, it had two different engines. One was the 1.5-litre Audi 80/Passat unit already referred to, but turned sideways and mated to a new transmission. It

fitted easily, since the engine had been designed short-but-tall to fit in-line ahead of the Audi 80 front axle line without excessive overhang. The smaller engine, with dimensions 69.5 x 72mm for a modest capacity of 1,093cc, delivered 50bhp compared with the bigger engine's 70bhp. Both engines were belt-driven SOHC but only the smaller one, all-new, had a cross-flow cylinder head layout. These were the engines, simple and effective, which would take Volkswagen well towards the turn of the 20th century – in fact, as front-line production engines they were destined to last as long as the Beetle's flat-4. The developments followed thick and fast during the 1970s, most notably with the appearance of the Golf GTI in 1976, with the engine's stroke increased by 3mm to take the capacity to 1,588cc, and Bosch K-Jetronic fuel injection to take the output to 110bhp. The near simultaneous shrinking of the smaller engine, by de-stroking to just 59mm, formed the 895cc power unit of the Golf's smaller companion

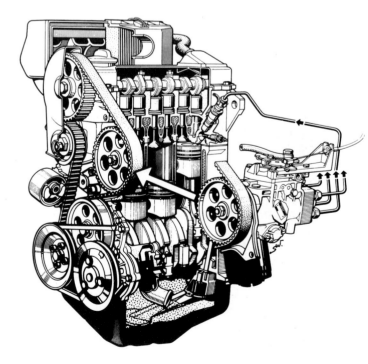

model, the Polo. Then, in 1978, came a brilliantly – or luckily – timed riposte to the energy crisis in the form of a dieselised version of the 1.5-litre engine, a new cylinder head bolted to an only slightly modified block to produce an economy engine *par excellence*. It gave Golf sales an incremental boost and did much to recommend the diesel engine to people who had previously viewed it with suspicion.

Meanwhile Audi itself, while still offering the 80, had moved up to the larger but mechanically similar 100, which had originally been launched in the late 1960s as an 'up-gunned' Super 90. The 4-cylinder in-line engine grew to an eventual 84 x 84.4mm (1,871cc) and in 1976 there arrived a new-generation 100 which, being bigger and heavier, needed more power. The 4-cylinder engine had a tiny stretch left in it, by boring-out to 86.5mm for a capacity of 1,984cc, but the question was where to go next, without completely changing the layout of the car, which Audi did not contemplate. An in-line 6-cylinder engine would have increased the front overhang too much; V6 engines were tried – Audi admitted at the time to running prototypes with Ford Cologne 2.8-litre V6s – but their weight led to excessive understeer. In the

The 1970s enthusiasm for five-cylinder engines was embraced by Audi, which found it could fit an in-line five-cylinder unit in the nose of the 100, with careful packaging. The alternative would have been a heavier V6, which Audi feared would upset the vehicle's balance and handling. The five-cylinder engine proved to suffer no notable problems of refinement, although it did have a distinctive noise. (Giles Chapman Library)

end the team succumbed to logic and produced an in-line 5-cylinder engine, developed from the 1.6-litre Audi equivalent of the Golf GTI engine, with dimensions 79.5 x 86.4mm for a capacity of 2,144cc, and a crankshaft with the pins at 144° spacing for even firing intervals. With Bosch injection, this engine delivered 136bhp and provided a platform from which some very high-performance units were later developed. In the 100, it proved quite adequately smooth without any resort to a balancer shaft. The author, writing in *Autocar* after a pre-announcement driving exercise in Germany, said it was 'about what you would expect – smoother than a 4-cylinder engine, not as smooth as a six', which with the benefit of hindsight – and especially the adoption of balancer shafts on more recent 5-cylinder engines – surely begs a question or two.

At that time the VW group was very close to Porsche, as evidenced by the ill-fated, poorly packaged and generally uninspiring mid-engined VW-Porsche, launched in the late 1960s with a choice of Porsche-developed 1.7-litre flat-4 and 2-litre flat-6 engines, and killed off in the mid-1970s. In its place came the much more sensible Porsche 924, front-engined and rear-driven, its price kept reasonably low through the use of what was in effect the 4-cylinder, 2-litre engine from the Audi 100. At the top end of its range, though, Porsche had more interesting ideas, first launching the 911 Turbo in 1974 – with 270bhp and 260 lb ft of torque which, in the first-generation car, had a nasty habit of arriving all in a rush. In 1977, Porsche struck out in another direction with the 928, complete with a brand-new V8 engine which (like the Chevrolet Vega) used the Nicasil process to allow the creation of an all-aluminium engine – except, that is, for the valves, the connecting rods, the twin overhead camshafts and the crankshaft. The V8 was extremely refined and deserved a better reception than it got – but even at that stage, the 911 was 'The Porsche' and nothing else, no matter what its qualities, was quite the same. And indeed, by the end of the decade, the naturally aspirated 911 engine had already grown to a nominal 3-litre capacity (95 x 70.4mm, 2,993cc) while the Turbo was already up to 3.3-litres (97 x 74.4mm, 3,281cc) and a full 300bhp.

Any discussion of turbocharging in the 1960s cannot pass without a look at what Saab was up to. The small Swedish company had passed from its early 2-strokes – capable of vivid performance in the hands of someone like Erik Carlsson – through the adaptation of the Ford V4 to the 96, and eventually to the commissioning of a new chain-driven SOHC slant-4 from Triumph in the UK, which went into the new, larger 99 with a capacity of 1,709cc (83.5 x 78mm) and an output of 80bhp. Both Saab and Triumph then set about developing this promising engine; in Saab's case it ended up with the same general configuration but without a part in common with the original, with a capacity now of 1,985cc (90 x 78mm) and an output of 95bhp in carburettor form, and up to 118bhp with Bosch fuel injection, and now built in the Saab-Scania factory in Sodertalje rather than in Britain. In the mid-1970s, Saab decided to turbocharge this engine and in 1977 the original 99 Turbo emerged, with Garrett T3 turbocharger, Bosch fuel injection, and 145bhp – and 233Nm of torque! Like most early turbo installations, the need to avoid detonation at high output involved dropping the compression ratio, in this case to 7.2:1 from the standard 9.2:1, with off-boost efficiency suffering as a result.

The 99 Turbo was by no means the first model to use the technology, as we have seen, but it is the one which seems to have entered motoring legend as the true 'pioneer'. This is perhaps because it initiated a process of development which has remained continuous as far as Saab is concerned, and it arrived at a time when many other manufacturers were already contemplating a move in the same direction: the turbo boom really took off during the 1980s, and will be considered in the next chapter.

In turn, Saab cannot be mentioned without a look at Volvo. The larger Swedish company had continued on its competent but undemonstrative way ever since its foundation in 1927, and may be judged to have entered the 'major league' in 1966 with the arrival of the 144. But the 144, like its predecessor the PV444/544 series and the 121 Amazon, depended on an essentially straightforward 4-cylinder OHV engine which broke no new technical ground. The same could be said even of the new engine series, the B20, introduced for 1968 complete with a 'one and a half' 6-cylinder derivative for the 164. During the 1970s, however, Volvo began to play catch-up. In 1974 it launched the B21 engine series with chain-driven SOHC, alloy head, a capacity of 2,127cc (92 x 80mm) and an output, with fuel injection, of up to 123bhp. At the same time, as told in more detail hereafter, Volvo entered a deal with Peugeot and Renault to develop a new 2.7-litre V6 engine, which Volvo designated B27 for the 264.

The Americans in Europe . . .

This was the decade in which the two largest European companies got their European acts together, although in different ways. Ford split engineering responsibilities between Britain and Germany, with Germany taking more responsibility for the larger products. GM simply closed down Vauxhall's passenger car engineering side and transferred all serious work to Opel in Germany.

Evidence of the Ford policy came with the decision to abandon the British-built Essex 3-litre V6 in favour of the Cologne-developed 2.3 and 2.8-litre units, in cars like the Granada and the Capri V6. Strangely, though, the first unit to appear in Britain was fitted to the Cortina (Series 3) 2.3 V6. The new and much larger Cortina 3 had appeared at the very beginning of the 1970s and its most significant power unit was a new belt-driven SOHC 2-litre engine (90.8 x 76.95mm, 1,993cc) which, through its export to the USA as already noted, became known as the Pinto engine. It also existed in 1.6-litre form, with slightly smaller bore and substantially reduced stroke (87.65 x 66mm, 1,593cc). These engines were also used in the 'hot' versions of the rear-driven Escort – the Escort Mexico and RS2000 – but the Kent OHV series continued as the main Escort power units, with evolved versions fitted to the new small front-driven Fiesta which was announced in 1975.

The swan-song for Vauxhall's last independently developed engines came in the 1970s, in the HC Viva and FE Victor. Towards the end of the decade, Vauxhalls became for the most part 'badge engineered' Opels, the Ascona becoming the Cavalier and the Rekord becoming the Carlton. Opel's long-established cam-in-head 4-cylinder and 6-cylinder

Late in the 1970s the hefty Ford 'Essex' 3-litre V6 gave way to a new family of V6 engines designed by Ford Germany in Cologne. The new engines, initially of 2.3 and 2.8-litre capacity – later opened out to 2.4 and 2.9 as seen here – were substantially lighter and more compact, saving space and improving economy in cars like the Capri and Granada. It is worth comparing these engines with the Essex shown earlier, and trying to work out exactly where the savings were achieved in units which do not look startlingly different . . . (Herridge & Sons Collection)

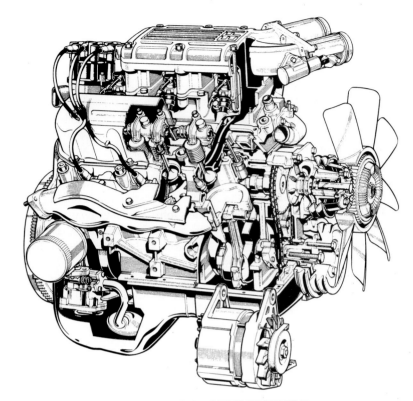

NEW FORD 2.4 LITRE V6 ENGINE

NEW FORD 2.9 LITRE V6 ENGINE

designs continued through the decade with progressive changes only, and no significant new developments.

France: **a mixed picture**

The French industry, in the form of Citroën, made a bright start to the 1970s with the announcement of two new models, the big SM sports coupé and the technically advanced GS medium-sized saloon. The SM's 90°, 2.7-litre V6 DOHC engine was created by Maserati's chief engineer, Alfieri, from an existing V8, but barely survived Peugeot's later takeover of Citroën, continuing only in Maserati's own Merak when the SM project was scrapped lock, stock and barrel. The GS engine was more significant by far, although ultimately it too represented a technical dead-end. It was the culmination of many years' work – some of it referred to in previous chapters – to fill the product gap between the flat-twin A-series engine and the 4-cylinder, 2-litre engine by now serving well in the DS. It emerged as an SOHC air-cooled flat-4, for all the world as though a modern interpretation of the VW Beetle concept, neatly shaped for installation ahead of the GS front axle line, driving the front wheels via a transaxle. Originally, the engine had dimensions of 74 x 58mm for a capacity of 1,015cc, but this proved rather lacking in torque for the GS and within a year the stroke had been increased to 65.6mm, taking the capacity to 1,129cc, and followed a year later still by a bore increase to 77mm, for a capacity of 1,222cc. These moves were certainly better appreciated in Britain where they had no effect on the car's fiscal rating.

As explained in the previous chapter, the innovative Citroën had been deeply interested in the Wankel rotary engine and at one stage had even created a joint venture with NSU to build the twin-rotor engine, but it all came to nothing even though the factory was built. Citroën did however produce two batches of Wankel-engined prototypes, the first being the M35 of 1970, a special coupé version of the Ami 8 with a single-rotor engine delivering 49bhp at 5,500rpm. Some 267 of these cars were loaned to selected high-mileage 'friends'. In 1974, there followed the GS birotor, with what amounted to a complete NSU Ro80 powertrain – complete with a three-speed semi-automatic gearbox – in an apparently standard GS body (and the GS had

certainly been designed with the Wankel in mind). The car actually made it into small-scale production, 874 units being built, but there was no denying that its fuel consumption was high – the official Citroën figure was 12.8 litres/100km (22.1mpg) and at the time this was more than sufficient to kill the entire programme. Citroën could not afford it any more.

Citroën's last move as an independent company was to launch the CX as a replacement for the DS, but the CX power units were little more than the DS engines turned sideways to drive the front wheels via a new transmission, creating far more space within the cabin and doing away with the long-standing curse of the DS, that the rear half of its engine was extremely difficult to work on. The larger of the CX engines was billed as a 2400 but was actually still the 2,347cc of the ultimate fuel-injected DS23. Citroën also created a 2.2-litre (2,175cc) diesel conversion of this engine for the CX, seeing an opening not only in the taxi market, but in an increasingly diesel-conscious Europe.

From that point on, Peugeot oversaw everything that was done at Citroën, and by degrees the two companies converged in terms of power unit engineering. Citroën's very last fling came in 1978 with the launch of the little Visa, with a choice of in-line flat-twin or transversely mounted 1,124cc 4-cylinder engine. The latter was Peugeot's existing small engine, but the twin was the ultimate extension of the A-series, in which the iron cylinder liners had been deleted and replaced with nickel-chrome plating. This was a spin-off, Citroën said, of the Wankel engine research programme, which allowed the pistons to run directly in the alloy bores, in turn permitting the engine to be enlarged to 77 x 70mm for a capacity of 652cc, enough to give it a 4CV rating in France. The engine was also equipped with solid-state ignition taking a timing signal from a flywheel position sensor, the first time this had been done in production, although within ten years it would be the norm. With the help of this system the little engine produced 36bhp at 5,500rpm, and thus 55bhp per litre – not bad for a funny little pushrod engine whose origins went back to the 1930s.

At the time it took over Citroën to form the PSA Group, Peugeot was itself in a state of change where engines were concerned. It continued to develop the solid OHV 504 engine, now opened out to nominal 2-litre capacity (88 x 81mm, 1,971cc) while it continued with the smaller OHC engines in the 304 series – but it had plans to replace the latter. Peugeot was also establishing itself as Mercedes' principal rival in the production of diesel passenger cars. There had been a rather crude diesel derivative of the 404, and now the 504 could be had in diesel form with a derivative of the petrol engine, with 1mm taken off the bore (for a capacity of 1,948cc) to ensure the cylinder walls were strong enough. With a Bosch fuel system the 504 delivered 56bhp compared with 93bhp for the petrol 'parent' but it did so with notable economy. Peugeot then developed an all-new 2.1-litre (90 x 83mm, 2,112cc) diesel engine and in 1977 bored out this unit by 4mm to 2,304cc and a

One 'oddball' engine of the 1970s was the 90-degree V6 jointly developed by Peugeot, Renault and Volvo for use in all their larger models (Peugeot 604, Renault 30, Volvo 264). It was said that the 90-degree angle was chosen to reduce engine height; some suspected it had begun life as a bigger V8 and lost two cylinders as a result of the first great energy crisis. In any event, it emerged as this all-alloy unit with chain-driven SOHC and vee-opposed valves. Although extensively developed (from 2.7 to 3-litre capacity, 24 valves, fuel injection, balancer shaft) the unit was never a great success.
(Ludvigsen Library)

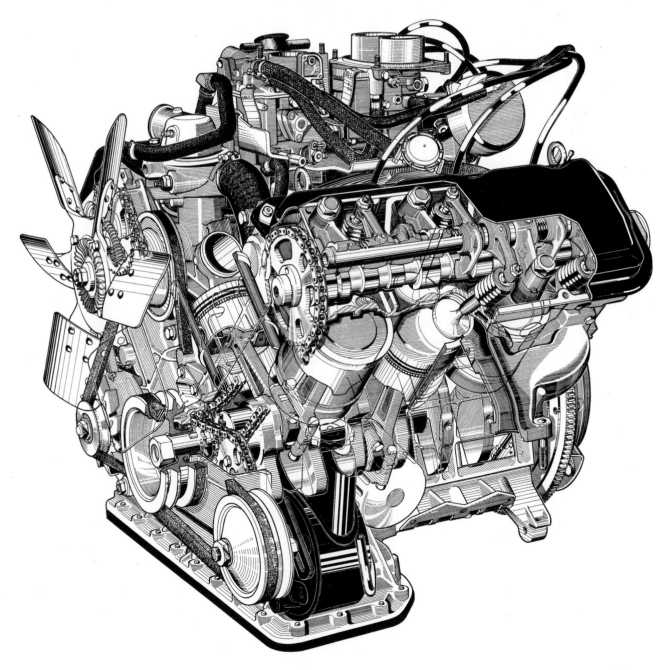

E.T.A.I.

Renault enjoyed more success with this J-series engine, a simple but strong belt-driven SOHC unit with opposed valves in hemispherical combustion chambers, and with the distributor driven directly from the end of the camshaft. The J-series served as the basis for a diesel conversion, and was also offered in a heavily turbocharged high-performance version, in the Renault 21. For well over a decade it was the workhorse of Renault's medium-large car range. (Herridge & Sons Collection)

more useful 70bhp – having meanwhile sold the 2.1-litre to Ford for use in the Granada!

Peugeot also addressed the extreme ends of its range through joint ventures with Renault. Early in the decade it launched its 104, replacing the 204, complete with an all-new engine made largely of aluminium alloy, and with an initial capacity of 954cc (70 x 62mm). For the sake of transverse front-drive packaging beneath a low bonnet line, the engine was inclined more nearly on its side (actually at 72°) than vertical, above its transmission. Like so many alloy-blocked, linered-engines, this unit proved to have a great deal of 'stretch', first being opened out to 1,124cc (72 x 69mm) and then appearing with dimensions of 75 x 69mm for a capacity of 1,218cc in the new Renault 14, in which the compactness of the unit was exploited by squeezing the spare wheel beneath the bonnet above the engine! Perhaps sadly, Renault did not persist with the 14 and never found another use for the engine. PSA continued to develop it, first with a larger capacity of 1,360cc (75 x 77mm) with 60bhp, and eventually through the 1980s and beyond, with a substantial reworking into a more conventional vertical configuration, producing the outstandingly successful TU-series.

Peugeot had in fact struck a deal with Renault to create a joint-venture engine factory at Douvrin in industrial northern France, where the small engine was being built alongside a much larger one – a 2.7-litre V6. This unit was the result of a wider-ranging agreement, taking in not only Peugeot and Renault but also Volvo. The result, which saw the light in the Peugeot 604 and Renault 30 of 1974, and in the Volvo 264, showed evidence of panic rethinking. It was a V6 with a 90° angle between the cylinder banks, rather than the 'ideal' 60°. Was this because the wider angle made the engine shallower and easier to fit beneath a low bonnet, as was suggested? Or could it possibly have been that the engine had originally been intended as a V8, to be shorn of two cylinders in the panic of the first great 'energy crisis' of the early 1970s? To this day, nobody then involved will say for certain, and the party line has been maintained. In any event, the result was a rather unsatisfactory unit with chain-driven single overhead camshafts and well over-square dimensions of 88 x 73mm, for a capacity of 2,664cc. The uneven firing intervals forced by the 'wrong' angle did nothing for its refinement, and neither was it particularly economical nor, initially, all that reliable. But the proponents persisted and eventually, with many modifications including a redesigned crankshaft with 30° offset pins to even out the firing intervals, enlargement to a full 3-litre capacity and the fitting of a balancer shaft, turned it into a respectable (but by then rather outdated) engine for such 1980s cars as the Citroën XM, Peugeot 605 and Renault Safrane. The Douvrin factory itself turned out to be a much sounder investment, and eventually produced other, far more successful Renault and PSA engines in significantly greater quantity.

Renault meanwhile, soldiered on with the 'Iron Cleon' C-series engine in all its many forms, and the all-alloy engine was launched with the 16, and now opened out to 1.65-litre capacity (79 x 84mm, 1,647cc) giving a much stronger performance. A more significant engine by far appeared in 1977, in the form of the first J-series unit, for the 20TS, replacing the 1,647cc alloy engine of the 20TL. The J-series, again Douvrin-built (but it was always a Renault engine) was all-alloy with 'wet' iron liners like its predecessor, but with a belt-driven SOHC operating opposed valves via rockers, and a larger capacity of 1,995cc (88 x 82mm). This was another engine with reserves of 'stretch' and it would serve Renault well, in its various forms, almost to the end of the century and in this initial form delivered 103bhp. Before the end of the decade it had already been translated into iron-blocked diesel form, as the J8S, with a capacity of 2,068mm and an output of 64bhp, enabling the company to claim its share of the medium-diesel market.

Italy: verve at all costs

The 1970s was a good decade for Alfa Romeo, technically at least. In 1972, Alfa Romeo staged two major launches of very different cars, the Alfasud and the Alfetta. While the Alfetta was a new rear-driven car (with the gearbox in unit with the rear final drive, as in the Porsche 924 and 928), but used the classic DOHC engine in 1.8-litre (80 x 89mm, 1,779cc) and eventually 2-litre (84 x 89mm, 1,962cc) forms, the Alfasud was a clean-sheet-of-paper small car created under the direction of Czech engineer Rudi Hruska. It emerged with front-wheel drive and a compact, water-cooled belt-driven SOHC flat-4 engine, iron-blocked and alloy-headed, initially 80 x 59mm for a capacity of 1,186cc, whose brilliance only truly emerged when it was driven. Although – as always, it seems – the flat-4 engine eventually lost out to the transverse in-line layout on the grounds of cost, the Alfasud engine was so immediately appealing, and so intrinsically sound, that it lasted into the 1990s and was evolved into substantially larger sizes and far greater power outputs than its initial 68bhp at 6,000rpm.

Associated with the 2000 DOHC engine came the first appearance of something which would eventually be a valuable engine-designer's tool. For export to the USA with its tightening emission rules, the Alfa Romeo Spider of the mid-1970s, with its 2000

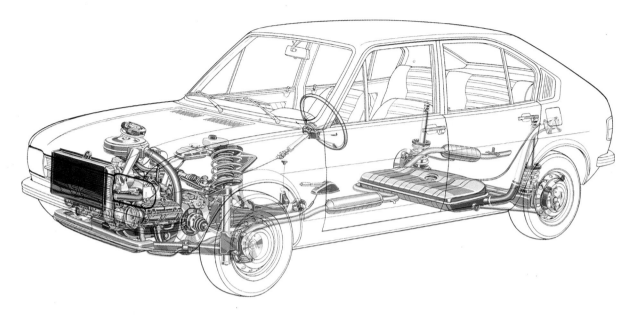

The Alfasud, with its 1.2-litre flat-four engine, appeared just when it seemed that engines of this configuration might go out of fashion. In contrast with the venerable VW Beetle unit, the Alfasud was water-cooled, had belt-driven SOHC and positively thrived on revs. By the 1990s it had been enlarged to 1.7 litres and developed into 16-valve versions, but eventually it gave way to newer in-line designs. (Giles Chapman Library)

engine, needed to be fitted with fuel injection rather than its European-specification double twin-choke Weber carburettors. But the single throttle of the EFI system, as opposed to the one-choke-per-cylinder of the carburettor setup, created cold-starting problems. These were eventually cured by fitting the inlet camshaft with a device – a variator – which retarded valve opening at low speed and load, reducing the valve overlap and making for easier starting. The normal timing could then be resumed at higher speed and load. Thus the first production example of variable inlet valve timing made its appearance, and was destined – twenty years later, and in more sophisticated form – for widespread use.

At the end of the decade, in 1979, there emerged yet another outstanding Alfa Romeo engine, this time a V6 of 2.5-litre (88 x 68.3mm, 2,492cc) and an output of 160bhp. It was a straightforward-looking engine, all-alloy with wet liners as was becoming the fashion, but it had a strong bottom end and well designed cylinder heads, each with a single belt-driven OHC operating vee-opposed valves via rockers. Like

the Alfasud unit, this engine had the capacity for a stretch to a full 3-litres, and subsequent swapping of cylinder heads for even more advanced designs proved that very large power outputs were possible. Certainly the engine was of a quality which ensured, once Fiat had taken responsibility for Alfa Romeo, that Fiat's own V6 was quickly consigned to history.

As for Fiat itself, the 1970s were something of an anticlimax after the hectic engine development activity of the 1960s. The in-line 2-cylinder OHV engine for the 126, the 500-replacement, was never going to shake the world. The new 132 simply inherited, in developed form, the DOHC engine from the 125 series. Eventually this engine was opened out, by lengthening the stroke, to a nominal 2-litre capacity (84 x 90mm, 1,995cc) and an output of 112bhp, and 122bhp with Bosch L-Jetronic injection.

The 131, which appeared in 1974 to replace the 124, was powered by a new OHV 4-cylinder engine with nominal capacities of 1.3 and 1.6 litres. Pragmatic engineering it may have been, but it also represented an abdication of Fiat's position in the front rank of technical development, to which it had devoted at least ten years of major effort. But then, the 1970s were a sad time for Fiat politically and socially, and probably the company did not feel it worth taking any technical risk whatever – which also explains the front-engine, rear-drive layout of the 131 at a time when most of its major competitors, other than the American-owned ones, were moving to front-drive. Eventually, like their predecessors in the

124, the 131 units were converted to belt-driven DOHC with completely new cylinder heads, but by now it was 1978 and the 131 looked outdated, whatever was done to its engines. Also in 1978, the 131 was offered with a choice of two 4-cylinder diesel engines, one of 1,995cc capacity and 60bhp, the other a massive 2,445cc and 72bhp.

Even while the DOHC engines were being installed in the 131 Super, a mid-range front-driven Fiat, a spiritual successor to the 128, finally appeared in the form of the Ritmo, or Strada in English-speaking markets. (The Fiat group was entering an era where it seemed to have a gift for coming up with one inappropriate or confusing name after another.) The Ritmo was essentially powered by a series of SOHC engines developed from the original 1,116cc engine from the 128. This was retained, as was the enlarged (bored out to 86mm) 1,290cc version first seen in the X1/9 mid-engined sports car. In a piece of pure comedy, this engine was further bored-out by 0.4mm, taking its capacity to 1,301cc, when the Italian government introduced differential *autostrada* speed limits with a break-point at 1,300cc! In exactly the same way, the 131-1300 unit, which had started life at 1,297cc, suddenly found itself with the extra 0.1mm bore needed to take it to 1,301cc. One wonders if any keen Italian policeman ever lifted a mid-range Fiat cylinder head and laid a ruler across the bore to see if the driver had been going 10km/hour faster than he was supposed to . . . The final stretch of the 128 engine involved a further increase in stroke, making the engine 86.4 x 63.9mm, for a capacity of 1,489cc and 75bhp. Tuned to deliver 85bhp, this engine also found its way into a revised X1/9.

As for Lancia, by the early 1970s, it was a shadow of its former self. Some of its spirit was kept alive by the rallying exploits of the Stratos, a car which had nothing to do with serious production. In 1972 the Flavia – which had already become the angular and nameless 2000 – was replaced by the Beta, whose DOHC engines came straight from the Fiat 132. In a final misjudged flurry of quasi-independence in 1976, there appeared the Gamma, a big car, spiritual successor to the Flaminia, but dogged from the start by the decision to engineer an all-new flat-4 engine to drive its front wheels. In its larger version, this engine had dimensions of 102 x 76mm for a capacity of 2,484cc and an output of 140bhp; there was also a narrower-bored (91.5mm) 2-litre version for the Italian market, in which cars over 2,000cc paid a heavy tax penalty. The sad fact was that prestige buyers in every significant export market – certainly in Germany, the UK, and the USA if Lancia was brave enough to try it – expected a car in this class to have six cylinders, no matter how good the big flat-4 might have been (and it wasn't that good anyway). Fiat/Lancia engineers at the Gamma's launch in Turin explained that the choice had lain 'between a flat-4 and a V6, therefore the flat-4 more or less chose itself', without venturing why a flat-6 had been out of the question, or indeed what would have been wrong with a lightweight V6. It was too late . . . and at the very end of the decade, there emerged the Lancia Delta, visibly from the same drawing board as the VW Golf, and Fiat engined, with no more than minor Lancia adaptations. The story was over.

Floundering in **Britain**

It might almost have been over in Britain too. During the 1970s, every surviving indigenous British manufacturer of significant size was drawn into the orbit of British Leyland, or whatever name was adopted for the combine with each successive consolidation and change of managing director. Basically, this meant that the group became responsible for the fortunes of Austin-Morris, Rover, Triumph and, for a time, Jaguar. The whole thing was such a mess that it is not really surprising nobody ever managed to make sense of it all. Strange decisions were taken, such as making Austin responsible for all front-driven budget-class models while Morris would do the rear-driven ones. This left Morris to die a slow death with the unloved Marina, launched in 1971 with a choice of A-series (1300) or B-series (1800) engines, and its repackaged descendant the Ital, which limped into the 1980s before the Morris name went the way of Riley and Wolseley before it.

The A-class also continued in the Mini, more or less unchanged throughout the decade. The 1970s was a period when the great game of the industry was guessing when and whether the Mini would be replaced, and the answer did not actually come until 1980. The B-series also continued, powering not only the 1800 but also its more stylish replacement the Princess. These cars also offered the transverse 6-cylinder 2200, the requirement for which had so cursed the 4-cylinder E-series, but there were pitifully few takers. The E-series itself was eventually lengthened in stroke to yield a capacity of 1,750cc for the Maxi and the Allegro.

For a long time, the Triumph engine range

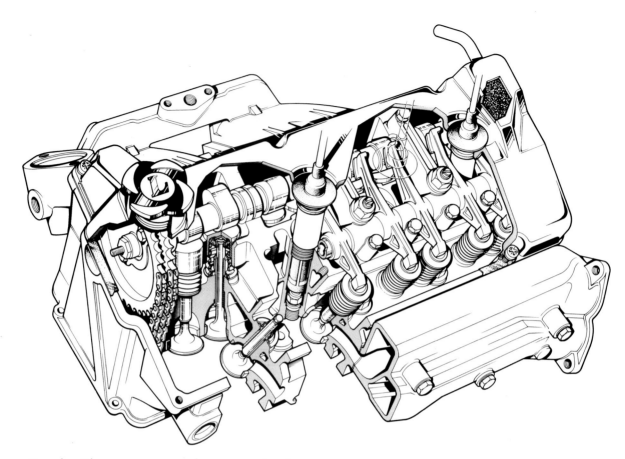

continued without any cross-reference to Austin-Morris, so that the Triumph 1300/Toledo engine formed a direct competitor for the A-series. The one advantage enjoyed by the Triumph engine was that it could be stretched to a nominal 1.5-litre capacity (73.7 x 83.4mm, 1,491cc) and in this form inflicted the ultimate indignity on the dying MG sports car range, by being substituted for the A-series engine in the final production version of the Midget, ostensibly to maintain performance levels in the US market against the onset of the emissions legislation. The MGB also continued, and was supplemented – for a while – by the MGB V8 GT with the 3.5-litre Rover engine. Only 2,591 were produced . . .

Meanwhile, Triumph pressed on with its own development of the Saab slant-4 engine which it had originally designed. In the rear-driven Dolomite, which shared a basic body shell with the rear-driven Toledo and the front-driven 1500 (née 1300) the Triumph evolution had bore and stroke of 87 x 78mm for a capacity of 1,854cc. It was then treated to a new 16-valve cylinder head in which the single overhead camshaft operated all the valves via rockers. In this form, as the Dolomite Sprint, it delivered 127bhp with the engine bored out to 90.3mm for a capacity of

An ingenious approach to the task of converting an eight-valve engine to 16 valves was seen in the Triumph Dolomite Sprint of the late 1970s, in which the single chain-driven camshaft operated one set of eight valves directly, and the opposing eight via rockers passing across the head. Finding room for the sparking plugs was something of a challenge as is evident in this view, but the engine worked well. (Herridge & Sons Collection)

1,998cc. Triumph had also conceived a plan to mate two of these engines to a single crankcase with a shorter-throw crankshaft, to make a 3-litre V8 engine. This emerged as the 86 x 64.5mm (2,997cc) Stag engine, which whatever its merits – and they turned out not to be many – was a waste of development resources for a group which already had the all-alloy Rover V8 on its books. Eventually, a minor industry developed substituting the Rover engine for the SOHC/bank Triumph unit in the Stag. In 8-valve form, this 2-litre engine powered the Triumph TR7, which was supposed to be the 'corporate' sports car that would assume the mantle of MG and Triumph in the all-important American market. It didn't.

One of the great BL Group projects of the 1970s

was to develop an all-new in-line 6-cylinder engine which would assume the roles of the unloved 2200 E-series, the by now elderly Rover 2200 4-cylinder, and the robust but even more elderly Triumph 2000/2500 6-cylinder OHV. The work was duly undertaken and preparations were made to put the new belt-driven SOHC engine into production at the Triumph factory in Canley, in two sizes, 2300 (81 x 76mm, 2,350cc) and 2600 (81 x 84mm, 2,597cc). The strange decision was taken, possibly to improve economy by reducing friction, that the engine should have only four main bearings, which did not help its operating refinement at a time when the opposition – not least BMW – was producing some extremely refined engines. In any event, the 2300/2600 were announced in new versions of the recently introduced SD1 3500, but in effect the engine was never seen again. It found no other application, nor did it survive very long. More development funds had been sluiced away to no purpose . . .

Jaguar soldiered on through this terrible time, bolstered only by the arrival of the long predicted V12 with its chain-driven SOHC per bank, and dimensions 90 x 70mm for a capacity of 5,343cc, announced in 1971, initially to power the E-type. Such an engine must have come under severe scrutiny during the 1973/74 energy crisis, but the money had been spent, the development work undertaken, and for many years it gave Jaguar a unique selling proposition and cachet. In 1975, it was further improved with the addition of fuel injection. Otherwise, Jaguar persisted with the good old – and already, it was old – XK engine in 3.4 and 4.2-litre forms. For them, relief was still some way off.

Rover continued to make a good thing of the 3.5-litre V8, deploying it to effect in the 3500 saloon, the Range Rover (from 1971) and the SD1 3500 (from 1976). The company hardly needed anything else, other than the continuing strength of the Land Rover; had anyone then told them that derivatives of the V8 would still be serving with great satisfaction into the 21st century, they would probably have thought them slightly deranged . . .

In Japan, consolidation

If one excepts Honda, which has already been discussed, Japan in the 1970s was still not quite ready to take a clear lead in technical matters. The concern of its industry appears to have been to make sure it was fully equipped to react to, and exploit, any good new idea that came out of Europe. This is not to say that in terms of product quality and reliability, Japanese engineers were not already clearly in the lead; they were.

Honda certainly was the exception, especially after Soichiro Honda – a great enthusiast for air-cooled engines, given all his motorcycle development experience – at last allowed his engineers free rein to work on liquid-cooled engines, following a famous 1969 conversation with Takeo Fujisawa. The rest, one might say, is history, leading in the 1970s to the original Civic (1972), the original 1.6-litre Accord (1976) and its coupé stablemate the Prelude (1978). Its repercussions also led to the voluntary abandoning of the 360cc microcar class from 1974 to 1981.

As mentioned in the previous chapter, Nissan never entered the microcar market but through the 1970s continued to build a comprehensive range starting with small cars (in Britain, the 1000 followed by the 100A Cherry) with a well over-square (73 x 59mm, 988cc) pushrod OHV engine. By the mid-1970s the range – even in simplified form – then extended up through the 120Y with a longer-stroke version of the Cherry OHV engine (73 x 70mm, 1,171cc) and then the 140J Violet with chain-driven SOHC engine of 1,428cc (83 x 66mm). Better known was the 160B/180B Bluebird, with the same engine first stroked to 73.7mm (1,595cc) and then bored and stroked to 1,770mm (85 x 78mm). The Japanese needed little teaching when it came to the 'numbers game' of adapting a single basic design to a number of different capacities. Nor did they have much to learn about the technique of passing 4-cylinder and 6-cylinder engines with the same main dimensions down a single machining line, in the interests of production economy. One of Datsun's most admired achievements in the 1970s was the engine that was merely 'one and a half' 160B Bluebird engines. With six cylinders this yielded 2,393cc, and the resulting engine went into the 240Z sports car, with celebrated effect. There were larger engines too, including the SOHC 2-litre 4-cylinder (89 x 80mm, 1,990cc) in the Laurel. They were sound, economical, reliable, and occasionally, extremely good, but not yet truly innovative.

An exactly parallel course was being followed by Toyota, whose range effectively began with the little rear-driven Publica (Nissan/Datsun was well ahead of Toyota in adopting front-wheel drive in its smaller cars), progressing through the best-selling but

Another flat-four engine family first extensively developed in the 1970s was to be found at Subaru in Japan. In the event, this turned out to be the most durable and highly-developed family of its kind, evolving into a whole series of designs with capacities

up to 2.2 litres, and with 16 valves, as well as 'one-and-a-half' flat-six equivalents. With the demise of the Alfasud engine, the Subaru family was destined to become the only flat-four series remaining in large-scale production. (Subaru)

extremely straightforward Corolla, which passed most of the 1970s with pushrod OHV engines. The year 1970 saw the original launch of the Carina/Celica series, destined to become a major part of Toyota's sales effort, especially overseas. SOHC engines crept into the Toyota range from the top downwards, logically enough. The bigger cars, the Crown and the Mark II, had entered the decade with them, and by the mid-1970s the hotter Celicas has followed suit, the 1600GT having a DOHC unit and 102bhp by way of distinction from the 1600ST with only 88bhp from one of Toyota's last mid-sized OHV units.

Even in 1970, both the Nissan and Toyota ranges extended up to true 'executive' cars, Nissan's President with a 3-litre, 6-cylinder SOHC unit of 130bhp, while the Toyota Century has a 150bhp 3-litre pushrod V8. Among the smaller Japanese marques, Mazda became celebrated for maintaining faith in the Wankel engine long after everyone else had given up on it, with Kenichi Yamamoto becoming its chief technical guru and advocate. During the 1970s Mazda offered twin-rotor Wankel engines in a remarkable assortment of machinery, not all of its appropriate: the RX-3 with its engine delivering 110bhp at 7,000rpm to what was essentially the fairly crude little 1300 chassis was certainly an experience – the author conducted the test-track session of the *Autocar* road test – but not one you would want to repeat all that often. The engine was much better in the RX-100 Cosmo and later in the RX-7 sports car . . . and there was Subaru, little more than a minicar maker in 1970, but one which in 1972 launched the idea of a tough four-wheel-drive 'go most places' estate car, powered by a new flat-4 engine which steadily evolved over the years, its descendants still going strong in the 21st century. There was also Daihatsu, yet another minicar-maker seeking to expand upwards, and producing in 1977 its first Charade, complete with the in-line 3-cylinder engine which has since become something of a company hallmark – and no longer alone in its seemingly odd configuration.

In summary

It would be easy to sum-up the 1970s as a thoroughly bad time from the point of view of the motor industry and even more of the engine designer. Worldwide, there was the affliction of the energy crises, the second one striking just when we seemed to be getting over the first. In the USA, there was the major upheaval caused by the Clean Air Act and the realisation that even if its provisions were postponed into the 1980s, they would not be abandoned and the industry had little choice but to make ready to comply. And in Britain, for a variety of reasons – some of them reflected in Italy – there was good reason to be gloomy about the future state of the national motor industry.

Yet in all this, there were pieces of silver lining to be found. The Clean Air Act may have seemed like an imposition and an over-reaction, but in truth emissions needed tackling, and the technologies developed in the process stood engine designers in good stead in later years. Technically, it was a decade in which the overhead camshaft, and the efficiency it brought, began to be taken for granted, and in which such concepts as multivalve cylinder heads and turbocharging began to be taken seriously, never to be entirely abandoned. One might, in retrospect, say that the suffering of the 1970s needed to be endured so that we would be in a position to make the 1980s much better.

10 The 1980s

Technology takes over

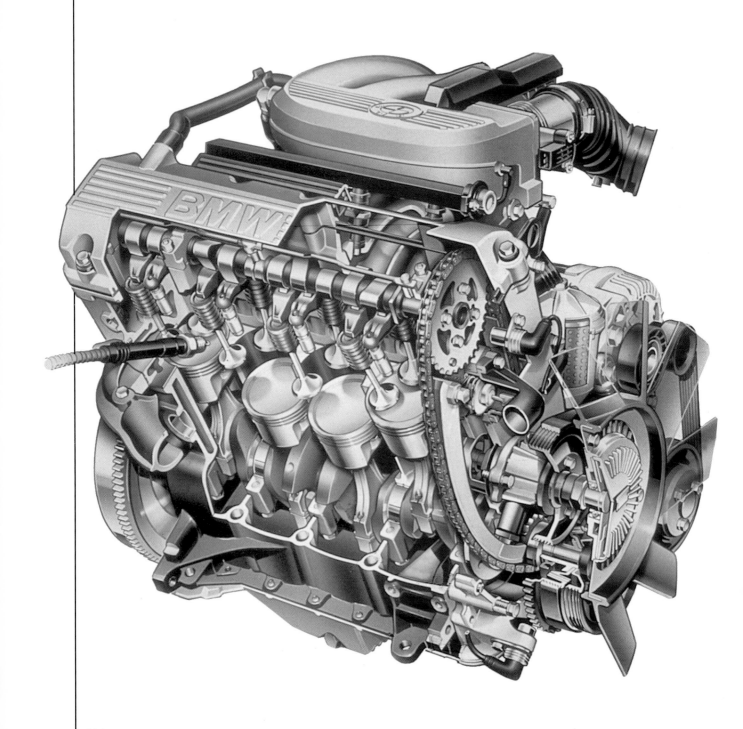

180

he previous chapter made the point that the 1970s had been hard times for car manufacturers and most of all for their engine designers. In the 1980s, things began to look better. There were no more political upsets on the scale of the 1970s – the next would come in the 1990s with the Gulf War, and even that would not be so traumatic from the point of view of its effect on oil prices. Furthermore, the exhaust emissions situation had been more or less resolved, for the time being at least. The car manufacturers had lost the argument but they had won a delay, and by 1980 they were ready, where necessary, with the appropriate technology, developed with all speed during the later 1970s.

The American industry trend to downsize for the sake of economy arose partly to keep in line with the Corporate Average Fuel Economy requirement – which stood at 20 miles/US gallon in 1980, and eased up to 27.5 miles/US gallon by 1990 (although it has stuck there ever since), and partly because in the aftermath of the 1978–79 energy crisis, even American car buyers were seriously interested in fuel economy. As a result, while the most typical American car of the early 1970s was an extremely large saloon with a V8 engine of around 5-litre capacity driving the rear wheels, by the early 1980s, it had become a medium-sized saloon with a V6 engine of around 3-litre capacity installed transversely and driving the front wheels. The traditional large V8 still existed, but the number of models on offer had shrunk dramatically.

New American cars for the 1981 model year had to meet the full Clean Air Act emission limits of 0.41 grams/mile HC, 3.4 grams/mile CO and 1 gram per mile of NOx. In practice, petrol-engined cars could only comply with these limits by fitting a three-way catalytic converter, and some form of fuel injection system working with an exhaust gas oxygen sensor (lambda sensor) in a closed control-loop mode to hold the air:fuel mixture ratio very precisely at around 14:1. Diesels could, at that time, just about scrape within the limit through being tuned to run the lowest possible NOx and use a one-way oxidising converter to take care of as much HC and CO as possible. An even lower limit would spell trouble for the diesel, as would any significant limit imposed on emissions of 'particulate matter' – strictly a diesel problem, at least in terms of the particle sizes anyone could measure in 1980.

The European and American manufacturers differed in their approach to fuel injection at that time. Europe's emission limits were relaxed compared with the US Federal standard and could still be met with carefully tuned engines breathing through carburettors. Hence injected cars in Europe tended to be up-market or high-performance models in which the main point of the injection was to increase power output. This in turn justified the use of multipoint systems, with separate injectors feeding pulses directly into the inlet port, to be sucked into the cylinder as soon as the valve opened. The technical debate in Europe revolved around whether it was satisfactory to inject simultaneously – one control pulse per two engine revolutions to all four, six or eight injectors – or to accept the extra cost of a 'sequential' system in which a separate control pulse was sent to each injector just before its inlet valve was about to open. It was accepted that this improved power output, fuel economy and exhaust emissions compared with simultaneous injection, but the generation and delivery of separate, accurately timed pulses made the control system significantly more expensive.

In America, the fact that virtually all cars were now fuel injected meant that low cost was a prime requirement so long as the emission limits were met. This led to the almost universal use of 'throttle body injection' (TBI) in which, in effect, the carburettor was replaced by a similar-looking unit into which the required amount of fuel was squirted by an injector (often, in practice, two injectors) rather than being sucked from a jet. The mixture then had to make its way through the entire inlet manifold and – as best it could – be distributed between the cylinders. It was a system which permitted positive closed-loop control of mixture strength, but otherwise suffered most of the disadvantages of the carburettor.

Opposite: The engine which revived BMW's fortunes in the most remarkable way managed to combine an elegant simplicity with high efficiency. The four-cylinder, eight-valve, SOHC unit seen here began life at 1.5-litre capacity and was opened out to a full 2-litres. A very similar layout was retained for the company's new six-cylinder in-line engines. (BMW)

For the most part, the manufacturers breathed a sigh of relief once they had met the 1981 emission limits with catalyst-equipped cars. For one thing, from 1982 the American limits remained essentially stable until the 1990s, freeing many engineers to work on other aspects of design. For another, it proved possible in nearly all cases to throw away the sometimes complex and occasionally unreliable devices used to meet the steadily tightening limits of the 1970s – the exhaust gas recirculation, the exhaust manifold air injection, the sometimes strange ignition timing calibrated to avoid the highest 'spikes' of emission at particular operating conditions, which led to many complaints of poor driveability.

There remained the question of which technologies the newly freed engineers were going to exploit in improving car engines. Here again, there was something of a split between Europe and America. By 1980, engineers everywhere were aware of the higher efficiency which could be achieved with overhead camshafts and cross-flow cylinder heads. But in America, engineers were reluctant to move at all quickly in this direction because logically, the main benefit was to enable a smaller, lighter engine to achieve adequate performance with better economy – at the cost of an expensive development programme. Of necessity this included, for the American market, a difficult and time-consuming test to certify emissions compliance. Now, while the average early-1980s American car buyer was interested in economy, he was not so keen as to pay a great deal extra for it, even less so if it involved advanced features which might not be altogether reliable or intelligible to his service station. He was already paying a good deal extra for this emission control equipment – why multiply the burden? This became an ever more popular argument as oil prices settled down and the 'pump' price of petrol (gasoline) in the USA became a modest fraction of what European drivers were paying. Thus, for the most part, American designers stayed faithful to pushrod OHV operation and were under no particular consumer pressure to do otherwise. In Europe, it was a very different matter.

There were also the questions of light alloy engine construction, multivalve layouts (three or four valves per cylinder rather than just two) and turbocharging. Alloy cylinder heads were becoming popular everywhere, but the Europeans were leading the way in aluminium blocks – and GM in particular could point back to unhappy experiences with the Buick V8 in the 1960s, and the Chevrolet Vega in the 1970s, as good reasons not to be in any hurry to go that way again. Multivalves, with their promise of higher specific power output, were firmly in the sights of many European manufacturers, but once again American experience was limited mainly to the Chevrolet Cosworth-Vega 16-valve, which had been made only on a small scale and aroused little enthusiasm. Turbocharging was a rather different

matter. It was seen as a 'strap-on' device which could increase output – especially torque – without greatly affecting emissions. Indeed, such evidence as there was suggested that turbo engines had slightly better emissions performance, all other things being equal. So American engine designers prepared to accept the turbocharger, at least for some specialised applications – the prospect was of a V6 turbo equalling the performance of a much bigger V8. It may seem strange that performance should matter so much in a market where speed limits were low and often strictly enforced, but 'acceleration on the freeway ramp' was still a valued quality.

America downsized, **down-powered** – but not for long

Of the 'big three' American manufacturers, Chrysler was the only one not to go the V6 route. In answer to the late 1970s energy crisis it undertook the design of a new 4-cylinder alloy-headed belt-driven SOHC engine of 2.2-litre (87.5 x 92mm, 2,213cc) capacity, for transverse installation in its new front-driven 'K-car', launched in 1981. To meet the demand which then existed for small, economical cars Chrysler, like Ford, filled the slot with imports from the former Chrysler Europe. Chrysler was also able to exploit its growing relationship with Mitsubishi in Japan, and for several years used a 4-cylinder SOHC Mitsubishi engine as an alternative to the 2.2-litre in the K-class. This Mitsubishi engine was among the first modern units to return to the Lanchester balancer shaft principle to make the big 4-cylinder acceptably smooth, mounting two shafts within the block and driving them at twice crankshaft speed.

The 2.2-litre engine was developed throughout the decade and provides a good example of how 'bread and butter' American engines evolved at this time. Being a relatively small engine in American terms, it began in 1981 by using an 'electronic feedback' carburettor and control unit to meet the emission limits. However, as the decade progressed the Environmental Protection Agency (EPA) began a programme of checking post-1981 cars to ensure continued conformity, and this was enough to prompt Chrysler into switching to TBI for some versions by 1984; production of carburettor engines continued until 1987, however. In 1984

Chrysler introduced a turbocharged version of the engine, for the Dodge Daytona, which delivered 142bhp instead of the standard 96bhp. In 1986, the engine was 'stretched' to 2.5-litre capacity by increasing the stroke, enabling it to use the existing cylinder head and achieve an output of 100bhp. This larger engine was also turbocharged, delivering up to 225bhp according to version.

Ford had had an engine since 1974 which was broadly equivalent to the Chrysler 2.2-litre, when it designed a 2.3-litre SOHC 4-cylinder unit – the Lima engine, which among other things, was the first American-designed engine to be fully metric – to replace the German-sourced 2.0-litre in the Pinto. This engine was now fitted to the Mustang and in 1983, in turbocharged form, even to the prestige Thunderbird. Ford also took its old in-line 6-cylinder engine and again removed two cylinders to create a completely different (and much cheaper) pushrod OHV 4-cylinder 2.3-litre which, from the mid-1980s, was fitted to the successful Tempo and Topaz models. However, the company still needed a V6 engine of suitable size for the American market and created it by taking the 5-litre (302cid) V8 and removing the two rearmost cylinders. With some adjustment of dimensions the resulting engine had a capacity of 3,797cc (231cid). What it also had, inevitably, was a less than ideal 90° angle between cylinder banks and was consequently noted for its unrefined operation until, in 1987, it was fitted with a single balancer shaft in the block, above the centrally mounted camshaft. This V6 then remained a mainstay of the Ford engine range until the end of the century. Higher in its range, naturally, Ford retained the V8 option for its larger cars, with two closely related units, the 5-litre (302cid) from which the V6 had been derived, and the 5.7-litre (351cid) for its top-range models including the Thunderbird.

Like its rivals, General Motors entered the 1980s with a fresh set of plans, including two new compact car platforms, the X-body and the slightly smaller J-body, to address its domestic-market need for smaller and more economical cars. To begin with, the only 4-cylinder engine available to GM the USA was a venerable all-iron, pushrod OHV 2.5-litre unit known affectionately – even then – as the 'Iron Duke'. This device was a relic of the 1960s and 1970s when 4-cylinder engines were strictly for the underprivileged, in the eyes of GM marketing executives. It produced only 90bhp and yet was really too heavy for the new cars, but it was pressed into service until more satisfactory 4-cylinder replacements could be developed. It was accompanied by a new 2.8-litre 60° V6 which proved amenable to 'stretch' – by stages, to 3.4-litre capacity, but by then in the 1990s – and a wide range of applications.

By the end of the decade GM was using a variety of 4-cylinder engines, some home-built and some imported, but by far the most technically significant was the Quad 4, which might be thought of as GM's step towards revolution for the 1980s, as the all-alloy Nova engine had been for the 1970s and the flat-6 air-cooled Corvair for the 1960s. The Quad 4 was a chain-driven DOHC 16-valve engine, almost wildly out of tune with the mainstream of American engine development. It was launched in 1987, to begin with in selected Buick and Oldsmobile models, with dimensions of 92 x 85mm for a capacity of 2,260cc, and an output of 150bhp at 5,200rpm: a specific output of over 66bhp per litre, close to what the best European engines were achieving at the time.

There were no such moves higher up the size range, at least not in the 1980s. Improvements were made to existing engines, including – again in 1987 – the addition of balancer shafts to the 90° V6 3.8-litre engine (see previous chapter). Even so, it is interesting to note that by GM's own figures, this engine was barely more powerful than the Quad 4, with 152bhp, although naturally its torque output was substantially greater. The decade had also seen this engine turbocharged to some effect. The most significant technical move in GM's V8 engine range was Cadillac's switch to a wet-linered alloy cylinder block (although it retained iron heads) for its new mainstay 4.1-litre V8 in 1982.

GM tried two more technical attempts to improve fuel economy in the early 1980s. One was the strange 8-6-4 engine, which deactivated two or four cylinders according to operating condition, so as to maintain the working cylinders at a load where they would burn fuel efficiently. Probably it was an idea well before its time. In any event, customers hated it and it suffered reliability problems. It did not last. Neither did GM's two big and related V6 and V8 diesel engines, both with dimensions 103 x 86mm and therefore with capacities of 4,294 and 5,736cc respectively. They would probably have been doomed anyway as fuel prices stabilised and then fell, but their poor reliability sealed their fate and, sadly, made the passenger car diesel engine something of a laughing-stock in the USA for the rest of the century.

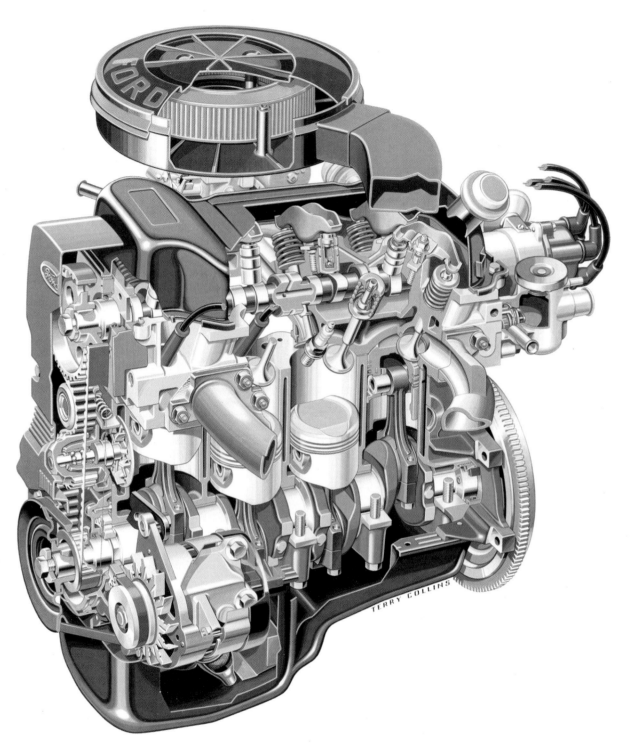

Despite the great care which went into its design and development, the Ford CVH engine proved to be less of an improvement on the OHV 'Kent' engine than had been hoped, and it did not enjoy a long life. Note here the single belt-driven overhead camshaft driving the eight valves via carefully angled rockers, so that both valves moved directly towards the geometric centre of the combustion chamber; also the considerably offset sparking plugs and rather oddly-shaped pistons. The five-bearing bottom end is substantial. (Ford)

America-in-Europe,
altogether different

As in America, so Ford of Europe entered the 1980s needing to reconfigure its engine range to suit the new requirement for extreme economy. For Ford, that meant two things: developing an up-to-date lower-range 4-cylinder engine, in the 1.4–1.6-litre class, and putting together a range of modern diesel engines.

In 1980, Ford announced an all-new 1.6-litre engine with belt-driven SOHC driving vee-opposed valves via rockers with hydraulic tappets, and carefully shaped pistons intended to create a shaped airflow within the piston when rising towards top dead centre. The basic idea, new at the time, was to encourage a horizontal tumbling motion, rather than a vertical swirl, to carry mixture to the sparking plug set well to one side of the cylinder centre. This new unit used an aluminium alloy head, surprisingly for the first time in a Ford of Europe engine. It was designated CVH, standing for Compound Valve angle Hemispherical chamber, and the intention was to produce versions of it in 1.1, 1.3 and 1.6-litre capacities, in both Europe and Detroit. The bore and stroke were given as 74 x 65mm (1,117cc), 80 x 64.5mm (1,296cc) and 80 x 79.5mm (1,597cc). The cylinder bore centres were spaced at 91.8mm.

The CVH was not, sadly, an unqualified success, although it served Ford of Europe more than adequately for a decade. When the first front-driven Escort was announced a few months after the engine itself, its 'base' 1100 unit was a pushrod OHV 1,117cc unit derived from the smaller Fiesta engine, itself owing much to the already elderly Kent. By the time a face-lifted Escort appeared in 1986, the main engine range consisted of 1.4-litre (77.2 x 74.3mm, 1,392cc) and 1.6-litre versions of the CVH, plus 1,117cc and 1,297cc versions of the old OHV Kent engine. Three things had happened. First, market experience had shown that a 1.4-litre engine was needed below the 1.6. Second, the CVH had proved in service not to be as economical as had been hoped, which mattered most at the lower end of the range. Third, the Kent engine had proved to have more life left in it than had been anticipated, it terms both of economy and of meeting the European emission limits – and it had the CVH well beaten on cost, with its simple cast-iron head.

Such considerations apart, the 1.6 in its 1986 form was also offered with fuel injection (Bosch K-Jetronic)

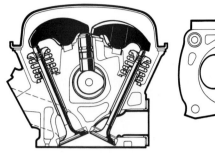

FORD HEMI

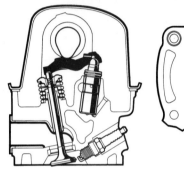

FORD WEDGE

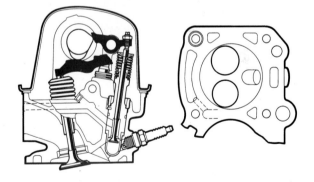

FORD CVCC

When the CVH engine was announced in 1980, Ford issued this comparison of three cylinder head layouts, the top being the CVH, the middle one the well established 'Pinto' engine with its in-line valves and wedge combustion chamber and, below, the company's proposed layout for a CVCC engine complete with third valve admitting air to a rich-mixture initial-combustion chamber. Note the large area of the CVH valves, but also the way the sparking plug is forced into a less than ideal position. (Ford)

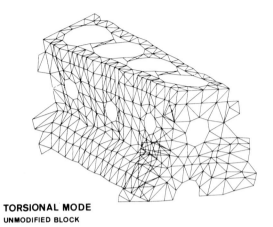

TORSIONAL MODE
UNMODIFIED BLOCK

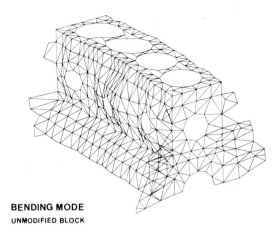

BENDING MODE
UNMODIFIED BLOCK

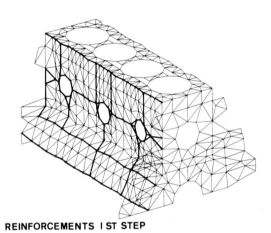

REINFORCEMENTS 1ST STEP

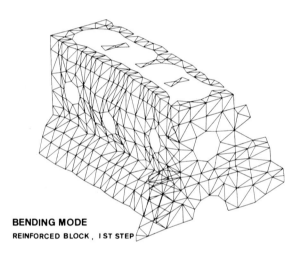

BENDING MODE
REINFORCED BLOCK, 1ST STEP

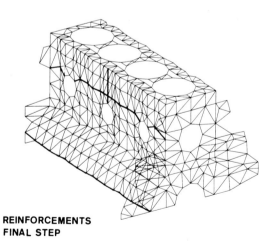

**REINFORCEMENTS
FINAL STEP**

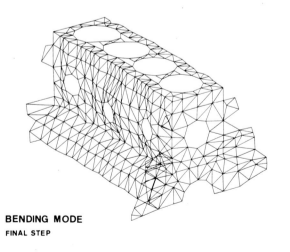

BENDING MODE
FINAL STEP

When the CVH was launched, Ford provided illustrations of the way the cylinder block had been analysed and stiffened using computer-based finite element analysis. Within a few years this kind of approach, and consequent saving of development time, would be taken for granted, but in 1980 it was an eye-opener. The illustration shows the effect of stiffening the block in two stages. As in all such illustrations, the actual distortion of the block is greatly exaggerated by the computer to make it more obvious and thus more easily analysed. (Ford)

and with turbocharging. The 1.6i engine delivered 105bhp, and the RS Turbo engine, 132bhp. In addition, the revised cars carried over the new 1600 diesel engine which had gone on sale in 1984, in both the Fiesta and the larger Escort/Orion. This all-iron diesel engine was a new unit with belt-driven SOHC and precisely square dimensions of 80mm bore and stroke, for a capacity of 1,598cc. The diesel system was typical of its day, with indirect injection into combustion prechambers, and the output was 54bhp, with excellent economy, if rather limited performance.

The 1980s saw little action where the larger Ford of Europe cars were concerned, save that the recently launched Sierra, replacing the final Cortina, used the 1.6 Pinto engine rather than the 1.6 CVH. Was this simply because the detail design of the latter was optimised for transverse front-drive installation? Technically, there was more interest to be found in the Sierra Cosworth, which on its 1988 announcement, had a belt-driven DOHC 16-valve conversion of the 2-litre Pinto engine, complete with a Garrett T03 turbocharger and intercooler, providing a slightly alarming 204bhp at 6,000rpm. Otherwise, for the Scorpio, the Cologne V6 engines were gently opened out from 2.3/2.8 to 2.4/2.9-litre capacity. But the RS Cosworth was a small-volume specialist car, and sales of the Granada were shrinking too.

Like Ford, GM's concern in Europe was essentially to put together a sensible range of modern small and medium-sized engines for its range, soon to consist

As exhaust emission legislation began to tighten, carburettor manufacturers sought ways of maintaining their position, almost regardless of complication. This was the Ford Variable Venturi Carburettor (VVC) for the CVH engine, in which a beam moves a carefully shaped block sideways within the carburettor body to create an 'ideal' airflow pattern matched to the position of the throttle valve below. The VVC gave considerable trouble in service and the final coming of fuel injection for all cars must have been a relief to some service engineers. (Ford)

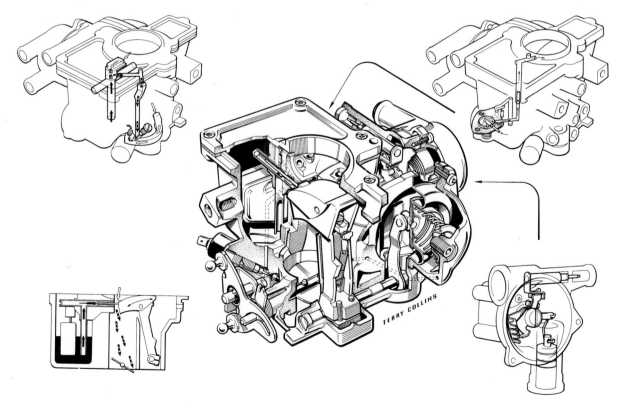

TERRY COLLINS

mainly of front-driven models. Among other things this meant the D-segment Ascona could, to a large extent, share powertrains with its smaller stablemates – something Ford had denied itself by making the Sierra rear-driven. By the arrival of the 1980s all former Vauxhall engines had effectively been consigned to history and the GM Europe range depended to begin with on existing Opel engines, and later in the decade on two new OHC engines, the 'Family One' and the slightly larger 'Family Two'. While for the sake of low cost, Opel's long-running pushrod OHV engines were retained for the lowest power requirements, in 1-litre and 1.2-litre form, the Family One started at 1.3-litres with dimensions 75 x 73.4mm, and belt-driven SOHC. This differed from the previous cam-in-head Opel engines in that the camshaft sat much closer to the valves, operating them via finger followers sitting on fulcrums on the opposite side. The result was a slightly taller engine but a more compact cylinder head; and the head itself was now aluminium rather than cast iron. The physically larger but otherwise very similar Family Two was also adapted for in-line rear-drive installation in the Rekord/Carlton 1800 of 1982. The 1,598cc version was also converted to diesel operation with a completely new iron head, the then customary Ricardo combustion prechamber layout, and an output of 54bhp, identical to that of its direct Ford rival. In 1986, GM announced changes to the Family engines, and a new design approach which it called LET – low end torque – implying that a fat torque curve was given precedence over high-end power, mainly through choice of valve timing.

The old cam-in-head engine with its larger cylinder block was retained for the rear-driven cars, appearing in 2.0E form with Bosch LE-Jetronic injection in 1983, delivering 110bhp. Meanwhile, the 6-cylinder versions of the cam-in-head engine also continued, with nominal capacities of 2.5 and 3.0-litres. These engines, of course, still had chain drives to their camshafts.

GM played the 'GTE game' in the performance market before ending the decade with three technically significant models. First, in 1988, came the Kadett/Astra 2.0 GTE 16v, a straight adaptation of the 8-valve SOHC unit, delivering 156bhp at 6,000rpm. At about the same time there briefly emerged a 24-valve adaptation of the 3-litre 6-cylinder engine, lovingly designed by Fritz Indra and delivering 201bhp with BMW-like refinement. It was not to last long, sadly, because V6s were on their way.

Finally, as though to prove that GM could match Ford's exploits with the Sierra Cosworth, there came the Lotus-Carlton – the 24-valve straight-6, opened out to 95 x 85mm (3,615cc) and boosted by twin Garrett T25 turbochargers to deliver 377bhp, which proved to be more than some people could handle.

Germany

The indigenous West German manufacturers meanwhile went from strength to strength. Audi consistently renewed its 80/90/100 model range and, if its remarkable unveiling of the Quattro at the 1981 Geneva Show was more to do with transmission than engine design, nonetheless proved the company's involvement with high-boost turbocharging, extracting – with intercooling – 200bhp from the 5-cylinder 2,144cc engine. As the decade progressed, intercooling seemed ever more desirable to engineers, enabling considerably more power to be extracted by increasing the charge density of the boosted air before it entered the engine. By late in the decade Audi's engines ranged from a 1.6-litre 4-cylinder to an all-alloy 32-valve V8 (81 x 86.4mm, 3,562cc) with 250bhp for the big V8 saloon. The company had also embraced the multivalve concept with enthusiasm, and several of its models gained 16 or 20 valves.

Nor did it ignore diesels, taking on Volkswagen's technology as evolved for the Golf D and extending it, again, to 5-cylinder engines. By 1989, it was seeking to prove that a diesel could offer high performance, as one of the first companies to move to the idea of turbocharging, and to the use of direct rather than indirect injection. By this means, it extracted 120bhp from its 5-cylinder 2.5-litre (81 x 95.5mm, 2,461cc) engine in the 100TDI. The one thing the company could not do, with the mechanical layout it had chosen, was to move to six cylinders or indeed to make its 5-cylinder engines any more substantial, which is why they tended to emerge unfashionably under-square. But Audi had plans to change all that.

BMW spent the 1980s relatively quietly, by the standards to which they had become accustomed. Of the available and apparently most interesting technologies, the company decided to leave turbocharging well alone – having had one experience of it in the 1970s as we have seen. In this, interestingly, BMW's thinking mirrored Honda's, since the Japanese company also set its face firmly against turbocharging except when marketing

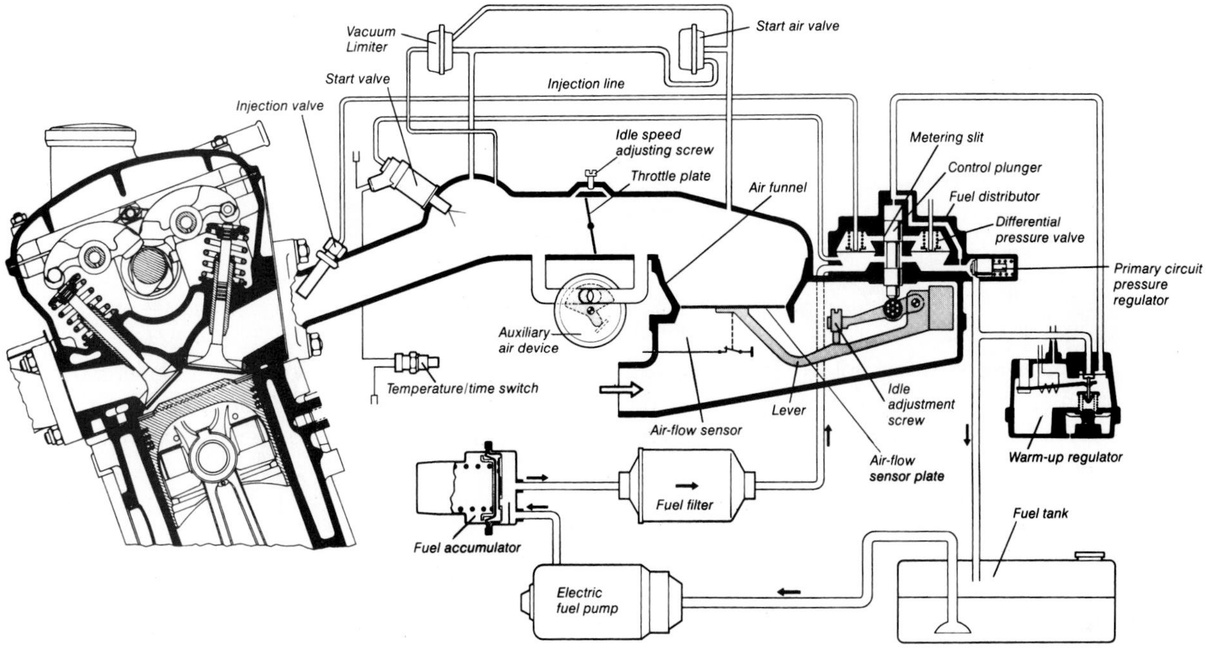
Vacuum Limiter
Start air valve
Start valve
Injection line
Injection valve
Idle speed adjusting screw
Throttle plate
Air funnel
Metering slit
Control plunger
Fuel distributor
Differential pressure valve
Primary circuit pressure regulator
Auxiliary air device
Temperature/time switch
Lever
Idle adjustment screw
Air-flow sensor
Air-flow sensor plate
Warm-up regulator
Fuel filter
Fuel accumulator
Fuel tank
Electric fuel pump

An ingenious non-electronic fuel injection system of the 1980s was Bosch's K-Jetronic, shown here as applied to the BMW 320i. The system depended on a balance-beam arrangement acted upon by the incoming airflow and the fuel pressure. It worked well by the standards of its day, but had to give way to electronically controlled systems as exhaust emission regulations became ever tighter. (BMW)

considerations made it absolutely essential – as it did, once or twice, in Japan.

BMW's approach to multivalves and to the diesel were also cautious. Only towards the very end of the decade did it move from two valves per cylinder to four. To begin with this was only in the 318iS, which to some extent, was a 3-series for markets where tax considerations favoured high specific output, and in the first generation of determinedly high performance M-models, including the original 4-cylinder M3, which offered 215bhp from 2,302cc (93.4 x 84mm), for a specific output of over 93bhp per litre. The 3.5-litre M5 delivered 315bhp, and the M635 CSi – which was not quite an M-car, but had a 4-valve engine – 260bhp. However, the principle had been established and the 1990s would see many further BMW moves in the multivalve direction.

It was likewise with the diesel. BMW realised it was losing sales in some markets by not being able to offer one, considered its options and came down in favour of a thoroughly conventional but carefully crafted 6-cylinder indirect injection unit – in 1983, just when the world was becoming excited about the prospect of direct injection. The engine was nominally 2.4-litre (80 x 81mm, 2,443cc) with chain-driven SOHC (still no toothed belts for BMW). As a plain diesel the engine produced 86bhp with – by diesel standards – exceptional refinement; with a turbocharger it managed 115bhp (and 222Nm of torque) for entirely acceptable performance in most circumstances.

By this time however, BMW had also moved in an entirely different direction to offer a combination of high performance and refinement, if not economy. It dusted off its plans for a V12 engine to rival Jaguar (and to trump Mercedes which had a similar project in the works). In 1986, the engine emerged fitted to the top version of the new 7-series, with dimensions of 84 x 75mm, which just happened to be the same as the 525. The V12 could in many ways be regarded as two 525 engines at a 60° angle, sharing a common crankcase and crankshaft, and indeed for the purposes of control – using the first 'drive-by-wire' electrical throttle linkage installed in a production car – treated the V12 in this way, with two separate Bosch management units which 'compared notes'.

This is certainly a good place to mention that by the end of the 1980s, the principle of combining control of multipoint (preferably sequential) fuel injection and ignition timing in a single unified electronic control unit – as demonstrated by the Bosch Motronic series – was already well established among top-range models in Europe; the BMW V12

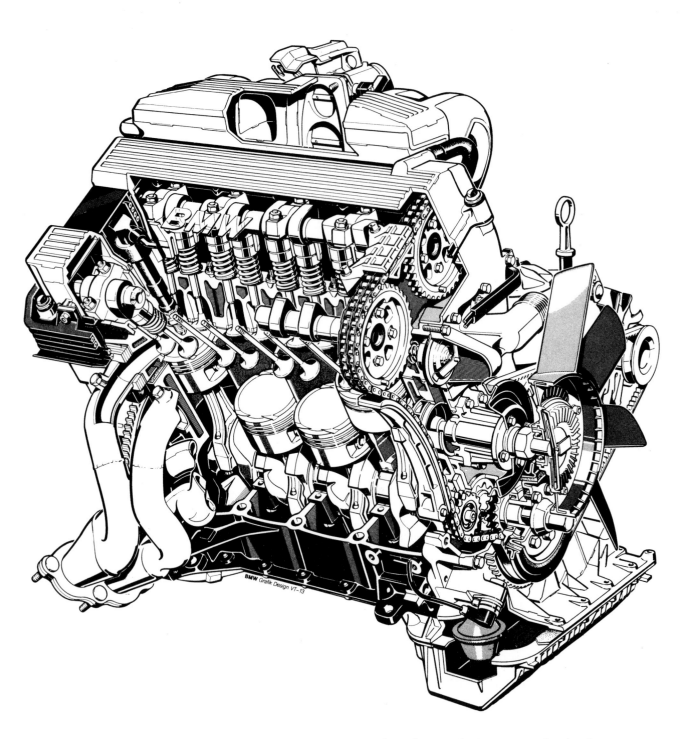

BMW was a fairly late convert to four valves per cylinder, but introduced this unit for the 318iS, a high-output model mainly for markets in which larger engines were heavily taxed, in 1989. The bottom end of the engine remained much the same, but the cylinder head, with its twin chain-driven camshafts, was of course entirely new. Before long, similar heads would appear on most of BMW's engines. (BMW)

simply took its application to another level. Engineers were still working out exactly how many functions could be entrusted to such a unit, so long as it was fed appropriate information from sensors.

Inevitably, Mercedes continued to maintain its high standard of engine design through the 1980s. It had actually set course at the very end of 1979 – for the 1980 model year – with an all-new 4-cylinder engine series, the M102, in which the cylinder block was somewhat (actually 15°) inclined to the right as viewed from the driving seat, and whose chain-driven SOHC now operated vee-opposed valves via rockers, rather than in-line valves directly. (As for BMW, so for Mercedes: chains were to be preferred, for refinement and durability.) The M102 designation spanned a large number of versions, from 1.8 to 2.5-litre capacity. In 1983, as a 2.3-litre, it was given Mercedes' first 16-valve cylinder head to reach production, in the 190E 2.3-16.

In 1985, the M102 layout was extended to the 6-cylinder M103 engines, which were thus effectively one-and-a-half W102s with the bore – rather than the 80.25mm stroke – adjusted to produce the right nominal capacity, of 2.6 or 3.0-litres. As the decade was reaching its end, there then emerged the M104, which was in effect a 3-litre M103 converted to take a 24-valve cylinder head, to produce 220 instead of 166bhp. As for the big V8 engines, they grew bigger, so that eventually the original 'small' 3.5 V8 had

become 4.2, and the 4.5 had become 5.6, both with aluminium alloy cylinder blocks. It certainly occurred to many observers that by Mercedes' refined standards, 5.6-litres was getting a bit big for a V8, but the answer would come in the 1990s.

There was a new look to Mercedes' diesel engines too, which took on the same 15° slant to their cylinder blocks. The 1980s engines came as neat pairs,

Mercedes's OM603 six-cylinder diesel engine, first seen in the G-Wagen SUV, was typical of the new generation of Mercedes engines, petrol or diesel, in being canted 15 degrees to the right for ease of access and a lower bonnet line. Details evident in this lengthwise cross-section include the beauty of the very strong seven-bearing bottom end, the duplex chain drive to the single overhead camshaft, the generous cooling around the valve area, and the in-line six-plunger injection pump – rotary diesel distributor pumps were making a strong impression in the mid-1980s but Mercedes took a lot of convincing. (Mercedes)

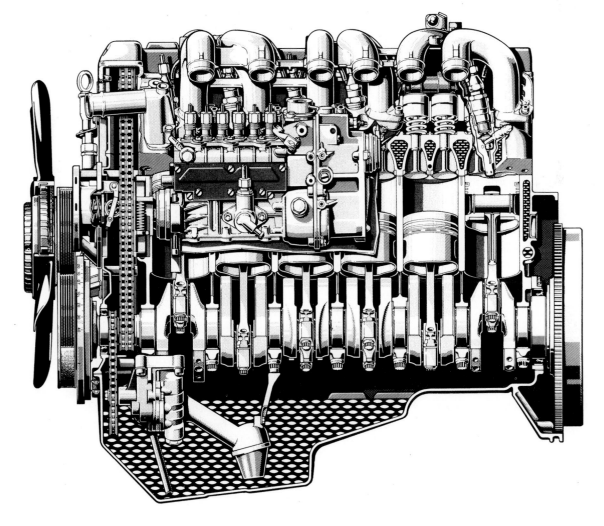

Volkswagen was not kindly disposed to four valves per cylinder in the early 1980s and stuck to the neat, simple but strong four-cylinder Golf engine as seen here – but in this case with the addition of the 'G-Lader' interlocking-spiral mechanical supercharger for installation in the Corrado G60. Simply shortening the housing reduced the output and the power consumption, and matched the unit to the smaller Polo engine for the G40. But the G-Lader failed to pass the test of large-scale service and vanished from the catalogue. (Volkswagen)

two 4-cylinder, two 5-cylinder and two 6-cylinder (OM601, 602 and 603 respectively). All but one had exactly the same cylinder dimensions, 87 x 84mm for nominal capacities of 2.0, 2.5 and 3.0-litres. The odd one out was a 2.2-litre 4-cylinder, the extra capacity gained by lengthening the stroke. For the 5 and 6-cylinder pairs, the differentiator was that one was turbocharged and the other naturally aspirated, the 300D Turbo delivering a healthy 143bhp – while direct injection, let alone common-rail, was still to come . . .

Volkswagen, having so dramatically changed technical direction – where engine design was concerned – during the 1970s with its two simple but effective SOHC engines for the Polo and Golf, it concentrated on growing its range of options, and its technology. From the original two engine sizes, a whole family had sprung, from 1,043cc for the Polo to a full 2-litre unit (82.5 x 92.8mm, 1,984cc) for the latest Passat, launched in 1988. Volkswagen was already deeply involved with the multivalve concept, having launched the 1.8-litre Golf GTI 16V with 129bhp in 1985, and similarly equipped the 2-litre Passat – so everyone was waiting for the Golf GTI 2.0 16V.

The company had, however, decided against turbocharging except for diesel engines – its diesel engine, still of 1.6-litre capacity, was producing 80bhp in turbo form by the end of the decade – and instead pinned its faith in the G-lader, a mechanical supercharger which depended for its operation on the progressive squeezing of air between the two elements of an interlocking spiral scroll as one moved eccentrically relative to the other. Certainly, the G-lader seemed to work, and had the advantage that its throughput could be matched to engine requirement simply by altering the depth of the scrolls; with the 1.8-litre, 8-valve Golf/Corrado engine it was good for 160bhp at 5,600rpm, and with no worries about turbo lag. Yet within a few years, without any explanation (although one suspects problems in manufacturing it in any volume), it had vanished from the catalogue . . .

Alongside Mercedes, down in Stuttgart, Porsche had embraced four valves per cylinder with great enthusiasm. Through the 1980s the 924 had grown into the 944, with 3-litre (104 x 88mm, 2,990cc), 16 valves, two balancer shafts and 211bhp; or alternatively with an 8-valve 2.5-litre turbocharged engine and 250bhp. And still there was more to come. The naturally aspirated 911 engine had grown to 3.6-litre capacity (100 x 76.4mm, 3,600cc exactly) and gained two plugs (but still only had two valves) per cylinder; the big 928 had been given a 32-valve layout in 1986 and now produced 320bhp from its 5-litre V8.

Not-so-dour **Swedes** ...

The 1980s turned out well for the two Swedish manufacturers. Saab, having been instrumental in establishing turbocharging as a viable technology, exploited it to great effect in the 900 and then in the 9000. Saab's presiding engines genius Per Gillbrand was also keen in four valves per cylinder, and by the end of the decade the 900 Turbo 16S with DOHC cylinder head and turbocharging to 0.85 bar was delivering 175bhp from 2-litre capacity. Saab had also long-stroked the 2-litre engine to a square configuration (90 x 90mm, 2,290cc), not only with 16 valves but also with two balancer shafts – it seemed more or less agreed in the industry that a 4-cylinder engine needed smoothing once it was bigger than 2 litres. The only thing Saab had yet to do, as the decade ended, was to add a turbo to the bigger-capacity engine. It had meanwhile also launched the first 'direct-ignition' system, with individual high-tension coils sitting directly over each sparking plug. This idea quickly became widely accepted for high-performance engines worldwide.

Volvo, in the midst of taking over the DAF concern and producing the new 400-series cars there, with Renault-supplied engines (including, by 1990, a turbo version with 120bhp from 1.7-litres) had also found the time to develop both 16-valve and turbocharged

versions of its tough 2.3-litre 4-cylinder engine. However, it only combined the two techniques in a smaller 2.0-litre unit which produced no less than 200bhp, compared with 155bhp for the 16-valve 740GLT and 170bhp for the 8-valve, 2.3-litre 740 Turbo. As for diesels, Volvo bought a specially developed 2.4-litre turbocharged 6-cylinder unit from Volkswagen, with 122bhp available.

Developments **in** **France**

PSA Peugeot-Citroën had established a strong position by the end of the 1980s, and had done it essentially with just two engine families, plus a small amount of help from the PRV V6, now looking rather elderly but at least developed to full 3-litre capacity, and provided with properly offset crankpins to even out the firing intervals, and a balancer shaft to compensate for its improper 90° angle between banks. But the PRV was really a side-issue, reserved for the low-volume Peugeot 605 and Citroën XM – the latter having arrived in 1989 to replace the CX.

The two key engines for PSA were the TU-series and the XU-series. The TU had been developed from the (literally) laid-back all-alloy engine in the 1970s 104. It was now decently upright, redesigned to be mated with an end-on gearbox rather than laying across the top of it, and was used in PSA's small and medium-sized twin models, the Citroën AX/Peugeot 205 and the Citroën BX/Peugeot 405, in sizes up to 1,360cc. Then for the latter pair, came the step up to 1,580cc, at which the XU-series began. The XU was an almost devastatingly simple 4-cylinder engine with belt-driven SOHC, in-line valves, and designed among other things, to be manufactured with a high degree of automation at PSA's new engine factory at Tremery in eastern France. Even the cylinder block casting had been studied to allow it to be made at a high rate and with little human intervention. As a final stroke of genius, the XU had been designed with the right degree of 'stretch' – and with the ability to be made as a petrol or diesel engine. As a petrol unit, it was all-alloy with removable wet linings: as a diesel, a block of exactly the same shape was cast in iron to withstand the greater compressive stresses. Then, as the diesel market grew steadily through the 1980s, PSA also turned the little TU engine into the 1.4-litre TUD lightweight diesel.

RELATIONS PUBLIQUES CITROEN

Although the XUD series was a highly successful diesel engine for the PSA group from the 1980s onwards, a larger engine was needed for diesel versions of the group's 'prestige' models. The Citroën XM was launched in 1989 *with a range of engines which included this 2.1-litre, four-cylinder diesel with belt-driven SOHC and three valves per cylinder, short enough for transverse installation in this front-wheel-drive car. (Citroën)*

Renault introduced two fundamentally new engines in the 1980s, the more significant being the F-series engine which first saw the light of day in the Volvo 480! In 1986, it also appeared in the Renault 21 which became one of the handful of cars to offer engines installed either transversely (the F-series) or in-line (the bigger J-series), using different sub-frames designed to pick up on the same body mounting

exploit its Formula 1 racing programme, Renault produced a multitude of turbocharged production engines during the 1980s. Almost every Renault model, from the little 5 to the big 30, had its turbo derivative, and many of these cars were extremely fast – perhaps the most impressive of all was the 175bhp 21 2.0 Turbo of 1989. The company also began to look seriously at multivalve engines although only two of its new designs – the 16-valve R19 and the 12-valve (three valves per cylinder) 21TI – had reached production by the end of the decade. There was more, much more to come.

Italy

In Fiat's hands, Alfa Romeo passed through the 1980s with its three existing engine ranges – the flat-4 Alfasud unit, the classic 4-cylinder twin-cam and the new V6. All were developed, the flat-4 being opened out by stages to 1.7-litre capacity from its original 1.2, for the Sprint and the 33. The twin-cam cylinder head was modified to accommodate two sparking plugs per cylinder, with some increase in output and decrease in emissions, while the V6 was enlarged to a full 3 litres. Two Turbo versions of the twin-cam were developed, a 1.8-litre for the 75 (the Giulietta replacement) and a 2-litre for the bigger, newer 164.

Fiat's major move of the 1980s was to introduce a new small-capacity, all-iron, belt-driven SOHC engine which it called the FIRE (Fully Integrated Robotised Engine) because it had been designed for virtually 'hands-free' production in a new factory at Termoli on the Adriatic coast. The FIRE was also ruthlessly optimised, with many fewer parts than the old 903cc engine which it more or less replaced, at first in a high-volume version of the Uno. Efficiency through simplicity, rather than leading-edge technology, was its hallmark, although the castings used for its cylinder block and head were advanced, the best that Teksid – Fiat's very capable foundry subsidiary – could provide. As time went on the FIRE was developed into both larger and smaller capacity versions and used in other Fiat models.

When it came to high technology, Fiat in the 1980s was inclined to experiment. In particular it took a long, hard look at mechanical supercharging in the form of the Volumex compressor, a sort of spiral-wound evolution of the familiar Roots compressor. Development work was carried out by Abarth and versions of both the 131 and the Argenta (the face-lifted 132) were produced in significant numbers, but the strand of development

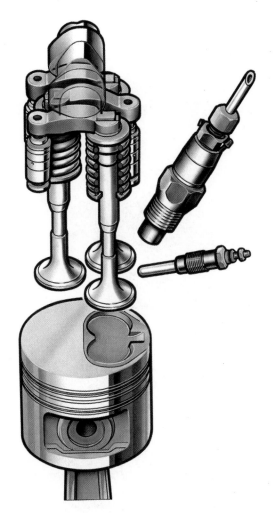

Interesting detail of the 2.1-litre Citroën diesel shows how the three valves per cylinder – two inlet, one exhaust – are operated via 'fingers' with hydraulic tappets from the single camshaft. As in most multi-valve diesel engines, the valves are upright – there is little scope for opposing them without reducing the compression ratio below the values needed for diesel combustion. Note also the positioning of the fuel injector, which injects into a pre-chamber where the glowplug is also sited. Note the shaped recess in the piston crown, not only for valve clearance but also to 'shape' the inflow from the pre-chamber. (Citroën)

points. The F-series was destined for a long life and a great deal of development, and its descendants still power many of Renault's 21st century models. The other new engine, the E-series, was a 1.4-litre unit designed for extremely high efficiency and initially fitted to the 19 when it was launched in 1988.

Possibly feeling the need both to justify and to

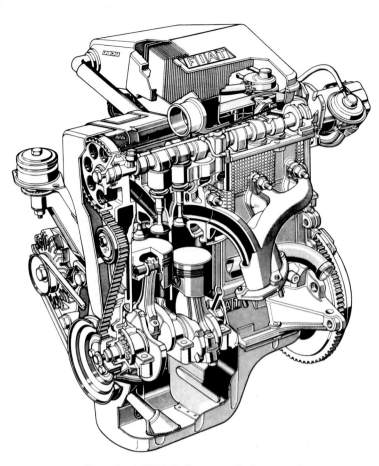

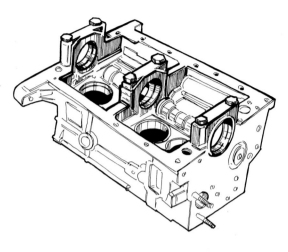

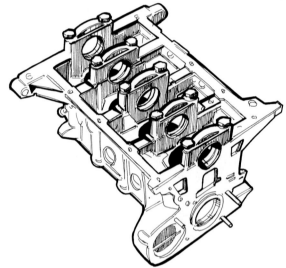

Above: Fiat's FIRE (Fully Integrated Robotised Engine) was ruthlessly simplified in order to be produced at low cost from an almost completely automated new factory at Termoli on the Adriatic coast. Note how almost everything in the engine is 'vertical' to facilitate machining prior to assembly; the belt-driven single overhead camshaft operates the vertical valves directly via bucket tappets. The unit shown is the smallest-capacity FIRE, of 750cc for the Panda, but larger engines look almost identical. (Fiat)

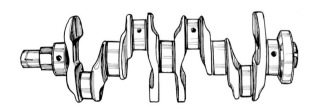

Above: Comparison of the upturned cylinder blocks for the 903cc OHV engine (top) and the FIRE (below) show more differences than the use of three main bearings in the older engine and five bearings for the new one. The way in which the parts count was reduced for the FIRE depended at least in part on the expertise of Fiat's Teksid foundry subsidiary, which cast many features into the complex and extremely stiff block. (Fiat)

Left: Another interesting comparison is between the crankshafts of the three-bearing 903cc and five-bearing FIRE. Although the latter is a more complex casting, it is also lighter, and bearing sizes were chosen to reduce friction losses as far as possible without sacrificing durability. Both crankshafts have four balance counterweights; a fully balanced shaft would have eight, one each side of each crankshaft throw. (Fiat)

petered out. In parallel came turbocharged versions of the Uno and of the big Croma, with 1.3 and 2.0-litre engines respectively. But it was only at the very end of the decade that Fiat announced its first 16-valve engine, a 1.6-litre unit for a high-performance version of the new Tipo which was launched in 1988.

With Italy being a country of high fuel taxation, Fiat took an early interest in diesel engines, as recounted in earlier chapters. In the early 1980s the company offered a 1.7-litre diesel-engined Strada and, more remarkably, a 1.3 diesel engine in the little 127 and the even smaller Panda. By the end of the decade it had moved on decisively to turbodiesels, with yet another small engine (this time a 1.4-litre) for the Uno 70TD, and a pioneering direct-injection 2-litre unit for the Croma.

It is worth noting, in passing, that Italy's policy of heavy annual taxation of cars with engines of more than 2-litre capacity led to some strange developments

A considerable contrast to the stark simplicity of the mass-produced Fiat FIRE is provided by the turbocharged 1.4-litre engine for the high performance Uno Turbo i.e. Although there are superficial similarities, for example the belt-driven SOHC operating the valves directly via bucket tappets, most of the detailing reveals that this is a performance-optimised engine – not least the cooling passages between the cylinder bores, and the way the valves are inclined rather than upright. And, of course, there is the substantial turbocharging system itself, and the use of electronic fuel injection rather than a carburettor. (Fiat)

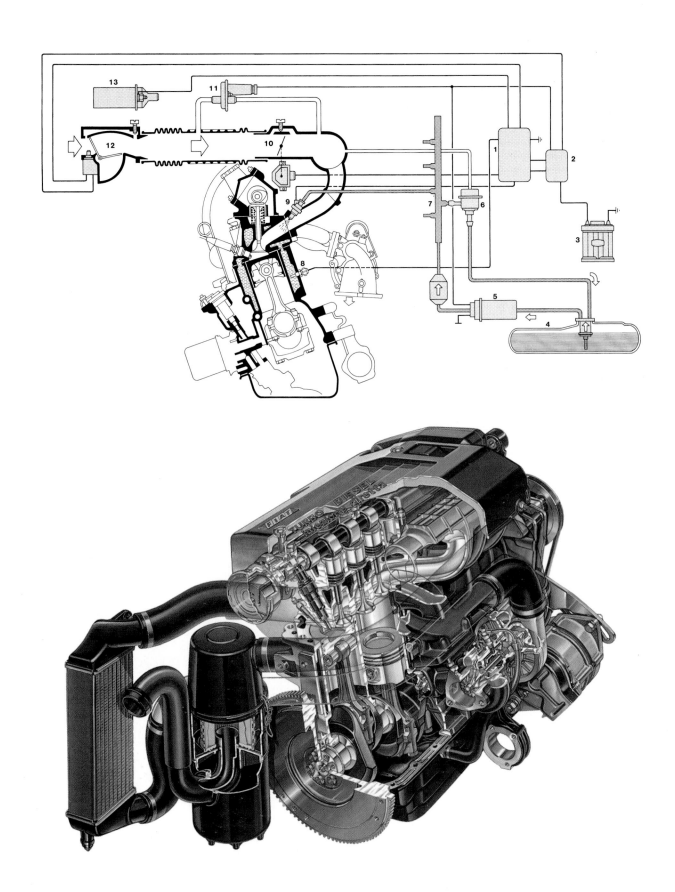

strictly for the home market. These included versions of the Ferrari 308 and the Maserati Biturbo with engine capacities reduced below 2,000cc, and turbocharged to restore something like a suitable level of performance. From Fiat's point of view, the policy meant that models with larger capacity engines were developed almost entirely for export.

A shrinking British presence

By the beginning of the 1980s, volume production engine development in Britain really involved only Austin-Rover – as the British Leyland group had become – and Jaguar. Austin-Rover, seeking a solution to the problem of its mainly elderly engine range, had already replaced the 1.8-litre B-series with the new O-series. In some respects at least this engine, in 1.7 and 2.0-litre sizes, with a common bore but different crankshafts, was a belt-driven SOHC conversion of the B-series with a new aluminium cylinder head, but there was rather more to it than that. The top-end design was Heron-head, with the camshaft directly operating the vertical, in-line valves and the combustion chambers formed entirely in the piston

crowns. A completely different approach was adopted for the next new engine, the 1.6-litre R-series, first seen in the Maestro: this was a development of the former E-series, still with a chain driven SOHC but with a revised combustion chamber shape. Alongside the R-series there continued the apparently ageless 1.3-litre A-series in its latest form. A year later, with the launch of the Montego, the smaller O-series engine had already metamorphosed into the 1.6-litre S-series which effectively replaced the R-series – the engine policy was becoming convoluted, although at least there was no lack of action.

Austin-Rover still had two more shots in its 1980s locker, both of them technically more significant. When the Rover 800 appeared in 1986 its top version was powered by a 2.5-litre 24-valve V6 engine developed by Honda, with whom Austin-Rover was by then deeply in partnership. However, the 820 versions were powered by a new 16-valve, 4-cylinder 2-litre engine, the M16, with belt-driven DOHC on an aluminium cylinder head. The M16 was actually a progressive development of the 2-litre O-series, and its lineage can therefore still be traced back to the B-series in some respects. With the M16 – and the Dolomite Sprint of the 1970s – Austin-Rover was actually involved in the multivalve scene rather earlier than some of its European competitors.

At the end of the 1980s there emerged a new small Austin-Rover engine, the K-series. This all-alloy unit was designed with its cylinder head, block and crankcase separately cast and assembled by means of long through-bolts pulling everything together, to minimise cost while also saving weight. The K-series was launched in 1.1 and 1.4-litre forms and with two different cylinder heads, one belt-driven SOHC driving in-line and inclined valves in a wedge-shaped combustion chamber, and the other belt-driven DOHC directly operating 16 valves. To avoid running the pistons directly in aluminium, the K-series was fitted with 'wet' cast-iron liners.

Austin-Rover did not ignore the 1980s fashion for turbocharging, producing versions of the Metro and the Maestro/Montego in turbocharged form, thus requiring turbo development programmes both for the A-series and the 2-litre O-series.

The 1980s saw Jaguar finally begin a slow farewell to the 6-cylinder DOHC XK engine. The company had begun the decade with a major reworking of its V12, adopting the special combustion chamber design developed by the Swiss engineer Michael May, with a higher compression ratio and better fuel economy. But the real change came in 1983 when the XJ-S coupé was announced with an all-new 6-cylinder engine, an all-alloy, chain-driven DOHC 24-valve unit of 3.6-litre capacity. This engine, the AJ6, was the result of a long story of evolution, with several changes of mind along the way, beginning in 1972. The AJ6 went into the new XJ40 saloon in 1986 and was accompanied by a 2.9-litre 12-valve SOHC derivative, which in effect used the same cylinder head as the V12 engine (but just one, obviously, rather than two).

The Japanese **race away**

The 1980s finally saw the Japanese manufacturers decide that in most respects, they had caught up with the Europeans and it was now time to race ahead. This was most evident in their approach to petrol engine design. By the end of the decade there was hardly a Japanese engine that did not have an SOHC engine operating opposed valves in a highly efficient combustion chamber. Most companies had tried three valves per cylinder as a first approach to the multivalve concept, but Japanese designers quickly decided that four valves per cylinder was the way to go. By 1984, this trend was well established and by 1989 the majority of Japanese petrol engines were using this layout. Only among the 1-litre engines, mostly for export models where cost was seen to matter most, was the change at all slow to come.

The only question, as the Japanese saw it, was how to arrange the valves. Toyota in particular decided to develop two distinct ranges of 4-valve engines, one 'economy' range in which the inlet and exhaust valves were at a narrow angle to each other – typically 25° or less – while the 'high-performance' range used an angle of around 45° or more. The narrow 'economy' angle created a compact and highly efficient combustion chamber, while the wide 'performance' angle made for straighter and easier gas flow through the engine, and made room for larger valves. Several of the economy engines used a single overhead camshaft to operate all 16 valves, while the performance engines were always DOHC. Almost to a man, Japanese designers decided toothed belts were the way to drive these camshafts. This was so even in Toyota's crowning glory of the decade, the exquisitely engineered all-alloy 32-valve 4.0-litre V8 for the

Lexus LS400. Although it used DOHC per cylinder bank, this engine used an economy head design with a 22° angle between the inlet and exhaust valves. With 245bhp and 353Nm of torque, it had enough performance anyway . . .

For their smaller engines, Japanese designers were very happy to use 3-cylinder engines. The Daihatsu Charade had extended the 3-cylinder options to include an extremely high-performance version with 12 valves and a turbocharger, as well as an extremely small diesel conversion; while Subaru also used three cylinders in the Justy. In part, the confidence to take this approach had been gained with the now highly developed cars in the microcar class, in which the permitted engine size had been increased from 360 to 550cc. Most of the cars in this class were now powered by tiny 3-cylinder engines, mainly multivalved – including one Mitsubishi model with five valves per cylinder – and sometimes turbocharged to take their output up to the 64bhp maximum allowed by the regulations. Among the larger cars, Subaru continued to develop its flat-4 engines (and added a flat-6 for the most powerful version of its XT coupé, together with a larger DOHC flat-4 for its big Legacy saloon). This engine layout had a special appeal for Subaru since it went so readily with four-wheel drive, one of the company's technical strong points. Mazda meanwhile pressed on with development of the Wankel engine, fitting twin-rotor engines to several of its 1980s models including the RX-7 sports car, but never making the breakthrough into large-scale production.

One trend which the Japanese had been slow to follow was the V6 engine, but they made up for it in the 1980s. First into the field was Nissan with a series of V6 engines for its Cedric/Gloria range (but, interestingly, the companion Skyline/Laurel family stayed with in-line 6-cylinder engines). By the end of the decade, all the major companies were offering V6 engines in a range of sizes up to 3-litre, and often with DOHC and 24 valves. The most advanced of these V6s was Honda's engine for the NS-X sports car, a 24-valve all-alloy unit which used the company's then newly developed VTEC system for altering valve timing and lift. VTEC was also used on the most powerful 16-valve, 1.6-litre 4-cylinder engines in the Honda Civic.

Honda had, on the other hand, set its face firmly against both turbocharging and the diesel engine, preferring to concentrate on making the naturally aspirated petrol engine as efficient and powerful

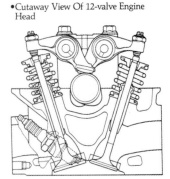

•Cutaway View Of 12-valve Engine Head

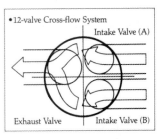

•12-valve Cross-flow System

Intake Valve (A)

Exhaust Valve   Intake Valve (B)

as possible. In this the company was definitely at odds with the rest of the Japanese industry. Turbocharged engines proliferated in all classes, often with neatly engineered twin-turbo installations in the larger units. As for passenger car diesels, the Japanese seemed eager to develop them simply because it would otherwise have left a gap in their technical armoury; but they had no significant home market demand to spur then on. Thus, there emerged a series of small and medium-sized diesels, mostly with four cylinders and none showing any great technical innovation, except for Mazda which made a determined attempt to establish the Swiss-invented Comprex pressure-wave supercharger as an alternative to turbocharging in its 4-cylinder, 2-litre diesel engine. But by the end of the decade, the Japanese still had not produced a diesel engine to rival the BMW or PSA units. Here, at least, Europe retained a technical lead. That could hardly be said in most other respects.

In summary

Yet again, a whole decade had seen the American engine designers moving in a different direction from their counterparts in Europe and Japan. To a large extent that was inevitable. The Americans had eyes

In the mid-1980s, Honda's mid-range models were powered by engines like this four-cylinder, 12-valve, 2-litre unit, announced in 1985 for the 1986 model-year Accord. Note the toothed-belt drive to the single overhead camshaft operating all twelve valves. This engine was fitted either with carburettors or with Honda's own electronic fuel injection system (PGM-FI) according to market. **(Honda)**

only for their home market and for their exhaust emission regulations. The Europeans and especially the Japanese proved they could meet those regulations when they needed to, but they also had to power cars for their own home markets where petrol was more expensive and fuel economy more highly valued. As the 1980s had progressed, the real price of gasoline at American pumps had steadily declined, taking with it any hope of a diesel market and any prospect of the US CAFE requirement becoming any more demanding. Thus, while the engine most frequently encountered in the USA was a 12-valve, pushrod OHV V6 of around 3.5-litre capacity, in Japan the OHC engine with four valves per cylinder was becoming the norm. The Europeans had the market, and therefore the technical lead in diesels – but also faced the prospect of European Community legislation on exhaust emissions becoming almost as tight as in the USA. Would that change the situation?

11 The 1990s
Emissions and **efficiency**

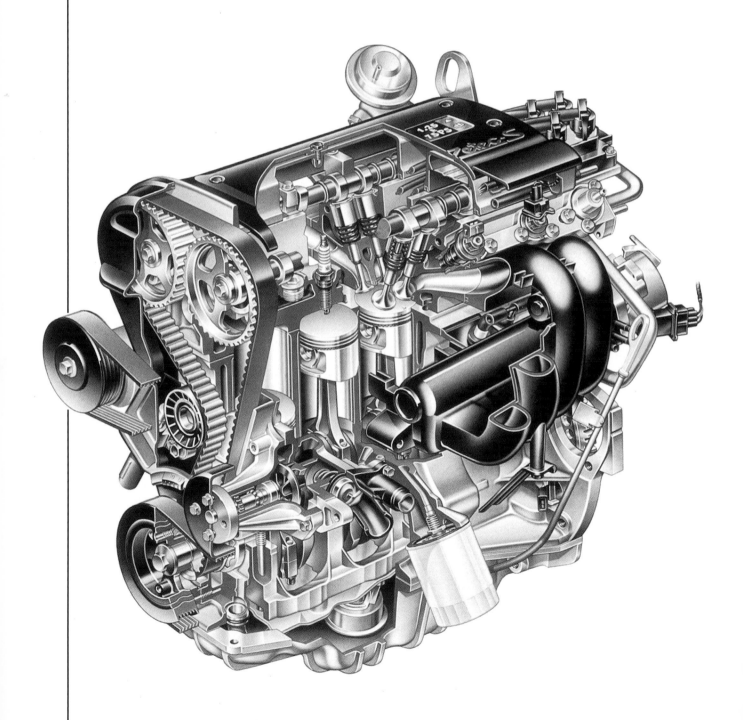

ow we come to the decade most of us remember – and possibly one of the most momentous in the history of the motor vehicle. Since 1990, the primacy of the internal combustion engine as its means of propulsion ceased to be taken for granted. At last, it had a serious rival: not the battery-powered electric vehicle – the 1990s were the years which saw that idea finally written-off, for most purposes, as the eagerly awaited 'miracle battery' predictably failed to materialise – but the fuel cell. In 1990, the idea of a fuel cell was something confined to the laboratory – or to spacecraft, or to huge emergency power packs for hospitals in earthquake-ridden Japan. By 2000, most engineers were prepared to grant that one day, the fuel cell would take over, and we would have a world of almost completely clean, electrically driven cars. When is that likely to happen? That is a question for the future, not for a history. But what was the reaction of the internal combustion engine design teams? In the main it was to rise to the challenge – to find ways of making engines cleaner, more efficient, smoother and quieter, but also more powerful and responsive. This was, in fact, the decade which set the agenda for IC engine design well into the 21st century.

Emissions: the looming European question

As we have seen, the 1980s saw engine designers in different parts of the world chase after different priorities. In the USA, the first priority was lower exhaust emissions. Nothing else mattered nearly as much, so long as the traditional American values of durability and 'lazy' power (which actually translates as torque, and for which there is 'no substitute for cubic inches') were maintained. In Japan, it often seemed as though people were chasing after technology for the sake of technology, although many Japanese engineers had a clearer vision than that: 'I want 100PS from a cubic foot of machinery', as Honda Chairman Nobuhiko Kawamoto once remarked to the author; and by the time he retired from his position, he had come fairly close. In Europe meanwhile, the emphasis had been on fuel economy, mainly because of the high taxes imposed by European governments. As we have seen, a second priority was to reduce costs while improving quality,

something which could be achieved by careful design. Controlling exhaust emissions came third – an important third, but third nonetheless.

That was about to change. In 1990, it was still possible to buy a new car in Europe equipped with a carburettor and relatively crude ignition. From January 1993, it would not be, because the European Community introduced a new set of exhaust emission regulations which made catalytic converters mandatory for petrol engines. Permitted emission levels were far lower under these new regulations, which brought Europe much closer to American and Japanese requirements. The regulations would apply from January 1992 for all newly designed cars; those already in production would not have to comply until January 1993. Among other things, this change meant that unleaded petrol would need to be made generally available, and that leaded petrol – incompatible with catalytic converters because it 'poisoned' them by overlaying the active surface of the catalyst – would eventually be phased out.

These regulations brought an end to any lingering hopes the European manufacturers might have had of being able to make small-capacity engines running 'lean burn' with an excess of air, without the added cost and higher fuel consumption resulting from the use of a three-way catalytic converter. There was no question that the lean-burn engines would have been more economical, since the catalyst would only work properly with the engine held at a strictly 'stoichiometric' mixture strength, in other words with just enough air to burn all the fuel – no more, no less, ensuring that the balance of exhaust gases would be exactly right (whatever happened in the engine) to reduce the harmful oxides of nitrogen to pure nitrogen and oxygen. The oxygen in turn oxidises the equally harmful carbon monoxide to 'harmless' carbon dioxide. Rather later, of course, carbon dioxide would itself become a villain, the main 'greenhouse gas'.

There was no question that lean-burn engines

Opposite: Ford's Zetec-SE engine was introduced in the mid-1990s as the group's standard small engine for European models, with a smallest displacement of 1.25 litres but capable of enlargement to 1.7 litres. This engine uses most of the advanced features which became common in Europe during the decade, including all light-alloy construction (including some magnesium), four vee-opposed valves per cylinder, direct acting camshafts, and careful attention paid to reducing both internal friction losses and noise. (Ford)

would have been more economical, because if there is more air than is strictly necessary in the combustion chamber, it is far more likely that all the available fuel will burn where it is supposed to. By general consent, an engine which is allowed to run lean-burn whenever the conditions are suitable can be up to 15 per cent more economical than one which is stoichiometric all the time.

There is, inevitably, more to it than that. The European mass-manufacturers may have been interested in economy, but they were certainly also interested in keeping costs as low as possible. So the lean-burn proponents generally failed to point out that no engine is lean-burn all the time: the higher the load, the closer it has to run to a stoichiometric mixture strength, which is reached at maximum power. And which engines are likely to run closest to full load most of the time? The smallest ones, the ones which struggle hardest to keep up with the traffic.

Beyond this, it was sadly evident that however low lean-burn engines might be in their emissions of

unburned hydrocarbon (HC) and carbon monoxide (CO), their downside was the formation of much larger amounts of oxides of nitrogen (NOx). This would not have been a problem if there had existed a catalytic converter able to reduce NOx to nitrogen and oxygen, but in 1990 the best researchers could offer were devices which gave results, but not especially good ones, in the laboratory. The challenge was to make the nitrogen part from the oxygen in conditions where there was already a lot of oxygen around: like hanging out washing to dry in the rain, as one engineer put it. Despite this challenge, NOx reduction devices were eventually developed – as we shall see – and carefully controlled lean-burn operation became possible, but in 1990 that wasn't the case.

The final argument which sank the European lean-burn argument was that the engines didn't work very well anyway. There were limits to how lean you could run an engine – how much extra air you could add to the mixture – without the risk of misfiring, in other words of a combustion chamber full of mixture sometimes failing to ignite. When that happened, as people with dodgy old engines and time-expired sparking plugs had known for years, the HC emissions could go sky-high. Occasionally, this would gather in the silencer until a stray spark fired the mixture therein, to cause a loud explosion and sometimes to blow the silencer apart. In a final technical fling, the Europeans worked at ways of detecting the onset of misfiring, as it was already possible to detect the onset of knocking. The most promising approach was to detect the small changes in engine speed which resulted from each missing power stroke, but the new regulations brought this line of research to a halt.

The regulations were carefully written to allow production of the diesel engine – which runs lean-burn except at full load, its power output controlled by the amount of fuel injected – to continue. In order to meet the lower emission limits imposed by 'Euro 1', light-duty diesel engines for cars became cleaner

In the early 1990s Ford and Orbital made a determined attempt to develop a two-stroke engine with acceptable exhaust emissions, fuel economy and durability, and fitted the three-cylinder, 1-litre engine seen here to a trial fleet of Fiestas. These demonstrated good performance and driveability, but these were really the least of the challenges involved, and ever tighter limits on NOx emissions in particular proved too much to overcome. (Ford)

simply by paying attention to detail design and, in some cases, by adding a simple one-way catalytic converter which ensured that any HC was properly reduced within the exhaust. The point was that the European regulations set a limit on the combined emission of HC and NOx: if you cleaned up the first, you had less cause to worry about the second. This situation would not last for ever, though, because the European legislators were already planning a tougher stance for 1996 and beyond. In fact, where emission regulations were concerned, Europe was setting out to catch up after years of lagging behind the rest of the developed world.

The tightening regulations also put a stop to any more thoughts about the superficially attractive alternative of the 2-stroke engine, compact and powerful in relation to its weight and bulk. In the early 1990s Ford worked with the engine developer Orbital to produce a small 3-cylinder 2-stroke engine which ran successfully in a trial fleet of Fiestas, but it could never hope consistently to achieve the NOx emission limits laid down in the European regulations of 1996, let alone the even tighter ones of 2000.

Petrol **problems**

The phasing-out of leaded petrol brought both benefits and problems. The benefit was to health, since by 1990 studies had made it clear that exhaust-borne lead was a hazard in some areas with heavy traffic. The problems were several. Some were simple to solve, as seen in the adoption of smaller filler necks and nozzles to prevent leaded petrol being put into catalyst-equipped cars by mistake (or occasionally, it seemed, out of sheer malevolence). More serious was the question of maintaining the octane rating of petrol at a reasonable level. In Britain, drivers had become used to having a choice of petrol with different 'star' system basically according to octane rating. (The fuel suppliers consistently argued that it wasn't good enough simply to advertise the RON itself since it wasn't the only important factor; but then the British do love to fudge such issues.) The old 5-star petrol, of RON 100 or better, had disappeared some time since, and the 1990s saw the remaining 'stars' vanish under the weight of a European standard which effectively established two categories, of around RON 95 for 'Premium' fuel and RON 98 for 'Super'. The distinction began to matter less, because as the decade progressed, more and more engines were able to adapt themselves to whatever fuel was put in the tank, by detecting the knock limit and retarding their ignition just enough to avoid it.

A more serious problem for older engines was that some of them had depended on the lead in petrol not only to raise the knock limit, but also to protect some highly loaded parts of the engine from wear, most notably the valve seats. Most poppet valves rotate to some extent as well as moving up and down, and when they close they exert a grinding effect on the seat. This is no problem if the valve seats are made of hard enough material, but in some older-generation engines they were not, but rather depended on a thin film of fuel-borne lead to act as a lubricant. With unleaded petrol, such engines soon suffer 'valve seat recession' as the valves began grinding away the seats, reducing valve clearance to the point where leakage could occur and the engine become ruined. Conversion kits were offered for some engines – at a price – but the simpler approach was to maintain a supply of leaded petrol for those cars that still needed it. Eventually, of course, the point was reached where there were far more cars on the road with catalytic converters, and elderly cars which needed leaded petrol became a minority (and still shrinking) interest at the bottom of the market. The most surprising thing, and a tribute to consumer ignorance or bloody-mindedness, was the number of owners whose 1980s cars would run perfectly happily on lead-free fuel, but who insisted on continuing to fill them with leaded – even when it was subjected to a penalising higher level of tax!

An associated problem then arose in that the single grade of unleaded petrol had an octane rating of around RON 96, not high enough for some 1980s (and earlier) cars with high compression engines. In order to survive, these had to be detuned, losing the edge of their performance. Some owners, taking their cue from the USA, instead added expensive 'octane improvers' to their fuel. By the end of the decade, lead in petrol was completely banned in most European countries, but by then the fuel suppliers had evolved 'lead replacement petrol' (LRP) which provided the same level of mechanical protection without using lead – but still only at RON 96. By this time, however, the suppliers were becoming more concerned with other challenges, such as 'reformulating' petrol to help reduce emissions, and removing sulphur to avoid 'poisoning' some of the new emission control devices being introduced. By and large, though, these were issues for the 21st century.

The evolution of
engine design

By 1990, the world of engine design seemed to have split into three. In the USA, if one left aside the question of exhaust emission control, most engines were still 'old fashioned', with pushrod-operated overhead valves and only two valves per cylinder. Low cost and high reliability remained higher priorities than outright efficiency or fuel economy. At the other extreme, the Japanese car manufacturers had eagerly developed engines with four valves per cylinder and other advanced features. Certainly, by 1990 any little company that specialised in making pushrods for Japanese engines had either diversified or gone out of business. Europe sat midway between the two, in some respects. Its engineers wanted to move ahead, chasing efficiency in the same way at the Japanese – squeezing the most out of the least, so to speak. Yet as we have seen, Europe was also the last bastion of the carburettor, because its exhaust emission regulations had yet to catch up. The truth was that by 1990, European engineers were generally honing their plans for more advanced engines, but wanted to wait until the market had settled down post-1992 and 'Euro 1'.

Progress in the USA

In the USA, the most popular engine configuration for passenger cars was now the V6, of 3-litre capacity and upwards, installed transversely in front-driven vehicles. The in-line 4-cylinder engine was reserved for entry level models from the US 'big three'. The stalwart V8, now mostly of around 5-litre capacity, was used mainly in a shrinking number of 'full-size' rear-driven models like the Chevrolet Impala and Ford Crown Victoria. Before accepting this as the American picture, however, two things are worth noting. One is that US-based car production now included a very large number of vehicles from the Toyota, Nissan and Honda factories which had been established there, and far more of these cars had advanced 4-cylinder engines. The other is that a large part of the US market was beginning to switch from conventional saloon cars to big 4WD 'recreational vehicles' (RVs) or to light pickup trucks, very popular in rural areas and increasingly offered with luxury specification – pickup trucks with hi-fi and air conditioning.

The important point was that such vehicles were not subject to the same stringent exhaust emission limits, or fuel economy requirements, as cars: they were indeed classified as 'light trucks' to which higher limits applied, if indeed there were limits at all. It was only at the end of the decade that light trucks in the USA became subject to a CAFE (Corporate Average Fuel Economy) requirement, and then it was set at 20.7mpg compared with 27.5mpg for cars. Thus the traditional American V8 did not die, it simply migrated from cars to light trucks which had been developed to offer 'muscle-car' levels of performance. For years through the 1990s, the Ford Model A light truck was actually the best-selling privately owned vehicle in the USA (and the best-selling car, much of the time, was the Honda Accord). Thus if one looks at engine production figures in the USA (and Canada, where Ford and GM maintained some large engine factories) through the 1990s, the V8s were still churned out in huge numbers. In 1997, the GM engine plant in Flint, Michigan, produced nearly 900,000 big V8s – backed by a further 450,000 from St Catherine's, Ontario. In the same year, Ford's V8 output from just two plants, at Romeo, Michigan and Windsor, Ontario, ran to well over a million. These were all big 'traditional' engines, the majority of them installed (along with some V10s) in light trucks, which millions of Americans were using as their main means of transport.

Eventually, the Americans too began building more engines with four valves per cylinder, including the General Motors Northstar DOHC 32V V8 which was seen as revolutionary when it first appeared and which became a mainstay of the Cadillac range, with other applications elsewhere. Lower down the size range, the Americans also realised they could develop high-technology V6 engines which would be equally suitable for their own mid-range cars and for European luxury models. This thinking gave rise to the Ford Duratec V6, as fitted to the European Mondeo and to the American Taurus. A DOHC 24V engine with capacities from 2.5 to 3.5-litres, the Duratec also found its way, in modified form, into the new smaller Jaguar models, alongside the Jaguar 4-litres, DOHC 32-valve V8. Meanwhile at General Motors, the closely equivalent Ecotec V6 range was developed for use both in Europe (Opel and Saab) and in the USA. By the end of the century, 4-valve heads were becoming far more

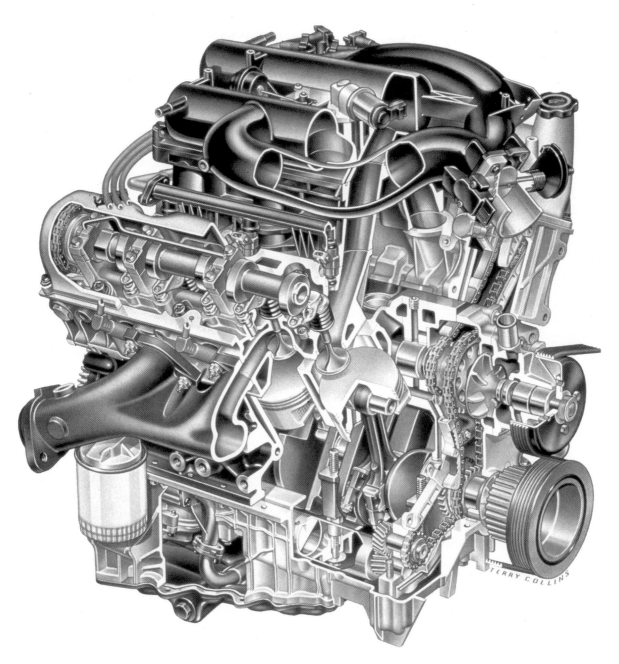

common in the USA, and Chrysler was using nothing else, except for the huge pushrod 8-litre V10 engine in the Viper sports car. Yet alongside, at GM and Ford, there remained some stalwart pushrod OHV V6 and V8 engines powering either 'base' car models or SUVs (sport-utility vehicles). And in a further interesting move, at the very end of the decade, GM decided to return to the straight-6 configuration for its new Vortec engine range, now with DOHC and 24 valves, for some of its SUVs.

The American taste for large, tough light trucks and Sport Utility Vehicles (SUVs) instead of conventional cars meant that engines like this Ford 4-litre V6, fitted to the Explorer SUV and other models, were produced in increasingly large numbers. The engine uses a single chain-driven camshaft per cylinder bank, with valve operation via fingers with hydraulic tappets, and just two in-line valves per cylinder. The large intake plenum chamber and long inlet manifold ducts show the care which went into optimising mid-range torque, important in an SUV. (Ford)

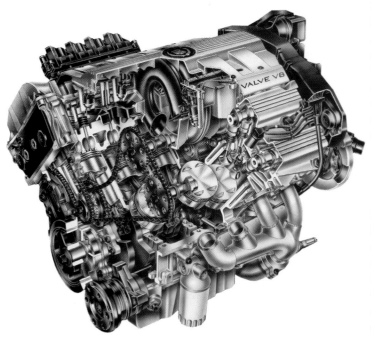

In 1992 General Motors launched a truly advanced V8 engine with four valves per cylinder, and called it the 'Northstar'. This cutaway view shows its basic construction with an alloy block fitted with cast-in-place cast-iron liners, single chain drive to the twin overhead camshafts per bank, and flat-topped pistons with cut-outs for valve clearance. As in most alloy-block engines, a substantial underframe beneath the block itself adds stiffness and houses the lower halves of the main bearings. (GM)

Tranverse cross-section of GM Northstar engine more clearly shows the conventional 90-degree angle between cylinder banks, and the layout of the valve gear and combustion chamber. Note the direct operation of the valves via bucket tappets – familiar practice in Europe but rare in American production engines. The Northstar was designed for transverse installation in large front-wheel-drive cars, and its detail layout is governed by the need for minimum length. (GM)

Technical **trends**

Aside from the USA, which continued to be something of a special case, the 1990s produced many interesting technical trends to contribute to internal combustion engine efficiency. The features were not always new. Some of them had been around for a long time, but the 1990s was the period in which they were suddenly seen as practical and worth doing. Many of them were also relatively subtle. The 1970s and 1980s had seen wide adoption of obvious things like four valves per cylinder and turbocharging. The 1990s produced a more varied list which included variable valve timing, variable inlet manifold geometry and lean-burn operation with direct petrol injection, together with the arrival of the common-rail diesel engine.

As mentioned in an earlier chapter, variable valve timing had been in production since the 1970s – and had been experimented with long before that – but suddenly in the 1990s it became a valuable tool for reducing exhaust emissions without loss of output or driveability, and indeed also for improving engine performance by combining the characteristics of 'peaky' high-speed, high power output engines with those of units designed more for mid-range torque. At first, valve timing variators tended to be fitted only to the inlet camshaft (the widespread adoption of the twin-cam layout had made variable valve timing much easier) and were often two-position, switching from one timing to another at a set speed and load. Advances in electronic engine management, and in the design of components, quickly made it possible to achieve continuously variable valve timing (within wide limits) according to need, and before long some

The 1990s saw an increasing willingness, especially in Europe, to engineer complex air intake systems to boost torque output over a wide spread of speeds. This arrangement, seen in the V6 engine fitted to the Peugeot 607, uses three electrically controlled, pneumatically operated valves to create three different intake duct lengths according to engine speed, switching automatically as each threshold is crossed. (Peugeot)

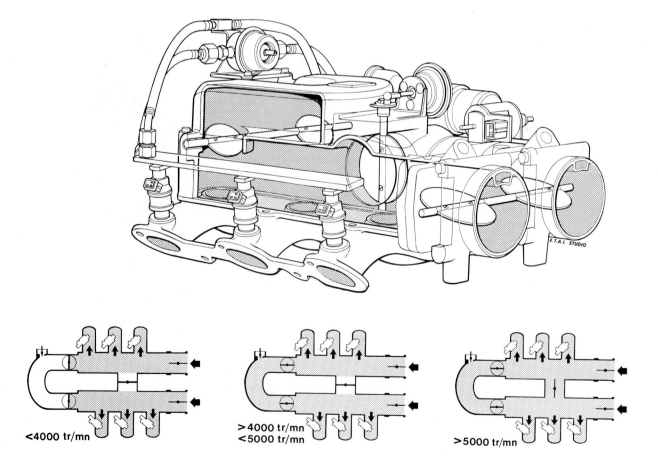

<4000 tr/mn

>4000 tr/mn
<5000 tr/mn

>5000 tr/mn

of the up-market manufacturers, notably BMW and Mercedes, began fitting variators to the exhaust camshaft as well.

Variable inlet manifold geometry is even more subtle, in effect tuning the acoustics of the manifold to optimise torque at different engine speeds. At high speed and load, short inlet ducts are best, but at moderate speeds they should ideally be much longer. It seems to have been the Opel in-line 6-cylinder 24V engine, mentioned in the previous chapter, which first made serious use of the idea, but within a year or two, many engine designers had followed suit. The accepted technique was to use a diverter valve (or series of valves) which would either force the air to travel through a long duct or allow it to 'short-circuit' at high speed.

By the mid-1960s, the problems of lean-burn, already referred to, had been largely overcome, at least in the laboratory. The answer to misfiring lay in two areas, the close (and variable) control of airflow within the cylinder during the compression stroke, and the sheer accuracy of control and speed of reaction which could now be achieved with modern sensors and electronic engine management systems. Control of airflow was made easier with two inlet ports per cylinder (in other words, in a 4-valve head) because the two ports could be made different in shape – one high-swirl and the other straight-through – and the latter could be shut off by a valve at low load, which is when lean-burn can be used. There is no point in designing an engine to operate lean-burn at maximum power, since the end result would be an engine which was larger and heavier than necessary). With extremely high swirl and accurate control, the technique which completed the picture was direct fuel injection, in a pattern directed carefully into the middle of the swirl motion. At last, researchers who had been studying the concept for 30 years found their dreams realised – and it proved possible, in the right conditions, to run engines with quite astonishingly lean mixtures, with air:fuel ratios of 40:1 or more. The remaining trick was to switch smoothly between this lean-burn operating state and a homogenous, stoichiometric mixture as soon as the driver hit the floor with the accelerator pedal . . .

As mentioned in the previous chapter, diesel engines with turbocharging and direct injection had been around in the 1980s, but during the 1990s it became ever less common to find a passenger car diesel engine that was not turbocharged. Diesels take very happily to turbocharging, since they do not have

to worry about a knock-limit as the diesel combustion process is started by what amounts to controlled detonation, and because their exhausts run cooler, giving the turbocharger components an easier time. It is fair to say that when enthusiasm for turbocharged petrol engines waned for several years during the 1990s, as people began to worry about high fuel consumption and doubtful durability, and the number of models on offer was greatly reduced, it was the diesel which mainly kept work on advanced turbochargers going. This work included the development of ever smaller units – the smaller, the lighter, therefore the less inertia and the faster the response to the accelerator, at the cost of running the rotor at astonishingly high speeds at full output – and into variable-geometry units which achieved much the same effect through greater complication, including the need for yet another controlling output from the engine management system.

Meanwhile, diesels moved on very quickly from direct fuel injection into the main combustion chamber, with injection pulses supplied from a rotary multi-piston pump, to the 'common-rail' principle, in which pressure, maintained in a supply gallery or rail is permanently connected to the injectors, which are individually operated by electronic control. Among other things this allows the injection to be made in stages rather than all at once, and 'pilot injection' has made common-rail diesels much quieter and more refined. At the same time the very high pressures which can be achieved with the common-rail system means that more fuel can be supplied in a given time, allowing engines to be more powerful, while fuel spray patterns can also be finely shaped, improving exhaust emissions.

4-valve cylinder heads: after 1990

Some provisos have to be made about the generally advanced standard of Japanese engine design in the early 1990s. While it is true that by 1990 the majority of Japanese engines had four valves per cylinder (although not always with twin overhead camshafts) and multipoint fuel injection, the Japanese were still making cars with old-technology power units, mainly for export to some markets – including, at that time, Europe – with less stringent emissions standards. In any case, the Japanese had not switched to 4-valve cylinder heads overnight, but had begun with their medium-sized and larger engines. By 1990, it was

An excellent example of the modern Japanese approach to engine design for small and medium cars is seen in the 1.6-litre, four-cylinder, 16-valve SOHC engine for the Civic series, equipped with one version of Honda's VTEC system for varying valve timing and lift (there are three such systems, with choice depending on application and requirement). The SOHC layout seen here is biased towards fuel economy rather than outright power, with a narrower angle between the valves than would be the case with a DOHC layout. (Honda)

almost impossible to find a 2-litre Japanese petrol engine with anything but a 4-valve head, but a number of the smaller mainstream Japanese cars were powered by engines with three valves per cylinder.

Entry-level versions of the then-current Nissan Sunny and of the Toyota Tercel and Corolla were thus powered, and indeed, early in the decade Mitsubishi launched new 4-cylinder, 12-valve engines, of 1.3 and 1.5-litre capacity, for the Colt and Lancer range. This approach did not last long, however, and Mitsubishi joined Nissan and Toyota in moving to 4-valve heads for almost everything. In some cases the 3-valve technology was passed on to industrial partners in Korea (Hyundai) and Malaysia (Proton) rather than be wasted. While this was going on, the engine size limit for the remarkable Japanese class of microcars was again increased, this time to 660cc, but still not enough to make them easy to sell outside the Japanese home market.

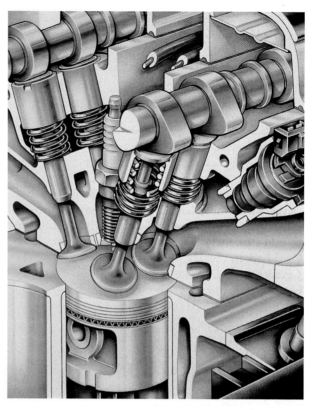

Among the larger Japanese engines, opinion still seemed to be divided between the merits of the straight-6 and V6. During the late 1980s, Honda had introduced a V6 for the Legend, but also an in-line 5-cylinder engine for some of its upper-mid range models, although these never came to Europe. Mitsubishi had committed to the V6, but Nissan and Toyota continued to offer a choice of V6 or in-line configuration, according to which model you bought. Nissan in particular introduced one very successful 24-valve DOHC V6, the QX series, in the mid-1990s, using it in many of its own models – including those built in the USA – and eventually also supplying it to Renault. For the top ends of their ranges, both Nissan and Toyota (or alternatively, Infiniti and Lexus, since these two artificially created luxury brands were now very much in business) had also created V8s. Toyota even went a stage further, in 1997, by introducing a DOHC 48-valve 5-litre (81 x 80.8mm, 4,996cc, 280bhp) V12, but by this time large and extravagant engines were falling out of favour (Jaguar had already dropped its long-running V12) and consequently the Toyota unit was introduced with little fanfare and confined to the home-market Century.

The Japanese engineers were among those most interested in the idea of the lean-burn engine with direct petrol injection, and in 1996 both Mitsubishi and Toyota launched such units, differing in some interesting details. For instance, Mitsubishi shaped its airflow through horizontal 'tumble', while Toyota chose vertical swirl. In both cases, NOx emissions continued to be a problem and the engines needed special catalytic converters to reduce them. Unfortunately these units were easily 'poisoned' by any sulphur impurity in fuel and the cars could only be sold where low-sulphur petrol was available. Despite this drawback, Mitsubishi in particular persevered and gradually extended its GDI (gasoline direct injection) principle to all engine sizes, from 660cc for its microcar to the 3.5-litre V6 for its

Shogun SUV. Eventually, most of the other Japanese manufacturers acknowledged the trend and joined it with interpretations of their own.

Europe – chasing emissions and efficiency

The situation in Europe was less easily defined, partly because so many manufacturers were still operating independently, and because so many of them had long histories. As already observed, European designers were tending to bide their time. They wanted to make sure the switch to catalytic converters was well under control before they moved with any real enthusiasm towards 4-valve heads and other advanced features. Nowhere was this more evident than among Europe's American-owned manufacturers. In 1990, Ford of Europe offered only one limited-production engine with four valves per cylinder (in the Sierra Cosworth), despite having stuck a toe in the water 20 years previously with the BDA version of the first-series Escort. True, it had taken to offering the Sierra and the Scorpio with a twin overhead camshaft version of its 2-

litre, 4-cylinder in-line engine, but still only with eight valves. Meanwhile, GM Europe had developed two 4-valve production engines, a 2-litre 4-cylinder unit (first seen in 1987) which went into sporting versions of the Opel Kadett/Vauxhall Astra and Opel Vectra/Vauxhall Cavalier, as well as the Calibra. As already discussed, both of the American-owned groups then went into partnership with their parents in the development of mid-range 24-valve V6 engines – the Duratec, which Ford sourced from its Cleveland plant in the USA, while GM decided to create a European production line at Ellesmere Port for the Ecotec V6. For smaller cars, Ford developed two new families of DOHC 16-valve 4-cylinder engine, the Zetec-E and the smaller, lighter Zetec-SE. For its part, GM evolved its Family One and Family Two engines into a unified range of Ecotec engines, all with four valves per cylinder, including a 3-cylinder, 12-valve, 1.0-litre unit for the Corsa. Opel was also early in the field with an advanced 16-valve direct-injection diesel engine.

Volkswagen had, more or less by popular demand, prepared a version of the 1.8-litre Golf GTI engine with a 16-valve head, delivering 129PS at 5,800rpm compared with the 107PS at 5,400rpm of the 8-valve version. (Comparisons are valid in this case because the 16-valve engine really was a fairly straightforward adaptation of the existing 8-valve unit.) Moving further into the 1990s, VW then developed a version of the 1.8-litre 4-cylinder engine to use five valves (three inlet, two exhaust) per cylinder, delivering 150bhp with the aid of turbocharging. At the same time the company re-invented the Lancia principle of the compact narrow-vee engine, developing a 2.8-litre V6 engine with just 15° between its interwoven cylinder banks. In an even more remarkable move, VW later lopped a single cylinder from this engine to produce a narrow-angle V5 of 2.3-litre capacity, a move which would surely have surprised Lancia himself – but it seemed to work well enough. Not content with this, VW busied itself towards the end of

the 1990s with work on further unusual engine configurations, including a W12. On the turbodiesel front, VW worked only with 4-cylinder engines, quickly moving to direct injection and then, creating an exception to the near-universal move to common-rail, adopted the alternative technology of the unit injection pump – an individual cam-operated high-pressure pump for each cylinder. Audi on the other hand developed its own range of high-output V6 direct-injection diesel engines for its larger cars, while adopting VW's five-valve per cylinder layout for many of its larger petrol engines, including a 2.7-litre 30-valve V6 and a 4.2-litre 40-valve V8.

BMW started the 1990s still faithful to the in-line 6-cylinder layout, single or doubled as the V12. It continued to develop both, but it was clear that for some purposes, the top 3.3-litre six was too small and the V12 was too big and expensive. Consequently, BMW bowed to the inevitable and developed a family of all-alloy DOHC 32-valve V8s with capacities from 3.5 up to 4.9 litres, mainly for the X5 SUV and for its larger specialised sports cars. Meanwhile, the company undertook the development of an all-new common-rail turbodiesel, a 6-cylinder, 2.9-litre 24-valve engine which attracted much admiration when it was launched, not only for its output of 193bhp but for its operating refinement. A 2-litre 4-cylinder

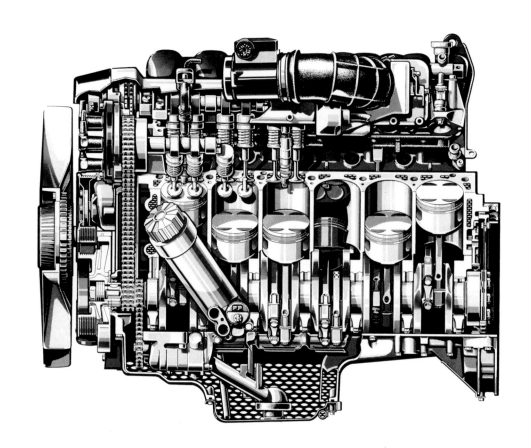

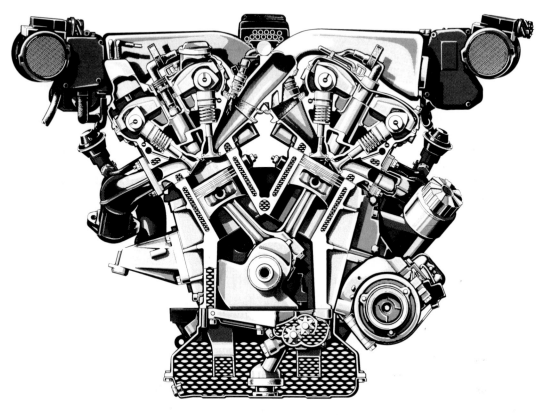

stablemate followed, and then a 3.9-litre 32-valve V8 delivering 245bhp – an output which would not have disgraced a petrol engine less than ten years previously.

While BMW had not considered a V6 engine at any price, in 1996 it astonished many onlookers by abandoning its highly developed straight-6 range in favour of a new family of all-alloy V6s with capacities of 2.6 and 3.2-litres. Even more remarkable was the company's careful choice, following much research, of a layout with three valves per cylinder (two inlet, one exhaust) and with two sparking plugs per cylinder, one opposite each inlet valve. Major advantages were claimed especially in terms of exhaust emissions performance. This development followed Mercedes' introduction, early in the decade, of its first ever automotive V12 engine, a 6-litre, DOHC 48-valve unit, as the top-range option for the big S-class. Through the 1990s, Mercedes moved first to adopt four valves per cylinder for its V8 engines, then by degrees switched its entire upper-engine range to the three valves per cylinder arrangement introduced with the V6s. Only the 4-cylinder engines retained the four-valve layout. Mercedes remained wary of turbocharging for petrol engines, even for its high-output AMG conversions, and preferred instead to offer some of its smaller engines in mechanically supercharged form, using a Roots-type blower supplied by Eaton.

There were no V6 diesels, however. Mercedes remained faithful to its 'modular' range of 4, 5 and 6-cylinder diesels through the 1990s, increasing the three capacities to 2.2, 2.7 and 3.2 litres, all with turbocharging, four valves per cylinder and common-rail technology, the 3.2-litre unit delivering 197bhp. Late in the decade, the icing on Mercedes' diesel cake emerged in the form of the 4-litre 32-valve V8 turbodiesel for the S-class, producing 250bhp and thus marginally out-gunning BMW.

In Sweden, the decade was notable for the swallowing of both the country's car manufacturers, Saab by General Motors and Volvo by Ford. Neither showed much sign of relinquishing its independence in matters of engine design, with Saab pursuing its turbo principles to the extent of a 230bhp version of the 2.3-litre 16-valve engine, and also taking the GM Ecotec V6 and suggesting some interesting ways of applying turbocharging to that unit. Volvo meanwhile had firmly established a family of solidly engineered 4, 5 and 6-cylinder in-line power units – managing to fit the 5-cylinder transversely into the 850 (later the S70), and the 6-cylinder into the S80, with the aid of extremely compact front-drive transmissions. By the later 1990s, Volvo had also recovered its taste for turbocharging, and especially for 'low pressure turbocharging' the aim of which was more to improve mid-range torque and engine efficiency than to boost top-end output. In the same way, Saab now varied the maximum boost on its 4-cylinder Turbo engines from version to version, depending on the target market.

Elsewhere in Europe

Fiat, not to be outdone where hot hatches were concerned, prepared a 16-valve version of its then-new Tipo, with a 1.8-litre version delivering 138PS. Fiat Auto – now of course including Alfa Romeo as well as Lancia – had a long history of enthusiasm for twin overhead camshafts, which continued in most Alfas and in the big Lancia Thema; 1990 saw the introduction of 4-valve heads for the 2-litre 4-cylinder engine in the Thema and also, intriguingly, for a version of the 1.7-litre flat-4 boxer engine in the Alfa 33, that somewhat maligned successor to the Alfasud. The days of the flat-4 engine were numbered, however, as a new range of Alfa Romeo models was prepared which would share their basic engine designs with Fiat and Lancia.

The in-line 4-cylinder Alfa Romeo engines, with their classic twin-cam cylinder heads of basic design dating back to the 1960s, had to wait a while before they joined the 16-valve club, not least because marketing insisted some means be found of marrying four valves per cylinder with the 'Twin Spark' cachet which had become part of the Alfa Romeo image. At the top of the Fiat Auto range, the early 1990s briefly saw the Lancia Thema 8.32, with a jewel of a 2.9-litre, 32-valve V8 engine developed by Ferrari, offering what now seems a modest 215PS (73PS per litre was seen differently at the time) at 6,750rpm.

Fiat was working towards a situation where, with some blurring of the edges, the lower end of its engine

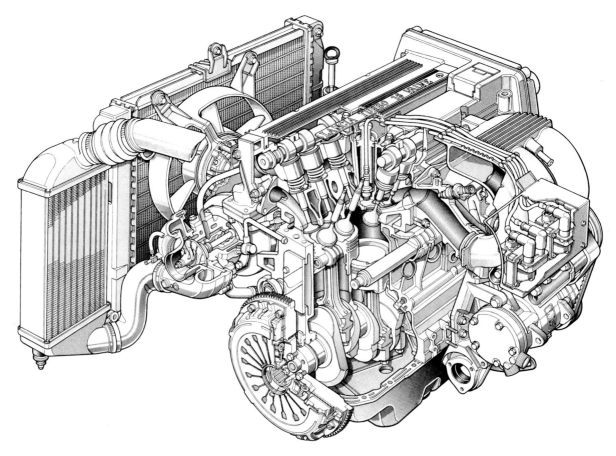

Not to be outdone in the specific power race, Fiat Auto developed this 2-litre 16-valve turbocharged engine producing 185bhp for its high-performance mid-sized models. Points to note in this remarkably detailed drawing include the turbocharger, itself complete with cooling system for its bearings, the air intercooler (to the left of the main radiator), and one of the two balancer shafts emerging from beneath the induction system. Note also the shape and short length of the induction passage, and the position of the injector. (Fiat Auto)

range would be based on the FIRE engine described earlier, while the top end would be catered for by variations on the Alfa Romeo V6, in differing capacities and with 24 valves. The middle ground was to be occupied by a family of 'modular' 4 and 5-cylinder in-line engines, all capable of being machined on the same line and all produced from a new factory at Pratola Serra, east of Naples. These engines spanned a wide range of capacities from 1.4-litres upwards (the FIRE being difficult to enlarge beyond 1,250cc) to a 20-valve 2.4-litre, delivering 160bhp. Early in the decade, Fiat had seemed keen on

turbocharged petrol engines with the Uno Turbo, the Lancia Delta Turbo, and turbo versions of almost everything in the range with a 2-litre engine. As pointed out in the previous chapter, Italian vehicle taxation heavily penalised any larger engine, so a 2-litre turbo was a good way of offering high performance without the penalty, a solution sought in the Alfa 75 and 164, the Fiat Croma, and the Lancia Thema. As the decade progressed this enthusiasm evaporated, except of course for turbodiesels. Fiat devoted an increasing proportion of its development effort to diesels and was actually the first manufacturer to put a common-rail engine on sale, in the form of the 140bhp 2.3-litre 5-cylinder JTD engine in the Alfa Romeo 156, although it was a close-run thing.

Among the French manufacturers, 1990 offered little evidence of enthusiasm for the four-valve layout. PSA (Peugeot-Citroën) powered their entire ranges with versions of just three petrol engines, if one excepts Citroën's flat-twin, air-cooled A-series which was soon to reach the end of its long life. The small engines, from 954cc upwards, were the Peugeot-developed TU series, the mid-range units from 1.6-litres upwards were the XU-series, and the top of the range was powered (in very small numbers) by the final 3-litre version of the PRV 3-litre V6. In 1990, the only PSA 4-valve head to have emerged was fitted to a version of the 1.9-litre XU engine, to create the Peugeot 405 Mi16, and a matching Citroën BX 16V. Renault had just one 4-valve engine, a derivative of the F-series for installation in a 16-valve version of the 19, to produce a rival for the high-powered Fiat Tipo 16V and Volkswagen Golf GTI 16V. Renault's engine delivered a claimed 140PS at no less than 6,500rpm; no wonder many people gained the impression in those days that 16-valve engines were inevitably high-revving screamers suitable only for sports-minded drivers.

Yet again, as the decade progressed, the French moved steadily towards evolving a range of 4-cylinder, 16-valve engines. The ever-pragmatic PSA was slowest, and many of its smaller engines in the TU series still had eight valves by the end of the century. But the TU had also been cleverly enlarged to 1.6-litre capacity – something its original design team surely never had in mind – and in this form it was given DOHC and 16 valves, to deliver 109bhp. The larger XU engine series was given over almost entirely to 16-valve configuration. As for diesel engines, PSA kept on with its 1.9-litre XUD series for an amazingly long time, the Tremery factory eventually producing up to a million a year in addition to the petrol versions. Then, quite suddenly it seemed, PSA played leap-frog with the technology, going directly from the indirect-injection XUD to the common-rail DW series, with no intervening stage of simple direct injection. There was no doubt, though, that development had been thorough and that the DW worked extremely well, with outstanding economy.

Renault spent much of the early 1990s carefully preparing its ground. It continued to develop those engines, the C, E, F and J-series which had in some cases appeared a long time previously, but where petrol engines were concerned its designers had embarked on the rather unusual course of creating a range of engines carefully tailored to specific needs, consequently with minimum weight and bulk but also, inevitably, with limited 'stretch' compared with many rivals. For the most part these new 4-cylinder engines were 16-valve units, although where low cost was a special concern, simplified 8-valve versions were also prepared. The smallest of these new engines was the nominally 1.2-litre D-series, while the K-series provided engines of 1.4 and 1.6-litre

capacity. These new engines embodied many technical features new to Renault, such as roller cam followers and weight-saving hollow camshafts. Meanwhile, the F-series, which had begun life many years previously in the Volvo 480 but had proved almost infinitely adaptable, served to fill the 1.8 and 2.0-litre slots. By this time there was actually nothing left of the original engine, in the manner of George Washington's axe, but it continued to serve not only as a high-output petrol engine but also as a diesel – steadily developed through a direct injection phase and into common-rail – and as Renault's direct-injection petrol (IDE) engine, the first lean-burn, direct injection engine to appear in Europe.

PSA and Renault also worked together on the development of an all-new, all-alloy 3-litre V6 engine, to replaced the little-loved PRV unit. The new engine – L-series in Renault terms – was a proper 60° V6, hence with no balance problems, and was a DOHC 24-valve design, for larger cars including the Peugeot 406 and 607, and the Renault Laguna and Espace.

UK in the 1990s

There was sadly little left of the independent UK engine development story after 1990. The K-series 'aluminium sandwich' engine continued in development and was successfully enlarged as far as 1.8-litres for the MGF sports car, also being fitted with an ingenious mechanism for varying both valve timing and lift in the process. The three final moves of the Rover development team were to adapt the layered K-series construction principle to an outstandingly light and compact 2.5-litre KV6 engine, and to engineer two strong diesel engines, the 2-litre L-series for car use and a 2.5-litre 5-cylinder turbodiesel for the Land Rover Discovery. Alongside, development continued on the seemingly ageless alloy V8, now opened out to a capacity of 4.6 litres (94 x 82mm, 4,552cc, 218bhp) for the Range Rover.

Jaguar's AJ6 engine sadly enjoyed a limited life. Having been launched in the 1980s in 2.9 and 3.6-litre form, it saw the 2.9-litre enlarged to 3.2-litre capacity for a revised XJ6 range, and the 3.6 in turn enlarged to a full 4 litres for an update of the XJ-S. In 1993, the long-serving V12 was enlarged to 6-litre capacity for the XJ V12 saloon, although the engine remained a 2-valve unit throughout its life, except in the prototype shop. The following year, the 4-litre AJ6 engine became the AJ16 with wide-ranging improvements, and yet the end was nigh, for in 1996

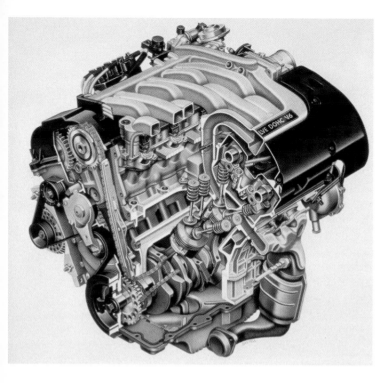

A 'mid-Atlantic' engine with several European applications, Ford's Duratec V6 was developed as a 2.5-litre 24-valve V6 capable of enlargement at least to 3-litre capacity. In Ford's European range it is fitted to the Mondeo and also forms the basis of the V6 engine used in the Jaguar X-type. Its design approach is typical 1990s, with evidence of special concern for durability (hence the name) and low maintenance requirements. (Ford)

first details were announced of the all-new AJ-V8 4-litre engine, to be built in a special section of the massive Ford engine plant at Bridgend. The final V12 emerged from Jaguar's old Radford factory in 1997, and later that year, the new XJ V8 was launched, spelling the end of in-line 6-cylinder Jaguar engines. From then on, however carefully the engines were redesigned in detail, they would come from Ford.

In summary

As I said in my introduction, there is a temptation to race from history into an attempt at crystal ball-gazing, but that was never the purpose of this work. Suffice it to say that by the end of the 1990s, engine design had to some extent settled down again after a period of upheaval. Engineers were no longer afraid to work in aluminium rather than cast iron. Most of them saw three or four valves per cylinder as an aid to efficiency, to lower emissions, increase specific power output and generally more satisfactory performance, rather than as a needless extra expense. Twin camshafts and multiple valves had in any case brought extra and often unanticipated advantages with them, such as the easy ability to exploit variable valve timing and to adjust in-cylinder airflow with the aid of swirl control valves. Along with the engines themselves, electronic control units have improved in accuracy, flexibility, and the ability to handle tasks which would have been inconceivable twenty years ago.

In Europe at least, the diesel engine had moved in ten short years from being a rather unwilling lump best suited to uncomplaining high-mileage professional drivers, to a smooth and powerful common-rail turbocharged unit worthy of consideration by anyone, given the European cost of motor fuel. In America, things are rather different, but one wonders how much longer they can remain so.

In Japan, the accent remains on sheer ingenuity, on

To replace the time-honoured XK engine which dated from the 1940s, Jaguar developed a new series of in-line six-cylinder engines, first the AJ6 and then the AJ16 shown here, a 4-litre 24-valve unit of all-alloy construction. Although the AJ16 performed well, and was developed into an extremely powerful mechanically supercharged unit also used by Aston Martin, it had a relatively short production life before being replaced by a more compact and stiffer V8. (Jaguar)

seeking higher efficiency even at the cost of additional complication. A European might ask himself if a certain system can ever be relied upon to work reliably; the Japanese reaction is to ensure that it does so, come what may. Yet there were signs at the 1999 Tokyo Motor Show that even the Japanese industry is looking for a clear path forward. That may be cars with hybrid drivelines, leading eventually to fuel cells – but even to suggest that is to forsake history for forecasting, and there are other places in which that should be done.

The AJ-V8, first seen in the S-type, was the effective replacement for the AJ16, and Jaguar's first engine of V8 configuration. Of all-alloy construction like its six-cylinder predecessor, with cylinder bores protected by the Nicasil process, this 90-degree V8 reflects modern design trends in its chain-driven valve gear (complete with variable inlet valve timing using variators in the camshaft sprockets) and combustion system. Points worth noting include the complicated but effective crossover induction system, and the extremely long poly-vee belt which drives all the main ancillaries. (Jaguar)

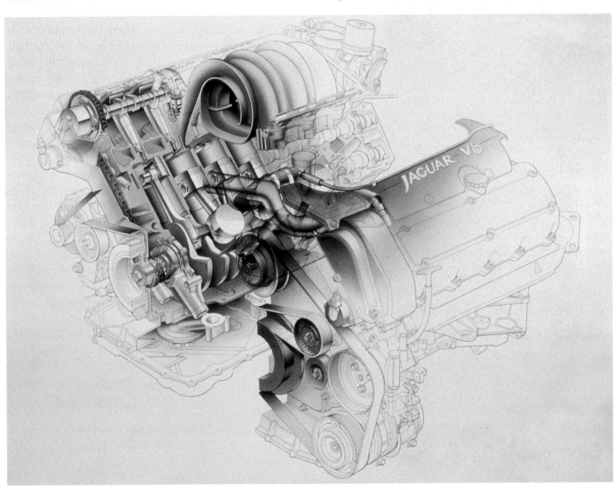

Index

Engines

AC 55
 6-cyl 56
Alfa Romeo 123, 151, 173, 195
 Giulietta 123, 124, 151
 1900 123
 2000 173
 flat-4 173, 174, 178, 195
 straight-8 90
 V6 159, 174, 195, 216
 4-cyl 123, 195, 215
 6-cyl 90
Allard 25
Aquila-Italiana 46
Auburn straight-8 79
Audi 188
 diesels 188, 213
 straight-8 69
 V6 213
 V6 diesel 213
 V8 188, 213
 4-cyl 38,167, 188
 5-cyl 167, 167, 188
 6-cyl 69, 167
Austin 71, 92
 4-cyl 54, 71, 72
 6-cyl 71, 111, 112
Austin Rover see also BMC/British Leyland
 A-series 199
 K-seres 199, 217
 M16 199
 O-series 199
 R-series 199
 S-series 199
 V6 199
 4-cyl 199
Ballot 2LS 4-cyl 67, 67
Bentley 7, 36
Benz 16, 17, 18
 flat-twin 20, 22, 40
 Parsifal 38
 Prince Henry 49
 1-cyl 18, 19
 4-cyl 38, 49
 6-cyl 38, 49, 68
 6/18 49
 16/50 68
 21/50 49
 25/65 49
 33/75 49
 82.200 49
BMC see also British Leyland 128-131,
 154-155
 A-series 93, 128, 128-129, 129, 131,
  154-155, 175-176
 B-series 128-131, 130, 154-155, 175, 199
 C-series 112, 128, 130, 154-155
 E-series 155, 155, 175, 177, 199
 4-cyl 128, 141, 155, 175
 6-cyl 128, 141, 154, 155, 175
BMW 87, 141-142, 163, 188, 210, 213
 M36 163
 M60 163
 318iS 189, 190
 320i 189
 diesels 189, 201
 straight-6 215
 V6 215
 V8 120, 163, 213, 215
 V12 163, 189, 213
 2-cyl 121
 4-cyl 87, 181, 189, 213
 6-cyl 87, 120, 163, 181, 189, 213
Bollée
 Type E 35
 4-cyl 24
Borgward 4-cyl 123

British Leyland (BL Group) see also
 BMC 175-177
 O-series 130, 199
 6-cyl 177
Buch diesel 37
Bugatti 7
 V16 77
Buick 45
 straight-8 78, 117
 2-cyl 46
 4-cyl 37, 46, 62
 6-cyl 46, 62
 V8 140, 182
Cadillac 99
 Type 51 46
 Type 452 77
 V8 45, 46, 49, 62, 100, 116, 141, 183
 V12 46, 77, 79
 V16 46, 77, 78, 96
Chadwick 6-cyl 36-37
Chevrolet 75
 Cosworth-Vega 16V 182
 H-series 46
 International Six 62, 64
 490 46
 copper-cooled 4-cyl 6, 62, 63, 64, 138
 flat-6 138, 183
 straight-6 140
 V8 47, 115
 4-cyl 62, 162
 6-cyl 62, 78
Chrysler 79, 99, 182-183
 Firepower V8 116
 straight-8 79
 V8 116,140-141
 V10 207
 300 series 117
 4-cyl 182
 6-cyl 64
Citroën see also PSA 80-81, 81,
 149-151, 170
 A-series 103, 104, 170, 216
 C-series 80
 GS birotor 170
 M35 170
 2400 170
 diesel 195
 flat-twin 81, 103-104, 150, 170, 216
 flat-4 151, 170
 V6 170
 V8 81, 170
 4-cyl 66, 80, 119, 170
 4-cyl diesel 82
 6-cyl 80-81, 103
Continental 54
Coventry Climax 94
Crosley 4-cyl 101

Daihatsu
 3-cyl 179, 200
 3-cyl diesel 200
Daimler (Britain) 42
 Double Six V12 94, 96
 straight-8 94
 V12 74
 4-cyl 42
 6-cyl 42, 74, 94
Daimler (Germany) 14, 14-17, 22, 69
 Standuhr (grandfather clock) 11, 17, 23
 6/40 69
 8/18 50
 24/110 69
 28/95 50
 38/70 50
 vee-twin 11, 22
 2-cyl 20
 4-cyl 19, 50, 69
 6-cyl 50, 69
Daimler-Benz see also Mercedes 68-69, 84

 straight-8 84-85, 99
 straight-6 68, 85
 4-cyl 85
 6-cyl 85
Daimler-Maybach
 vee-twin 18
 4-cyl in-line 19
Darracq 2-cyl 40
Datsun - see Nissan
De Dion-Bouton 23, 25, 33-34, 37, 41, 50
 10CV 68
 14CV 50
 20CV 50
 1-cyl 22, 22-24, 29, 33
 2-cyl 29, 30, 31
 4-cyl 31, 33, 50
 V8 32, 33, 45-46, 50
De Soto straight-8 79
Delage 106
 straight-8 82
 6-cyl 103
Delahaye 106
 6-cyl 82, 103
DKW 2-stroke 69, 88, 123, 144
Dodge
 straight-8 79
 4-cyl 47
 6-cyl 64
Duesenberg straight-8 47, 79-80, 80

Erskin Six 26

Ferrari 7
 V8 215
Fiat/Fiat Auto 90-91, 151-153, 174-175,
 194-197, 215, 216
 FIRE 195, 196, 216
 JTD 216
 S61 40
 Series 3 24HP 39
 Uno Turbo 197, 199
 124 151, 174
 128 152, 153, 175
 131 175, 194
 132 174
 500 91, 91,107-108
 508C 91-92
 1100 107-108
 1300 126
 1400 108, 123
 1400D 124
 1500 107, 126
 1900 123
 2100 126
 diesels 197, 199, 216
 flat-4 215
 V6 159, 174
 V8 124
 V12 69
 2-cyl 39, 126, 174
 4-cyl 39, 39, 51, 69, 90-92, 91, 123,
  125, 125-126, 151, 153, 174, 215
 4-cyl diesel 175, 197, 199
 5-cyl diesel 216
 6-cyl 69, 90, 92, 107, 126, 151
Ford 75, 94, 99-100, 111
 Duratec 206, 212, 218
 Lima 183
 Model A 65
 Model-T 29, 45, 50
 X-8 63
 Zephyr V12 100
 V6 183, 206, 207, 207, 218
 V8 77, 78-79, 101, 117, 141, 183, 206-207
 V12 101
 1-cyl 25
 2-cyl 25, 37
 4-cyl 37, 64, 65, 78, 183
 6-cyl 37, 103, 138, 183

Ford of Britain 145, 147-148, 168, 172
 Essex 147, 148, 168
 Kent 147, 162, 168, 184-185
 E93/100E 95, 131
 105E 95, 131, 132, 147-148
 V4 146, 147-148, 168
 V6 147, 168, 168
 V8 131
 4-cyl 95, 131
 6-cyl 131
Ford of Europe 185, 212, 218
 CVCC 185
 CVH 184, 185, 185, 187, 187
 Zetec-E 213
 Zetec-SE 203, 212, 213
 1600 diesel 187
 diesels 185, 187
 2-stroke 204, 205
 3-cyl 205
 4-cyl 185, 213
Ford France V8 103
Ford Germany 145-146, 168
 Pinto 168, 183, 185, 187
 V4 145, 146
 V6 146, 167-168, 187
Ford-Cosworth BDA 148, 212
Franklin
 V12 79
 6-cyl 62

General Motors 46, 99, 117, 162, 183,
 187-188
 Family One 188, 213
 Family Two 188, 213
 'Iron Duke' 183
 LET 188
 Northstar 206, 208
 Nova 162, 183
 Quad 4 183
 Vortec207
 8-6-4 183
 straight-6 188, 207
 V6 139, 140, 163, 183, 206-207
 V6 diesel 183
 V8 17, 138, 206-207, 208
 V8 diesel 183
 V8 'small block' 117
 3-cyl 213
 4-cyl 183
 6-cyl 188, 207
GM Europe
 Ecotec 206 213, 215
 V6 206, 213, 215
 4-cyl 213
Goggomobil
 V8 142
 4-cyl 142
Gregoire 106

Hillman 94
 straight-8 73
Hispano-Suiza
 V12 82
 6-cyl 82
Honda 156, 177, 200
 CVCC 6, 160-161, 161
 S800 137, 156
 VTEC 6, 200, 211
 V6 199, 200, 212
 2-cyl 156
 4-cyl 200, 201, 211
 5-cyl 212
Horch
 straight-8 69
 V12 88
 4-cyl 38, 38, 69
 6-cyl 38
Hotchkiss 106
Humber 73, 94

20/55 74
1-cyl 41
4-cyl 73, 111
6-cyl 74, 94, 111
Hyundai 211

Infiniti V8 212
Isotta-Fraschini
    Tipo 8 47
    straight-8 52
    4-cyl 47

Jaguar 177, 199-200
    AJ6 200, 217-218
    AJ16 217, 219
    AJ-V8 218, 219
    XK 99, 109, 111, 113, 124, 133, 177,
        199, 219
    SS100 94
    V8 206, 218
    V12 177, 189, 199, 212, 217-218
    6-cyl 99, 109, 199-200
Jowett flat-4 111, 111
Julien 1-cyl 104
Lagonda V12 96-97
Lanchester
    flat-twin 24, 25, 29
    straight-8 74
    6-cyl 40HP 74
Lancia 51-52, 75, 126, 128, 140, 153, 175
    Alfa 40
    Artena V4 92
    Astura 233 V8 92
    Augusta V4 92
    Beta 40
    Dialfa 40
    Theta 5
    B10 126
    flat-4 153, 175
    V4 70, 71, 92, 153, 153
    V6 126, 126, 128
    V8 70-71, 92
    V12 70
    4-cyl 51, 53, 126
Lexus V8 212
Lincoln 115
    V8 79, 101
    V12 79, 100
Lotus 7
Lycoming 65
    straight-8 80
    V12 79

Marmon V16 77
Maserati 7
Mathis 106
    6-cyl 103
Maudslay 36, 41
    3-cyl 36
    4-cyl 36
    6-cyl 36
Maybach 17-19, 36, 39
    straight-8 88
    V12 69, 87
    2-cyl 19
    4-cyl 19, 39
    5-cyl 39
    6-cyl 69, 88
Mazda 179, 200
    4-cyl diesel 201
Mercedes-Benz (see also Daimler-Benz)
    36, 85, 135, 142, 144, 163, 165,
        190-192, 210
    M100 142, 165
    M102 191
    M103 191
    M104 191
    M108/M114 142
    M110 163
    M115 142
    M116 142-143, 165
    M117 163
    M121 121, 142
    M127 123
    M136 106
    M180 121, 142
    M186 121, 121, 142
    M189 123

M198 121
M199 121, 123
OM601 192
OM602 192
OM603 191, 192
OM617 165
OM621 121, 142
OM636 106
W102 191
W115 142
220D 165
240D 165
300D Turbo 192
diesels 87, 215
straight-8 69, 85, 123
V8 142-143, 163, 165, 191
V8 turbo dieel 215
V12 189, 215
2.6l diesel 87
4-cyl 69, 85, 106, 121, 142, 190, 192
4-cyl diesel 215
5-cyl diesel 165, 192, 215
6-cyl 69, 80, 82, 83, 84, 85, 121,
    142-143, 163, 165, 192
6-cyl diesel 215
Mercedes-Knight 50
MG 6-cyl 92
Mitsubishi 211
    V6 212
    3-cyl 200
    4-cyl 182, 211
Morris 94
    4-cyl 72, 93, 130
    6-cyl 72
Mors 29
    V4 24

Napier 6-cyl 32-33, 42
Nissan (Datsun) 177, 211
    QX series 212
    240Z - 6
    V6 200, 212
    4-cyl 177
    6-cyl 177, 179, 200, 212
NSU 143-144, 170
    2-cyl 143
    4-cyl 143

Oldsmobile
    Rocket V8 100, 101, 117
    straight-8 78
    V8 47, 139-140
    4-cyl 47, 62
    6-cyl 47, 62
Opel 148, 188
    4-cyl 69, 88, 148, 168
    6-cyl 69, 88, 148, 168
Orbital 2-stroke 204, 205

Packard
    straight-8 65, 79, 117
    V8 117
    V12 (Twin Six) 47, 49, 65, 77, 79
    6-cyl 47, 65
Panhard et Levassor 50
    flat-twin 119, 120
    2-cyl 24
    4-cyl 50
    6-cyl 50
Peugeot see also PSA 37, 82, 119, 119,
    149, 170-172
    diesels 171
    Grand Prix 50
    7CV 50
    12CV 50
    V6 168, 171, 173, 209
    2-cyl 24, 37-38
    4-cyl 38, 50, 66, 106
    6-cyl 50, 82
Pierce-Arrow
    V12 79
    6-cyl 37
Plymouth 64
    6-cyl 79
Pontiac
    straight-6 140
    straight-8 78
    V8 78

6-cyl 62, 78, 140
Porsche 193
    flat-4 167
    flat-6 167
    V8 167, 193
Proton 211
PSA see also Peugeot 193, 216-217
    DW-sereies 217
    PRV V6 193, 217
    TU-series 173, 193, 216-217
    TUD-series 193
    XU-series 193, 217
    XUD-series 194, 217
    V6 193, 217
    4-cyl 193
    4-cyl diesel 194

Renault 36, 50, 66, 82, 148-149, 173,
    193, 217
    AT 37
    C-series 'Iron Cleon' 148, 173, 217
    D-series 217
    E-series 195, 217
    F-series 195, 217
    J-series 172, 173, 195, 217
    K-series 217
    'Ventoux' 119
    16TS 150
    40CV 66
    45CV DQ 51
    straight-8 66, 82
    V6 168, 171, 173, 217
    4-cyl 37, 51, 66, 82, 104, 105, 149, 217
    6-cyl 37, 51, 66, 82
Riley 55
    Nine 59, 73
    vee-twin 41
    4-cyl 72, 92
    6-cyl 72
Rolls-Royce 33-34, 74, 95-96
    straight-six 34
    V8 142
    V12 94
    6-cyl 96, 112, 142
Rootes Group 132, 155-156
    4-cyl 132
    6-cyl 132-133
Rover 73, 74, 112, 217
    KV6 217
    L-series 217
    16/50 74
    diesels 217
    flat-twin 74
    gas turbine 113
    V8 139-140, 176-177, 217
    1-cyl 41
    2-cyl 56
    4-cyl 56, 113, 155, 177
    5-cyl turbo diesel 217
    6-cyl 74, 94, 112-113

Saab 167-168, 193, 215
    96V4 145, 168
    slant-4 176
    2-stroke 145, 147, 167
Salmson 106
    Type D 67
    4-cyl 82
Serpollet
    flat-4 steam 41
Simca
    flat-twin 119, 120
    4-cyl 106
Singer 72-73, 94
    10HP 56
SK Simplex 2-cyl 35
Skoda 4-cyl 123
Standard see also Triumph
    4-cyl 108, 131
    6-cyl 94
Stanley flat-twin steam 41
Studebaker V8 117
Subaru
    flat-4 178,179, 200
    flat-six 200
    3-cyl 200
Sunbeam
    12/16HP 56

14/18HP 56
16/50 74
1-cyl 41
6-cyl 74

Talbot-Lago 6-cyl 119
Tatra V8 123
Toyota 177-179, 200, 211
    V6 212
    V8 179, 200
    V12 212
    6-cyl 212
Triumph 74, 176-177
    SS100 94
    2300/2600 177
    slant-4 168, 176
    V8 176
    4-cyl 94, 133, 134, 176
    6-cyl 94, 134, 155, 177

Vauxhall 56, 74, 131, 168
    A09 56
    A11/A12 56
    B10 56
    D-type 56, 74
    E-type 56, 75
    H-type 94
    M-type 74
    OD-type 75
    Prince Henry 56
    30/98 56, 74-75
    1-cyl 42
    3-cyl 42-43
    4-cyl 42-43, 56, 74, 94, 111, 131-132,
        148
    6-cyl 56, 75, 94, 111, 132, 148
Volkswagen 165, 192-193, 213
    Golf 166, 192, 192
    Golf GTI 213
    Golf diesel 166, 167, 188
    Polo 192
    Type 64 107
    412LS 165
    diesels 213
    flat-4 88, 88, 107, 107, 123, 144,
        165-166
    flat-6 144-145
    V5 213
    V6 213
    W12 7, 213
    4-cyl 165-166, 213, 213
    4-cyl diesel 213
    6-cyl diesel 193
Volvo 168, 193, 215
    B20 168
    B21 168
    B27 168
    V6 168, 171, 173
    740GLT 193
    740 Turbo 193
    4-cyl 168, 193, 215
    5-cyl 215
    6-cyl 168, 215

Wankel 143,143-144, 150, 162, 165,
    170, 179, 200
White steam 41
White & Poppe 54, 73-74
Willys 101
    4-cyl 103
    6-cyl 103
Wilson-Pilcher
    flat-4 40
    flat-6 40
Wolseley 55, 72, 94, 111
    1-cyl 41
Wolseley-Siddeley 55
    4-cyl 41

Cars

AC 56, 141
Alfa Romeo 40, 51, 69, 90, 123, 151,
    173, 195
    Alfasud 173, 174, 195, 215
    Alfetta 173
    Giulia Super 151

Giulietta 123-124, 151, 195
Spider 173
Sprint 195
Tipo 103 151
8C2300 90
33 195, 215
75 195, 216
156 216
164 195, 216
1500 123
2600 151
Aston Martin 219
Auburn 66, 79
Audi 38, 88, 144, 165
Quattro 188
Super 90 167
Type M 69
Type R 69
70 144
80/80L/80LS 165-167, 188
90 144, 188
100 167, 188
Austin see also BMC/British Leyland
A30 129
A40 111
A70/A90 Westminster 111-112, 130, 155
A135 111
Eight 130
Maxi 155
Seven 54, 71, 74, 129
Sixteen 71
Twelve 71
Twenty 71
3-litre 155
1100 154
1300 154
1800 130
Austin-Healey
Midget 130
Sprite 130
100 130
3000 112
Austin-Morris 175
Austin-Rover 199
Maestro 199
Metro 199
Montego 199
Auto Union 88
Autobianchi
A111 153
A112 153

Ballot 82
2LS 67
Benz
Type S 68
Velo 21
16/50
BMC see also British Leyland/BL
Farina saloons 154
Maxi 155
Mini 128-130, 154, 156
Mini Cooper 154
Mini Cooper S 154
1100/1300 128, 154-155
1800 155
BMW 87, 141, 188-189
Isetta 121
M-models 189
M3 189
M5 189
M635 CSi 189
SD1 3500 177
X5 213
3-series 189
7-series 189
303 87
315 87
318iS 189, 190
319 87
320/326 series 87
320i 189
328 87
329 87
335 87
501 120
502 120
503 120

600 121
700 121
1500 141
1800 141
1800TI 141
3200 L/S/Cs 120
Borgward Isabella 123
Bristol 407 141
British Leyland/BL see also BMC 175, 199
Allegro 175
Maxi 175
Mini 175
Princess 155, 175
1800 175
2200 175
Buick 25, 37, 46, 99
Roadmaster 117
Skylark 138
Special 117

Cadillac 25, 37, 46
Eldorado 117
Fleetwood Eldorado 141
Chevrolet 25, 46, 103
Biscayne 140
Corvair 138
Impala 206
Vega 162-163, 167, 182
Chrysler 47, 99, 103
Imperial 116
New Yorker 116
Citroën 170
Ami 6 150
Ami 8 170
Caddy 66
Dyane 150
Project F 150
Project G 150
Traction Avant 81-82, 103-104, 119
AX 193
B2 66
BX 193
BX 16V 217
C-type 66
C60 150
CX 151, 170, 193
DS 119, 150-151
DS21 150
DS23 170
GS 150, 170
M35 170
SM 170
XM 173, 193-194
2CV 81, 103-104, 106, 113, 126, 150
2CV6 150
15CV 103
Cord 66, 79
810/812 80

DAF 193
Daihatsu 156, 179
Charade 179, 200
Daimler (Britain) 41-42
Daimler (Germany) 20, 99
Darracq, Italy 40
Datsun
1000 156
1600 157
de Tomaso 141
DeDion-Bouton 24, 41
Delage 82
Delahaye 82
Dixi 87
3/20 87
DKW 69, 88
F102 144
Dodge 103
Charger 141
Daytona 183
Viper 207
Duesenberg 66, 79
Model J 80
Model SJ 80
Duryea 25

Edsel 117

Facel Vega 141
Ferrari 308 199
Fiat 39, 69, 151-152, 194-197
Argenta Abarth 194
Campagnola 123
Croma 197, 216
Nouva 500 125-126, 174
Panda 196-197
Ritmo 175
Sport Spider 151
Strada 175, 197
Taxi 51
Tipo 197, 215
Tipo 16V 217
Tipo 1 51
Tipo 2/2B 51
Tipo 3/3A 51
Tipo 4 51
Tipo 5 51
Turbina 113
Uno 195, 197
Uno Turbo 197, 199, 216
Uno 70TD 197
X1/9 152, 175
124 151-152, 174-175
124 Coupé 152
124 Special T 152
125 152, 174
126 174
127 197
128 152-153, 175
130 153
131 174-175
131 Abarth 194
131 Super 175
132 174-175
500 Topolino 90-91, 97, 107, 126
500C 126
501 69
505 69
508 Balilla 90
508 Sport 90-91
508C 91
509 69
510 69
518 Ardita 90
519 69
520 69
527 90
600 125-126
850 151-152
1100 92, 107
1300 126
1400 123
1400D 124
1500 90, 107, 126
1500E 90
1900 123
2100 126
2800 92
Ford 43, 123, 168
Anglia E93A/100E 95
Anglia 105E 95, 131-132, 147
Capri 162, 168
Capri V6 168
Consul 131
Consul Classic 147
Consul Cortina 147
Corsair 146
Corsair 2000E 148
Corsair V4 148
Cortina 155, 162, 187
Cortina 3 162, 168
Cortina 1200 147
Cortina 1500 147
Cortina GT 147
Crown Victoria 206
Escort 168, 185, 187, 212
Escort Mexico 168
Escort RS2000 168
Escort Twin Cam 147
Explorer 207
Falcon 138
Fiesta 168, 185, 204-205
Fordor 101
Granada 168, 172, 187
Lotus-Cortina 147, 152
Mercury 101

Model A 37, 63, 65, 75, 78-79
Model A light truck 206
Model B 37, 79
Model C 37
Model F 37
Model N 37
Model T 37, 45-46, 63-65, 75, 78-79, 166
Model Y 94
Model 18 79
Mondeo 206, 218
Mustang 103, 183
Mustang II 163
Orion 187
Pilot 131
Pinto 162-163, 183, 185, 187
Popular 100E 95
Quadricycle 25
RS Cosworth 187
Scorpio 187, 212
Sierra 187, 188
Sierra Cosworth 187-188, 212
Taunus 12M/15M 145-146, 206
Tempo 183
Ten 94-95
Thunderbird 183
Topaz 183
Transit 146
Tudor 101
Victoria 117
Zephyr 131, 148
Zephyr Mark 4 148
Zodiac 148, 155
Zodiac Mark 2 131,

General Motors 25, 37, 103, 168
Goggomobil 142
S1004 142
Gordon-Keeble 141

Hillman
Imp 156
Minx 111, 132
Hispano-Suiza 82
Type 68/68bis 82
Holland Spyker 32
Honda 156, 177, 206
Accord 177, 201, 206
Civic 160, 177, 200, 211
Legend 212
Prelude 177
NS-X 200
N360 156
N600 156
S800 156
Horch 38
Hotchkiss 82, 119
Hudson 65, 99
Humber 24, 94
Hawk 111, 132
Humberette 41
Super Snipe 111, 132
8/18 73
9/20 73
14/40 73
Hyundai 211

Infiniti 212
Iso 141
Isotta-Fraschini 52

Jaguar 175, 177, 199-200
E-type 177
S-type 219
X-type 218
XJ-S 200, 217
XJ V8 218
XJ V12 217
XJ6 217
XJ40 200
XK120 111, 133
Jensen 141
Jowett
Javelin 111
Jupiter 111

Lancia 69, 153
Appia 126
Aprilia 92, 108